Expert Learning
for
Law Students

Expert Learning
for
Law Students

Michael Hunter Schwartz
CHARLESTON SCHOOL OF LAW

CAROLINA ACADEMIC PRESS
Durham, North Carolina

ISBN 1-59460-113-5
LCCN 2005926645

CAROLINA ACADEMIC PRESS
700 Kent Street
Durham, North Carolina 27701
Telephone (919) 489-7486
Fax (919) 493-5668
www.cap-press.com

Printed in the United States of America

Contents

Preface

For years, law professors, law schools and even the Law School Admissions Council (the creators of that bane of every aspiring law student's life, the LSAT) have known that a student's LSAT score and undergraduate grades do not really tell you whether the student will succeed in law school. There are students who had high LSAT scores and excellent undergraduate grades and nevertheless failed out of law school. There are students who had relatively lower LSAT scores and lower undergraduate grades and graduated at or near the top of their law school classes. And there are, in fact, law students who studied incredibly hard and still did not do well. If one were to look only at the entrance credentials and effort level of both groups of students, one might be baffled by these outcomes. Looking at how they studied and learned law, however, clears up the confusion.

The successful students studied differently. Not harder, but differently. The successful students were, as we will see, "Expert Learners." Ask any law professor and she will tell you—we can spot expert law students from miles away. Some students just seem to be better at being law students. These expert learners approach their law studies with confidence, resourcefulness, diligence and planning. They are in control of their own learning, figuring out for themselves what they need to do to learn and study law. They know when they understand and know when they need help, and they even prepare better for meetings with their professors and ask better questions. They do better in law school than their peers, seem to have an easier time of it and enjoy the experience more.

We law professors can cite countless examples of students who were either much better or much worse at being law students than their peers. We know that the students who are better at being law students do better in law school, and we even can describe the characteristics typical of the better students. The fact that we know all of this, however, has been largely irrelevant over the 110-year history of legal education. It's as if we all had agreed that expert law students are simply born that way and that students cannot be taught to be experts.

Meanwhile, the rest of the educational world has been investigating expert learning. In fields as diverse as medical education, graduate statistics education, undergraduate education and even K–12 education, researchers have been discovering not only that expert learning skills predict student outcomes, but also that students can be successfully taught to be expert learners. As a result, instructional programs designed to teach students to be expert learners have popped up in colleges, graduate programs, undergraduate schools and high schools. Legal education, however, has entirely ignored this important research—until now.

Until Summer 2001, I was like every other law professor in this country. I enjoyed the expert law students. I tried to tell all my students to do what I perceived the expert students to be doing and had no success whatsoever in getting the novices to act like experts. In Summer 2001, I was granted a leave of absence from my teaching obligations and was given the resources to figure out what makes the expert students expert, whether novices can be taught to be experts and how to teach the novices to be experts.

This textbook and the accompanying workbook are the result. This project, in many ways, has a singular message to you, its readers: you can be an expert learner of the law!

The text is organized into two parts. Part I provides background information about law school, about how humans learn and about expert learning. It then explains how to perform each aspect of expert learning and helps students become expert in their own learning preferences. Part II focuses on specific learning strategies needed by new law students.

You may want to re-read certain chapters in Part II of this book once you have started law school. For example, Chapters 12 and 13, dealing with strategies for organizing and memorizing, will be helpful once you have attended a few classes and need to begin making sense of all the new material you are learning. Likewise, Chapters 14 through 17 will ease your transition into writing law school exams and papers but may be most meaningful to you once classes have started.

All of the chapters conclude with a list of references you may find helpful and a set of reflection questions designed to help you make what you are learning become a part of who you are and develop the high-level self-reflection skills that expert learners possess. The reflection questions are reproduced in the workbook with space for you to respond. By responding to the questions you will gain the particular insights possible only when you are forced to put your thoughts in writing. Beginning with the skills addressed in Chapter 5, the workbook has exercises that you can do on your own to begin developing your expert learning skills. Those exercises are organized and numbered by chapter. For example, the exercises relating to Chapter 5 are labeled 5-1, 5-2, 5-3, etc.

Of course, no preface is without a thank you or two. I therefore wish to thank my wife, Dr. Stacey Hunter Schwartz, for pointing me in the right direction and giving me the support I have needed to get there, my daughters, Kendra and Samantha, for being the amazing humans they are, and my deans, Maryann Jones and James Hogg, for the opportunity to blaze a trail where none existed. Finally, I owe thank yous to the many readers who provided suggestions, edits and helpful comments during the process, including Professor Gerry Hess of Gonzaga University School of Law, Professor Vernellia Randall of Dayton University College of Law, and the following colleagues at Western State: Professors Carole Buckner, Glenn Koppel, Constance Hood, Susan Keller, Niccol Kording, Paula Manning, Kevin Mohr, Brent Romney and Greg Sergienko.

Michael Hunter Schwartz, April 2003

Part I

Basic Principles

Chapter 1

Introduction to Expert Learning

There is a better way to study law, to prepare for the bar exam, to learn anything at all. That way, known as "Expert Learning," allows students to learn more, learn better and perform better than their peers. Expert learning, however, is not magic. You hold all the power within yourself to decide whether you wish to become an expert learner; you must be willing to make the necessary demands on yourself.

Expert learners have three characteristics. First, they **actively engage** with the material to be learned. They are *not* passive readers/listeners. Second, they **take responsibility** for their own learning. They view learning as something they do for themselves, not as something that is done for them or to them. Third, they practice "**self-regulated learning**;" they use specific processes to guide their own learning.

Self-regulated learning (SRL) is itself best understood as a cycle, consisting of three phases: (1) a **planning phase**, where the students decide what they want to learn and how they can best learn it, (2) a **monitoring and implementing phase**, where the students put their plan into action while constantly assessing whether they are "getting it", and (3) an **evaluation phase**, where the students determine whether their plan has produced efficient and optimal learning.

The planning phase of SRL sets the stage for learning. During this phase, students analyze the learning task, set learning goals (making sure these goals are very clear) and plan learning strategies (considering a variety of ways to approach the learning task). During the monitoring and implementing phase, students implement the plan while monitoring themselves to make sure they're making progress toward their learning goals. During the evaluation phase, students determine how well their chosen strategies worked and how those strategies might be improved. Engaging in this cycle of planning, implementation, monitoring and evaluating causes the students to be constantly reflecting on their learning. These students take control over their own learning and become experts not only in the general principles of learning, but also in what learning approaches work best for them. The students also become experts in knowing when they are learning and when they are not and how to get the help they need when they are not learning.

What Expert Learners Know and Do

Years of academic studies of expert learning and expert learners have helped educational psychologists develop a prototype of expert learners, a list of the skills and knowledge that expert learners possess. Expert learners are said to:

1. Control their own learning processes
2. Be active, not passive, in their approach to learning
3. Be motivated (i.e., enjoy learning, have specific short-term and long-term goals, etc.)
4. Be disciplined (i.e., have learned good habits and use them consistently)
5. Be more aware of themselves as learners (i.e., know their own strengths and weaknesses)
6. Initiate opportunities to learn
7. Set specific learning goals for themselves
8. Have a large repertoire of learning strategies from which to choose
9. Know not only *what* to learn but *how* to learn
10. Plan their approach to learning
11. Monitor their learning while it's happening (i.e., notice when they're not learning and adjust their learning approach)
12. Be more adaptive because they do self-monitor while learning
13. Reflect more upon their own learning
14. Evaluate the effectiveness of learning approaches and strategies
15. Be more sensitive to the demands of specific academic tasks
16. Use learning strategies selectively and strategically
17. Attribute failures to correctable causes and attribute successes to personal competence

Professors Peggy Ertmer and Timothy Newby of Purdue University, two of the leading authors in the expert learning field, summarize these ideas by explaining that expert learners

> are aware of the knowledge and skills they possess, or are lacking, and use appropriate strategies to actively implement or acquire them. This type of learner is self-directed and goal oriented, purposefully seeking out needed information, incorporating and applying a variety of strategic behaviors to optimize academic performance.... By using the knowledge they have gained of themselves as learners, of task requirements, and of specific strategy use, they can deliberately select, control, and monitor strategies to achieve desired goals and objectives. By being consciously aware of themselves as problem solvers and by monitoring and controlling their thought processes, these learners are able to perform at a more expert level, regardless of the amount of specific domain knowledge possessed.[1]

Evidence That Expert Learning Improves Student Performance

Given expert learners' extraordinary skill in learning, it should not be surprising at all to learn that expert learners learn more, get better grades, remember what they have learned longer and enjoy learning more.

Studies conducted at every level of education have reached the same conclusion. Educational psychologists have conducted studies of law students, medical students, stu-

1. Peggy A. Ertmer & Timothy J. Newby, *The Expert Learner: Strategic, Self-Regulated and Reflective*, 24 INSTRUCTIONAL SCIENCE 1, 5–6 (1996).

dents working towards graduate degrees in statistics, undergraduate students and even high school and younger students. Those studies have looked at SRL as a whole, as well as at various aspects of SRL. Uniformly, those studies have found that SRL skills are a better predictor of educational success than traditional measures of aptitude, such as the SAT and LSAT. In fact, studies have found that students who use even one aspect of SRL, such as goal setting, invoking self-efficacy or self-monitoring, outperform those who do not.

Studies also confirm that students can be taught to be expert learners. Students who have never even considered engaging in self-regulation can learn to be experts. In fact, with the proper instruction, students can make expert learning a part of who they are. Students who learn expert learning skills report that the things they have learned have changed not only how they study, but also how they work and live (because both work and life require continuous learning).

According to the experts in teaching students to be expert learners, the best place to start expert learning instruction is by helping students understand their educational context, to explain to them what they need to learn in their educational program and how their professors will try to teach them. The next chapter does just that; it is a short introduction to how law is taught and the expectations of law professors about their students. The purpose of this discussion is to help students see their role in the educational process in which they are engaged, to help them understand what will be happening and what they are expected to be doing and learning.

Reflection Questions

1. How are novice self-regulated learners different from expert self-regulated learners?

2. Why do self-regulated learners achieve higher grades than students who are not self-regulated learners?

3. In what ways do you already do things that expert self-regulated learners do? In what ways do you not do the things expert learners do?

4. How can you improve as a learner based on what you have read so far?

References

Peggy A. Ertmer & Timothy J. Newby, *The Expert Learner: Strategic, Self-Regulated and Reflective*, 24 INSTRUCTIONAL SCIENCE 1 (1996).

Gerald F. Hess, *The Legal Educator's Guide to Periodicals on Teaching and Learning*, 67 UMKC L. REV. 367 (1998).

Barbara K. Hofer, Shirley L. Yu and Paul R. Pintrich, *Teaching College Students to Be Self-Regulated Learners* in SELF REGULATED LEARNING: FROM TEACHING TO SELF-REFLECTIVE PRACTICE 57 (D.H. Schunk, B. Zimmerman, eds.1998).

Reinhard W. Lindner and Bruce Harris, *Self-Regulated Learning: Its Assessment and Instructional Implications*, 16 EDUCATIONAL RESEARCH QUARTERLY 29 (1992).

Bridget Murray, *Getting Smart About Learning Is Her Lesson,* 29 APA MONITOR (April 1998).

James R. P. Ogloff, David R. Lyon, Kevin S. Douglas, V. Gordon Rose, *Annual Nebraska Survey & Survey of Legal Education: Article More Than "Learning to Think Like a Lawyer:" The Empirical Research on Legal Education,* 34 CREIGHTON L. REV. 73 (2000).

Paul R. Pintrich, *Understanding Self-Regulated Learning* in UNDERSTANDING SELF-REGULATED LEARNING 3 (P. Pintrich, ed. 1995).

Paul R. Pintrich, David A.F. Smith, Teresa Garcia and Wilbert J. McKeachie, *Reliability and Predictive Validity of the Motivated Strategies for Learning Questionnaire,* EDUCATIONAL AND PSYCHOLOGICAL MEASUREMENT, #53, 83–92 (1993).

Gregory Schraw & David W. Brooks, *Helping Students Self-Regulate in Math and Science Courses: Improving the Will and the Skill,* http://www.ccci.unl.edu/chau/SR/Self Reg. html.

Bruce C. Howard, Steven McGee, Regina Shia, Namsoo Shin Hong, *The Influence of Metacognitive Self-Regulation and Ability Levels on Problem Solving* (American Educational Research Association 2001), http://www.google.com/search?q=cache:0h2dcI-IZS0Y:www.cet.edu/research/papers/regulation/AERA2001BHsral.pdf++college+and+achievement+%22self-regulate%22&hl=enhttp://www.cet.edu/research/papers/regulation/AERA2001BHsral.pdf.

Claire E. Weinstein and Richard E. Mayer, *The Teaching of Learning Strategies,* in HANDBOOK OF RESEARCH ON TEACHING (M.C. Wittriock, ed. 1986).

Claire E. Weinstein & Gretchen Van Mater Stone, *Broadening Our Conception of General Education: The Self-Regulated Learner,* 81 NEW DIRECTIONS IN COMMUNITY COLLEGES 31 (1993).

Barry J. Zimmerman, *Developing Self-Fulfilling Cycles of Academic Regulation: An Analysis of Exemplary Instructional Models* in SELF REGULATED LEARNING: FROM TEACHING TO SELF-REFLECTIVE PRACTICE 1 (D.H. Schunk, B. Zimmerman, eds.1998).

Chapter 2

Introduction to Law School Instruction

To be in a position to apply expert learning principles to your legal education, you need to know what you can expect to encounter in law school. Law school teaching methods are dramatically different from the other teaching methods you have encountered in your academic career. In law school, the expectations on the students are high; students who take command over their own education, who act upon their learning rather than passively receiving it, excel. In many respects, your only choice is whether to take control over your learning or to perform far below your capability.

The Goals of Legal Education

For many years, law professors, law school deans and practicing attorneys have struggled to define exactly what are the educational objectives of legal education. Of course, in the largest sense, there is only one goal and it's one that is simply stated: *produce graduates ready to be lawyers*. That goal statement, however, is so broad, encompassing so many skills, so much knowledge and such particular values, that it offers prospective law students little insight into their imminent law school experience. From a very different perspective, legal scholars and practicing attorneys have developed long lists of knowledge, skills and values that law school graduates should possess. These lists are also not particularly helpful because they are so detailed, so intricate and so dependent on the reader already being a lawyer that showing such a list to a prospective law student may overwhelm the student.

Acquiring Knowledge in Law School

What you need to know at this early stage of your legal education is that law school instruction and testing require you to acquire enormous amounts of knowledge (information). You need to learn a vast repertoire of new terminology, hundreds of rules of law and case holdings, and the mental steps involved in performing a wide variety of skills. You also need to learn how all this information is interrelated and how it is different.

Acquiring Skills

Even if you learn perfectly every bit of information presented to you in your texts and classes, you still may fail to do well in law school. This seeming contradiction is not really a contradiction at all and, in fact, it is the single most important thing you need to know about the goals of legal education. Although knowledge is crucial to success in law school, the goal of legal education is to teach you skills. In other words, what you need to learn is how to **apply** the knowledge you acquire and to do so **in writing**.

This point is crucial and often overlooked by new law students. Every semester since I started teaching law in 1991, there are a few students who come to see me and express shock at the low grades they received for my course. In each instance, the student has said something like, "But I knew the law cold. I knew it backwards and forwards and every other which way." Some students have even asked me to test their knowledge on the spot so that I would know how much they knew. These students were smart enough to realize that they had to assimilate vast amounts of knowledge to succeed in law school. They failed to realize, however, that such knowledge was not enough.

Law school does require you to acquire knowledge but only so that you can demonstrate your skills. To understand this relationship between skills and knowledge, forget about law school for a moment. Think about a skill that you have learned, such as playing the piano, performing a sport (such as basketball) or even doing long division. In each instance, knowledge was crucial. In piano, you needed to know, among other things, what the musical notes are and where each note is located on your piano. In basketball, you needed to know, among other things, all the rules of the game and who your teammates are and what skills they possess. To do long division, you needed to know, among other things, what a division problem looks like and the steps involved in performing long division.

In each of these settings, however, such knowledge was not enough to be able to perform the tasks. Those skills required you to practice their performance and seek out and obtain feedback on how you were performing, and they did not come quickly or easily. In learning piano, you needed to spend endless hours practicing both on your own and while an expert, your piano teacher, watched and listened and gave you feedback on the positioning of your hands and fingers, your use of the pedals and your transitions between notes. To learn to play basketball, you needed to devote countless hours practicing your shooting, passing, rebounding and defending both on your own and while an expert, your coach, watched and gave you feedback on the positioning of your hands, arms, feet and eyes, your assessment of what was happening and your anticipation of what was about to happen on the basketball floor, and the positioning of your body in relation to the other players with whom you were playing. Even long division required you to practice hundreds of long division problems, both on your own and while a teacher (and/or parent) watched and gave you feedback on your computations (the dividing, multiplying and subtracting involved in doing long division), on the extent to which you were following the procedure required to perform long division (e.g., did you remember the correct next step) and on how you could check your work for accuracy (such as by multiplying your result by the dividend).

From this discussion, a pattern or set of best practices for acquiring new skills should be evident to you: (1) acquiring new skills requires you to **practice** those skills over and over; (2) acquiring new skills requires you to seek out and **obtain feedback** from experts; and (3) acquiring new skills requires a large **expenditure of time** by you and does not necessarily come easily or quickly.

In law school, while students must learn many skills, the principal skills they must learn are legal reasoning and expressing their reasoning in writing. As you will learn in these materials, legal reasoning and expressing legal reasoning in writing are multi-faceted skills. Like other skills, they require you to possess vast stores of knowledge, but, also like other skills, these skills require you to combine and use knowledge in ways that, while similar to skills you already possess, are unique. For this reason, for most students, these skills come neither quickly nor easily; they are the product of countless hours of study and practice and require you to make frequent efforts to obtain feedback from your peers and professors. Moreover, law schools assume that students possess the skills and knowledge necessary to make it possible for them to learn what they need to learn in law school.

The Skills and Knowledge Law Schools Assume You Already Possess

Law schools, as graduate schools and perhaps by necessity, assume that law students possess certain skills and knowledge before they come to law school. Those skills and that knowledge fall within five major categories: reading comprehension skills, writing skills, learning skills, knowledge about the legal system and teachability.

First, law schools assume that entering law students possess excellent reading comprehension skills. Law students must digest enormous amounts of reading material in short periods of time. The reading material is abstract, complicated, and, sometimes, dry. Much of it includes language that is either unfamiliar to non-lawyers or uses familiar language in unfamiliar ways. For this reason, new law students who are concerned about their reading comprehension skills should devote particular attention to Chapter 9 of this book. Based on research into how successful law students and lawyers read and understand court opinions, Chapter 9 teaches you how to apply well-established reading comprehension techniques to the task of comprehending law school reading assignments.

Second, law schools assume students enter law school with excellent writing skills. Specifically, law schools assume that entering students possess excellent knowledge and skill regarding grammar, usage, paragraphing, punctuation, organization and other related writing skills. You therefore need to either possess those skills or work to enhance your existing skills before you start law school. Fortunately, there are many resources available to you to help you enhance your writing skills. In addition to the excellent resources reflected in the bibliography at the end of this chapter, many colleges and universities have developed websites that are accessible to anyone interested in enhancing her writing skills. Four excellent websites are:

http://webster.comment.edu/grammar/index.htm

http://owl.english.purdue.edu/handouts/index.html

http://www.ucalgary.ca/UofC/eduweb/grammar/and

http://cwx.prenhall.com/bookbind/pubbooks/biays/.[1]

---

1. I am grateful to my colleague, Professor Mark Patrick, the writing instructor/specialist at my law school, for these suggestions.

Third, law schools assume that you possess excellent learning skills, including organization, memorization, examination preparation and other learning skills. This book addresses the learning skills you need to possess or develop. If you adopt the practices explained and demonstrated in this book, you will possess the learning skills you need.

Fourth, law schools assume you possess basic knowledge of legal civics, including knowledge of how cases move through our legal system, court hierarchies, the concepts of precedent and appeal, how statutes become law, the roles lawyers commonly play and the work they do, the state and federal constitutions and their roles within our legal system and the relationships between federal and state law and between our state and federal court systems. Fortunately, any of the legal civics resources identified in the bibliography at the end of this chapter suffice to fill in any gaps in your knowledge in any of these areas.

Finally, law schools assume you are teachable. In other words, because law school skills, at least in some respects, are unique and difficult to learn, law students need to be open to feedback, eager to learn, willing to change and unafraid of criticism. It also means that you must be ready to deal with the unique aspects of law school instruction, which the rest of this chapter addresses.

The Four Main Units of Law School Instruction

Rules, Court Opinions, Public Policies and Hypotheticals
and the Integration of these Units

Law school instruction principally deals with four related units of instruction taught together as an integrated whole: rules of law, court opinions, public policies and hypotheticals. Each law school class focus on a particular bodies of rules, court opinions, public policies and hypotheticals; thus, a criminal law class will focus almost exclusively on the rules, court opinions, public policies and hypotheticals that make up the criminal law whereas a tort law course will focus almost exclusively on tort law.

The discussion below explains what each of the units of instruction are, how each unit works and how all the units work together in law school instruction.

Rules of Law

A rule of law is an abstract statement of fact describing **a context in which the rule applies** (unless the rule applies in all contexts), a **set of required circumstances** and setting forth the **legal consequence** if that required set of circumstances exists; in many cases, a rule also identifies a limited abstract context in which it applies.

For example, consider a simplified version of a rule of contract law known as the statute of frauds. The rule is:

> A contract for the sale of land is not enforceable unless it is in writing and signed by the parties to it.

On its face, this rule seems extraordinarily simple. Close examination reveals that the rule is much more complicated, providing details about the context in which the rule applies, the required set of circumstances and the legal consequence if the required circumstances are not met:

The context in which the rule applies:
(1) The parties have a contract, and
(2) The contract is for the sale of land

The required set of circumstances:
(1) The contract must be in writing, and
(2) The writing must be signed

The consequence if the required circumstances are not present:
The contract is not enforceable.

Note that, as explained above, the context and set of circumstances are abstract. There is no reference to a particular contract, to a particular piece of land or to particular parties; rather, the rule applies to any contract, to any piece of land and to any set of parties.

Consider another example. Under one definition of the crime of larceny, a person may be held criminally liable for larceny if she commits a trespassory taking and carrying of the personal property of another with the intent to steal. As we saw with the statute of frauds, this simple sentence communicates a complicated rule that addresses the context, required set of circumstances and a consequence:

The context in which the rule applies:
(1) Personal property is involved
(2) The personal property belongs to someone other than the defendant

The required set of circumstances:
(1) The defendant takes the other person's personal property
(2) The defendant carries it away
(3) The defendant possesses a particular mental state with respect to these actions: intent to steal the property

The consequence if the required circumstances are present:
The defendant will be held criminally liable.

Note again that the words of the rule describe abstract sets of facts. Rather than describing a particular piece of personal property, such as a car or a watch or a painting, the rule refers to the abstraction, "personal property." Similarly, rather than describing a particular instance of taking (pick pocketing or removing an item from an unlocked, unoccupied car), the rule refers to the general act, "taking."

As I explain below, rules are only sometimes taught in isolation from court opinions and without consideration of their application to particular disputes or events. Nevertheless, they are a separate unit by which students learn to become lawyers and with which students must become familiar and adept at understanding and using. Law students must become adept at reading rules, a much more complex process than it sounds, because of the degree of attention to detail required and the importance of breaking rules down into subparts, as explained in Chapter 12.

The need for attention to detail and of breaking down rules can be seen by considering a definition of murder:

Murder is the unlawful killing of another human being with malice aforethought, and malice aforethought can be shown by an intent to kill, by an intent to inflict grievous bodily harm, by an abandoned and malignant (depraved) heart or by application of the felony murder rule.

Rules must be broken down into sub-parts so that a judge can ascertain whether the state has proven everything it must prove. With respect to murder, for example, the definition translates to five required elements of proof, i.e., things the state must prove. The last of these elements can be proven in any of four alternative ways. Here's an outline of the required elements:

(1) there has been a killing,
(2) the killing was unlawful,
(3) it was a human being who was killed,
(4) the person killed was someone other than the person who did the killing, and
(5) the murder was committed with "malice aforethought"
    a. intent to kill
    b. intent to inflict grievous bodily harm
    c. acting with an abandoned and malignant heart with respect to the potentially consequences of your actions OR
    d. committing a killing that requires application of the felony murder rule.

The details are important because the **definitions** of the words used, the choice of **conjunctions** (i.e., *and, or, but*) and the **punctuation** (the location of the commas) can change how a court would apply this definition to determine whether a particular accused defendant is guilty. To be able to apply this rule to determine whether the defendant has committed a murder, the court also needs definitions of "unlawful" (Does that include killings made in self-defense? In defense of one's home? To keep someone from stealing one's new car?), "killing" (Does that include people who would have imminently died from natural causes anyway?), "human being" (Does that include an unborn fetus?), "intent," "grievous bodily harm," "depraved heart," "felony" and the "felony murder rule." In addition, the court must understand the implications of the "and" between the words "abandoned" and "malignant" in the definition and the implications of the word "or" near the end of the definition. In Chapter 12 of this book, you will learn how lawyers **deconstruct** rules (break rules into organized elements). For now, you simply need to know that rule deconstruction is a skill you study and must develop in law school.

The skill is particularly crucial because law school exams require law students to apply rules to particular fact patterns in ways similar but not identical to how judges do it. Accordingly, law school exams assume that, you, as a law student, have developed the skills of identifying and understanding the legal implications of details—definitions, conjunctions and punctuation—and of breaking rules into their subparts so well that you are able to apply each subpart to a hypothetical factual situation.

Court Opinions

A court opinion is a published document created by a judge or a set of judges acting together in which the author describes the nature and facts of the dispute before the court, the parties, the relevant rules of law and precedents (past decided court opinions), the court's decision and the reasons for the court's decision. Law school texts, called "casebooks," consist mostly of court opinions that the editors of the casebook have selected, edited and organized. A case is selected because it established an important new rule, because its results or reasoning have had particular influence on other courts, because of its notoriety or its interesting facts, because the court's discussion of the issues was particularly insightful or even, sometimes, because the court's discussion was particularly lacking in insight. In fact, in reading court opinions, it is often a productive learning technique to try to figure out why the casebook editor selected the case. Appendix B at the end of this book contains both a casebook version of a case and a full, unedited version.

Lawyers analyze and use a court opinion by focusing on its **holding** and the court's reasoning in reaching that holding. A holding is a statement of the precedential significance of a court opinion. It is a statement about how courts should use the court opinion to resolve future disputes. Holdings typically identify the key applicable principle of law (the rule) and the key facts. Sometimes courts explicitly state a holding, and sometimes courts do not. In either case, a lawyer's task includes defining that holding, that statement of the precedential effect of the opinion, in a way that favors the lawyer's client. Given a court opinion that seems to favor the lawyer's client, the lawyer will try to articulate the holding as **broadly** as possible, to argue that the court opinion should produce the same result for the lawyer's client that it produced in the precedent case. In contrast, a lawyer facing an unfavorable court opinion will articulate the holding as **narrowly** as possible, arguing that the opinion only applies if the facts are exactly the same as the facts in the case for which the court opinion was written and therefore does not apply to the lawyer's situation.

Once again, language choices, organization and, at least sometimes, punctuation are crucial. Judges carefully write and rewrite their opinions, knowing that lawyers will use those opinions as a basis for making arguments in connection with future disputes. However, because language is an imperfect tool for expressing one's ideas and because judges do not and cannot anticipate either all of the analogous disputes that will arise or all the ways in which a lawyer might attempt to explain the significance of a particular opinion, the ability to define the future applicability of a court opinion is a crucial skill for lawyers and law students.

Students, therefore, study cases as sources of rules, as examples of how to apply rules, and as ends in themselves. Consequently, you must become expert at learning from cases. In fact, as Chapter 9 of this book explains, successful law students read court opinions differently than their less successful peers. You will learn to read court opinions the way that successful law students do so in Chapter 9.

Public Policies

Most generally, a public policy is a statement about what the speaker (the judge, a lawyer or a legal commentator) believes is good for society. For example, encouraging people to drive their cars carefully is a statement of public policy; that policy is reflected in hundreds of traffic laws, such as speed limits, restrictions on passing and signaling requirements. Lawyers, judges and law professors use the term public policy more specifically as a way of describing **the social good served by a rule of law or by a precedent**. For example, the rule making people liable for the injuries they cause by driving their cars carelessly can be said to serve the social good described in the above policy statement. Similarly, the rule requiring contracts for the sale of land to be in a signed writing serves the social good of encouraging people to act cautiously and carefully when they make contracts for the sale of land, which are very economically significant contracts for most people.

Public policies are important to law students for two different reasons. First, they explain the "whys" of the rules and holdings. Studies of learning have shown that knowing the whys of a rule helps the reader understand it and how to apply it. Secondly, lawyers use public policies to bolster their arguments in court. A lawyer will try to convince a court that a result favoring her clients would better serve society than a result in favor of her opponent's client. If the public policy of the applicable rule supports her argument, the lawyer will note that fact for the court. Thus, in a breach of contract suit, a lawyer trying to help her client avoid liability under an *oral* agreement for the sale of land might argue that granting relief to her opponent's client would contravene the policy for the rule requiring a *written* agreement. The lawyer representing the other party probably would have to argue a different policy, depending upon the facts of the case. For example, if the other party relied on the contract in a substantial way (building a house on the land), the lawyer would make a fairness policy argument, arguing that it would be unjust not to enforce the contract given the client's expenditure of so much money.

Students therefore must learn to discern the policies that underlie the rules and court opinions they are studying. Sometimes, courts and legislators explicitly state the policy underlying their decisions; many times, however, courts are not so explicit. Students therefore must learn to derive the underlying policies by reasoning out the social good the court or legislature must have had in mind. Chapter 9 provides guidance to students in developing this skill.

Hypotheticals

The term "hypothetical" is shorthand for the term "hypothetical question." It consists of a statement of a set of facts that gives rise to one or more legal disputes. A hypothetical may be as short as a sentence or as long as three pages. It may involve multiple parties or just two. Law professors write their hypotheticals by using court opinions not assigned to the students (usually with some modifications), by changing key facts in the court opinions assigned to the students, by adapting newspaper stories or by simply coming up with a story from scratch and making the hypothetical an appropriate length and degree of difficulty.

The student's tasks in response to a hypothetical are to identify the legal questions raised, to identify each fact that is relevant to the resolution of each legal question raised, to articulate all of the potentially applicable law, i.e., the relevant rules or case holdings, to explain how lawyers representing each of the parties would argue for a result favoring their respective clients and to predict how a court would decide the matter and explain why. Law professors and lawyers refer to these last parts, where the student articulates the parties' arguments and predicts the result and explains why, as the **legal analysis**; it is, by far, the most important part. While students must know the rules and case holdings and be able to identify the legal questions, they are ultimately evaluated as law students and lawyers by how well they perform legal analysis. In large part, law school exams and bar exams test students' ability to perform each of the skills identified in the preceding sentence and students' possession of the knowledge necessary to perform those skills (such as the knowledge of the rules and holdings).

Professors ask students in class to analyze hypotheticals as a way of testing the students' understanding of the court opinions they have read and as a way of helping the students practice the skills on which they will be tested on their examinations. These shorter hypotheticals are usually stated verbally and usually relate directly to the court opinions or rules on which the class is working.

Examination hypotheticals are almost always longer and almost never identify the relevant court opinions or rules. It is common for an exam hypothetical to conclude with one or more **calls of the question**. A call of the question is a statement of the students' assignment with respect to the question. It may be very broad, such as a statement that the students should "discuss the issues." It also may consist of a set of narrow questions, such as a list of objections to the admission of evidence on an evidence law examination, and a request that the students analyze the outcome of each objection.

How Rules, Court Opinions, Policies and Hypotheticals Are Integrated in Law School Instruction

As the foregoing discussion of rules, court opinions, public policy and hypotheticals suggests, students seldom study any of these units of instruction in isolation. The rules come from the court opinions (or from statutes or secondary sources), and they are often applied in the court opinions. The court opinions or statutes explicitly state the relevant policy considerations or the students must derive the policies by thinking through the rationale underlying the holdings or statutes. Finally, the hypotheticals require knowledge and application of the rules, holdings and policies. This integration, however, is not always evident to law students because of the technique by which most law professors teach law—the "Socratic" Method.

The "Socratic" Method and What It Assumes Students Will Be Doing

First-year law school instruction is most commonly described as "Socratic" in technique.[2] This method is characterized by little lecture and lots of questions by the professor to the students. Professors select one student (or, occasionally two or three) and ask the student to describe aspects of a rule or court opinion the class is studying. For court opinions, many professors require the selected student to identify the relevant facts, the court's holding and the policy underlying it; for rules, many professors require the selected student to break the rule down into a set of sub-requirements and articulate the policy underlying the rule. The professor then focuses on the application of the holding or rule by asking the selected student to apply the rule or holding to a hypothetical or series of hypotheticals. This questioning places significant demands on students in terms of class preparation. Professors assume the students will come to class having carefully read and briefed (more on both of these topics later) all the assigned court opinions. Some professors have even been known to simply walk out of class and leave the students to fend for themselves if the professor deems the students unprepared for class.

Because students are called on individually and must speak and think while their peers and their instructor are listening, there is a performance aspect to law school classroom experiences. This performance aspect may, at first glance, seem intimidating

---

2. There is evidence that upper division law school courses are more often taught using lecture methodologies.

and may be anxiety provoking. The most important thing for students to do is to treat this experience as neither more significant nor less significant than it really is. On the one hand, your performance in this context has very little, if any, bearing on your grades or your opportunities for extracurricular experiences, such as moot court and law review, and says virtually nothing about what kind of lawyer you will be. There is certainly no evidence that the students who say smart (or just many) things in class get the better grades. Consequently, students should never sacrifice necessary learning activities, such as listening in class, doing all the work for all their classes, studying for examinations and timely completing their papers simply to appear smart to their peers and their professors when called on in class.

On the other hand, the experience is not meaningless. By speaking in class, you are actively engaging in your own learning, and it is well established that active learners outperform passive ones on every measure of success. In fact, your preparation in class helps you take in your new learning, because, as I explain in the next chapter, students retain new learning better when they have connected it to prior learning. Moreover, when you speak in class, you give yourself an opportunity to practice your new skills and get feedback on your efforts from your professor. Certainly, one telling characteristic of all expert law students is that they seek and obtain as much practice and feedback as possible. In fact, for some students, as you will learn in this book, articulating their understandings out loud is an essential part of their learning process (if you are such a person, frequent participation in class may be necessary). Finally, because you are getting feedback (and in many law school classes, this oral feedback is all you get other than your results on your examinations), you are gaining information about your level of understanding and your approach to learning the material.

The Socratic Method requires students to learn vicariously because, while the selected student is being questioned, all the rest of the students in the class are not directly involved. Law professors *assume* that all the students in the class are playing along, answering the professor's questions in their heads and learning from the selected student's answers to the questions and the professor's responses to the student's answers. The non-selected students, therefore, must learn what they need to learn from this vicarious experience of watching the professor question one of their peers. They must practice by trying to answer the professor's questions in their heads and apply the professor's feedback and corrections to their answers. The vicarious nature of the experience means that the demand on students to self-evaluate their performance and regulate their own learning is particularly high; it is very unlikely professors have any idea whether any particular student has learned most of the material.

The method also involves self-teaching because professors assume students will learn all they need to learn by watching and by studying on their own or in groups. In fact, law professors seldom tell students the relationships among the concepts studied in the course, expecting students to figure those relationships out themselves. In most instances, professors also do not tell the students how to identify legal issues or how to perform legal analysis, leaving it to the students to figure these things out for themselves. In fact, this method's most traditional practitioners refuse to answer student questions, believing students should figure out the answers on their own; in more than half of all law school classes, students' first feedback on their development of law school skills is their grades on their midterms and finals. Consequently, law students, perhaps even more than their peers in other educational settings, must self-regulate their own learning. In short, each law student is the only person in a position to assess whether the student actually has learned what she needs to learn.

Law students, law professors, practicing lawyers and judges all have commented on the difficulty and discomfort this methodology produces in new law students. Part of that discomfort likely does stem from this approach to law school instruction. It also stems from the differences between college and law school, the competitiveness of many law students and because learning any new skill, particularly an intellectual one like legal reasoning, is very stressful.

Law School Stress

While nearly all law students regard law school as stimulating, most also experience it as stressful. If you feel stress during your first year in law school, you are in the majority. This discussion is not offered to scare you or to try to dissuade you from law school. The goal of this book, in fact, is to give you a set of tools that will allow you to both enjoy and succeed in law school. I have chosen to address the issue of law school stress to let you know that you are not alone and to help you understand the sources of the stress so that you can better deal with them.

First, as noted above, the nature of law school teaching produces stress. Students are on the spot in class, are expected to learn vicariously and, ultimately, must bear a much larger responsibility for their own learning than they ever have born in their lives. Moreover, most students are not told that they must learn vicariously or teach themselves. They either must figure it out on their own or suffer the consequence: poor grades. By reading this book, you will know what to expect and you will learn not only how to teach yourself, but also how to get the help you need when you cannot learn vicariously or on your own.

Second, law school is an educational culture shock, particularly for students who attend law school right out of college. In many college courses, particularly those in the social science areas, much of the learning involves memorizing and much of the tests demand little more than regurgitation of learned material. In law school, students must memorize and be able to regurgitate even larger amounts of material, yet this regurgitation does not ensure even passing grades. Unfortunately, such knowledge, while essential, is insufficient to achieve success on law school exams and papers because law school exams and papers require *application* of the knowledge. By reading this book, you will develop an approach to learning that greatly increases the likelihood that you will develop those application skills.

Third, law school requires a significant amount of challenging work. Many students come to law school having succeeded in college without having had to work very hard. The difficulty of the work combined with the quantity of work can be daunting. Many law students devote as much as 50 hours per week to their studies. For this reason, finding balance between school work and other interests is crucial, and developing the time management skills addressed throughout this book will improve the quality of your law school living. If you master the skills in this book, you will be the kind of student who works smarter, not harder.

Fourth, in many law schools, the students are very competitive. Students who have succeeded in all of their past educational endeavors quickly discover that all of their peers in law school also have always succeeded. In addition, some employers give enormous weight to students' law school grades, which increases the grade pressure on students. The issue requires students to constantly focus on why they are in law school—to join an amazing profession. Five years after students graduate, their law school grades have become irrelevant; clients do not chose their lawyers based on the lawyers' law school grades but, rather, based on their qualities as lawyers and people. Moreover, many of the most rewarding jobs held by lawyers are much less grade-dependant. While there is no doubt that this book is designed to help students get good grades in law school, its ultimate purpose is to help students *learn well* in law school and for the rest of their lives.

Finally, law school exams and papers are not merely different from college exams and papers. Law school exams and papers are also harder. Law school exams and papers demand significant skills and the skills demanded are ones many (perhaps most) students did not possess before they came to law school. On law school exams and papers, students must be able to identify previously unseen problems by type, draw analogies, apply rules and cases and predict outcomes in disputes their professors (experts in the subject area) have designed not to have obvious outcomes.

While the demands of law school inevitably produce discomfort, the picture is not really a bleak one. Knowing you will encounter stress and knowing it is normal and survivable (and most students survive just fine) makes the stress easier to deal with it. Law school is also exciting and stimulating. Learning new things, if you are open to the experience, is one of the greatest gifts of being a human being. Plus, the learning and thinking skills you acquire will serve you for the rest of your life, even if you never practice law.

Having learned how law is taught, knowing that law school makes particularly significant demands on students, and understanding that expert self-regulating learners outperform novices, you are ready to begin your study of self-regulated learning.

Reflection Questions

1. How will law school be different from your undergraduate or other graduate studies?

2. How is law tested?

3. Explain what it means to say learning in law school involves vicarious learning and self-teaching and what these two characteristics of law school learning demand of law students.

4. Why is law school stressful?

5. How will the differences between law school and your past educational experiences change how you will study and learn?

References

E. Allan Farnsworth, *An Introduction to the Legal System of the United States* (3rd ed.) (Oceana Publications, Inc., 1996).

Toni M. Fine, *American Legal Systems: A Resource and Reference Guide.*

Margaret Z. Johns and Rex R. Perschbacher, *The United States Legal System* (Carolina Academic Press, 2002).

Lawrence S. Krieger, *What We're Not Telling Law Students—And Lawyers—That They Really Need to Know: Some Thoughts Toward Revitalizing the Profession from Its Roots,* 13 J. L. & Health 1 (1999).

Terri LeClercq, *Legal Writing Style* (2nd ed.) (Aspen Law and Business 2000).

Bridget A. Mahoney, *Distress Among the Legal Profession: What Law Schools Can Do About It,* 15 Notre Dame J.L. Ethics & Pub. Pol. 307 (2001).

Making Docile Lawyers: An Essay on the Pacification of Law Students, 111 Harv. L. Rev. 2027 (1998).

Cathleen A. Roach, *A River Runs Through It: Tapping into the Information Stream to Move Students from Isolation to Autonomy,* 36 Ariz. L. Rev. 667 (1994).

Richard C. Wydick, *Plain English for Lawyers* (4th ed.) (Carolina Academic Press, 1998).

Chapter 3

How Humans Learn

Not only do expert learners know what to expect from their educational experiences (a topic addressed in the previous chapter), but also they know how they learn. In the past one hundred years, educational psychologists have gained considerable insight into how human beings learn. In particular, the two most influential movements in educational psychology research, **Cognitivism** and **Constructivism**, have together created a revolution in our understanding of human learning across all educational contexts. Expert learning is itself grounded in understandings based on these theories. More importantly, expert learners, by understanding how learning occurs within their brains, are better able to make learning choices most likely to produce optimal results.

Cognitivism

Prior to 1950, the only model for understanding how humans learn was behaviorism. According to the behaviorist model of human learning, a student has learned something when she makes the desired response to a specific stimulus. Thus, a student has learned to perform long division when, in response to a problem requiring long division (a stimulus), the student properly performs it (the desired response). The role of instruction, according to this view, is to strengthen the connection between the stimulus and the desired response by rewarding the learner when she responds properly and punishing the learner when she performs improperly. The focus of this view is on what the instructor observes rather than on what occurs within a learner's mind. In other words, the focus is on the response and not on the mental activity that causes a learner to develop the ability to make the desired response.

In the late 1950s, learning theory shifted away from behavioral models and away from the focus on learning as an observable event to a set of models of human learning collectively referred to as cognitivism. Cognitivists focus on what occurs within the human brain during learning, explaining learning in terms of how the brain processes and retains new learning. These explanations or models of how human learning occurs are called "**information processing theories**." Cognitivists equate learning with the active storage in a student's long-term memory (a part of the brain) in an organized, meaningful and useable manner.

Learning, according to cognitivists, involves a mental process believed to occur according to the sequence described below. Although, as described below, the sequence appears linear, moving from one place along the line to the next and then to the next and so on, the process is likely more circular and interactive. Also, although information processing is described as a theory or model, there is considerable research evidence supporting its accuracy.

Computers are the analogy upon which information processing theories are based. Hundreds of pieces of information[1] reach our senses every moment. The information registers in our brains (our "sensory registers") for a brief moment. We can pay attention, however, to only a few of these pieces of information at any given moment, a process known as "**selective attention.**"[2]

The information to which we pay attention passes into our **short-term memory,** also known as our "working memory." Only small amounts of information can be retained in working memory and only for a limited time. Introductory psychology textbooks note the fact that telephone numbers consist of seven digits precisely because studies of short-term memory show that seven bits of information (plus or minus three bits) is the maximum capacity of short-term memory. Most of us have noticed that we usually can remember a new phone number for only 10–20 seconds unless we do something to help us remember it, such as saying it out loud several times.

By **encoding**[3] information in a meaningful way, the information becomes stored in **long-term memory.** The more deeply we think about new information, the more likely we are to remember it. In fact, one goal of instruction is to help students learn the material so well that they can recall it with minimal attention, which is known as "**overlearning.**" Overlearning, in turn, produces what educational psychologists call "**automaticity.**" For every high level intellectual skill, such as those you will be learning in law school, there are sub-skills for which students require automaticity so that they can focus brain power on the more difficult skill. For example, most adults have overlearned and developed automaticity with respect to reading; they are able to read and process the meaning of sentences and paragraphs without focusing on "sounding out" the words used or the meaning of unfamiliar words. Most people also have experienced automaticity with respect to the act of driving home from school or work; most of us have had the experience of driving our cars home from school or work and, when we arrived at home, have had the strange sensation of not being able to recall doing so, of being unable to recall getting on the freeway, identifying the freeway exit and getting off the freeway and then making the series of turns necessary to get to our homes. We were able to do so because we have overlearned the route home and the skills involved in driving.

---

1. The term "information" can be misleading. It does not simply refer to what might be called rote knowledge, such as being able to state the capitals of all 50 states in the United States. Rather, the term refers to all learning at all intellectual levels, including synthesis of information, analysis and problem solving.

2. For example, as I wrote this section of this textbook, my brain received sensory inputs from the *sounds* of passing cars, backing trucks and barking dogs, from the *feel* of the computer keys against my fingers and of the hard chair on which I am sitting, from what I see as I read my notes and the articles and books from which I am working and from the *taste* of the coffee I am sipping as I work. No person possibly could attend to all of these inputs and write anything. Instead, I selectively attended to each input as I wrote.

3. Encoding refers to how we store the information in long-term memory. As a law professor, when I cannot recall the name of a student in my class, I often finds myself able to recall the length of the student's name, the degree to which the student's name is a common one or the first letter of the student's name. This recall suggests how I store my students' names in long-term memory, by the length, commonness or first letter of their names.

Schema Theory

Cognitivists also believe the brain does not merely store information in long-term memory; the brain organizes long-term memories in structures called "schemata." Experts believe schemata are organized like a card catalog (to use an outdated library term) or a database. In other words, each piece of information has its own slot or place within a larger structure. The folder system developed as part of Microsoft's Windows software both assumes the existence of such schemata and replicates human schemata. For example, I have stored this portion of my text in a folder I have labeled "ELLS Textbook," which is inside a folder I have labeled "ELLS" which is inside a folder I have labeled "Research Projects," which is inside a folder my employer has created for me labeled "michaels." Similarly, a law library database might classify this text by a number of "fields": author, title, topic, year of publication, etc. Schema theory assumes our brains store information in a similar way.

The database analogy is particularly accurate because it captures another aspect of schema theory. Humans often store learning in multiple ways, particularly when they want to be able to recall it readily. For example, I can recall the name of the novel, *The World According to Garp,* by recalling its author, by recalling its plot, by recalling any of several of the characters in the novel and by recalling the friend with whom I shared a love of the book. Storing learning in multiple ways, which is known as "deep processing," allows easier recall. Theorists believe learning in multiple ways improves recall either because it strengthens the memory trace (the process of moving to gather the information) or because it creates more mental paths to the information.

Schemata do not only store information like folders or card catalogs. Schemata also are like entire computer programs in that the organized material includes structures that reflect how to perform skills. Thus, most adults who can play a musical instrument, such as the piano, have developed a schema for performing all the mental and physical steps involved. These steps include identifying each mark on the sheet of music, knowing what each mark means and understanding the relationships among: the marks, the black and white keys, their hands, the necessary fingering to reach all the keys, the pedals below the keys and their feet. In addition, schemata are like theories in that they allow us to make predictions and to draw inferences. Thus, all of us have developed schemata for what makes food appear particularly appetizing—the colors, odors and shapes of the items on a plate allow us to predict whether we will enjoy a meal.

To use prior learning to analyze a problem or perform a skill, the learning must be **recalled** from long-term memory into short-term memory. In this sense, short-term memory and long-term memory are seen as engaging in a continuous discussion or exchange in which learning passes back and forth between them. When we encode new learning, it moves from short-term memory into long-term memory; when we recall the procedure involved in working a long division problem, the procedure moves from long-term memory into short-term memory so we can implement it. Finally, retrieved information passes through a response generator that sends an appropriate message to the parts of the body that need to act on or communicate in the environment. Figure 1 shows a cognitivist model of human learning.

As this model reflects, learners receive information from their environment, attend to information upon which they wish to focus, encode information they wish to retain, retrieve encoded information when they are ready to use it and use that information to generate a response to an environmental event. Thus, for example, students learning the

Figure 1: A Cognitivist Model of How Humans Learn

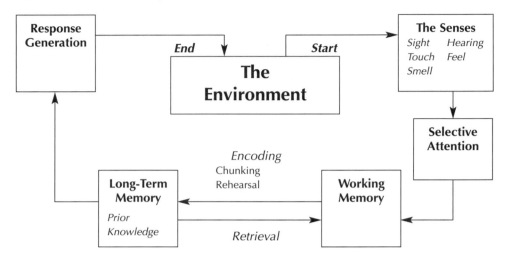

above model would see it in this text, focus on it so that it enters their working memory, use a technique to help them encode it (such as trying to draw it for themselves or creating a mnemonic to remember each of the parts), later retrieve the encoded model from long-term memory by thinking about it (if, for example, they were taking a test on it) and then use that recollection to direct their fingers to correctly answer the test question.

Taken together, this view of human learning has the following crucial implications for students who wish to become expert learners:

- ✓ Students must make active efforts to encode their new learning.
- ✓ Students must become experts at the various techniques for encoding new learning.
- ✓ As much as possible, students should try to draw analogies between what they are learning and what they already know so the new learning can connect to the prior learning already stored in their long-term memory.
- ✓ Students should try to organize their learning so that it can be readily stored in a schema.
- ✓ Students need to engage in "deep processing" so that they develop automaticity with respect to knowledge and skills.
- ✓ Students should encode their new learning in multiple ways to allow easier recall.

Constructivism

Constructivism is a learning theory of even more recent vintage, having just gained prominence in the past 20 years. Constructivists view learning and knowledge as being created by each individual from her experience. They view what others assert to be "absolute truths," such as the idea that the sun is a star, as "truths for now," negotiated and agreed upon by experts in the field.

Constructivists, therefore, do not believe instructors transmit knowledge. Rather, they believe each learner continually creates her own images of what the world is "like" from her experiences and her interpretations of her experiences. For constructivists, therefore, a crucial factor in learning is providing students with opportunities to develop personal interpretations of experiences, to make for themselves a set of understandings about what they are learning. Constructivists also emphasize the importance of real-world experiences. They argue that students learn best when they are thrust into **authentic experiences**, when they do what practitioners in the field do. Thus, constructivists argue that students should learn to be contracts lawyers by working with clients who have real contracts problems or, at least, by working with real contracts.

Finally, constructivists emphasize the importance of student-to-student interaction. They believe students should be given opportunities to work with their peers in small groups to find meaning and learn, rather than being forced to learn and find meaning solely on their own. Such groups, called "cooperative learning groups" by education experts, have been proven to be one of the most powerful learning tools in existence. These groups are so effective because they allow students to obtain access to multiple perspectives with respect to a problem or issue and thereby to develop the more complex approaches and understandings required to address complicated problems. Most of us can find the value of this insight from recalling a meeting or discussion in which we have participated in which the group as a whole developed a better understanding of a problem or a better solution than any individual had been able to come up with on his or her own. Of course, such results are the product of groups that know how to work together, how to subdue ego in service of the goal of obtaining the best results possible, how to develop "positive interdependence," where each member of the group invests in the success of every other member of the group, and how to develop "accountability," where each member of the group holds every other member of the group responsible for performing her or his share of the group work. Groups that do not develop these qualities are dysfunctional, and dysfunctional groups are no more productive or valuable than dysfunctional families or working on one's own.

This view of human learning also has important implications for students seeking to become expert learners:

- ✓ Students should strive to make their learning personally meaningful, to make sense for themselves of what they are learning.
- ✓ Students should seek authentic experiences or to make what they are learning as close to "real world" as possible.
- ✓ Students should participate in small work groups and should try to foster group identity, mutual commitment and mutual accountability.

Reflection Questions

1. Given your own experiences as a learner and what you have learned in this chapter, how do you learn? In other words, what aspects of Cognitivism and Constructivism are consistent with your own learning experiences and what aspects of your own learning cannot be explained by either of these learning theories?

2. How will what you have learned about Cognitivism influence how you study law?

3.   How will what you have learned about schema theory influence how you study law?

4.   How will what you have learned about Constructivism influence how you study law?

References

Marcy Perkins Driscoll, PSYCHOLOGY OF LEARNING FOR INSTRUCTION (1994).

Peggy A. Ertmer & Timothy Newby, *Behaviorism, Cognitivism, Constructivism: Comparing Critical Features from an Instructional Design Perspective,* 6 PERFORMANCE IMPROVEMENT Q. 50 (1993).

Dale H. Schunk, LEARNING THEORIES: AN EDUCATIONAL PERSPECTIVE (2d ed. 1996).

Michael Hunter Schwartz, *Teaching Law by Design: How Learning Theory and Instructional Design Can Inform and Reform Law Teaching,* 38 SAN DIEGO L. REV. 347 (2001).

Patricia L. Smith & Tillman J. Ragan, INSTRUCTIONAL DESIGN (1999).

Chapter 4

The Self-Regulated Learning (SRL) Cycle

Self-Regulated Learning, as explained above, is a cycle in which a student actively controls her behavior, motivation and cognition, as she is engaging in academic tasks. Professor Barry Zimmerman, one of the leading authors in the field, explains:

> Self-regulated learners view academic learning as something they do for themselves rather than as something that is done to or for them. They believe academic learning is a proactive activity, requiring self-initiated motivational and behavioral processes.... Unlike their less skilled peers, self-regulated learners control their own learning experiences through processes such as goal-setting, self-monitoring, and strategic thinking.[1]

Actually, those who teach for a living have encountered students who possess excellent self-regulation skills:

> Teachers know self-regulated academic learners when they see them—these students are interested in the subject matter; well-prepared; and ready with comments, questions, ideas, and insights; they are problem finders and problem solvers, unafraid to fail or to admit they do not understand, driven to rectify failure and to construct understanding.[2]

The SRL cycle involves three phases: *forethought, performance* and *reflection,* each of which has multiple components. Figure 2 depicts the cycle and all the components of the three phases; each of the phases is detailed below.

The Forethought Phase

The **forethought phase** consists of all the thinking the student does before she starts engaging in a learning task. It is the preparation phase, although the term "preparation" misleadingly makes it sound as if the activities in which the student is engaged during the forethought phase are not as important or as demanding as the tasks in which the

---

1. Barry J. Zimmerman, *Developing Self-Fulfilling Cycles of Academic Regulation: An Analysis of Exemplary Instructional Models* in SELF-REGULATED LEARNING: FROM TEACHING TO SELF-REFLECTIVE PRACTICE 1, (1998).

2. Barry J. Zimmerman & Andrew S. Paulsen, *Self-Monitoring During Collegiate Studying: An Invaluable Tool for Academic Self-Regulation* in NEW DIRECTIONS IN COLLEGE TEACHING AND LEARNING: UNDERSTANDING SELF-REGULATED LEARNING 13 (No. 65:1995).

Figure 2: The Self-Regulated Learning Cycle

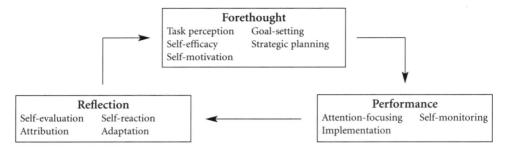

student will later engage. In fact, each of the activities involved in the forethought phase has been shown independently to improve a student's educational results. In other words, students who use even one of the activities required by the forethought phase obtain higher grades than those who were not so trained and did not engage in that activity.

The forethought phase includes five activities or sub-phases:

(1) **Perceiving the task,**
(2) **Classifying the task,**
(3) **Invoking intrinsic interest and self-efficacy,**
(4) **Goal setting,** and
(5) **Planning strategies.**

As the numbering implies, expert self-regulated learners typically engage in these activities in a particular sequence, although the sequence is not exactly linear in the sense that particular learners combine activities (particularly as they become skilled at them), develop automaticity in performing the activities, and alter the order to their particular preferences. These changes in ordering and use occur because expert learners alter their approaches to learning based on their particular learning needs and preferences and based on their reflections on their learning, both while the learning task is in progress and after it has been completed. In other words, expert learners see each learning task as an opportunity to reflect upon and sharpen their learning skills.

At the outset of a learning experience, all learners, expert and otherwise, **perceive the task.** In other words, they recognize that a task has been required of them. For example, before you started reading these materials, you noticed them in your syllabus. Expert self-regulated learners then **classify the learning task,** noting the type(s) of skills required by the task (e.g., reading for understanding, memorizing, problem-solving, writing) and the subject area of the task (e.g., history, geology). An expert learner, therefore, would classify the task in which you are engaged in right now as a reading comprehension task (reading to learn the concepts described in this chapter) and classify the subject area as "self-regulated learning" or "expert learning" or, more generally, "educational psychology."

Having identified and classified the learning task, the learner reacts to it. In part, she considers how much the task interests her intrinsically. Expert self-regulated learners **invoke intrinsic interest** by determining the relevance of the task, both to the course and to their reasons for undertaking the particular educational endeavor in which they are engaged (e.g., becoming a lawyer). An expert learner would regard reading this book as interesting simply because learning interests them or because of the relevance of self-regulated learning to their success in law school.

At about the same time, the student also assesses her **self-efficacy** for accomplishing the task. Self-efficacy refers to "students' beliefs about whether they have the ability to successfully master an academic task." Self-efficacy has been proven to be a particularly powerful predictor of educational success.[3] Expert learners consciously *invoke* self-efficacy by recalling past successes with similar tasks. In the context of reading this book, an expert learner would recall other courses in which they had to learn from a text, such as history, social science or even some hard science courses. Self-efficacy is a product of the intersection of students' past educational experiences, their perception of the degree of difficulty of the task and their perception of the adequacy of their development of the skill(s) required by the task. Thus, an expert learner would consider how well prepared she feels to learn about self-regulated learning, given its only modest difficulty, and would weigh how skilled she is in learning from texts.

The self-regulating learner then sets a goal, a specific outcome she desires, for the task. Expert self-regulated learners generally **set learning goals** that, most commonly, focus on mastery of the material rather than on grades. These goals have specific standards to measure their mastery, are short term and moderately difficult to achieve. An appropriate goal for the material in this chapter might be: "By the first day of class, I will be able to list the three phases of the SRL cycle and explain what each generally involves without error, and be able to list the sub-tasks of each phase and explain generally what each sub-task requires with 80% accuracy." This goal is appropriate because it is demanding but not too hard, because it is a short-term goal and because it is concrete.

The final and crucial step of the forethought phase involves devising and tailoring a strategic approach to achieving the student's goal. The student, having classified the task according to what it demands and its subject area, engages in **strategy selection** by identifying possible strategies most appropriate to her goals, reviewing her own learning preferences and making predictions of outcomes based on the various strategies she is considering and then by choosing the learning strategy(ies) she will be employing. Learning strategies are so many, so varied and so task dependent that a list here is impossible. At this stage of your study of the SRL Cycle, you only need to know that learning strategies are task-specific (different depending on the task), many in number (several for each type of learning), and learner-specific (dependent on your learning preferences, personality type and learning goals).

Strategy selection also includes identifying motivational strategies (the thoughts that will help you stay focused on the task as you progress through it, such as your interest in the task and reasons for mastering it and your past successes with similar tasks) and environmental strategies (e.g., removing distractions, forming study groups).

The Performance Phase

The performance phase is the implementation phase of the cycle. It involves not only the learning activities themselves, but also the mental processes that affect students' ef-

---

3. Anastasia S. Hagan & Claire Ellen Weinstein, *Achievement Goals, Self-Regulated Learning, and the Role of the Classroom Context* in NEW DIRECTIONS IN COLLEGE TEACHING AND LEARNING: UNDERSTANDING SELF-REGULATED LEARNING 45 (No. 65:1995).

forts to concentrate and otherwise implement those activities. There are three tasks that make up this phase:

(1) **attention-focusing,**
(2) implementation of **the learning activity** itself (including the student's mental process for performing the activity properly), and
(3) the **self-monitoring** the student performs as she implements her strategies and begins to learn.

All three of these phases occur, more or less, at the same time. In other words, the student focuses her attention and monitors her learning throughout her performance of the learning activities.

Attention-focusing increases the likelihood that studying endeavors will be productive. Self-regulated learners use strategies to focus and preserve their attention on their learning tasks. These strategies include both motivational control strategies (which help the students find the push within themselves to do the necessary work) and emotional control strategies (which help the students control feelings of inadequacy and anxiety when progress is slow and feelings of overconfidence and wavering focus when the learning is going particularly well).

The learning activity itself involves engaging in the learning strategy(ies) selected by the student. Self-regulated learners possess a wide variety of learning strategies, and they have learned them in such a way that they can readily use them without regard for the subject area (e.g., history, educational psychology, the construction industry, law) in which the task happens to fall. They use verbalizations of task requirements (e.g., first, I will do this, than I will do that, etc.) and visualizations (e.g., picturing what a good diagram of a concept looks like before drawing one) to ensure they perform the tasks correctly.

There is general agreement that the self-monitoring aspect of the performance phase is crucial. The student's goals and strategy decisions set criteria for this monitoring, which includes monitoring both the effectiveness of the selected strategies for achieving the student's learning goal and the time and effort the strategy is requiring and then weighing the two against each other. Expert self-regulated learners monitor their learning continuously and perform the monitoring very close in time to the event being monitored.

The Reflection Phase

The reflection phase of the cycle guides the students as to their future learning endeavors. The student reflects on what she did and how effective it was and then considers the implications of her experience for future learning activities.

This phase includes four facets:

(1) **self-evaluation,**
(2) **attribution,**
(3) **self-reaction,** and
(4) **adaptation.**

Self-evaluation involves comparing one's performance with a standard, either in terms of the standard set by the learner or the instructor's objectives or in comparison to other learners. Expert self-regulated learners evaluate how they are doing accurately and immediately after they have completed their learning activities.

Having evaluated her performance, the self-regulated learner develops attributions about the causes of her results. An attribution is the student's explanation for why she performed well or poorly. Although students' personal beliefs and the results of others greatly influence students' attributions, self-regulated learners are much more likely to attribute failures to correctable causes, such as insufficient effort or incorrect selection of learning technique(s), and to attribute successes to personal competence. These attributions lead self-regulated learners to try again and to try harder when they fail; in contrast, novice learners are more likely to attribute their failures to ability and, therefore, are more likely to give up and stop trying.

Attributions are closely connected to the next facet, self-reactions, which are the student's emotional feelings about herself as a result of her results and of her attributions of the causes of her results. Self-regulated learners generally feel better about themselves as learners, even when they encounter learning difficulties, and therefore are more likely to persist to success.

The students' attributions influence their adaptations because, having identified the sources of the errors, they are able to brainstorm and select the necessary adjustments for future learning endeavors. Self-regulated learners are therefore more adaptive because they recognize both that learning difficult skills may require many practice cycles and that systematic variations in approaches will help them overcome learning difficulties.

Reflection Questions

1. At various times in this chapter, as well as in Chapter 1, self-regulated learners are described as "proactive," "in control," "strategic," "consciously aware," "goal oriented" and "driven to rectify failure and to construct understanding." To what extent are these characterizations an outgrowth of engaging in the behaviors described as a part of the SRL cycle?

2. What aspects of the SRL cycle make sense to you? Why? (What have you observed in your life as a student that makes you believe that these aspects will work for your law school studies?) What aspects of the SRL cycle do not make sense to you? Why? (What have you observed in your life as a student that makes you believe that these aspects will not work for your law school studies?)

References

Peggy A. Ertmer & Timothy J. Newby, *The Expert Learner: Strategic, Self-Regulated and Reflective*, 24 INSTRUCTIONAL SCIENCE 1 (1996).

Anastasia S. Hagan & Claire Ellen Weinstein, *Achievement Goals, Self-Regulated Learning, and the Role of the Classroom Context* in NEW DIRECTIONS IN COLLEGE TEACHING AND LEARNING: UNDERSTANDING SELF-REGULATED LEARNING 45 (No. 65:1995).

Barbara K. Hofer, Shirley L. Yu and Paul R. Pintrich, *Teaching College Students to Be Self-Regulated Learners* in SELF REGULATED LEARNING: FROM TEACHING TO SELF-REFLECTIVE PRACTICE 57 (D.H. Schunk, B. Zimmerman, eds.1998).

Reinhard W. Lindner and Bruce Harris, *Self-Regulated Learning: Its Assessment and Instructional Implications,* 16 EDUCATIONAL RESEARCH QUARTERLY 29 (1992).

Bridget Murray, *Getting Smart About Learning Is Her Lesson,* 29 APA MONITOR (April 1998).

Paul R. Pintrich, *Understanding Self-Regulated Learning* in UNDERSTANDING SELF-REGULATED LEARNING 3 (P. Pintrich, ed. 1995).

Rochester Institute of Technology, http://www.rit.edu/~609www/ch/faculty/self-reg.htm.

Stephen Stoynoff, *Self-Regulated Learning Strategies of International Students: A Study of High- and Low-Achievers,* COLLEGE STUDENT JOURNAL 329 (1997).

Claire E. Weinstein and Richard E. Mayer, *The Teaching of Learning Strategies,* in HANDBOOK OF RESEARCH ON TEACHING (M.C. Wittriock, ed. 1986).

Barry J. Zimmerman, *Developing Self-Fulfilling Cycles of Academic Regulation: An Analysis of Exemplary Instructional Models* in SELF REGULATED LEARNING: FROM TEACHING TO SELF-REFLECTIVE PRACTICE 1 (D.H. Schunk, B. Zimmerman, eds.1998).

Barry J. Zimmerman & Andrew S. Paulsen, *Self-Monitoring During Collegiate Studying: An Invaluable Tool for Academic Self-Regulation* in NEW DIRECTIONS IN COLLEGE TEACHING AND LEARNING: UNDERSTANDING SELF-REGULATED LEARNING 13 (No. 65:1995).

Chapter 5

The Forethought Phase
of the SRL Cycle

The forethought phase sets the table for the rest of the cycle; it is the preparatory phase of the SRL Cycle, and the goal for the student is to get ready to learn so that her learning is as efficient and successful as possible. The danger of omitting this phase is similar to the danger of building a home without plans or of having plans but failing to consider all relevant construction issues (cost, timeline for completion, region [are there tornado or earthquake safety issues to consider?], style preferences, etc.). The result will likely fall far short of what it could have been.

In many ways, students may perceive this phase as a process of simply being explicit, of forcing themselves to make conscious, thoughtful decisions about their studying plans as opposed to "just studying." In fact, in the beginning, they may feel that some of these steps require them to be excessively conscious, to act unnaturally. They may even feel these acts are needlessly time consuming at first. Once they understand cognitive theory, however, they know that they can do something about this feeling. Thus, one of the goals for the first semester of law school should be to overlearn these steps, to develop automaticity in their use so that they become natural and speedy.

Just as the overall self-regulatory process can be seen as a cyclical process, so can the forethought phase itself be seen as a process. The learner moves through this process in a fairly linear, straightforward way. The purpose of the forethought phase is to prepare the learner to begin learning. The learner comes to grips with what she needs to learn and how she will go about doing so. The forethought phase consists of the following activities: perceiving the task, classifying the learning task, invoking self-interest and efficacy, setting learning goals, and identifying learning strategies choices and selecting from among them. This phase can be shown graphically as a linear process through which the student progresses. Figure 3 below depicts this process as a series of steps and identifies the questions implicated by each step.

Step 1: Perceiving the Task

(1) What is the assignment?
(2) By when must it be completed?

As reflected in the information-processing model above, learning tasks, like all mental tasks, begin with perception and the choice by the learner to focus on the task. Thus, the first task for a learner, **perceiving the task**, is to recognize the need for engaging in learning and to choose to attend to that task. The learner determines that she must do something (get ready for an examination, read a textbook, memorize course material) and her deadline for completing the task. For example, a syllabus for a Criminal Law class might include the following two entries, among many others:

<blockquote>"Week 1   The Mental State   pp. 118–165"</blockquote>

and

<blockquote>"Week 8   Midterm Examination   Be prepared"</blockquote>

To succeed in this course, the student needs to perceive that the first entry is a reading assignment related to something called "The Mental State" and the other entry is a disclosure of when students will be taking their midterm and therefore actually is an assignment of all the tasks necessary to be prepared to take the examination by the eighth week of class.

Having perceived a task, learners, even novice self-regulators, then contemplate what's involved in performing the task.

Step 2: Classifying the Learning Task

(1) What is the subject area in which the task falls?
(2) What types of learning are involved?

Not all learning tasks are alike, and different tasks require different learning strategies. Expert learners take vastly different approaches depending upon whether they are reading an economics textbook, writing a paper, researching a question, memorizing formulae in preparation for a chemistry test or learning a new musical piece to play on a musical instrument in front of an audience. As a few examples, a reading assignment might require organizational strategies, such as outlining or creating graphic organizers, and comprehension strategies, such as pre-reading and questioning; a writing task might require different organizational strategies and would require editing strategies; a memorization task might require selection from a wide variety of strategies, such as rehearsal (reviewing flashcards), summarizing or mnemonics, the choice of which would depend upon the purpose in memorizing, the planned use of the memorized information and the student's possession of contextual information.

By **classifying the learning task** at the outset, the student can decide which approach would be most effective. The first classification is a simple one, requiring less than five seconds—identifying the subject area in which the task falls. In the first weeks of law school, students will receive many assignments and have significant and seemingly overwhelming demands placed on their time. Consequently, students will need to take a few moments and make sure their studying gets done and identify, each time, the subject area on which they will be working.

A somewhat harder classification involves identifying the nature of the assignment. Law school learning tasks do not vary as much as college tasks vary. However, in law school, students will have multiple tasks to complete every single day and so must determine exactly what each task demands so that they can select from among the strategies best suited to each task's successful completion.

Figure 3: The Five Steps of the Forethought Phase

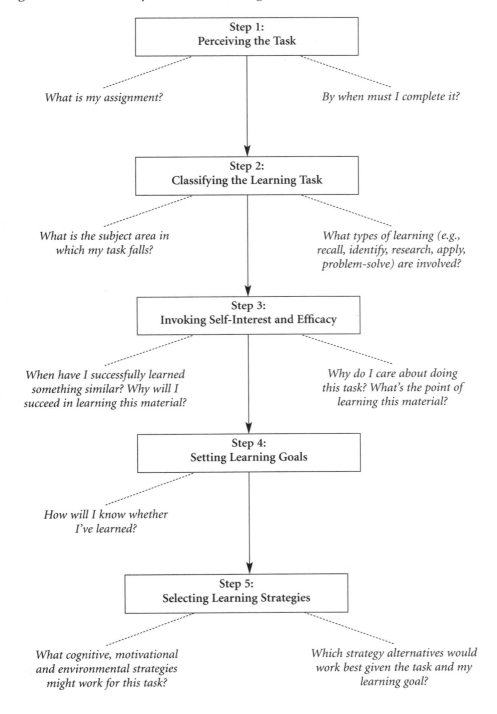

Law school learning tasks fall within one of five categories: **reading comprehension, research, synthesis, problem-solving** and **exam preparation**, which includes aspects of memorization, organization, concept learning (known by law students as issue spotting) and two types of principle learning (application of rules to facts and applying and distinguishing cases). The discussion below describes in general terms these various types of learning activities. This discussion, by necessity, does not describe **how** to perform these tasks; that discussion will come later. At this stage, the focus is for classification purposes.

Legal Reading Comprehension

Reading comprehension tasks in law school most often involve reading and understanding court opinions and statutes. These assignments are the typical day-to-day assignments students receive from their law professors. Law professors give these assignments and expect the students not only to read the cases and rules but also to understand them.

The good news is that educational psychologists have developed a vast body of knowledge with respect to the techniques best suited to helping students enhance their reading comprehension. In fact, some students may already be familiar with the SQ3R method of reading. SQ3R describes an approach to reading non-legal texts that has been shown to be an effective tool for enhancing student reading comprehension. Moreover, recent studies of law students reveal that successful law students and lawyers read court opinions differently than their less successful peers. Later in this book, these techniques will be described.

Research

Research involves discovering what the applicable law is. Typically, it involves working through a procedure in which what the student finds governs the next step (or, more accurately, the next branch of steps) of the procedure. For example, if, during an early step, the student learns of an applicable statute, the student would then find the statute and cases applying the statute. On the other hand, if the student determines there is no applicable statute, he or she will have to search an index of cases organized by subject area. Because research skills involve what educational psychologists call "procedural learning," a crucial technique for developing these skills involves memorizing the procedure, including all the decision and information steps that could lead in different directions. Techniques for doing so are presented later in this text.

Synthesis

Synthesis, in the law school context, refers to making sense of a set of cases all of which at least appear to address the same subject but which also appear to be in conflict. It involves reconciling the conflicts among the cases or recognizing that the cases cannot be reconciled. Synthesis tasks are typically an implicit, rather than an explicit, part of law school assignments. In legal writing or first-year professional skills courses, students must reconcile a set of cases as part of a larger problem-solving, hypothetical-based task. In other words, in such courses, students are given a hypothetical set of facts. Their task, in part, is to research and find the relevant statutes and court opinions. Once the student has found the relevant statutes and court opinions, the student must make sense of them, reconciling or at least understanding any potential conflicts among them. Once she does so, she is able to use the cases and statutes to analyze the hypothetical facts.

Problem Solving

The entire process of reading a hypothetical set of facts, determining the body of applicable law (or, more likely, the bodies of applicable law), researching and synthesizing the law (or using the law as the student has learned and synthesized it throughout a course), and then analyzing how lawyers representing each of the hypothetical parties would argue the analysis of the facts and predicting an outcome is collectively referred to as problem-solving. Typically, as noted above, the student is given only the hypothetical set of facts and then is asked to analyze those facts as lawyers representing all the parties described in the facts would do. Law school papers and examinations, as well as bar examinations, almost exclusively test students' problem-solving skills. The evidence that the student has engaged in all these learning activities is his or her written product, the paper or essay. For this reason, writing skills in general and legal writing skills in particular are crucial to law school success. At the same time, it is easy to erroneously perceive law school exams and papers and the bar exam as principally a writing enterprise. In fact, it is more accurate to understand law school exams and papers as being based on the assumption that all law students are good writers and even more accurate to say that law school exams and papers are a hybrid enterprise in which good, organized thinking is likely to produce good, organized writing.

Educational psychologists and law professors have developed approaches to such problem-solving tasks that make this process somewhat easier; those techniques are one of the subjects addressed later in this book.

Exam Preparation

Finally, most law school courses have final exams, and many have midterms for which the students must be preparing throughout the semester. Exam preparation includes the reading comprehension, synthesis and problem-solving tasks described above and three other main tasks: **memorization and organization**, **concept learning**, **principle learning**, and **exam writing**. Few professors, however, assign preparation activities; they just schedule tests. ***Students must perceive the need to engage in exam preparation activities on their own***, must sequence and schedule them on their own and must monitor their occurrence and effectiveness on their own. Because successful preparation for law school examinations requires students to engage in each of these types of learning tasks, each is described in some detail below.

Memorization and organization. Because law school exams require students to recall and use the rules, holdings, policies and syntheses they have learned and developed over the course of the semester, memorization of each is a prerequisite to success. It is common for law professors, who are not necessarily experts in human learning, to assert that students should not memorize the rules. They do not literally mean that students should not know the rules and holdings; rather, what they are communicating is that students need to memorize and to do more than merely memorize. Students also need to understand what the words mean and how to apply the rules and holdings. Of course, because law school exams test the ability to apply the law, "legal reasoning skills," students also must have memorized how to perform these skills.

Moreover, it is not enough to have memorized and to understand the rules, holdings, policies and syntheses. While students need to know every tree in the forest (all the rules, holdings, policies and syntheses), they must also understand the forest. Law school exams require seeing the big picture, seeing how the material all fits together. One reason for understanding the material relationships among the concepts has already been addressed in connection with the above discussion of schema theory; understanding the relationships among concepts makes the memory trace stronger. In addition, knowing the relationships among the concepts makes it easier to identify which of the concepts are being tested by a particular examination hypothetical.

Concept learning. Even flawless memorization and excellent organization are insufficient factors to achieve law school success. While both memorization and organization are prerequisites for success, even a student who has performed these two tasks flawlessly might not pass her law school examinations. That's because grades on law school exams are based on the extent to which the student demonstrates her development of legal reasoning and law school exam writing skills. Moreover, a crucial sub-skill of legal reasoning is the ability to read the hypothetical question(s) on examinations and classify the legal disputes within the subject area. No law school examination tests every concept studied over the course of the semester. For example, in a criminal law class, students will study dozens of different crimes. On criminal law examinations, however, students likely will be tested on less than one-half of those crimes. A colleague of mine once described this testing phenomenon as "the traffic cop approach." Traffic cops know that, if they appear on the highway and give tickets to a select few they catch, everyone will slow down because of the threat of being caught. Similarly, by threatening to test every concept the students have studied, law professors get students to slow down and study every concept.

Law professors and law students use the term "issue spotting" to describe this process of identifying which of the concepts learned are actually being tested on a particular exam, and educational psychologists use the term "concept learning" to describe the same process. Regardless of the label, the process requires sifting the facts in the hypothetical to determine which concepts a reasonable lawyer would regard as "at issue." It is impossible, at this early stage of your legal education, to explain the nuances of issue spotting or for the student to fully understand what is involved and why it is a difficult skill to master. For now, students simply need to understand that they must plan studying activities that prepare them to deploy this skill on their examinations and that there are studying and learning practices for preparing. The best practices include the organizational strategies and other concept-learning strategies addressed later in this book. In addition, students striving to build their issue spotting skills need to practice the skill itself, to identify the key aspects or attributes of each concept and to come up with examples, non-examples and debatable examples of the concept.

Principle learning. Law school examinations, as I have explained, require students to apply the rules, holdings and policies they have learned to previously unseen facts. Educational psychologists refer to this application process as principle learning. Principle learning, in law school, involves demonstrating, in writing, the student's reasoning process. The student explains how a lawyer in the real world might argue that the requirements of a particular rule or holding are met and how another lawyer might argue that the requirements of a rule or holding are not met. The student's explanation would include a prediction of how a judge or jury might decide between the lawyers' arguments and an explanation of that prediction. Learning this skill (or, perhaps more accurately, these skills), which lawyers and law professors, perhaps a bit sloppily, call "application," "analysis," "legal reasoning," or, even more abstractly, "thinking like a lawyer," will be the major focus of the first year of law school and is the focus of the later chapters in this book. Learning this skill really does take at least one full year for most students. Like other difficult-to-learn skills, such as calculus skills or the skills involved in mastering a musical instrument or a sport, application requires law students to know what to do, to know why they are doing it and both to practice the skill on their own and to seek out opportunities for "coached" practice, where the student gets feedback from peers or experts.

Law school exam writing. Although, in many respects, law school examination writing is the sum of organization, memorization, concept learning and principle learning, it also really is a skill in and of itself. Part of the skill involves thoughtful combination and coordination of the skills addressed above. Law school exam writing also involves time and stress management, planning and outlining and general writing sub-skills. In fact, this text devotes a large portion of a chapter, Chapter 16, to detailing strategies for developing the skill of writing a law school exam. By far, the most important strategy involves writing practice essay exam answers for each of the courses that have essay exam questions.

Exercise 5-1 in the Expert Learning for Law Students Workbook (hereinafter the "Workbook") will help develop the ability to identify and classify learning tasks. Because Exercise 5-1 will be the first such exercise, a few words on learning skills are warranted. Learning any skill requires practice. Consequently, there is a Workbook companion to this book to allow students to try out the new skills and begin to develop them. The workbook is designed so that the reader can use it in conjunction with this text, with the reader feeling free to flip back and forth between this book and the exercises.

Once the student knows what it is that she or he must be learning, Step 2 is completed, and it is time to address the psychological aspects of the forethought phase.

Step 3: Invoking Self-Interest and Self-Efficacy

(1) Why do I care about doing this task? What's the point of learning this material?
(2) When have I successfully learned something similar? Why will I succeed in learning this material?

Ironically, while Step 3 is the step students are most likely to skip, it is, in fact, the step that is best correlated with improvements in student outcomes. Some law students find it awkward or artificial to force themselves to think about why they are interested in what they are learning and why they believe they will succeed in learning it. Unfortunately, giving such short shrift to Step 3 is a big mistake. Although it seems like the least significant step, it may, in fact, be the most significant one.

There are literally thousands of studies showing that students who get themselves interested in what they are learning (invoke self-interest) and who believe they will succeed in learning (invoke self-efficacy) outperform those who do not. For example, most people who have taken freshman psychology classes have heard of the studies showing that many pre-teen girls develop low self-efficacy for doing math and therefore do not perform as well in math classes as they are capable of performing. There are even studies showing that students who receive falsified positive information about their capability outperform those who do not receive such information or who receive negative information about their capability. These results make sense because learning is a product of effort, persistence and strategy selection. Students who are interested in the subject matter and believe they will learn are more likely to try hard, to persist in the face of the inevitable difficulties in learning anything new and to try alternative strategies if their initial strategy choices prove erroneous. As a result of this effort, persistence and strategic behavior, the students are more likely to learn what they need to learn. They then develop greater interest in what they are learning (because the understanding they gain makes the material more interesting) and greater self-efficacy (because they have succeeded) and therefore study more, persist more and use more strategic behaviors. In other words, self-interest and self-efficacy create a cycle of learning that leads to success in learning enterprises. Figure 4 on the next page depicts that cycle.

Invoking Self-Interest

Students can invoke self-interest by adopting one of four strategies. First, they can invoke interest in learning for its own sake. Visit any grade school and you will find classrooms full of students who are excited by learning because growth, change and success are rewards in themselves. In fact, many law students who wait a few years after graduating from college before attending law school report that the absence from school taught them to appreciate the excitement of learning. Studies of students who are expert learners suggest that expert learners enjoy learning for its own sake much more than their peers do.

Second, students can invoke the interest in law that led them to attend law school. Everything one does in law school is part of a process of getting ready to be a successful lawyer. Most people chose to attend law school because becoming a lawyer was a dream. Recalling that dream often helps students find interest in what they are learning.

Third, students can enjoy the excitement and challenge particular to law school learning. Learning in law school is a challenge for almost everyone. It is much like learning to play a sport or a musical instrument well in that it requires hard work and much practice and it is not easy to learn. At the same time, learning in law school is exciting. At least part of the discussion throughout law school revolves around questions of what the law should be. For example, law students might discuss why the framers of the Constitution chose to create a right of free speech and what the limits of that right should be or whether, given that the Constitution has no explicit mention of a right to privacy, whether we have such a right. Most people seldom have time to contemplate these questions.

Finally, it is always helpful for students to imagine how they will use what they are learning both in their lives right now and in their future lives as lawyers. This process

Figure 4: The Self-Interest/Self-Efficacy/Better Studying/Better Results Cycle

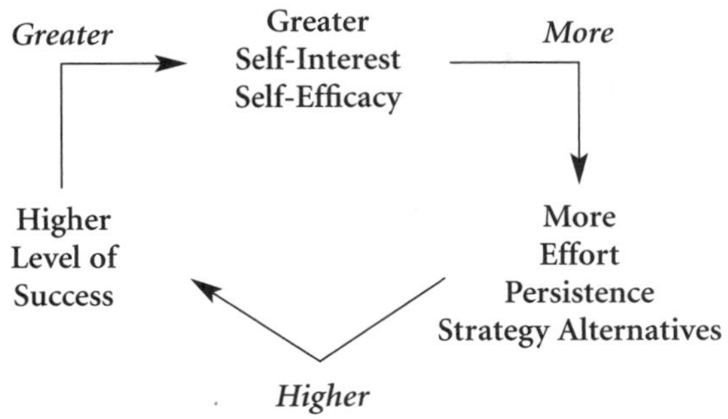

does require some thought. For example, students who plan to practice criminal law or family law or environmental law may have difficulty developing interest in their study of contract law. They can do so, however, by recognizing that, in their day-to-day activities, they are making dozens of contracts (contracts to buy homes, cars, groceries, dinners, medical and dental services, etc.), for which knowledge of contract law may help in some way. Moreover, lawyers who practice criminal law sign contracts with their clients and their employers (the District Attorney's or Public Defender's offices, for example) and on behalf of their clients or the public (plea agreements). Similarly, family law practitioners not only sign client and employment contracts, but also draft custody and divorce agreements, and environmental lawyers make contracts with clients, employers and, on behalf of their clients, contracts with governmental regulatory agencies, such as the Environmental Protection Agency (EPA). Considering how to use the information helps students develop an interest in it.

Invoking Self-Efficacy

Invoking self-efficacy is no more difficult than invoking self-interest. It simply is a matter of identifying past successes and drawing analogies between those successes and particular law school tasks. Most broadly, nearly all of us can point to a past experience in which we struggled and, eventually, succeeded in learning something we found difficult to learn—a sport, a musical instrument, calculus, philosophy, a job task. All that is required is that the task be one that did not come easy. We can recall the struggle, the need for hours and hours of practice, and the self-doubt. Hopefully, we can also recall the triumph of succeeding over that adversity.

Invoking self-efficacy is more a matter of remembering to do so than a matter of intellectual struggle. Try this exercise right now: Remember something you have learned that did not come easy to you at first. What made it hard? How did you manage to learn? How did learning it make you feel?

Exercise 5-2 in the Workbook is designed to help develop the ability to invoke self-interest and self-efficacy. Once a student has decided that she wants to learn and can succeed at doing it, she is now ready to set learning goals.

Step 4: Setting Learning Goals

(1) How will I know whether I've learned?

Most psychologists would agree that goal setting is not a process that is limited or should be limited to learning experiences. Rather, the process of setting achievable, challenging goals and breaking them into manageable sub-goals where necessary is a process that serves us well in all phases of our lives. We benefit because we have created a plan of action and a standard for measuring whether we have achieved it.

In educational settings, goal setting has been shown to be a crucial prerequisite to success. Students have been shown to perform as much as 30% better when they set appropriate goals and use those goals to monitor their achievement. In fact, in one study, students who set proper goals (as explained below) outperformed those who did not do so *(even though the goal-setting students actually studied significantly less)*. These results stem from the fact that setting proper goals creates a blueprint for students, establishing the standard against which students can plan their studying and measure their results. Goals also help students know when they have to make an "online adjustment in their studying" (a change of approaches while the studying is ongoing) so that changes occur before learning issues have become problems.

According to the studies of effective goal setting, effective goals meet the following four criteria, each of which I will explain and exemplify below by using examples from both within and outside the educational setting:

(1) They must be concrete. In other words, the goal must describe what the student will be learning in terms of the behavioral evidence that the learning has occurred and the criteria by which mastery will be measured.

(2) They must be short-term.

(3) They must be challenging.

(4) They must be realistic, i.e., achievable.

Goal Setting Rule #1: The Goal Must Be Concrete

A goal must be behavioral and have explicit criteria for its achievement so that the student can know what she needs to do to achieve it. An abstract life goal, for example — "I will exercise more," gives the speaker little guidance as to what she should do. What constitutes exercise? Is playing ball with a child exercise? Is weight-lifting exercise? How frequently must the person exercise to be able to say she is exercising "more"? Does "more" refer to the duration of each exercise experience or the number of exercise experiences per week or month? A behavioral, criterion-based goal would be: "I will do aerobic exercise for twenty-five minutes three times per week." Now, the speaker knows what constitutes exercise, how much exercise is minimally required each time and how often she should do it.

Likewise, an abstract educational goal, such as "I will learn the forethought phase of the SRL cycle," is as problematic as the initial exercise goal above; it fails to give the student a method for knowing what she should know and be able to do when she's done. What does "learn" mean? Must the student be able to recite each of the five steps from memory or select them from a list? Must she be able to explain what each step involves?

How accurate must her recitation be? How will she know if she has accurately "learned" the forethought phase? An appropriate set of behavioral, criterion-based goals that would capture the same basic idea as the original "learn the forethought phase" goal would be:

(1) "By the end of the first day of class, I will be able to list the five steps of the forethought phase and paraphrase the questions for each with 100% accuracy as measured by comparing my recitation with Figure 3."

(2) "By the end of the first day of class, I will be able to recite in my own words how I will perform each of the steps and the key information about each of the five steps with 80% accuracy as measured by comparing my recitation with my notes from this chapter."

(3) "By the end of the first day of class, given an assignment for this class, I will able, with 100% accuracy, to accurately classify it as a reading comprehension, research, synthesis, problem-solving or exam preparation task."

(4) "By the end of the first day of class, given a learning task for this class, I will identify why I am interested in that task and why I believe I will succeed at it."

(5) "By the end of the first day of class, given a learning task for this class, I will, with 80% accuracy, be able to set a learning goal that is behavioral and has explicit criteria for its achievement, is short-term, is challenging and is realistic."

Notice that each of these goals refers to *observable* behaviors (reciting, classifying, identifying, etc.). Note also that most have standards of performance. Some, those for which measurement is impossible because they are really attitudinal goals, do not. Those tasks I thought could be mastered perfectly, such as the list of forethought steps and questions, have 100% accuracy as the measure; those learning tasks that are more difficult and more complex, such as all the information about each of the steps, have an 80% standard, reflecting that higher degree of difficulty. I selected 80% because it is the standard measure of mastery according to traditional educational standards. Finally, notice the number of goals I set and the fact that I included both knowledge goals (e.g., the list of steps) and skill goals (being able to set proper learning goals). Students sometimes forget to include both types of goals.

Goal Setting Rule #2: The Goal Must Be Short-Term

While most people and most students set long-term goals, such as becoming a lawyer and learning everything in a course, learning goals must be short term so that the student can evaluate them close in time to when setting them. This approach allows more effective evaluation of learning and ensures that most study sessions are productive. For example, the above goals with respect to the forethought phase of the SRL Cycle all focus on what the learner would be able to do by the end of the class session in which the student will focus on the skills and knowledge in question. Of course, some goals, such as memorizing all the necessary law for a final examination, cannot be achieved in one session or even a few sessions. The key for such goals is to break them into short-term sub-goals, such as memorizing a defined portion of the rules. Thus, for a Criminal Law class, a student might set one goal of memorizing all the homicide rules and a second goal of memorizing all the theft rules.

Goal Setting Rule #3: The Goal Must Be Challenging

Studies also show that it is important to set challenging goals. Goals should encourage the student to stretch herself. Students who set goals that are too easy often become bored and may even lose interest before completing them. Note for example that I combined memorizing the steps with memorizing the questions that go with the steps because I thought that memorizing the steps alone would be too easy.

Goal Setting Rule #4: The Goal Must Be Realistic

Just as the goals cannot be too easy, they also cannot be too hard or unachievable. It would be impossible, for example, to memorize everything in this chapter with 100% accuracy. Such a goal would lead to frustration and disappointment. Students need to set achievable standards. Likewise, time goals should be realistic. A 100-page law school reading assignment cannot be completed in only one or two hours. A student might be able to finish turning the pages within that time, but the retention and understanding would be so low that, in effect, most of the time would have been wasted.

A Few Final Thoughts about Setting Goals

Generally, goal setting requires some thought. Students cannot simply look at an assignment in a law school syllabus (which may only list the pages to be read) and set a goal for it because they do not know what it is they must learn. To create behavioral, criterion-based, challenging yet achievable goals for such an assignment, they would need to look over the assigned materials and get a feel for the topic, the length of the assignment and the complexity of the topic. They also, of course, would want to consider any instructional objectives provided by the instructor. Students should then draft a set of goals. Finally, they should check their goals against the four criteria by which goals are measured. Exercise 5-3 in the Workbook assists students in learning to set appropriate goals.

Step 5: Selecting Strategies

(1) What cognitive, motivational and environmental strategies might work for this task?
(2) Which strategy alternatives would work best given the task and my learning goal?

The final, crucial step involves creating the student's plan for learning. The student (1) must decide the techniques she will use to learn, known as **cognitive strategies**, (2) must decide how, when, where and with whom she will use those strategies, known as **environmental strategies**, and (3) must plan how she will maintain her focus and attention and how she will deal with difficulties in learning, known as **motivational strategies**.

Motivational and Environmental Strategies

Within certain parameters, motivational and environmental strategies are a matter of personal preference and control. Students are in the best position to know what will get themselves started on their studying, what they should say to themselves while they are studying to help them stay focused, what materials they need to study and where, when, how long and with whom they should study. A few best practices with respect to motivational and environmental strategies are worth noting, however.

Students need to plan for those moments when they are having difficulty focusing on their work, when they feel tired, burned out, anxious, etc. The acts of invoking self-interest and self-efficacy and of setting short-term goals are techniques that address some of these issues some of the time. Nevertheless, many students find it helpful to plan their own **rewards** for completing certain steps in a learning process, such as planning a ten-minute break for a phone call to a friend or loved one after finishing memorization of some defined portion of the materials. Another effective technique is to develop **self-talk**, a term educational psychologists have developed to describe things students say to themselves to keep themselves on task and focused, such as "First, I will do this, then I will do that..." or "Keep your eyes on the prize (the law school diploma)" or "I know I can do this; this is just like when I...."

Similarly, studies of student learning have identified characteristics of appropriate studying locales: quiet, free from distraction and ready access to help. As described in Chapter 6, however, students vary in their learning styles. There are many students who prefer to study in locales that have none of these characteristics (i.e., in loud, distracting environments where there is no one nearby to turn to for help). For these reasons, sometimes, the law school's law library may not an optimal study locale. While it is quiet and peers can be a source of help, the law library can also be distracting because peers and friends may interfere with a student's focus or distract her from studying. A home office also involves trade-offs; it can be quiet and help may be available via e-mail from peers and professors, but family members can be a source of distraction.

There are also best practices in terms of the amount and length of time for study. Overwhelmingly, studies have shown that mere time on task is not a predictor of success in academic matters such as law school. Every law professor knows of a student who studied endlessly, but who did not do well in law school because her studying was not productive. Productive study requires a student to be well-rested and able to focus. It also requires taking short breaks every hour or two.

Expert learners take breaks and space their learning activities out over time rather than trying to cram all their studying together at once because studies of student learning show that **spaced study** produces better and more efficient learning. Spaced study is superior to cram studying because it allows students to:

(1) build their skills, by practicing, obtaining feedback on their practice and thereby increasing their skill level;

(2) identify gaps in their understanding and skills while there is still time to rectify them;

(3) obtain help from their instructors and peers, behaviors that are typical of expert learners; and

(4) rest before their examinations because studies show that, on examinations like law school tests that require creative thought, students perform better if they are well-rested.

Finally, the choice to study with others and with whom to study requires careful consideration. Other students, as described later in this book, are an excellent source of practice and feedback as part of exam preparation activities. Peers also are helpful sources for dealing with areas of confusion and getting the necessary social and emotional support. Seeking such help from peers is highly correlated with educational achievement. Moreover, students often benefit even more from helping their peers; forcing oneself to understand something well enough to explain it to a peer is one of the most productive learning enterprises in which a student can engage. For this reason, nearly all students need to include peer work in their study plans.

Such activities can become counter-productive, however, if students select peers who are not similarly committed to their own learning and therefore are unwilling to do their share of the necessary work, if there are social conflicts with those peers or if the presence of peers distracts the students from doing those tasks on which each student must work alone. Expert students recognize when peer studying is necessary and appropriate and when it may be a distraction, and they adjust accordingly.

Having learned what environmental and motivational strategies are, students are now ready to develop and practice using these skills. Exercise 5-4 in the Workbook will allow for practice in identifying environmental and motivational strategies.

Cognitive Strategies

There are a large number of cognitive strategies for each of the types of learning. In fact, there are as many 50 cognitive strategies that learners can use. Figure 5 is a list including definitions of most, but not all, of the strategies explored in this book.

Considering Figure 5, an example that includes at least some familiar strategies should give the student a feel for the variety of choices available to expert learners. To memorize the five steps of the forethought phase, one set of techniques is collectively referred to as rehearsal. Strategies in this category include: repeating the list over and over again and making and testing oneself with flashcards. A second set of techniques is known as mnemonics. Most students are familiar with the mnemonic technique that involves creating a word or phrase based on the first letter of each item. There are actually three other mnemonic techniques. A third set of techniques is known as organizational techniques, which include breaking down the information into clusters, outlining the material and creating graphic organizers (such as the flowchart depicted in Figure 3). In fact, there are at least four different types of graphic organizers commonly used. A fourth set of techniques is called elaborative techniques. These techniques involve drawing analogies between new learning and the student's prior learning. All of these techniques are described and explained later in this book. For now, this list should give the student some insight into the wide variety of approaches available to her for each type of learning task.

The student's task during the select strategies step of the forethought phase, of course, is to decide which strategies would be most productive for the learning task in which she is about to engage.

Figure 5: Cognitive Strategies Relevant to Law School Learning

Type of Strategy	Strategy Name	Brief Description
Pre-reading	Opinion pre-reading	Learning activities before reading an opinion
Reading	Opinion reading	Learning activities while reading
Note-taking from texts	Opinion briefing	Activities to record understanding of an opinion
Classroom learning	Class preparation	Activities to prepare for class and take notes
Assistance	Self-help	Restudying, using supplemental resources
	Peer help	Using cooperative learning techniques
	Professorial help	Approaching professors with planned questions
Organizational	Deconstructing rules	Breaking rules into their sub-parts
	Outlining	Creating a subject outline
	Timelines	Dividing a line into time periods to show key events
	Comparison charts	Creating a table listing items to be compared along the left side and comparison topics across the top
	Hierarchy charts	Connecting high level concept to sub-concepts
	Flowcharts	Showing a process
	Mind maps	Connecting a central concept and all related concepts
Memorization	Analogizing	Connecting new learning to prior learning
	Chunking & clustering	Reducing info into memorable pieces
	Imagery	Associating new learning with a memorable image
	Mnemonics	Techniques to create artificial memory associations
	Flashcards	Index cards to facilitate easy testing of concepts
	Paraphrasing	Restating rules and holdings in one's own words
	Examples & non-examples	Learning concepts by creating unmistakable examples and non-examples of them
Time management	Creating calendars	Working backwards from due date to plan project
Stress management	Invoking self-efficacy	Recalling past successes with difficult tasks
	Overlearning	Insuring ready recall by overstudying
	Reframing	Substituting positive for self-defeating thoughts
	Planning attention-focusing	Planning strategies for re-focusing if you become distracted during an exam
	Deep breathing and progressive relaxation	Engaging in deep breathing and systematically tensing and relaxing each muscle in the body
Research	Research logs	Recording research results to compare strategies
	Research planning	Developing steps for a particular research task
Legal writing	Outlining	Planning the org. of a paper or essay exam answer
	Check-listing	Developing questions to ask while editing a paper
	Multi-pronged reading aloud	Reading a paper aloud several times with different focuses each time
	Emulating experts	Selectively and consciously adapting experts' work on the same type of project
Issue spotting	Reorganizing	Finding alternative relations among course concepts
	Practice	Practicing attending to details and identifying issues
Essay exam writing	Using IRAC+	Using expanded IRAC format
	Practice	Write multiple practice essay exams in each subject
Exam preparation	Instructor study	Identifying areas of emphasis and preference
	Overlearning	Acquiring knowledge to a level of automaticity
	Self-created hypos	Creating exam-type questions on one's own
	Learning from tests	Using feedback from instructors to improve

An Introduction to the Factors the Student Should Weigh in Making Cognitive Strategy Selections

There are three factors that bear on the question of what cognitive strategy would be most appropriate for any particular learning task:

(1) The demands of, benefits of and limitations of each possible strategy.
(2) The learning goal(s), the time available to complete the task and the importance of the task relative to alternative uses of the student's time.
(3) The student's learning style and, to a lesser degree, familiarity, experiences and comfort with each of the possible strategies.

Each cognitive strategy facilitates different aspects of learning and each has its own limitations. For example, using an elaboration technique is useful for connecting new learning to prior learning but does not help create a schema for a body of new information. Creating a graphic organizer helps develop a schema for new learning but does not really allow students to include a great deal of detail. Preparing an outline allows students to include an unlimited amount of detail but inhibits the ability to see the big picture or develop a schema for the new learning. Thus, in selecting a cognitive strategy, students should consider the benefits and detriments of each possible strategy.

Students also need to consider their learning goal(s), the time they have to complete the task and the importance of the task. The learning goal, of course, creates the standard by which the student measures success and therefore should weigh heavily in the choice of strategies. Students need to select strategies that will work to achieve their goal. At the same time, some strategies with which they may be most comfortable, such as reading and re-reading class notes, may require considerably more time and effort but may only produce a marginal learning gain or may even be less productive than other uses of study time. The time available to complete the task, therefore, is a consideration. The importance of the task must also be considered. As explained in Chapter 2, while students need to be prepared for class to help retain new learning and to benefit from the opportunity for in-class feedback from the professor, it is important not to assign disproportionate value to the experience of appearing smart to peers in class. Consequently, students should not prepare for class in a way that interferes with the other learning activities they should be doing.

The final factor students should consider is their individual learning profiles. Learning style, strategy preferences and experiences and comfort with each of the strategies affect learning. As part of their study of the materials in the next chapter in this book, students should take online assessments of their learning and personality styles. The materials detail how this self-knowledge should influence students' strategy selections. These materials explain that each of us has a set of approaches with which we are most comfortable and, all other things being equal, a strategy that best suits one's learning and personality styles is better than a strategy that is antithetical to one's learning and personality styles. However, all other things are only sometimes equal. Some strategies are better for some purposes, regardless of individual styles. Moreover, the more techniques a student masters through practice, the more choices she will have when encountering a previously unseen learning experience. Most significantly, as discussed in Chapter 4, each learning experience offers students additional information about what works best for that student with respect to a particular learning task; that information is crucial to future technique selections. In fact, the most successful students will alter the techniques they learn in this book both as they are using them and in planning future learning activities, based on the results they obtain.

In short, more than anything else, expert learners are expert in how they learn best. While students will be developing that expertise through their activities in reading this book and as they apply the skills to learning activities in law school classes, work and personal life, they will not complete their conversion into the status of learning expert for about one year, after having had the chance to hone their learning strategies through use and adaptation.

Time Management

Law school classes require incredible amounts of work; in general, new law students are expected to devote 3–4 hour outside of class for every one hour in class for each of their law school subjects. As a result, almost all law students feel pressed for time.

In Appendix A of the book, you will find a time management/self-monitoring log that you can use to plan your studying. Many students have found such logs incredibly helpful. But there are many other ways to manage your time. Here are some keys to effective time management:

- ✓ *Take the time to consciously plan your time.* Take control of your time by having a schedule and sticking to it. Start with your list of tasks, set learning goals and then assign times for achieving each of your goals.
- ✓ *Work backward from deadlines.* Successful time managers work backwards from deadlines to insure that they finish tasks with plenty of time for revisions and necessary help.
- ✓ *Work on the most challenging work when you are freshest.* Be sure to spend your time carefully. Figuring out new, difficult material is more challenging than converting a course outline to flashcards for memorization purposes; plan accordingly.
- ✓ *Safeguard blocks of time.* Say no to people and activities that interfere with your designated study times.
- ✓ *Be willing to adjust and adapt.* Change any aspect of your schedule that is not working for you.

Reflection Questions

1. How will you know what learning tasks in which you should be engaging?

2. Why are you going to law school?

3. What courses will you be taking in your first semester of law school? (Find out if you do not already know) What do you find interesting about each subject? (Find out what each course basically deals with—e.g., contract law deals with private disputes between parties relating to promises the courts deem enforceable and then brainstorm determine why that subject might interest you.)

4. Why is self-efficacy so highly correlated with student success? Can you think of a time when your self-efficacy influenced your results on a test, project or task?

5. Why are effective learning goals concrete, short-term, challenging and realistic?

6. Why does spaced study produce better learning than cramming?

7. What are the obstacles to your time management in law school? What will be are the keys to success in managing your time?

8. What motivational, environmental and cognitive strategies have been most effective in your past learning exercises?

References

Albert Bandura & Dale H. Schunk, *Cultivating Competence, Self-Efficacy, and Intrinsic Interest Through Proximal Self-Motivation*, 41(3) Journal of Personality and Social Psychology 586 (1981).

John P. Barker and Joanne P. Olson, *Medical Students' Learning Strategies: Evaluation of First-Year Changes*, http://www.msstate.edu/org/mas/ejour2.html.

Martin M. Chemers, Li-tze Hu & Ben F. Garcia, *Academic Self-Efficacy and First-Year College Student Performance and Adjustment*, 93(1) Journal of Educational Psychology 55 (2001).

Stephen R. Covey, The Seven Habits of Highly Effective People (1989).

Anastacia S. Hagan & Clare Ellen Weinstein, *Achievement Goals, Self-Regulated Learning and the Role of the Classroom Context* in Understanding Self-Regulated Learning 43 (P. Pintrich, ed. 1995).

Teresa Garcia, *The Role of Motivational Strategies in Self-Regulated Learning* in Understanding Self-Regulated Learning 29 (P. Pintrich, ed. 1995).

Barbara K. Hofer, Shirley L. Yu and Paul R. Pintrich, *Teaching College Students to Be Self-Regulated Learners* in Self Regulated Learning: From Teaching to Self-Reflective Practice 57 (D.H. Schunk, B. Zimmerman, eds. 1998).

Robert W. Lent, Steven D. Brown and Kevin C. Larkin, *Self-Efficacy in the Prediction of Academic Performance and Perceived Career Options* 33(3) Journal of Counseling Psychology 265 (1986).

Karen D. Multon, Steven D. Brown & Robert W. Lent, *Relationship of Self-Efficacy Beliefs to Academic Outcomes: A Meta-Analytic Investigation*, 38(1) J Counseling Psychology 30 (1991).

Frank Van Overwalle & Machteld De Metsenaere, *The Effects of Attribution-Based Intervention and Study Strategy Training on Academic Achievement in College Freshmen*, 60 Britain Journal of Educational Psychology 301–304, 305–308 (1990).

LaVergne Trawick & Lyn Corso, *Expanding the Volitional Resources of Urban Community College Students* in Understanding Self-Regulated Learning 57 (P. Pintrich, ed. 1995).

Philip H. Winne and A.F. Hadwin, *Studying as Self-Regulated Learning* in Metacognition in Educational Theory and Practice 279 (D.J. Hacker, J. Dunlosky and A.C. Graesser 1997).

Christopher A. Wolters, *Self-Regulated Learning and College Students' Regulation of Motivation*, 90(2) JOURNAL OF EDUCATIONAL PSYCHOLOGY 224 (1998).

Robert E. Wood & Edwin A. Locke, *The Relation of Self-Efficacy and Grade Goals to Academic Performance*, 47 EDUCATIONAL AND PSYCHOLOGICAL MEASUREMENT 1013 (1987).

Barry J. Zimmerman, *A Social-Cognitive View of Self-Regulated Academic Learning*, 81 JOURNAL OF EDUCATIONAL PSYCHOLOGY 329–339 (1989).

Barry J. Zimmerman, *Developing Self-Fulfilling Cycles of Academic Regulation: An Analysis of Exemplary Instructional Models* in SELF REGULATED LEARNING: FROM TEACHING TO SELF-REFLECTIVE PRACTICE 1 (D.H. Schunk, B. Zimmerman, eds.1998).

Barry J. Zimmerman, Sebastian Bonner and Robert Kovach, DEVELOPING SELF-REGULATED LEARNERS: BEYOND ACHIEVEMENT TO SELF-EFFICACY (1996).

Barry J. Zimmerman & Andrew S. Paulsen, *Self-Monitoring During Collegiate Studying: An Invaluable Tool for Academic Self-Regulation* in NEW DIRECTIONS IN COLLEGE TEACHING AND LEARNING: UNDERSTANDING SELF-REGULATED LEARNING 13 (No. 65:1995).

Chapter 6

Know Thyself: Personality Types and Learning Styles

Expert self-regulated learners know themselves well. Not only do they know how to learn and what strategies work best to produce learning, but, also, they know how they personally best learn and how they prefer to learn. As explained in Chapter 5, the student's learning style and personality type are significant considerations in evaluating strategy options. While the student's preferences and comfort zones should not lead her to select strategies that would be unproductive or inefficient, both factors warrant consideration where multiple strategies are possible and each option is, more or less, equally productive and equally efficient. Moreover, in the evaluation phase (as explained in Chapter 8), part of the evaluation process involves analyzing the causes of the student's success or failure and the efficiency of the learning strategies she selected. In making this evaluation, the student will need to consider her comfort with the learning strategies she adopted in light of her personality type and learning style preferences.

Introduction to Personality Types and Learning Styles

Psychologists use the term **personality type** to describe the basic psychological, social and perceptual characteristics that a person brings to the learning environment. The best known way to classify personality types is according to four matched sets of preferences: (1) whether a person prefers to process new information from the outer world or through their own inner mental world, (2) whether a person prefers to approach problem-solving by focusing on observed facts or by relying on intuition, (3) whether a person prefers to base decisions, form opinions and make judgments objectively by weighing cause and effect and using logic or by weighing personal and social values, and (4) whether a person prefers to deal with the world in a structured, organized way where things are settled or in a flexible, spontaneous way. These characteristics give insights into a student's core approaches to learning.

Educational psychologists use the term **learning style** to describe a student's preference for methods of learning. One learning styles inventory involves classifying the student according to the student's preferences with respect to one of four categories commonly used in educational settings: graphic images, written words, spoken words or experience/tactile learning. In other words, some people enjoy and learn best from the various graphics in this text, some enjoy learning from reading the textual materials and from writing about what they are learning, some will prefer hearing the information and others will want to apply it so they can see its relevance right away.

Another inventory, developed based on the work of Dr. David Kolb of Case Western Reserve University, characterizes the student in terms of her learning preferences according to two pairs of opposite inclinations: (1) whether the student prefers to learn by doing or to learn by watching, and (2) whether the student prefers thinking or feeling. Based on these preferences, the student is classified as an enthusiastic learner, a practical learner, an imaginative learner or a logical learner.

A personality type or learning style does not describe students' strengths or weaknesses in terms of whether they will succeed as learners, especially because no particular type or style is better or worse for learning anything. Law school itself involves activities that meet the preferences of most people, regardless of their learning style. Moreover, results from such assessments produce, at most, a set of suggestions or ideas; they give students guidance in their preferences, not mandates for how they should go about being students. In other words, a particular personality type or learning style is not a box that limits students to particular approaches but, rather, a guide that points students towards particular approaches, all other things being equal. In addition, few people prefer to learn all things in the same way.

Personality Types

Based on the theories of Carl Jung, one of the most influential psychologists in the past century, personality typing has been the subject of literally hundreds of studies. There are many tests designed to classify people's personality types, most of which are based, in large or small part, on the Myers-Briggs Type Indicator (MBTI). The web address in this text (below) is to an MBTI derivative test, a test created by a team of psychologists and mathematicians based on the MBTI categories. These questions classify you according to four pairs or categories and give you an indication of the strength of those classifications. You will be given a four-letter code that reflects your classification for each pair. It is important to remember that no person falls into any classification entirely or prefers everything to be structured only one way. These classifications indicate preferences, not exclusive categories. Here's a bit more information about these categories.

As explained above, the first classification deals with how you process new information, where you prefer to focus your attention in the learning process. You are classified as an extrovert (E) or as an introvert (I). Extroverts prefer to think aloud, enjoy projects more than tests and enjoy engaging in peer teaching. They prefer action and are goal-oriented and innovative. Introverts are reflective and observational. They enjoy abstract reasoning and time for reflection, and they require time to think before speaking.

Learning implications of being an extrovert. Extroverts need to make their learning experiences more active; they should try to talk in class, participate in group discussions and work on group projects. Where possible, they should arrange experiences in which they can teach their peers. They also, however, should find areas in which they are able to work on their own and force themselves to anticipate issues and problems. They should make particular effort to learn legal theories, such as policies and concepts, and they should strive to connect the theories and concepts to their own experiences.

Learning implications of being an introvert. Introverts need to give themselves time to think things through and not allow themselves to feel pressured into measuring themselves by how well they do in classroom exchanges with their professors. To make these experiences less stressful and more productive, they should anticipate questions before class. Finally, introverts should make sure their study time includes opportunities for quiet reflection and writing. They find all types of graphic organizers to be helpful learning tools.

The second classification deals with how you approach solving a problem, how you prefer to acquire information, how you find out information about the world around you. You are classified either as **sensing** (S) or **intuitive** (N). Sensing people prefer to work with observable facts within what is given. They are realistic and practical and can handle and work with large numbers of facts. Intuitive people tend to look at the big picture and try to grasp the essential patterns and concepts but are impatient with details. They enjoy complexity and follow their inspirations, regardless of data.

Learning implications of being a sensing student. Sensing students should strive to find, through their peers, their instructors or supplemental materials, both concrete examples of and the practical implications of the concepts they are learning. They should strive to find the procedural aspects of the skills they are learning and to find multiple opportunities for drill and practice. They also should monitor their learning closely, paying particular attention to whether they understand what they are reading.

Learning implications of being an intuitive student. Students who are intuitive need to force themselves to attend to facts and details and to focus in class. They should seek out the many opportunities in law school for self-directed learning. In addition, they need to force themselves to develop the rationales for their insights. Finally, they should create their own graphic organizers to help themselves make sense of the concepts they are learning.

The third classification deals with how you make decisions, reach conclusions and form opinions. You are classified as either **thinking** (T) or **feeling** (F). Persons who rely on a thinking approach strive to make decisions objectively; they like to weigh evidence, seek objective truth and discover the logic of things. People who rely on a feeling approach base their decisions on their values or the value of others. Logic is not as important to such persons as are values. While feeling people tend to be sympathetic and kind in dealing with people, they do not base their decisions on *emotions.* Feeling people base their decisions on whether the chosen result is consistent with their values.

Learning implications of being a thinking student. Students in this category find motivation from discerning the reasons or logic underlying concepts and therefore should strive to understand the "whys" underlying the rules they are studying in law school. They also need to understand the reasons underlying the learning activities in which they are engaging and to see the relationships among (the structure of) the knowledge and skills they are learning. Finally, they need to help themselves identify human factors underlying legal decision-making.

Learning implications of being a feeling student. To make their law school learning meaningful to them, feeling students need to identify for themselves the human aspects of the materials they are studying, to identify the values motivating the parties to the lawsuits about which they are reading. They also need to seek out feedback and reinforcement from teachers and peers. Therefore, group work can be particularly effective for such students. Lastly, they need to force themselves to recognize the significance of long-term societal goals and not just short-term, individual-focused goals.

The fourth and final classification deals with how you interact with the outside world or bring structure to your life. You are classified as either focused on **judgment** or as focused on **perception**. People who prefer judging prefer their lives to be planned, organized and ordered. They like to make decisions, complete projects and regulate and control their lives. Persons who are focused on perception enjoy living flexibly and spontaneously. They like to adjust their goals and plans "on the fly" and prefer general parameters to rules.

Learning implications of being a perceiving student. These students need to get themselves organized, they need to plan, and they need to avoid procrastination. For this reason, tasks need to be broken into smaller tasks and sub-tasks and these students also need to set deadlines for themselves. They also need to make sure they are decisive in instances where quick decisions are necessary, such as on law school and bar examinations.

Learning implications of being a judging student. Judging law students also should set goals and sub-goals for themselves and develop schedules. At the same time, they need to try their hands at dealing with problems that go "outside the box" to enhance their ability to adapt to new experiences, a helpful skill on many law school essay examinations. They also need to force themselves to keep an open mind in analyzing problems, to make sure they consider alternatives not immediately apparent to them.

Now that you understand the basics of the typologies, you are ready to take an MBTI test. There are many free online versions of the MBTI-type test. Two such websites are: http://www.humanmetrics.com/cgi-win/JTypes1.htm and http://www.personalitytype. com/quiz.html. When the test is finished, you will be given a four-letter code corresponding to the pairs described above. Both websites also provide some helpful information about the implications of your personality type. Below is some additional information about learning preferences according to the corresponding four-letter code.

Population Breakdown

Here's roughly how the United States' population breaks down in terms of the sixteen four letter categories:

ISTJ	9%	INTJ	3%	ESTJ	14%	ENTJ	4%
ISTP	6%	INTP	4%	ESTP	14%	ENTP	5%
ISFJ	9%	INFJ	3%	ESFJ	13%	ENFJ	4%
ISFP	6%	INFP	4%	ESFP	9%	ENFP	7%

Additional Information about Potential Strengths and Weakness for Law School Studying of Each Four-Letter Classification

ISTJ. ISTJs possess some important strengths for their law school studies. They are serious about their studies, and get their work done. They do their work accurately and methodically and are thoughtful. Such discipline and thoughtfulness are keys to success in law school because the workload is so demanding. ISTJs tend to analyze legal issues logically and systematically and to use the evidence described in fact patterns well. They are less likely to become stressed during examinations

ISTJs, however, need to guard against focusing so hard at mastering each of the trees of legal subjects (each of the rules of law) that they lose sight of the forest (the big picture of the area of law they are learning). They also need to open themselves up to change; all learning involves change and, therefore, unless inhibited, ISTJ's tendency to resist change may inhibit their development of lawyering skills. In working with other students on projects and in study groups, ISTJs need to force themselves to listen to peers who have more creative and innovative ideas and to express their appreciation for the people with whom they are working rather than keeping such feelings to themselves. On examinations, they need to resist their inclination to see only one side of issues.

ISTP. ISTPs also possess analytical and practical strengths that are likely to prove helpful with their law school studies and tests. They tend to be logical and fact-focused, a crucial pair of skills on law school exams. They also are seldom procrastinators and therefore are likely to timely complete all of their law school work. Likewise, ISTPs are often efficient, in the sense that they strive to find the best way of limiting the amount of effort required for each task. They are curious, and they are effective at finding the core of things.

ISTPs' search for efficiency, though, may lead them to cut necessary corners. They need to force themselves to carefully plan their studies and law school assignments and then to stick to that plan. Because ISTPs tend to get bored easily, they need to commit themselves to peers, such as members of their study groups, to make sure they complete the necessary work. Finally, ISTPs need to open up to their peers and professors, especially if and when they are struggling with their law school studies (and most law students do struggle at times), or they may not get the help they need.

ISFJ. ISFJs possess great common sense, focus well on facts and have great memories for the many nitty-gritty details of some bodies of law. All of these skills are helpful on law school exams, particularly law school multiple-choice tests. ISFJs are hard working and diligent, are great planners and follow-through on their plans, helpful attributes given the workload demands of law school. They also generally work well in groups because they tend to be helpful and warm.

There are risks, however, in being an ISFJ law student. ISFJs need to budget extra time for tasks because they are likely to spend a lot of time on planning and do each task so meticulously. ISFJs need to carefully select their study partners because they sometimes get taken advantage of and too often try to rescue others in trouble. They also have a tendency to be too literal and, consequently, to miss subtleties. Finally, they need to force themselves to think more globally on assignments and essay exams and, by doing so, develop the less obvious approaches and arguments.

ISFP. ISFPs make good study group members because they are sensitive to others, patient and flexible. They are interested and enthusiastic learners and are excellent at enjoying the learning moment for itself. For this reason, they usually set good short-term learning goals, plan strategies for achieving those goals and achieve them in one setting. They tend to be very hard workers. They have particular skills in adaptation and improvisation, both of which are excellent attributes for law students, almost all of whom by necessity develop new ways of learning.

ISFPs need to guard against their tendency to see feedback as discouragement rather than as a tool for getting better. On law school essay exams and papers, they need to make sure they analyze objectively and with skepticism. A key to law school success for ISFPs is planning and organizing their study time and study resources.

INTJ. INTJ's natural inclination towards perfectionism is their gift (and their curse, as explained below). It is a gift because it drives them to mastery and causes them to take full responsibility for their own success, two critical attributes of successful law students. So much of traditional law school instruction requires students to self-teach; INTJs are well equipped for these demands. INTJs are great at developing original legal arguments and ideas and learn legal theory readily. They have insight and vision and are very energetic.

INTJ's perfectionism is their curse because perfection in learning endeavors as difficult as law school is nearly impossible, and, as a result, there is some risk INTJs will be too hard on themselves and their law school peers. Another issue is that INTJs tend to miss details and ignore common sense when either conflicts with their original ideas. As a result, on law school exams, they may develop and make an original argument at the expense of making the obvious, necessary and sometimes better argument. They also tend to miss out on the benefits of learning from others, and, given their inclination towards single-mindedness, the choice to work alone is likely to interfere with their success. Finally, when they do work in groups, to be productive, contributing members, INTJs need to respect the feelings of others, even if they regard those feelings as illogical.

INTP. INTPs are intellectual, logical and, at times, creative at a brilliant level. These are great attributes for a law student. INTPs also are precise and insist upon logic. They enjoy the type of hairsplitting that is sometimes necessary to correctly analyze legal issues. They work well independently. INTP's skill in finding flaws in arguments and ideas is an excellent tool for reading court opinions and self-editing their law school essays and papers.

On the other hand, INTPs tend to be impatient with details and sometimes lack follow-through; they may not finish all of their law school assignments, class preparation or exam studying. They have a tendency to get stuck on small flaws and not finish what they have started; as a result, their grades suffer because deadlines in law school tend to be enforced through severe penalties. Finally, because some of INTPs' ideas are complex, they sometimes have trouble communicating them to others; because law school essays and papers succeed only to the extent readers can follow the argument, INTPs need to be careful to explain all the steps of their reasoning.

INFJ. INFJs possess strengths that, when harnessed, can help them succeed in law school. They tend to be intense, committed and idealistic. They are original thinkers and delve deeply into situations, making it easier for them to identify difficult legal issues and develop more in-depth arguments on law school exams and papers. They make good leaders and work well on group projects.

INFJs' focus, however, can tend to develop into an unhelpful single mindedness. On law school examinations, they need to make sure they attend to all the facts and not just those that support their theories. They need to make sure they take care of the routine tasks of law school and not just the activities they find stimulating. They need to make sure they analyze everything objectively. They need to be open to feedback and avoid hypersensitivity.

INFP. People who are INFPs possess excellent long-range vision, and they have many skills necessary to manage their law school workload: flexibility, adaptability and commitment to their long-term goals. They communicate well in writing and prefer that mode. They can be very convincing, a trait helpful in nearly all law school writing.

INFPs need to make sure they are being logical and fact driven when taking law school exams. They tend to procrastinate the operational aspects of projects, such as law school papers, and they spend too much time refining and polishing their ideas and not enough time actually researching, writing, and editing. Because they tend to be perfectionists and self-critical, INFPs need to guard against feelings of inadequacy, remain open to feedback and avoid translating failures in learning, which are a normal part of law school, into negatives.

ESTJ. ESTJs possess many skills that are readily adaptable to law school studies. Their conscientiousness, enjoyment of structure, and strong memorization and organizational skills ensure they finish their law school projects on time and done well. They are logical, objective and analytical and therefore, in law school, they quickly develop legal reasoning skills.

ESTJs are less comfortable with and struggle more to understand legal theory. They have a tendency towards being rigid and have trouble seeing gray areas, which, with the difficult and ambiguous legal problems on law school exams and assigned as law school papers, is a significant problem. By becoming more adaptable and listening to others' ideas (particularly the ideas of people who are very different from them), they can gain insights they might have had trouble seeing on their own and thereby harness their skills, limit their potential issues and excel in law school.

ESTP. ESTPs have particular skill in understanding underlying principles, making it easier for them to understand legal rules and their application. They are effective in group settings because they tend to be outgoing and diplomatic. They do well with high stress situations, like law school, because they are easy-going and realistic. They also pay attention to details, a helpful trait for a detail-oriented field like law. Finally, they tend to be high-energy people.

ESTPs must discipline themselves into planning; their tendency to move from putting out the fire on one task to putting out the fire on another task simply will not work in law school and will be even less effective on the bar exam. They need to budget their time, limit their commitments or risk being overrun and overwhelmed by the demands of law school. Finally, they need to discipline themselves to complete the boring details. In short, for ESTPs, law school success is all about time management, goal setting and self-discipline.

ESFJ. ESFJs, being people persons, both work well in law school study groups and feel a strong need to participate in them. Their study group peers appreciate their conscientiousness and graciousness, and the ESFJs satisfy their craving for connection and relationships in the context of law school, which tends to be a competitive and individualistic environment. ESFJs are great at identifying and remembering facts and are very well organized, two crucial traits for law school success.

ESFJs tend to place others ahead of themselves, an extremely risky behavior in law school, during which time and energy are such precious commodities. They also must force themselves to overcome their natural reluctance to ask for help when they need it and to be open to constructive criticism. Finally, they need to slow themselves down from time-to-time to make sure they have analyzed legal problems fully and from all angles; in particular, they should try to look for new or different ways of doing things.

ESFP. ESFPs are realistic, have good common sense and are good observers. They adapt well to new environments so their transition to the law school world is not as difficult as it is for some of their peers. Because they get along well with others, they make good group members. They also are persuasive, an important skill for most law school courses, and they are excellent at details.

ESFPs, however, have difficulty disciplining themselves to the workload demands of law school. They do well when they use organizational and time management strategies to help them set goals and achieve them. By doing so, ESFPs can strike an appropriate balance between work and play and between social concerns and educational needs. When they do not discipline themselves, on the other hand, ESFPs are risk for not finishing tasks, even law school itself. ESFPs learn best from hands-on experiences and therefore should strive to find the practical applications of what they are learning in their first-year coursework and seek out clinical and other real-world learning experiences later in law school.

ENTJ. ENTJs make great leaders of study groups — they have lots of vision, are great long-term planners and organize people very well. They are logical and driven; consequently, both legal reasoning and the workload necessary to develop the skill come naturally to them. They work efficiently, research well and enjoy theory, truth and mastery.

Because ENTJs are so focused, they sometimes move too quickly and miss information. Their leadership inclinations can be problematic for group projects because they sometimes ignore the input of others. They need to force themselves to seek feedback and then force themselves to learn from it. Thus, for ENTJs, their rule of thumb should be, "don't miss out on information."

ENTP. ENTPs do not shy away from the challenges of law school; rather, they enjoy them. They are enthusiastic learners and enjoy new ideas and multiple possibilities, which law professors love to introduce regularly into class discussions. Of all their skills, ENTPs' analytic skills, their ability to recognize flaws in arguments readily and to intuit arguments on both sides of issues most directly translates to law school success.

ENTPs do worse with the mundane aspects of law school. They have a hard time with the details, the day-to-day labor, and they ignore the easy and best way to do things because they prefer innovation for its own sake. They are more likely to skip the preparation so they can go right to the aspect of a task that interests them. Unfortunately, in law school, the details and the sweat matter as much as the ideas so ENTPs must discipline themselves.

ENFJ. ENFJs have the natural organizational skills and ability to see beyond the obvious that are typical of successful law students. They also possess the abilities to be consistently productive and responsible about their work, which enable them to finish their work in law school and do it well. They are people lovers and value relationships, making them cooperative study group members. They also read people well.

ENFJs' people focus can be their undoing in law school. They sometimes become overworked or disillusioned when things are not working well. They do not always address their own needs and, as a result, their studies may suffer. They need to be careful not to make assumptions and to make sure they have and understand all the facts. They also need to force themselves to learn from criticism rather than become upset by it.

ENFP. ENFPs possess excellent pattern recognition skills and therefore have the potential to be excellent at identifying legal issues, both on exams and in law practice. They also are original thinkers and notice details better than most, both of which are critical to success on law school exams. They also are sensitive, adaptive and resourceful.

ENFPs, however, often lose interest or focus once they have hatched their original idea. They need to develop time management and organizational skills to make sure they take care of everything they need to do to ready themselves for exams and to write and edit their law school papers. They greatly need to focus on follow-through because it does not come naturally to them. They prefer to work with others and benefit greatly from working with people who possess better discipline and attention to the details involved in finishing any project, even if that project is getting ready for an examination.

If you are interested in learning more about the implications of your four-letter code, there are numerous websites from which you can learn more about your type. Try the following four websites: http://typelogic.com/, http:///knowyourtype.com/intro.html, http://www.wncc.nevada.edu/studentservices/counseling/styles_types/2_16_personality_types.html and http://www.capt.org/Using_Type/Workplace.cfm.

Learning Styles

Learning style refers to your preferences in how you acquire new learning. There are numerous learning style classifications, none of which yet has prevalence among educators. All learning styles experts agree that, while students should know their styles so they can adapt to their learning tasks, no particular learning style is more or less conducive to success. One set of classifications used by a number of post-secondary educational institutions around the country is known as VARK, which refers to four categories of learning styles: Visual, Aural, Read/write and Kinesthetic. In fact, there is a fifth learning style, which probably is, in fact, the most predominate: multi-modal, meaning the student learns readily in several of the above modes. It is also common to collapse the visual and read/write categories into one single category.

Visual learners prefer to see concepts depicted graphically through their inter-relationships. They like all forms of graphic organizers, including flowcharts, concept maps, hierarchy charts and comparison charts. They need to translate written and spoken information into graphic form and then translate their graphics into the written and spoken word.

Aural learners (also known as "auditory learners") prefer to learn from hearing their instructors, their peers and even themselves speak. In fact, they often must read aloud or speak aloud written materials to remember them. They also like to participate in group activities in which group members discuss what they have been learning.

Read/write learners prefer the printed word. They like to learn from texts and other written materials and to express themselves in writing as well.

Kinesthetic learners learn best through experience, not only by touching and feeling, but also through experience, whether the experience is actual, exemplary or simulated. They also like to learn through movement, which is seldom possible in law school.

Multi-modal learners make up as much as 50–70% of the population. Multi-modal learners may prefer two, three or may even be most comfortable using all four strategies. There is even some evidence that multi-modal learners prefer using multiple strategies for each learning experience, which is probably a good practice for all types of learners.

The VARK website, http://www.vark-learn.com/, includes the online assessment instrument on which these materials are based, additional information about the four categories, and printable "help sheets" which offer suggestions as to how your particular learning style might influence your approach to studying. Another website that uses categories identical to the VARK categories in all ways other than their labels also provides some excellent study recommendations; that website is: http://www.metamath.com/lsweb/fourls.htm. The website located at: http://ccc.commnet.edu/faculty/~simonds/styles/compensate.htm discusses nine different learning styles and suggests strategies for overcoming a weakness in any of those nine areas.

Another learning styles approach, originally developed by Dr. David Kolb of Case Western University, assigns a student to one of four learning style categories depending on whether the student is more oriented towards feeling or thinking and whether she is more comfortable doing something new on her own or watching someone else do it first. For example, students who are more emotional, intuitive, accepting, risk-taking, opinionated and people-oriented are classified as "feeling-oriented" whereas students who prefer logic, analysis, theory, planning, organization and calculation are denominated "thinkers." Likewise, students who prefer listening, reacting, asking questions, thinking up ideas, deliberating and digesting are labeled "watching-oriented" whereas people who prefer action, experimentation, change, doing, answering questions and finding solutions are labeled "doing-oriented."

Students are then placed in one of four quadrants: **enthusiastic** (more feeling and action oriented), **imaginative** (feeling and watching oriented), **practical** (thinking and doing oriented) or **logical** (thinking and watching oriented). All four types have potential assets and liabilities for studying law.

Enthusiastic learners are likely to be inspired by talking about their legal studies with others and therefore initiate and maintain study groups well. They are excited to try new things, manage their time, even on exams, well and are likely to adjust to law school more easily than most. They need to look for the practical applications of what they are learning. They may, however, fail to organize their exam answers before beginning to write, may have trouble finishing projects, may take on too many projects and may, at times, lack focus. They also may have to work harder at understanding and learning to use legal theory.

Imaginative learners have the advantages of being good at seeing the big picture, of being good imitators and therefore comfortable learning in the vicarious atmosphere common in law school teaching. They are effective at developing creative arguments, an excellent skill for law school exams and papers, and their orientation towards deliberating may help them identify legal problems well. They need to guard against allowing relationships, even study group relationships, to interfere with their studies. They may avoid doing new things necessary to law school success, such as the suggestions in this text, and they may have trouble starting assignments and reaching conclusions on legal questions that require conclusions.

Practical learners' strengths include the ability to recognize and work within the "game" aspect of law school examinations. They also tend to be skilled at drawing inferences from facts, a skill crucial to success on many law school examinations. They are inclined to act independently (such as by writing practice exams even if they are not told to do so) and then seek feedback. They also manage their time well, even on exams. Practical learners' greatest liability is that they may tend towards being too general. On exams, they have to guard against providing general conclusions and leaving out steps in their reasoning. On their course outlines, they may leave out important details, such as exceptions and fine distinctions about the effect or consequence of a rule of law.

Finally, logical learners organize well. They develop good course and exam answer and paper outlines. They quickly see the relevance of facts, seldom make careless errors and synthesize well. They tend to understand theory readily. Their skill in organization can work against them, however. They need to make sure they do not spend so much time on organizing their essays that they do not have time to finish them. They need to make sure their course outlines are not too detailed. They also need to force themselves to learn from their peers and to stop themselves from dismissing creative arguments too readily.

One website that addresses Kolb's ideas is http://facultyweb.cortland.edu/andersmd/learning/Kolb.htm. Another website that addresses both Kolb's ideas as well as all the other theories addressed above and more is http://www.nwlink.com/~donclark/hrd/styles.html#kolb.

Reflection Questions

1. What is my four-letter personality type? How might my personality type influence how I go about studying law?

2. What have I learned about my learning style(s)? How might my learning style(s) influence how I go about studying law?

3. Throughout this text, you will find a number of lists of things, such as the steps involved in performing the forethought phase, the list of types of law school learning activities and the list of learning styles. For which personality types and learning styles have these lists been designed?

4. You will also find many graphic images in this text. For which personality types and learning styles have these graphics been designed?

References

Robin A. Boyle & Rita Dunn, *Teaching Law Students Through Individual Learning Styles*, 62 ALB. L. REV. 213 (1998).

Gerald F. Hess & Steve Friedland, TECHNIQUES FOR TEACHING LAW (1999).

M.H. Sam Jacobson, *A Primer on Learning Styles: Reaching Every Student*, 25 SEATTLE UNIV. L. REV. 139 (2001).

Presentation and Conference materials: Kristina L. Niedringhaus and Peter E. Thorsett, *Multiple Personalities: Using Technology to Teach Everyone*, 2002 Conference for Law School Computing (2002).

Vernellia R. Randall, *The Myers-Briggs Type Indicator, First-Year Law Students and Performance*, 26 CUMBERLAND L. REV. 26 (1995).

Paul D. Tieger and Barbara Barron-Tieger, DO WHAT YOU ARE (3d ed. 2001).

http://www.capt.org/Using_Type/Workplace.cfm

http://ccc.commnet.edu/faculty/~simonds/styles/compensate.htm

http://facultyweb.cortland.edu/andersmd/learning/Kolb.htm.

http://www.humanmetrics.com/cgi-win/JTypes1.htm

http:///knowyourtype.com/intro.html

http://www.metamath.com/lsweb/fourls.htm.

http://www.nwlink.com/~donclark/hrd/styles.html#kolb

http://typelogic.com/

http://www.vark-learn.com/

http://www.wncc.nevada.edu/studentservices/counseling/styles_types/2_16_personality_
    types.html

Chapter 7

The Performance Phase of the SRL Cycle

Unlike the forethought phase, the performance phase of the cycle does not involve a set of independent steps through which the student moves. Rather, students sometimes engage in each of the three tasks of the performance phase—attention-focusing, implementation and self-monitoring—at the same time and sometimes one at a time but in no particular order. In other words, while you are implementing your learning strategies, you also repeatedly should focus your attention and monitor your learning progress. Thus, a graphic depiction of this phase would not appear as a line, but, rather, as an interlocked set of ovals as in Figure 6 below.

Figure 6: The Performance Phase

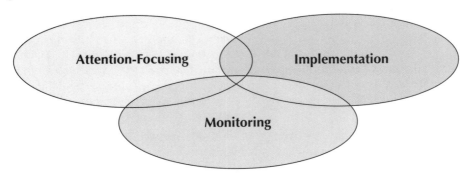

For the purposes of this discussion, however, it is helpful to consider each of these tasks independently.

Attention-Focusing

Students need to track their attention whenever they are engaged in learning, regardless of whether they are reading a text or participating in a classroom experience. As described in Chapter 3, the cognitive model of human learning begins with the assumption that the learner successfully has focused her attention on the learning task; otherwise, the new learning never even reaches her short-term memory. Almost all of us have had the experience of engaging in **pseudo-studying**. Pseudo-studying is an activity that looks like studying from the outside but actually involves no learning. For example, many of use have had the experience of reading a page in a textbook over and over again without taking in anything or have spent hours in the library supposedly studying with a friend during which we have actually devoted most of the time to socializing. In college, such wastes of time are not always problematic; in law school, however, frequent pseudo-studying results in poor performance.

Pseudo-studying is usually a result of poor attention-monitoring caused by boredom, fatigue or self-doubt. Expert self-regulated learners do not, therefore, allow themselves to be distracted by self-doubt, fatigue or boredom. Rather, they use one or more of the following **volitional control** techniques to focus their attention on the learning activities in which they are engaged:

(1) Following each step of a procedure sequentially and checking off each step as they go (systematic guides);
(2) Verbalizing (out loud) what they are about to do (self-guiding verbalizations);
(3) Developing mental images of what they are trying to do as they are doing it (imagery); and
(4) Praising themselves as they work (positive self-talk).

Most cognitive strategies follow a linear procedure that can serve as a **systematic guide** to the learner's actions and thereby help the learner retain his or her focus. In other words, the procedure serves as a control on the learner's actions. For example, creating a comparison chart (a type of graphic organizer used to help learners understand the comparisons between two similar concepts or items) requires the learner to (1) decide to create a comparison chart, (2) identify and list the number of things (e.g., three cases) being compared, (3) identify and list the number of characteristics (e.g., parties to the cases and years the cases were decided) by which the learner will compare the things being compared, and (4) create a chart with the items being compared (the cases). A learner would focus his or her attention on the task of creating such a chart by following the procedure from first step to the last step, checking off each step as he or she completes it. Because this approach occupies the learner's brain, it inhibits other thoughts, such as self-doubt, from invading the learner's consciousness and distracting his or her focus.

To focus attention, the learner might also (or alternatively) use **self-guiding verbalizations**. In other words, the student would verbally state out loud each step before performing it. Thus, the learner might say, "First, I will identify the number of things to be compared." The act of verbally stating a plan of action out loud recalls that step of the procedure into the student's working memory so the student can implement it accurately.

Another approach would involve using **imagery**, picturing a comparison chart the student had seen some time in the past or picturing what a successful product of his or her efforts would look like. The student would retain the image in his or her mind the entire time that student is engaged in the learning strategy. The student would use the image both as a guide to keep focused on creating the comparison chart on which he or she is working and as a tool to help him or her avoid distractions. As many successful athletes have discovered, imagining a good result increases the likelihood it will occur.

Finally, as many athletes also have discovered, **positive self-talk**, praising oneself as one works, increases the likelihood of success. Coaches actually teach athletes to make encouraging statements to themselves as they are engaging in their sports (e.g., "Nice shot!"). Students who engage in such positive self-talk are much less likely to create obstacles to their own learning, such as procrastination, low effort or spreading themselves too thin.

Exercise 7-1 in the Workbook focuses on helping to develop these tools for maintaining focus during learning experiences.

In addition, expert learners use the above strategies in conjunction with **motivational control**, which keep students on task by making sure the student knows why she is engaged in the learning task, and **emotional control**, which involves being vigilant against either undue anxiety about or overconfidence about the likely success of the learning project.

Implementation

This part of the performance phase involves actually performing the learning tasks. Part II of this text, Chapters 9–16, describes the learning strategies most helpful to law students. Each chapter describes the strategies, explains how to perform them, and identifies the strengths, weaknesses and uses of the strategies. Thus, at this stage of the study of SRL, the student simply needs to be aware that this part of the performance phase involves performing those activities.

Self-Monitoring

In the context of the performance phase, the most significant distinction between naïve self-regulated learners and their expert peers is that the experts more closely and more accurately self-monitor their learning. In fact, studies of both undergraduate and graduate students found that students who simply filled out a self-monitoring log (similar to the log in Appendix A to this text) achieved significantly higher grades than those who did not do so.

Expert learners self-monitor five things—their comprehension, their efficiency, their environmental strategy choices, their help seeking, and their attention. Once students become expert at self-monitoring and at SRL (once they have developed automaticity in SRL and in the cognitive strategies they are using), much of the monitoring occurs offline (on a less conscious level). In other words, expert self-regulated learners are always vigilant about their comprehension and their efficiency, and they intensely self-monitor only when they have identified a deficit in a particular area of their comprehension or efficiency.

The monitoring process often causes expert learners to change or modify their approaches and techniques during the learning process. Expert learners do not merely observe their learning; they evaluate it with a purpose in mind—achieving their learning goals. Consequently, expert learners change their approaches whenever their self-monitoring reveals that those approaches are not working.

Monitoring of Comprehension

First and foremost, expert self-regulated learners monitor their comprehension. They keep track of personal indicators of success as they are engaging in the implementation of their learning strategies. The expert students can tell when they are getting it and when they are not, and they can and do use this information to alter their approaches before they get poor grades. Many naïve self-regulators, in contrast, overestimate their understanding and therefore fail to study as thoroughly as they need to study.

Monitoring of Efficiency

Second, expert learners monitor not only whether they are learning, but, also, *how efficiently* they are learning. They evaluate how long they are studying and how much effort that studying is requiring and then weigh those two factors against the effectiveness of the process and the importance of the learning task. This effort gives the student information upon which to modify his or her strategies to streamline them (when it is appropriate to do so) and to prepare themselves for the time and effort certain difficult tasks will require (and therefore plan similar learning activities in the future).

Monitoring of Environmental Strategies

Third, expert learners monitor their environmental strategies, paying attention to where they are studying, when they are studying (including the time taken for study breaks) and with whom they are studying. As discussed in Chapter 5, all of these considerations are important to students' success. Expert learners make sure that they actually study when they plan to study, that they take scheduled breaks to allow themselves spaced learning experiences, that the location in which they have chosen to study facilitates their learning and that their study partners enhance their learning.

Monitoring of Help-Seeking

Fourth, expert learners monitor their own help-seeking activities. Having identified a comprehension difficulty (and such difficulties arise for all learners in all educational settings), they monitor their efforts to get the help they need from their instructors and peers. In fact, expert learners keep asking different peers and instructors until they are sure they understand. Some peers and even some teachers are better than others in providing such help; expert learners find out this information and act accordingly.

Monitoring of Attention

Finally, expert learners monitor their attention even as they are focusing it using the strategies discussed above. Expert learners know that unfocused study is, generally, a waste of time because it does not produce learning. They therefore make sure that they are able to pay attention (e.g., that they are not too tired, that they do not need a study break, and that their study location is not distracting).

Appendix A to this text, the "Time Management/Self-Monitoring Log" is a tool for facilitating this self-monitoring. It allows the student to record his or her efforts to study and their outcomes.

The Time Management/Self-Monitoring log contained in Appendix A and reproduced in the Workbook has been designed to help students develop self-monitoring skills and is an excellent tool for planning their studying and self-monitoring the process. In fact, studies of students who have completed such forms for entire courses show that students who do so outperform those who do not at a statistically significant level. To help students begin to develop their ability to use the log to self-monitor their learning, Exercise 7-2 in the Workbook directs student to fill out the log for the reading in the next chapter dealing with the reflection phase of the SRL cycle.

Reflection Questions

1. For each of the four techniques for focusing attention, explain why that technique helps learners to focus their attention.

2. Why is self-monitoring so crucial for expert learning?

3. Recall a learning experience that did not go as well as you would have liked. Was there a point in time before you received your grade when you knew things were not going well?

4. If your answer to the above question is "yes," how did you know? Why were you unable to address the issue(s) productively?

5. If your answer to the above question is "no," why do you think you were unaware that you were having a learning difficulty?

6. Why is monitoring for help seeking so important to success in law school?

References

Peggy A. Ertmer & Timothy J. Newby, *The Expert Learner: Strategic, Self-Regulated and Reflective*, 24 INSTRUCTIONAL SCIENCE 1 (1996).

Barbara K. Hofer, Shirley L. Yu & Paul Pintrich, *Teaching College Students to Be Self-Regulated Learners* in SELF-REGULATED LEARNING: FROM TEACHING TO SELF-REFLECTIVE PRACTICE 57, 76 (1998).

William Y. Lan, *Teaching Self-Monitoring Skills* in Statistics in SELF-REGULATED LEARNING: FROM TEACHING TO SELF-REFLECTIVE PRACTICE 86 (1998).

William Y. Lan, *The Effects of Self-Monitoring on Students' Course Performance, Use of learning Strategies, Attitude, Self-Judgment Ability, and Knowledge Representation*, 64(2) JOURNAL OF EXPERIMENTAL EDUCATION 101 (1997).

Mark Morgan, *Self-Monitoring of Attained Subgoals in Private Study*, 77(6) JOURNAL OF EDUCATIONAL PSYCHOLOGY 623 (1985).

Bridget Murray, *Teaching Students How to Learn: College Students Often Struggle to Find Effective Learning Strategies, But Professors Can Help*, MONITOR ON PSYCHOLOGY, Volume 31, No. 6, June 2000 http://www.apa.org/monitor/jun00/howtolearn.html.

Philip H. Winne & Denise B. Stockley, *Computing Technologies as Sites for Developing Self-Regulated Learning* in SELF-REGULATED LEARNING: FROM TEACHING TO SELF-REFLECTIVE PRACTICE 106 (1998).

Claire E. Weinstein & Gretchen Van Mater Stone, *Broadening Our Conception of General Education: The Self-Regulated Learner,* 81 NEW DIRECTIONS IN COMMUNITY COLLEGES 31 (1993).

Barry J. Zimmerman, *A Social-Cognitive View of Self-Regulated Academic Learning,* 81 JOURNAL OF EDUCATIONAL PSYCHOLOGY 329–339 (1989).

Barry J. Zimmerman, *Developing Self-Fulfilling Cycles of Academic Regulation: An Analysis of Exemplary Instructional Models* in SELF-REGULATED LEARNING: FROM TEACHING TO SELF-REFLECTIVE PRACTICE 1 (D.H. Schunk, B. Zimmerman, eds. 1998).

Barry J. Zimmerman, Sebastian Bonner and Robert Kovach, DEVELOPING SELF-REGULATED LEARNERS: BEYOND ACHIEVEMENT TO SELF-EFFICACY (1996).

Barry J. Zimmerman & Andrew S. Paulsen, *Self-Monitoring During Collegiate Studying: An Invaluable Tool for Academic Self-Regulation* in NEW DIRECTIONS IN COLLEGE TEACHING AND LEARNING: UNDERSTANDING SELF-REGULATED LEARNING 13 (No. 65:1995).

Chapter 8

The Reflection
Phase of the SRL Cycle

The reflection phase of the self-regulated learning cycle is the analytical phase of the cycle. Once expert learners complete the learning task during the performance phase, they reflect upon the experience, analyzing what they did, how they did it, how well they did it, why they did as well as they did, how they feel about how they did and how they will do things in the future. Like the forethought phase, it is easy to contemplate omitting the reflection phase but erroneous to do so. It can be easy to contemplate omitting this phase because the learning task is over at this point, and the learner, already anticipating the next learning task, may want to move on.

Studies of expert learners have found that this phase is a crucial prerequisite to successful future learning tasks. This phase creates the foundation upon which students invoke self-efficacy in the future. During the self-reflection phase, expert learners both develop data about their learning outcomes and figure out the causes of those outcomes in terms of their strategy selections. Thus, the reflection phase reinforces expert learners' sense that learning is a matter of planning, strategic choice and persistence rather than a matter of innate ability. In fact, in a series of studies, including a study of Belgian law students, researchers taught students that their success was a matter of strategy selection and persistence, rather than aptitude. The control groups for these studies received no such instruction. The researchers found that the students who had been taught that success was a matter of persistence and strategy selection consistently outperformed the students in the control groups.

Moreover, during the reflection phase, students plan how, for future similar learning tasks, they will modify their cognitive, environmental and motivational strategies based on their learning outcomes. Students weigh how well they learned and how quickly they learned and then modify their approaches to improve efficacy and efficiency. Thus, the reflection phase will play a large role in determining the success or failure of future learning endeavors. In fact, as the constructivist model of human learning suggests, students only really become experts as learners when they take full control over their own learning process, devising learning strategies that make sense for their particular set of preferences and understandings.

The reflection phase consists of four tasks: **self-evaluation**, **attribution**, **self-reaction** and **adaptation**, each of which is described in detail below. This phase is similar to the forethought phase in the sense that it is a linear process, in which the learner moves from task to task, using information developed during a prior task to perform the next task. Two aspects of this phase are important to recognize at the outset. First, because SRL is a cyclical process, the reflection phase inevitably leads the learner back to the forethought phase. Second, some academic tasks require multiple cycles through the three phases of SRL as the learners work towards developing the requisite level of mastery and identifying the best strategy or set of strategies.

Figure 7 below depicts this sequence and identifies the questions implicated by each step.

Figure 7: The Four Steps of the Reflection Phase of the SRL Cycle

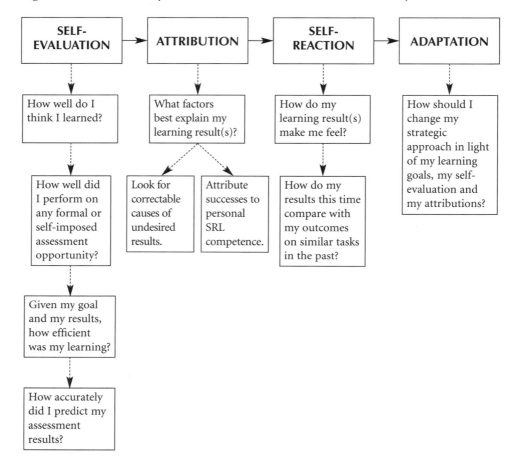

Self-Evaluation

How well do I think I learned?
How well did I perform on any formal or self-imposed assessment opportunity?
Given my goal and my results, how efficient was my learning?
How accurate was my self-perception as a predictor of my performance?

One of the easiest ways to distinguish expert learners from novices is in terms of their efforts at self-evaluation. Expert learners evaluate their learning frequently, in multiple ways, objectively and according to explicit criteria. On the other hand, novice learners evaluate their learning seldom, in no more than one way, based only on subjective beliefs and not according to any particular criteria. These differences influence all of the other steps of the reflection phase, enhancing the expert learners' sense of empowerment and efficacy (as they figure out the causes of their successes and failures, celebrate their successes and determine how to correct any failures) while contributing to the naïve learners' feelings of discouragement and powerlessness.

Expert learners assess their learning experiences in four ways: internally, on their own; externally, through formal or self-imposed assessment events; according to their own criteria, by weighing their outcomes against their goals and the time and effort the learning required; and reflectively, by comparing their predicted outcomes with their actual outcomes.

Internal Evaluation: How Well Do I Think I Learned?

Expert learners begin their self-evaluations with an internal assessment. They ask themselves whether they have achieved their learning goals—whether they have mastered the material. This evaluation is really the only one possible in real world contexts, such as the practice of law, making it particularly crucial that the student learn to accurately evaluate her learning. In fact, internal self-evaluation is one of the techniques used by expert practicing attorneys to help them avoid malpractice. Expert attorneys know when they know something and, more importantly, they know when they do not know. This knowledge guides expert practioners in how they practice law, informing many decisions, such as decisions about which cases to take and which to reject, decisions as to when to ask for help with a client's problem and when to keep struggling to figure it out, and decisions as to when to do more research and when the research process is complete.

External Evaluation: How Well Did I Perform on Any Formal or Self-Imposed Assessment Opportunity?

Studies have found a significant difference between expert learners and their peers with respect to external evaluation. Expert learners seek out opportunities for external evaluation. They take practice tests, for example, whenever it is possible to do so and they request professorial or peer evaluation of their efforts or they evaluate their efforts themselves. Expert learners are the students who choose to take the optional tests and do the optional exercises. Novice learners, in contrast, miss these opportunities or even consciously try to avoid them because they fear the outcome, may not see the value in such activities or are overconfident.

Because new law students are working towards acquiring a new skill, opportunities for practice and feedback are crucial to their success. Opportunities for such practice and feedback are available from many different sources. Many law schools provide students with copies of past essay exams and answers. In addition, the common law school practice of forming study groups creates opportunities for peer testing and feedback. Finally, students can test themselves.

Criteria-Based Evaluation: Given My Goal and My Results, How Efficient Was My Learning?

At this stage of the self-evaluation process, the learner weighs the degree to which her results suggest she has achieved her goals against the time and effort she used in implementing her learning strategy. An optimal set of learning strategies (environmental, motivational and cognitive) not only produces learning, but also is as efficient as possible. Because law students, like everyone else, only have a limited amount of time, they need to assess their learning strategies not only for whether they produced optimal learning but also for whether the strategies caused the student to learn the material as quickly as possible. In this sense, expert learners act as their own efficiency experts.

Reflective Evaluation: How Accurately Did I Predict My Assessment Results?

Finally, expert learners self-evaluate by reflecting on the accuracy of their internal self-assessment. Because, as explained above, internal self-evaluation is such a crucial skill for practitioners in all fields, expert learners use reflective evaluation to help them fine-tune their self-assessment skills.

One technique that can be particularly effective in helping students build their self-assessment skills is for students to graph their outcome predictions against their actual outcomes. Figure 8 depicts below a fictional version of such a graph in which, for each exam, the student records both her predictions (light gray) and her outcomes (black). The student records a prediction as to the student's performance before taking the test and then records the actual results after the test and then reflect on the reasons why the two are different.

Figure 8: Example of How to Graph Predicted Outcomes against Actual Outcomes

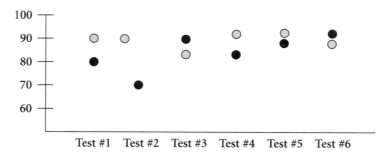

Note that, by graphing the predictions and outcomes together, the student gets a visual sense of when her predictions are far off and can visually see as her predictions become more accurate over time.

Exercise 8-1 in the workbook provides an opportunity for you to practice your self-evaluation skills.

Attribution

What factors best explain my learning result(s)?
Look for correctable causes of undesired results. Attribute successes to personal SRL
competence.

Attributions are students' explanations as to the cause(s) of their learning results. Having achieved or failed to achieve a learning goal, the student tries to understand the causes of this outcome. Expert learners attribute their successes to personal learning competence, to their successful and persistent implementation of their learning strategies, and attribute their failures to correctable causes, such as errors in strategy selection, implementation errors or insufficient practice. Novices, in contrast, attribute their successes and failures to ability.

These differences explain why attributions are important to law school success; attributions greatly influence persistence. Some learning tasks, particularly tasks that involve the development of high-level intellectual skills (such as legal analysis) require multiple SRL cycles to develop mastery. Like learning to play a sport or a musical instrument, learning to perform legal analysis often involves multiple instances of meager learning results. Because novices believe successes and failures are caused by ability, they are likely to give up and stop trying if they fail to learn on the first try. In contrast, expert learners, who recognize that their failures are due to correctable causes and expect that some learning tasks will require many SRL cycles, persevere and, eventually, learn.

Novices' attributions of success to personal competence do not ultimately serve them well. There is some evidence that novices' ability-based attributions lead to over-confidence or failures to study; the novices see great effort as unnecessary. Expert learners' attributions of success to personal SRL competence, on the other hand, help them create a cycle of positive and dedicated learning efforts.

There is no real magic to making attributions in the sense that at least a part of the process involves self-perception and attitude. Learners must choose to make the proper attributions. The more difficult task is making **accurate** attributions, because accuracy helps ensure that future learning efforts succeed. The keys are **reflection** and **brainstorming**.

First, learners need to give themselves time to reflect on their just-completed learning process. They need to trace their learning process from its inception, looking for errors and inefficiencies. They need to consider the difficulty of the learning task and the possibility that they did not learn simply because the task necessitates cycling through several or even many attempts to learn.

Second, learners need to brainstorm the possibilities. Human error is just as much a part of the learning process as it is of anything else in life. Each phase of the SRL cycle involves possibilities for miscalculation. At the same time, as noted above, some failures to learn simply are inevitable given the nature of the learning task. Consequently, learners need to review their process with a checklist of possible causes in mind, such as the checklist in Figure 9 below.

Exercise 8-2 in the Workbook will allow you to use Figure 9 to develop attributions about a past learning experience.

Figure 9: Checklist of Possible Causes of Failures to Learn

Possible problems in the forethought phase

___ Failure to set appropriate goal (learner set no goal or set improper one)
___ Incorrect assessment of the learning task (learner erroneously classified the task)
___ Failure to invoke self-efficacy (learner failed to identify past success in similar learning enterprises)
___ Failure to develop intrinsic interest in the learning task (learner did not determine why he or she needed to learn the material)
___ Poor motivational strategy choices (learner could not stay motivated)
___ Poor environmental choices (learner made bad location, timing, rest sequence choices)
___ Poor cognitive strategy choices (the strategy choices proved unsuited to the learning task or the learner should have used additional strategies)

Possible problems in the performance phase

___ Incorrect implementation of strategy choices (the learner incorrectly used the strategies)
___ Failure to maintain focused attention (learner was unable to focus during implementation)
___ Failure to self-monitor (learner failed to recognize a breakdown in the learning process while it was ongoing)
___ Insufficient persistence (learning task simply requires multiple learning cycles)

Possible problems in the reflection phase

___ Failure to pursue opportunities for self-assessment (student did not take advantage of or create opportunities for practice and feedback)
___ Inaccurate self-assessment (student incorrectly assessed how well she learned)

Self-Reaction

How do my learning results make me feel about myself?
How do my results this time compare with my outcomes on similar tasks in the past?

Because this step is inevitable for nearly all learners, it is considered a part of the process. For example, having attributed a failure to learn either to ability or to correctable causes, the learner considers what those results mean for him or herself. Because expert learners have not attributed the failure to a lack of ability, they experience no negative self-reaction. Novice learners, however, perceive failures to learn as personal defeats, as saying something about their intelligence or capacity to learn. As a result, expert learners retain their sense of self-efficacy, regardless of their outcomes, whereas novices' self-efficacy is outcome-dependent and therefore considerably more vulnerable. In fact, there is some evidence that learners transfer this sense of agency or lack thereof, of control over their environment or of lack of control, outside the learning context. Expert learners usually tend to perceive themselves as able and competent, whereas novice learners often do not.

One way for learners to facilitate a positive self-reaction is to compare their outcome on the task at hand with their outcome on past, similar tasks. If the learner has failed to learn what he or she needed to learn but can point to a past success, the learner is more likely to react to this result positively and with confidence about a long-term resolution. Even if the learner can only point to past failures to learn, this comparison can allow the learner to see improvement, to recognize the progress he or she has made towards achieving her goals. Exercise 8-3 in the Workbook provides an opportunity for the student to reflect on her self-reaction to a successful learning experience she has had and to an unsuccessful learning experience she has had.

Adaptation

How should I change my strategic approach in light of my learning goals, my self-evaluation and my attributions?

The adaptation step is, perhaps, the most constructivist aspect of the SRL cycle. Ultimately, it is the learner who is the expert in his or her own learning. The learner is in the best position to figure out the causes and the solutions for failures to learn or inefficiencies in the learning process. However, it is much easier to make learners aware of the need to engage in this process than to explain how to do it.

There are, however, three characteristics of good adaptations. First, good adaptations are **tied to the student's original learning goals**. The goals set the standards by which the learner measures her performance during self-monitoring and self-evaluation. Consequently, the goals also set the standard at which the learner is aiming through his or her modifications of her learning approach.

Second, good adaptations **reflect the learner's self-evaluation** of his or her learning. While excellence is a worthy aspiration, perfection is not. In many instances, there is no failure to learn at all and therefore no need for adaptation. In many others, the learner has not fallen very far short of her learning goals and therefore a major overhaul is unnecessary. If the learning deficiency is a small one, only a small adjustment is appropriate. In still other situations, the issue is one of efficiency, not effectiveness, and again only small adjustments may be in order.

Finally, good adaptations are **systematic**. Rather than changing every aspect of the learning process after a failure, expert learners know that they may need several or even many SRL cycles to master a difficult learning task. Consequently, expert learners make smaller adjustments (unless the whole process went wrong from the outset), planning to adjust their approaches as they develop more information and practice their new skills more. Exercise 8-4 in the Workbook addresses the development of your adaptation skills.

Conclusion: Completion of the Reflection Phase— Onto the Next Forethought Phase

As the foregoing discussion reflects, learning, whether it is self-regulated or not, requires persistence, thoughtfulness and a high degree of motivation. Expert learners possess this motivation because they know they will eventually learn. As they cycle through the reflection phase, they anticipate the forethought phase, developing self-efficacy and strategic plans that will influence how they go about the performance phase. For this reason, the degree to which students engage in self-regulated learning determines, ultimately, not only whether learning occurs, but, also, whether the learner enjoys the process and sees the learning experience as a positive or a negative one. SRL allows students to command their own learning and to ensure that they achieve the goals that led them to enter the academic enterprise in the first place.

Reflection Questions

1. How does the reflection phase influence the forethought and the performance phases?

2. Many novice learners never engage in any of the behaviors described in this chapter. Why do novice learners avoid these behaviors?

3. Have you ever engaged in the behaviors described in this chapter? Describe what you did.

4. In what sense is the reflection phase the most self-empowering phase of the SRL cycle?

References

Deborah L. Butler, *A Strategic Content Learning Approach to Promoting Self-Regulated Learning by Students with Learning Disabilities* in SELF REGULATED LEARNING: FROM TEACHING TO SELF-REFLECTIVE PRACTICE 160 (D.H. Schunk, B. Zimmerman, eds. 1998).

Arthur L. Costa & Lawrence E. Lowery, TECHNIQUES FOR TEACHING THINKING (1989).

Peggy A. Ertmer & Timothy J. Newby, *The Expert Learner: Strategic, Self-Regulated and Reflective*, 24 INSTRUCTIONAL SCIENCE 1 (1996).

Friedrich Fösterling, *Attributional Retraining: A Review*, 98(3) PSYCHOLOGICAL BULLETIN 495 (1985).

Barbara K. Hofer, Shirley L. Yu and Paul R. Pintrich, *Teaching College Students to Be Self-Regulated Learners* in SELF REGULATED LEARNING: FROM TEACHING TO SELF-REFLECTIVE PRACTICE 57 (D.H. Schunk, B. Zimmerman, eds. 1998).

Frances O'Tuel & Ruth K. Bullard, DEVELOPING HIGHER ORDER THINKING IN THE CONTENT AREAS K–12 50 (1993).

Claire E. Weinstein & Gretchen Van Mater Stone, *Broadening Our Conception of General Education: The Self-Regulated Learner*, 81 NEW DIRECTIONS IN COMMUNITY COLLEGES 31 (1993).

Timothy Wilson & Patricia Linville, 49(1) JOURNAL OF PERSONALITY AND SOCIAL PSYCHOLOGY, 287 (1985).

Barry J. Zimmerman, *Developing Self-Fulfilling Cycles of Academic Regulation: An Analysis of Exemplary Instructional Models* in SELF REGULATED LEARNING: FROM TEACHING TO SELF-REFLECTIVE PRACTICE 1 (D.H. Schunk, B. Zimmerman, eds. 1998).

Barry J. Zimmerman, Sebastian Bonner and Robert Kovach, DEVELOPING SELF-REGULATED LEARNERS: BEYOND ACHIEVEMENT TO SELF-EFFICACY (1996).

Part II

Learning Strategies for Law Students

Chapter 9

Strategies for Reading and Briefing Court Opinions

Introduction

As explained in Chapter 2, cases are not only one of the four main units of instruction, but they are also often the axis around which the other three units revolve. Students and lawyers read cases as source material for rules and holdings, as exemplars to help them understand the application of the rules to particular facts, as springboards for discussing the policy rationales for the rules and holdings, and as models from which hypothetical variations can be taken. Consequently, expertise in reading cases is crucial to student success.

This assertion stems both from general studies of best practices for reading textual materials and from studies of case reading by lawyers, law students and law professors. In an important law review article authored by a writing instructor at Seattle University School of Law, Laurel Currie Oates summarized the results of previous case reading studies as well as her own efforts to study law student case reading techniques.[1] Taken together, these studies reveal that novices read cases differently than experts and that successful law students read cases differently than their less successful peers and more like the experts.

The process of effectively reading cases actually involves three, equally important steps:

(1) **pre-reading strategies,**
(2) **reading strategies** and
(2) **briefing strategies.**

Each of these strategies is separately addressed below. Many law texts recommend that students simply read and re-read their assigned cases over and over until the student understands the cases. Other law texts simply state that students must brief cases and then list what the students should include in their briefs. The approach described here takes no more time than these approaches, but it is much more stimulating (because students are not simply passively reading and re-reading) and much more pro-

---

1. Laurel Currie Oates, *Beating the Odds: Reading Strategies of Law Students Admitted Through Alternative Admissions Programs*, 83 Iowa L. Rev. 139 (1997).

ductive (by helping students both understand cases and develop useful case briefs as part of their class preparation).

Pre-Reading Strategies

The goal of pre-reading strategies is to ensure that your actual reading of the case goes as smoothly as possible. Many law students feel as though they have no idea what parts of the case are important, what they are supposed to get from the cases, and, as a result, they have trouble understanding them. By engaging in pre-reading activities, you ensure that you have the background knowledge you need to be able to avoid these problems.

There are six pre-reading strategies that expert law students use that their less successful peers do not. You already have learned about and know how to perform one of those five activities—setting a learning goal. Professor Oates' study revealed that successful law students read cases with a purpose or goal in mind whereas their less successful peers do not. That information should not be surprising to you because you already have learned that setting mastery learning goals improves grades. Thus, before beginning to read a set of assigned, expert learners set a mastery learning goal.

Second, Professor Oates' comparison of successful and unsuccessful students revealed that the successful students keep in mind, even before they start reading the cases, that court opinions do not state absolute truths. Rather, court opinions are really just pieces of persuasive writing in which the author (a judge) is trying to convince his or her audience (lawyers, other judges and law professors) that the decision he or she is describing is a correct one. Successful students recognize that opinions create meaning (both for the parties involved in the case being described in the opinion and for future lawyers, judges and parties who will read the opinion and be influenced by it). Judges tell a story about what happened between the parties and what the court decided.

For example, a famous judge once began a famous opinion with the following sentence: "The defendant styles herself 'a creator of fashions.'"[2] The famous judge then ruled against the defendant. As another famous judge, Richard Posner, pointed out in his biography of Benjamin Cardozo, the author of the opinion, "Cardozo has subtly loaded the dice against the defendant by implying that she may be a phony."[3] To see Posner's point, imagine how different the opinion would have read had Cardozo chosen this sentence as his first one: "Defendant is a well-known fashion expert," which would have been an equally-plausible description of the defendant at the time Judge Cardozo issued his opinion.

Professor Oates also found that the successful students recognized that their task in reading a case was not merely to pull information from it, but, rather, to construct meaning from it for themselves. In other words, expert students and lawyers recognize that case reading is a matter of interpretation, not unlike the interpretation of a poem or novel, and therefore students must make the opinions they read meaningful to themselves. This statement does not suggest that students must force themselves to agree with decisions they dislike or alter their understandings of court opinions to fit their values. What it does mean is that students should not see themselves in a passive role,

---

2. *Wood v. Lucy, Lady Duff-Gordon*, 222 N.Y. 88, 118 N.E. 214 (1917).
3. Richard Posner, Cardozo, A Study in Reputation 95 (1990).

receiving wisdom from judges through court opinions. Rather, successful law students adopt an active role as they get ready to read, planning to develop for themselves an understanding of what the opinion means.

To see this point, imagine two lawyers (representing opposing parties to a lawsuit) who are dealing with a particular prior decision, a precedent. It is very likely one lawyer will perceive the precedent to be favorable to his or her client, and the other lawyer will perceive the precedent to be unfavorable. In order to convince a judge to view the precedent in a way that favors their respective clients, the lawyers will try to convince the judge to interpret the precedent in a way that favors their respective clients. The lawyer for whose client the precedent is favorable will try to convince the judge that the proper interpretation is that the facts of the precedent case and the case at hand are identical or are similar in every important way. The lawyer for whose client the precedent is unfavorable will identify differences between the facts in the precedent case and the facts in the case at hand and try to convince the judge that those differences are important ones and require the judge not to follow the precedent. In other words, as reflected in Figure 10 below, the first lawyer will try to stretch the precedent to fit around the case at hand, and the second lawyer will try to shrink the precedent by squeezing it so tight that it cannot fit the case at hand.

Figure 10: How Lawyers Work with Precedents: Stretching and Squeezing

An example from outside the legal context may help. Imagine an employer who previously allowed an employee to go home early from work because the employee received a call informing the employee that her mother had died. We'll call this situation "the precedent." Now, a second employee's mother has become seriously, but not mortally, ill. The second employee asks to go home. This second employee hopes the employer applies the precedent broadly to cover all situations involving serious family health matters (a broad interpretation). The second employee's immediate supervisor, however, may want the second employee to stay and therefore may hope the employer applies the precedent narrowly to cover only deaths in the family or at least only deaths and life-threatening situations. The differences in interpreting this employment precedent are mirrored every day by lawyers as they interpret court opinions.

While expert law students recognize that judges' opinions create meaning and that lawyers create meaning as they read and interpret those opinions, expert law students also know that they will understand the possible meanings of the court opinions they are reading much more readily if they have developed prior knowledge about the subject area before they do the reading.

Developing Knowledge about the Subject of the Case(s)

Knowing something beforehand about what the student is about to read makes it easier for the student to understand and recall it. The new information from the opinion is stored in the brain through the connection to this prior knowledge. Perhaps more precisely, by possessing prior knowledge about a topic, the student possesses a schema for taking in that new learning. For this reason, it is helpful not only to have prior knowledge about a subject, but also to have **prior organized knowledge** about it. Expert students gather this knowledge from a variety of sources.

Information from course syllabi and casebook tables of contents. First, students can gain a feel for the organization of a set of cases by looking at their course syllabus and the table of contents of their casebook. The syllabus, for example, may list assigned materials by topic. Similarly, the authors of one of the most frequently used contracts texts[4] divided their text into six chapters, entitling Chapter 1 of their text "Remedies for Breach of Contract" and entitling Chapter 2 "Grounds for Enforcing Promises." They also divided Chapter 1 into five topical sections, entitled: "The Goals of Contract Damages," "Limitations on Damages," "Alternate Interests: Reliance and Restitution," "Contractual Controls on the Damage Remedy," and "Enforcement in Equity."[5] From this information, a student can draw tentative inferences and gain insight into the structure of contracts law:

(1) remedies is a major topic in contract law,
(2) there is more than one remedy for breach of contract,
(3) the above five topics are major topics within the larger subject of remedies,
(4) people cannot recover unlimited damages,
(5) reliance and restitution are in some way alternates,
(6) parties at least sometimes try to control damages in their contracts, and
(7) contracts can be enforced in equity (whatever equity is).

The structural information suggested by this table of contents can be shown in outline form:

I.   Remedies for breach of contract
    A.   Goals of contract damages
    B.   Limitations on damages
    C.   Alternate interests
        1.   Reliance
        2.   Restitution
    D.   Contractual controls on the damage remedy
    E.   Enforcement in equity
II.   Grounds for enforcing promises

---

4. John P. Dawson, William Burnett Harvey & Stanley D. Henderson, CONTRACTS: CASES AND COMMENT (7th ed. 1998).
5. *Id.* at xiii.

Information from supplemental texts' tables of contents. If the professor's syllabus and the table of contents of the outline prove unhelpful, students can find similar information in the table of contents in a hornbook (a large text explaining in detail an entire subject area, like contracts law), a commercial outline (a shorter book, depicting, usually in outline form, the major points of law in an area) or some other supplemental text. As the above outline suggests, students can gain insight into the hierarchies among the topics they are studying by reviewing such texts. For example, most first-year law students read cases addressing disputes within which one of the parties claims to be the victim of a tort called "intentional infliction of emotional distress." If a student were to look up this tort in the table of contents of *Prosser and Keeton on Torts,* perhaps the best-known torts hornbook, that student would be able to figure out that this topic falls within the larger subject of intentional torts and the sub-topic of intentional torts against persons (as opposed to intentional torts against property). This observation will help the student develop a partial schema for torts that can be depicted in the form of the hierarchy chart in Figure 12 on the next page. Over time, the student will be adding to, modifying and revising their schema for this area of law, but this pre-reading activity would give the student some structure for understanding how intentional infliction of emotional distress fits within the larger subject area of tort law.

Information from casebook topical introductions. Another source of information may be found in the introduction to the chapter or chapter section in which the assigned cases fall. Even if the introductory reading is not assigned, it is worth reading. The introduction may provide an overview of the subject area, and, in some cases, may outline the key legal principles the student will be learning. For example, in Stephen C. Yeazell's Civil Procedure casebook, the Introductory Materials to Part A, Chapter II, section B ("The Modern Constitutional Formulation of Power") gives students guidance as to the connections between what they have read and what they are about to read.[6] It also foreshadows some of the issues in the cases the students are about to read. Thus, students can more readily connect their new learning to the prior learning and predict what they will be learning from the cases they are about to read. The Introductory Note to Chapter 1, Section 4 of the Contracts text referenced above goes one step further than the Yeazell introduction; it includes quotations from court opinions that both articulate the prevailing rule and identify major policy concerns with respect to this area of law.[7]

Information from the questions and notes following the case. Prior knowledge can also be acquired from the questions and comments that follow the case or the set of cases. Although authors of casebooks probably intend that students consider the questions only after reading the cases, there is nothing that prevents students from reading the questions beforehand. In fact, doing so makes cases easier to understand and gives guidance as to the key points. Most reading comprehension experts actually recommend that students read such questions first, regardless of the subject matter being studied.

The benefits of this approach can best be seen by considering an example. The fourth case in Joseph G. Cook and Paul Marcus' *Criminal Law* casebook is a hard-to-understand but well-known case called *Bowers v. Hardwick.* The opinion is difficult because it comes very early in the text (when students still know little about criminal law), because it addresses a Constitutional law issue (which are usually more difficult), because it is a

---

6. Stephen C. Yeazell, Civil Procedure, 94 (5th ed. 2000).
7. Dawson, Harvey & Henderson, *supra* note 12, at 127–129.

*Figure 11: A Partial Hierarchy Chart Depiction of New Law Students'
Torts Schema*

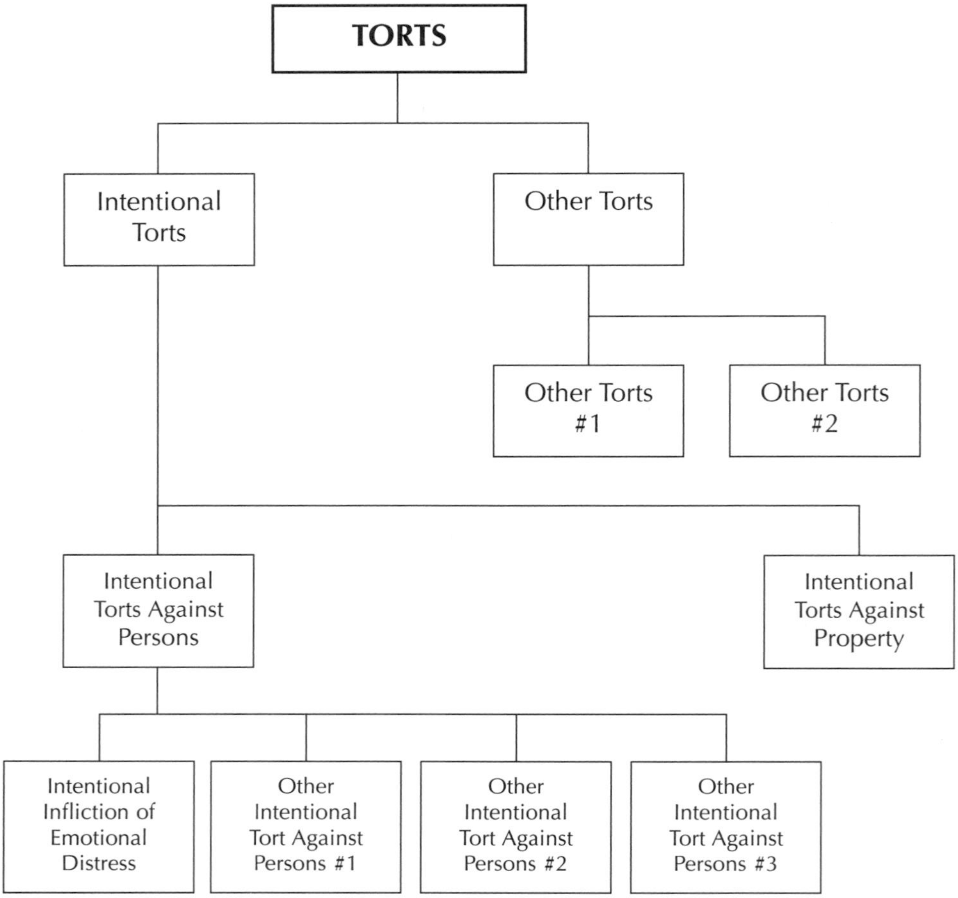

Supreme Court opinion (which are usually more complicated) and because it includes a majority opinion (a majority opinion expresses what most of the justices hearing a case decided), two concurring opinions (a concurring opinion expresses agreement with the result reached by the majority but offers different or additional reasons for reaching that result) and a dissenting opinion (a dissenting opinion expresses the views of a justice or justices who disagree with the majority's decision). The questions after the case, however, make reading the case easier. The questions state the issue in the case and give the student some guidance as to the structure of the analytical approach of the majority opinion, describe some weaknesses in the majority's reasoning, provide some historical context for the opinion, set forth a key basis for the court's decision and point out an argument the court chose not to address.[8] Thus, students who read the questions first have a great advantage; they know for what to look.

Information from the substantive portions of supplemental texts. Finally, many law students find it helpful to read about the subject area they are studying in a horn-

---

8. *See* Joseph G. Cook and Paul Marcus, CRIMINAL LAW, 26–27 (4th ed. 2001).

book or other supplemental text before they read the cases. Doing so helps students identify the key points in the opinions. For example, one of the cases in the Cook & Marcus *Criminal Law* text is *State v. Thompson*,[9] a 1977 case decided by the Washington Supreme Court. *State v. Thompson* is in the portion of the Cook and Marcus text that deals with the felony murder rule, a rule that authorizes courts to treat as murders accidental killings that occur during certain felonies. A student who read the felony murder section of a well-known hornbook, Wayne R. LaFave and Austin W. Scott, Jr.'s *Criminal Law,* would not only find out how other courts have dealt with the issue in *State v. Thompson*, but would also see that case cited in a footnote in the relevant section of the hornbook with a summary of the principle for which the case stands.

Reading hornbooks before reading the cases also helps students discern the reasons that the casebook authors included the cases they included in their books. Hornbooks usually identify when there is a disagreement among the state courts with respect to a particular point of law and the rules the differing courts have adopted. For example, the reference to *State v. Thompson* suggests that a number of states have reached a different result than that court reached. This information allows students to consider the possibility that the case was included because the author of the casebook disagrees with the opinion. If so, the students can anticipate that their professor may ask them to critique the case and argue whether it was a good decision as a matter of public policy.

One caveat is worth noting—many law faculty express distaste or outright hostility to the use of supplemental texts. Part of this concern stems from the fact that, by necessity, every law school class only addresses a portion of the particular body of law under study. It would be impossible, in fact, to cover all of contracts or torts or civil procedure law, even in a two-semester course. Thus, some professors have a well-founded concern that their students will either confuse themselves by knowing more law than they need to know or by learning the wrong portion of the body of law. Moreover, many professors are seeking to teach their students applying and distinguishing skills and therefore need to confine the course materials (and the useable cases) to those cases reproduced in students' texts. These concerns, however, do not relate at all to the above recommendations. Even the most strident anti-supplemental text professor is unlikely to object to the idea of reading a hornbook for the sole purpose of developing prior knowledge so that the case reading experience is more productive.

Previewing the Case

Previewing a case allows the student to sharpen her focus on it and to develop a schema for understanding it. It is much like skimming a text, as the point is to identify the key topics addressed by the case. To perform this activity, the student identifies and reads all the headings in the case. The student then reads the first sentence of each paragraph in the case; in most instances, that sentence is a topic sentence that states the point of the paragraph. For example, consider a case found in most contracts casebooks, *Parker v. Twentieth Century-Fox Film Corporation* (*see* Appendix B for a version of the case as it might appear in a Contracts casebook). On the next page of this book are the first four paragraphs of the opinion in its casebook form. For ease of student

---

9. *Id.* at 444.

reference, the first sentence in each paragraph appears in bold-italic font. Included in the bold-italic font sentences are many of the most important facts in the case.

First Excerpt from *Parker v. Twentieth Century-Fox Film Corporation*

Burke, J—Defendant Twentieth Century-Fox Film Corporation appeals from a summary judgment granting to plaintiff the recovery of agreed compensation under a written contract for her services as an actress in a motion picture. As will appear, we have concluded that the trial court correctly ruled in plaintiff's favor and that the judgment should be affirmed.

Plaintiff is well known as an actress, and in the contract between plaintiff and defendant is sometimes referred to as the "Artist." Under the contract dated August 6, 1965, plaintiff was to play the female lead in defendant's contemplated production of a motion picture entitled "Bloomer Girl." The contract provided that defendant would pay plaintiff a minimum "guaranteed compensation" of $ 53,571.42 per week for 14 weeks commencing May 23, 1966, for a total of $ 750,000. Prior to May 1966 defendant decided not to produce the picture and by a letter dated April 4, 1966, it notified plaintiff of that decision and that it would not "comply with our obligations to you under" the written contract.

By the same letter and with the professed purpose "to avoid any damage to you," defendant instead offered to employ plaintiff as the leading actress in another film tentatively entitled "Big Country, Big Man" (hereinafter, "Big Country"). The compensation offered was identical, as were 31 of the 34 numbered provisions or articles of the original contract.

Unlike "Bloomer Girl," however, which was to have been a musical production, "Big Country" was a dramatic "western type" movie. "Bloomer Girl" was to have been filmed in California; "Big Country" was to be produced in Australia. Also, certain terms in the proffered contract varied from those of the original. Plaintiff was given one week within which to accept; she did not and the offer lapsed. Plaintiff then commenced this action seeking recovery of the agreed guaranteed compensation.

Looking solely at the first sentence of each of these paragraphs, a student already knows these important facts:

1. The defendant lost in the trial court and is appealing that decision.
2. The plaintiff recovered damages for the defendant's breach of a contract to use plaintiff as an actress in a movie.
3. The defendant offered to give plaintiff a role in another movie so that plaintiff would not suffer any damage because of defendant's breach.
4. The other movie offered plaintiff was a western whereas the original movie promised plaintiff was a musical.

The next four first sentences are equally revealing. Below are four more paragraphs from the opinion in its casebook form with the first sentence again appearing in bold italic font. Taken together, these sentences tell the students a lot of information about the rules relied upon by the court and about the holding in the case. This important information makes understanding the full text of the opinion much easier.

Looking solely at the first sentence of each of these paragraphs, a student now knows these four important points about the case:

(1) The defendant's only argument for avoiding liability for breaching its contract with plaintiff is that plaintiff improperly rejected defendant's offer of alternative employment.

(2) The general rule regarding damages for breach by an employer of an employment contract: the amount of salary agreed upon for the period of service, less

the amount which the employer affirmatively proves the employee has earned or with reasonable effort might have earned from other employment.

(3) The court agrees with the trial court's conclusion that the plaintiff's damages should not be reduced simply because she turned down an offer of employment in a film called "Big Country."

(4) The "Big Country" offer was inferior because it altered rights plaintiff had under her original contract.

Moreover, if the student obtains access to the opinion in its original form, which students can do by going to their law library or doing a search online, the opinion also will include a summary (an overall description of what the case addresses) and mini-summaries of the case's main points linked to the portion of the opinion being summarized. Both the summary and the mini-summaries are also worth reading as part of the preview. Neither, however, is a substitute for reading the full text of the opinion, as either or both may be inaccurate, incomplete or misleading (because they are not written by the judges who wrote the opinions but, rather, by employees of the legal publishers).

The full text of *Parker v. Twentieth Century-Fox Film Corporation* includes such summaries (*see* Appendix B, which also contains the full text of the opinion without the summaries). An overall summary would explain that the California Supreme Court ruled in favor of Parker's contention that the fact that she turned down an opportunity to star in a western-style movie could not be used by the defendant to reduce the amount she recovers as damages for the defendant's breach of a contract to star her in a musical movie. Likewise, the mini-summaries would include, among other things, statements of the rule the court applied. Again, it bears repeating that these summaries are authored, not by the judges, but by employees of the legal publishers, and they therefore are not a substitute for reading the case in full. At the same time, this information is quite helpful to a lawyer (or law student) reading the case for the first time.

By the time a student has finished developing knowledge about the subject area and previewing the case(s), the student has developed some excellent hypotheses about what the student should be getting from the case(s).

Noting Details

Experts in case reading are more likely than novices to note the date of an opinion, the names of the parties, the court issuing the opinion and the author of the opinion. Experts do so because they know that legal decision-making can be influenced by all of these factors. For example, judges, like everyone else, are influenced by the society in which they live. To understand some decisions, therefore, one needs to consider the date on which the court made the decision because the date will suggest the historical context (e.g., war or peace), the economic situation (e.g., The Great Depression) or technological developments (such as developments that make it easy for parties to quickly communicate even if they reside great distances from each other) that may have influenced the decision. Likewise, the identities and statuses of the parties (powerful or powerless, famous or infamous), the court that issued the opinion (a lower court in a conservative state such as Alabama or a higher court in a progressive state such as New York), and the author of the opinion (some judges are famous for their innovations or for the high quality of their opinions) all may be used to explain a difficult-to-understand decision. Figure 12 below gives the first few lines of *Parker v. Twentieth Century-Fox Film Corpora-*

Second Excerpt from *Parker v. Twentieth Century-Fox Film Corporation*

As stated, defendant's sole defense to this action which resulted from its deliberate breach of contract, is that, in rejecting defendant's substitute offer of employment, plaintiff unreasonably refused to mitigate damages.

The general rule is that the measure of recovery by a wrongfully discharged employee is the amount of salary agreed upon for the period of service, less the amount which the employer affirmatively proves the employee has earned or with reasonable effort might have earned from other employment (*citations omitted*). However, before projected earnings from other employment opportunities not sought or accepted by the discharged employee can be applied in mitigation, the employer must show that the other employment was comparable, or substantially similar, to that of which the employee has been deprived. The employee's rejection of or failure to seek other available employment of a different or inferior kind may not be resorted to in order to mitigate damages (*citations omitted*).

Applying the foregoing rules to the record in the present case...it is clear that the trial court correctly ruled that plaintiff's failure to accept defendant's tendered substitute employment could not be applied in mitigation of damages because the offer of the "Big Country" lead was of employment both different and inferior, and that no factual dispute was presented on that issue. The mere circumstance that "Bloomer Girl" was to be a musical review calling upon plaintiff's talents as a dancer as well as an actress, and was to be produced in the City of Los Angeles, whereas "Big Country" was a straight dramatic role in a "Western Type" story taking place in an opal mine in Australia, demonstrates the difference in kind between the two employments; the female lead as a dramatic actress in a western style motion picture can by no stretch of imagination be considered the equivalent of or substantially similar to the lead in a song-and-dance production.

Additionally, the substitute "Big Country" offer proposed to eliminate or impair the director and screenplay approvals accorded to plaintiff under the original "Bloomer Girl" contract, and thus constituted an offer of inferior employment. No expertise or judicial notice is required in order to hold that the deprivation or infringement of an employee's rights held under an original employment contract converts the available "other employment" relied upon by the employer to mitigate damages, into inferior employment which the employee need not seek or accept.

Figure 12: Key Details in Parker v. Twentieth Century-Fox Film Corporation

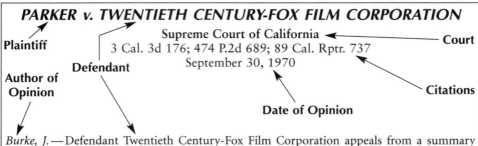

PARKER v. TWENTIETH CENTURY-FOX FILM CORPORATION

Plaintiff

Defendant

Author of Opinion

Supreme Court of California
3 Cal. 3d 176; 474 P.2d 689; 89 Cal. Rptr. 737
September 30, 1970

Court

Citations

Date of Opinion

Burke, J. — Defendant Twentieth Century-Fox Film Corporation appeals from a summary judgment granting to plaintiff the recovery of agreed compensation under a written contract for her services as an actress in a motion picture. As will appear, we have concluded that the trial court correctly ruled in plaintiff's favor and that the judgment should be affirmed.

tion. The date, the names of the parties, the court and the author of the opinion are all labeled.

The "citations" for the *Parker* case are also labeled to show what the letters and numbers mean. The citation includes the following information about where the student can find the opinion: the name of the reporter (a "reporter" is a hardcover book that includes the full texts of certain specified court opinions), the number of the series within that reporter (e.g., first, second or third series), the number of the volume within that series and the page number on which the case begins. Thus, the *Parker* case has, among its citations, this citation: 3 Cal.3d 176, which tells the reader that she can find this case in volume **3** of a reporter called the California Reports (the reference to **Cal.**), within the third series of California Reports, on page **176**.

Generating Questions

Finally, the last and perhaps the most important step in the process involves coming up with questions the student expects to be answered by the case(s). Coming up with questions improves comprehension because it causes students to be **active readers** of the material they are reading. If students are looking for the answers to their questions in the materials they are reading, they are actively engaged. Moreover, such questioning assists students in self-monitoring for comprehension by increasing the students' awareness of whether they are getting what they expect to get from the material. In other words, if the case is not providing answers to a student's questions, the student knows something is going wrong, and the student can compensate for the problem before it becomes a serious one.

Questions may be **memory** questions or **think-type** questions. Memory questions are questions that focus on the important points in the court's opinion: who the parties are, what rules the court stated and what the court held. Think-type questions are questions that require the student to use what he or she is reading in a new way. While memory questions are helpful tools for getting ready for classroom discussions, think-type questions are much more important to students' learning. In fact, it is often best to convert a memory question (Who were the parties in *Parker v. Twentieth Century-Fox Corporation*?) into a think-type question that incorporates a memory aspect (Who could I substitute as a party in place of Ms. Parker and change the result the court reached?)

Thinking questions can be further classified into **comprehension** questions and **connection questions**, both of which warrant inclusion in students' question lists. Comprehension questions focus on whether the student understands what he or she is learning. **Question stems** (a question stem is a prompt that students can use to start their thinking questions) that are useful for coming up with good comprehension questions are:

- Describe _____ (the facts in _____ case, the holding in _____ case, etc.) in your own words.
- What does _____ (a concept or term of art used to describe the subject area) mean?
- Why is this _____ important?
- Why did the court decide _____?

Here are some comprehension questions for *Parker v. Twentieth Century-Fox Corporation*:

1. What did the *Parker* court hold?
2. What does "mitigation" mean?
3. Why is mitigation important?
4. Why did the California Supreme Court hold in favor of Ms. Parker?

Connection questions link new reading to ideas students learned previously in the course or before they came to law school. As explained in the discussion of Cognitivism in Chapter 3, making such connections increases retention, comprehension, and ease of recall and use. Question stems that are common to connection questions include:

- Why is _____ (this case, this excerpt from a law review article, this entire topic) in this casebook?
- How does this concept tie in to _____ concept (that you learned before law school, that you learned in another law school class, that you already learned in this class)?
- How are this case and _____ case similar?
- How are this case and _____ case different?
- What is the difference between _____ and _____ (two similar concepts that have different legal implications)?
- What are the strengths and weaknesses of the court's reasoning?
- What are the benefits and detriments of the court's conclusion?

Connection questions for *Parker v. Twentieth Century-Fox Corporation* would include:

1. Why is *Parker v. Twentieth Century-Fox Corporation* in my casebook?
2. How does the mitigation concept relate to contributory negligence law (a somewhat similar concept in torts law)? How does mitigation relate to the measure of damages materials we just finished studying in Contracts and is it common to study these concepts in this order?
3. How are *Parker v. Twentieth Century-Fox Corporation* and *Rockingham County v. Luten Bridge Company* (a case Contracts students typically read immediately before they read *Parker*) similar? How are they different?
4. What is the difference between mitigation and forseeability (a concept that Contracts students study either immediately before or immediately after mitigation)?
5. What are the strengths and weaknesses of the *Parker* court's reasoning?
6. What are the benefits and detriments of the *Parker* court's conclusion?

As the student is reading, she will be looking for answers to her comprehension and connection questions as well as generating and answering additional questions based on what the student is reading.

Exercise 9-1 in the Workbook provides an opportunity for students to use these pre-reading strategies in connection with two of the cases the students must read for their first week of law school.

Reading Strategies

Having prepared to understand the case, the expert law student now begins to read it. Once again, there are differences between what novices do while they are reading and what experts do. Novice law school learners are much more likely to simply read through the case, highlighting things they feel are important as they read. In many instances, the student ends up highlighting so much that the student has not actually accomplished the goal that led the student to use a highlighting pen, reducing the case to a more manageable amount of material.

For this reason, expert law students force themselves to read every court opinion more than once and to avoid marking the case at all (with notes or highlighting) the first time they are reading the opinion. During that initial reading, expert law students are simply trying to get a feel for the overall story and how the case comes out.

There are two other things that distinguish effective case reading from ineffective case reading: the extent of student engagement with the text and the degree to which the student pays attention to the details of the opinion.

Engaging with Court Opinions

Expert law school learners are highly engaged case readers. First, they are engaged by the act of trying to achieve their learning goal and by their monitoring of their progress towards that goal. Because they are self-monitoring for comprehension, expert learners are always asking themselves whether they understand what they are reading. They make this evaluation both on a sentence-by-sentence basis and in terms of the big picture, the two or three major points addressed by the opinion.

Second, expert learners are engaged by the task of finding answers to the questions they posed during the pre-reading stage. Expert learners, therefore, read cases with a much greater sense of purpose than their less successful peers. Instead of simply reading and re-reading, expert learners look for answers to their questions as they are reading and also use a technique called a "**text lookback**" in which students, after completing their initial reading of the assigned materials, skim the assignment looking for the parts of the reading that answer each of their questions. For example, one of the comprehension think-type questions generated above was "What does 'mitigation' mean?" While reading the case the first time, therefore, the student would be looking for an answer to this question. If the student did not find an answer during this initial read, the student would re-read the section of the case in which the court discussed mitigation to look for the answer.

Third, expert readers develop graphic depictions, known in the field as **representation imagery**, to help them make sense of difficult aspects of the opinions they are reading. Representation imagery is a particularly useful tool for organizing a convoluted set of facts, such as cases involving complicated party relationships, intricate contractual relations, or a difficult-to-follow timeline. For example, a timeline of the *Parker* case reveals why no one argued that Ms. Parker should have had to look for employment with a different filmmaker after Twentieth Century cancelled *Bloomer Girl;* there was so little time between Twentieth Century's notice of default and the date on which filming was scheduled to commence that she could not have found an alternative opportunity in time. In fact, it seems likely that, had she found an alternative film, that opportunity would not have replaced *Bloomer Girl* but, instead, would have simply been scheduled so she could be in both *Bloomer Girl* and the other film. Figure 13 shows this timeline.

Figure 13: Timeline for Facts in Parker v. Twentieth Century-Fox Corporation

August 1965	April 4, 1966	May 23, 1966	September 1970
Parties sign contract	*20th Century cancels contract*	*Filming of "Bloomer Girl" to start*	*Date of Supreme Court's opinion*

Similarly, to make sense of another well-known Contracts case,[10] students need to grapple with familial relationships across three generations, including at least two re-marriages. The court's opinion, in fact, begins by reciting the relevant family history as follows:

> Natale and Carmela Castiglia were married in 1919 in Colorado. Carmela had three children, John, Rosie and Christie, by a previous marriage. Rosie was married to Nick Norcia. Natale had one grandchild, plaintiff Carmen Monarco, the son of a deceased daughter by a previous marriage. Natale and Carmela moved to California where they invested their assets, amounting to approximately $ 4,000, in a half interest in agricultural property. Rosie and Nick Norcia acquired the other half interest. Christie, then in his early teens, moved with the family to California. Plaintiff remained in Colorado. In 1926, Christie, then 18 years old, decided to leave the home of his mother and stepfather and seek an independent living. Natale and Carmela, however, wanted him to stay with them and participate in the family venture. They made an oral proposal to Christie that if he stayed home and worked they would keep their property in joint tenancy so that it would pass to the survivor who would leave it to Christie by will except for small devises to John and Rosie. In performance of this agreement Christie remained home and worked diligently in the family venture. Natale and Carmela placed all of their property in joint tenancy and in 1941 both executed wills leaving all their property to Christie with the exception of small devises to Rosie and John and $500 to plaintiff. The venture was successful, so that at the time of Natale's death his and Carmela's interest was worth approximately $100,000. Shortly before his death Natale became dissatisfied with the agreement and determined to leave his half of the joint property to his grandson, the plaintiff. Without informing Christie or Carmela he arranged the necessary conveyances to terminate the joint tenancies and executed a will leaving all of his property to plaintiff. This will was probated and the court entered its decree distributing the property to plaintiff.

One way to make sense of these facts is by drawing a family tree as reflected in Figure 14.

Fourth, expert learners engage in a **dialogue** with their cases and court opinions. As they read, they are **evaluating** the opinions, looking for flaws in the courts' reasoning, descriptions of the facts, statements of law and assertions about what are the

---

10. *Monarco v. LoGreco*, 35 Cal.2d 621, 220 P.2d 737 (1950).

Figure 14: The Familial Relationships among the Parties to
Monarco v. LoGreco*

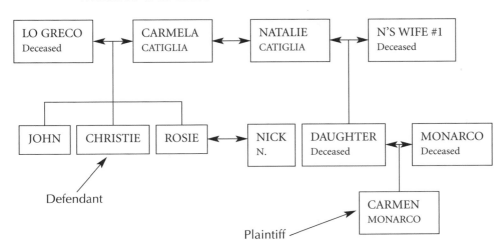

* This chart is based on a version of the chart developed by professor Kevin Mohr of Western State University College of Law. Professor Mohr granted permission for the use of this chart in this text.

public interests implicated by the parties' dispute. They even **argue** with the opinions, making notes on their casebooks indicating their disagreements. For example, consider Figure 15 on the following page. Figure 15 shows an excerpt from the *Parker* case and some comments an expert learner might write on his or her casebook or, at least, think.

Notice that these comments reflect a view of court opinions that is typical of expert law students (as explained above): courts do not simply report "truth" but, instead, construct meaning. Students are free to do the same and, in fact, should do the same and should question the court's version of the truth. In other words, note that the student questions the judge's use of phrases like "it is clear," "mere circumstance" and "by no stretch of the imagination" and the certainty such phrases communicate.

Lastly, expert learners continue to pose (and answer) questions while they are reading. Question stems that raise thinking questions particularly applicable to this stage of the case reading process include:

- If I changed _____ (a key fact in the case) to _____ (a different fact) would the court have reached the same result? (Students should ask this question in multiple forms to generate their own hypotheticals, both hypotheticals that would result in the same conclusion the court reached in its opinion and hypotheticals that would result in the opposite conclusion.)
- How might I use the facts in the case to better argue for the result the court reached?
- How might I use the facts in the case to argue for a different result?
- What must the losing party have argued? (Often, courts, like the *Parker* court, make it sound as if the result in the case was inevitable, but, of course, a lawyer representing the losing party thought the question was close enough that the case warranted an appeal. In fact, the full text of *Parker* includes a dissenting opinion.)
- Did the court reach the correct conclusion? Why or why not?

Figure 15: A Sample Dialogue with
      Parker v. Twentieth Century-Fox Corporation

> [I]t is clear that the trial court correctly ruled that plaintiff's failure to accept defendant's tendered substitute employment could not be applied in mitigation of damages because the offer of the "Big Country" lead was of employment both different and inferior, and that no factual dispute was presented on that issue. The mere circumstance that "Bloomer Girl" was to be a musical review calling upon plaintiff's talents as a dancer as well as an actress, and was to be produced in the City of Los Angeles, whereas "Big Country" was a straight dramatic role in a "Western Type" story taking place in an opal mine in Australia, demonstrates the difference in kind between the two employments; the female lead as a dramatic actress in a western style motion picture can by no stretch of imagination be considered the equivalent of or substantially similar to the lead in a song-and-dance production.

If you need to say, "It is clear," it often isn't!

I can imagine that some actresses might see a lead role in two movies as fairly close to equal.

I'd rather film in Aust. than L.A.

I don't buy it; where does the court explain why these differences matter?

Such questions for the *Parker* case might include:

1. What if "Bloomer Girl" had been a drama instead of a musical? What if both films were to have been filmed in Los Angeles? What if Ms. Parker had been given the same director and screenplay approvals for "Big Country, Big Man"?
2. What if Ms. Parker was not an actress but, rather, was a director and had been hired to direct "Bloomer Girl" and offered the same position for "Big Country, Big Man"?
3. Why did the court believe it was important that the fact that "Bloomer Girl" was a musical and "Big Country, Big Man" was a western? Why was the filming location important? Why were the approvals important? Can I explain the significance of these facts in greater detail?
4. What must Twentieth Century have argued?
5. Was the *Parker* court right? Why?

Attention to Detail

Most students, even relatively novice learners, have developed strategies for dealing with am unfamiliar term or word. As a general rule, most readers either simply infer meaning from the context in which the word appears or ignore the word. Legal reading is different in this crucial respect. Law students need to read word-by-word and sentence-by-sentence, making sure that, in addition to getting the big picture and main ideas, they also understand everything else. This need for attention to detail stems from two characteristics of the lawyering process.

First, lawyering, like any other field, has its own vocabulary. All lawyers know this terminology, and, the more quickly new law students learn this terminology, the more easily they will assimilate into their new role. Mastering the terminology from the outset, looking up and committing to memory every new word and term and every familiar word and term used in an unfamiliar way, makes future case reading efforts easier and quicker. Mastery of legal terminology also helps students write better case briefs, legal writing papers, and essay examination answers.

Second, for lawyers, every word often matters. Lawyers (and law professors) work very hard to be as precise as possible in their writing, although even they often fail. Lawyers expend so much effort on precision because slight nuances in meaning can change the legal implications of what the lawyer has written.

Consider, for example, a contract drafted by a team of hundreds of lawyers representing every major insurance company in this country. The contract promised that the insurance companies would pay the costs of defending lawsuits and any judgments awarded in lawsuits that allege "property damage" caused by products manufactured by the companies that purchased this insurance. The insurance attorneys did not define the term "property damage," presumably because they thought (as you might think reading the words) that the term "property damage" is unambiguous. However, 20–30 years after these policies were drafted, homeowners and business owners sued manufacturers of asbestos insulation, which had purchased the policies in question, claiming that the presence of undamaged asbestos insulation in their homes and office buildings reduced the value of the homes and buildings. By the time these lawsuits were filed, experts had determined that asbestos insulation was dangerous, even life-threatening, if the insulation was damaged in any way. The insurance companies pointed out that the insulation at issue in all these lawsuits was not itself damaged and had not physically damaged the homes and buildings. Thus, according to the insurance companies, there was no "property damage," and they did not have to defend the lawsuits or pay the claims. The manufacturers convinced the courts, however, that the phrase "property damage" included any type of harm (a synonym of the word "damage") to property and that a reduction in the value of property *was* a harm to property. Because the courts agreed, the insurance companies were required to pay literally hundreds of millions of dollars to defend and resolve the lawsuits.

For these reasons, expert law students read casebooks differently than they read their college texts. First, they read their casebooks word-by-word. They work with a **law dictionary** and an **English dictionary** right next to them as they read, looking up both unfamiliar words and phrases and familiar words and phrases used in an unfamiliar way. For example, in the excerpt from the casebook version of the *Parker* case in Figure 16 on the next page, the words a new law student should be looking up are highlighted.

Second, expert law students also read line by line, making sure they understand each sentence before they move onto the next one. Consider the following sentence from the above excerpt of *Parker*:

"Plaintiff moved for summary judgment under Code of Civil Procedure section 437c, the motion was granted, and summary judgment for $ 750,000 plus interest was entered in plaintiff's favor."

Expert students would not only look up each word in this sentence separately but also would make sure they understand what the sentence as a whole means. Thus, an expert law student would translate the above sentence to mean,

"Relying on California's statute dealing with such requests, Ms. Parker's attorneys asked the judge to decide the case in her favor without ever letting a jury hear the matter, arguing that there was no real disagreement among the parties about what happened and that the only real dispute involved how the law applied to the facts of the case, and the judge agreed and ruled in Ms. Parker's favor and published a document that stated that Twentieth Century must pay

Figure 16: Excerpt from Parker v. Twentieth Century-Fox Corporation *with the Words New Law Students Should Look up Highlighted*

The complaint sets forth two causes of action. The first is for money due under the contract; the second, based upon the same allegations as the first, is for damages resulting from defendant's breach of contract. Defendant in its answer admits the existence and validity of the contract, that plaintiff complied with all the conditions, covenants and promises and stood ready to complete the performance, and that defendant breached and "anticipatorily repudiated" the contract. It denies, however, that any money is due to plaintiff either under the contract or as a result of its breach, and pleads as an affirmative defense to both causes of action plaintiff's allegedly deliberate failure to mitigate damages, asserting that she unreasonably refused to accept its offer of the leading role in "Big Country."

Plaintiff moved for summary judgment under Code of Civil Procedure section 437c, the motion was granted, and summary judgment for $750,000 plus interest was entered in plaintiff's favor. This appeal by defendant followed.

As stated, defendant's sole defense to this action which resulted from its deliberate breach of contract is that in rejecting defendant's substitute offer of employment plaintiff unreasonably refused to mitigate damages.

The general rule is that the measure of recovery by a wrongfully discharged employee is the amount of salary agreed upon for the period of service, less the amount which the employer affirmatively proves the employee has earned or with reasonable effort might have earned from other employment. (*citations omitted*) However, before projected earnings from other employment opportunities not sought or accepted by the discharged employee can be applied in mitigation, the employer must show that the other employment was comparable, or substantially similar, to that of which the employee has been deprived; the employee's rejection of or failure to seek other available employment of a different or inferior kind may not be resorted to in order to mitigate damages. (*citations omitted*).

Ms. Parker $750,000 plus interest on that money from the time Twentieth Century first owed the money to Ms. Parker until the time it pays her."

Exercise 9-2 in the Workbook provides an opportunity to use these reading strategies in connection with two of the cases a student may need to read for the first week of law school.

Conclusion Regarding
Pre-Reading and Reading Strategies

There is no question that, in the beginning, these pre-reading and reading strategies will involve considerable effort. In fact, most law professors expect new law students to spend hundreds of hours studying, particularly in their first year of law school, as they develop their case reading skills. The investment of time is a good one. In the long run, the approach to reading in this chapter will help you understand the cases better and more quickly and perform better in classroom discussions and on examinations. Below is a one page synopsis of the above reading and pre-reading strategies. It may be helpful to copy it and use it as a bookmark.

Summary Sheet for
Pre-Reading and Reading Strategies

Pre-Reading Strategies

✓ Set a mastery comprehension goal.

✓ Recognize and keep in mind that courts are creating meaning by their opinions and lawyers are creating meaning when they read opinions.

✓ Develop some knowledge about the subject of the cases by:

   (1) Gaining insight about the relationships among the concepts addressed in the cases from the organization of the syllabus and of the tables of contents of the casebook and a supplemental text;

   (2) Getting background information by reading an introduction to the topic if the casebook has one;

   (3) Developing some insight into the important points by reading the questions and comments following the case before reading the case; and

   (4) Learning about the subject by reading about it in a supplemental text.

✓ Preview the opinion before reading it by reading the headings and the first sentence of each paragraph of the opinion.

✓ Be conscious of background details that might explain the decision: the court, the author of the opinion, the historical context and the parties' statuses.

✓ Generate questions expected to be answered by the opinion.

Reading Strategies

✓ Read the entire opinion once all the way through without making a mark on it and then read it in depth.

✓ Monitor learning at all times to make sure learning goals are being achieved.

✓ Search the opinion for answers to pre-reading questions.

✓ Develop graphic depictions of key facts.

✓ Dialogue with the opinion, arguing with the court's reasoning and assertions.

✓ Continue to generate questions and search for answers to those questions.

✓ Attend to the details of the opinion on a word-by-word basis (using dictionaries).

Briefing Strategies

It is worth noting, at the outset, that there is one absolute with respect to case briefing; while there are commercial sources of case briefs for most casebooks, expert law students do not use them. Expert students know that learning requires active efforts on their part and that briefing cases on their own is an active experience whereas reading someone else's case briefs is a passive one. The act of reading and briefing the cases strengthens the memory trace for students. Reading and briefing is particularly important for students whose learning style or personality type causes them to prefer active, real-world experiences, including kinesthetic learners and students whose personality type is extroverted, sensing, thinking and/or feeling.

Expert law students also recognize three important things about their briefing efforts even before they start writing them. First, expert students know that a good case brief starts with a careful, thoughtful, active pre-reading and reading of a case.

Second, they understand that a case brief is no more and no less than a tool for learning; it is a written record of their understanding of the key components of a case. It is no more than a tool for learning because few, if any, professors assign grades to their students' case briefs or test briefing skills on examinations (although a few do so, the likely percentage of law professors who do so is less than 1%). It is no less than a tool for learning in the sense that, although briefs are not graded, their creation is not a meaningless exercise. A case brief helps the student impose structure on a court opinion by reorganizing the narrative of the opinion into sub-categories common to every opinion. The end result of a good case brief is a product students can memorize and use on their examinations.

Third, expert students know that different professors demand different things from students' case briefs and adjust accordingly. These differences are reflected in the kinds of questions their professors ask during classroom discussions and in the professors' expectations in terms of student performance on examinations. Very few law professors care about what students actually have written in their briefs; rather, they care about how students respond to their questions. Some professors want students to perform in class as if they have created detailed briefs that include each of the elements described below and more. Others want much less. Moreover, professors vary in the degree of detail they expect and in their preferences for how students express each of the elements. These differences reflect, in some instances, professor idiosyncrasies and, in others, differences among legal experts as to what is important in cases and what law students should be learning.

This text adopts a student-centered perspective on these differences. The categories below reflect the author's sense, from reviewing many different forms, as to a workable compromise among them. Where possible, the text notes common professor differences and suggests common student adaptations. It is not possible, however, to cover every possible professor preference and therefore students will have to adapt this approach to their particular professors' preferences. Of course, expert learners know that learning always requiring adapting one's learning to the instructional approach of the instructor.

A case brief has at least five elements: (1) **Facts**, (2) **Issue**, (3) **Holding**, (4) **Rationale** and (5) **Synthesis**. In addition, many cases include a **Dissent** and/or **Concurrence**, each of which need to be summarized in a case brief. The facts are the events that transpired before anyone went to court and what transpired within the judicial system. The issue is the legal question(s) in dispute and discussed in the opinion. The holding describes the precedential effect of the case in terms of a generalized statement about the legal consequences of a particular action or set of actions by a particular party or set of parties. The rationale is the set of reasons offered by the court for its holding, including the rule(s), the application of the rule(s) to the facts, the analogies to and distinctions from precedential authority and public policy(ies). Synthesis involves reconciling the case the student has just read and briefed with other cases the student has studied. Finally, students must summarize the key points in any dissent or concurrence. A dissenting opinion is an opinion written by a judge who disagrees with the conclusion reached by the other judges; the disagreeing judge explains his or her reasons for disagreeing. A concurring opinion is an opinion authored by judge who agrees with the conclusion reached by the other judges but has different or additional reasons for reaching that conclusion.

It is worthwhile for law students to commit these five elements to memory because doing so will save them time in briefing cases. They can be remembered with the following mnemonic: Fine Idiots Happily Relate to Simplicity. As you will learn in Chapter 11 of this book, this mnemonic technique, in which the learner creates a phrase using the first letter of each item in a list to be memorized, is known as the "single use coding method."

Each of the elements is addressed below. A warning at the outset is worth noting: because the elements of a case brief are related, are seldom labeled and are often mixed with each other throughout court opinions, students initially experience some difficulty in identifying them. Case briefing is an example of a skill that requires many, many cycles to master.

Facts

The facts of a case identify what transpired and how the parties ended up in the court that is issuing the opinion that the law student is analyzing. Nearly all law professors expect students to include facts in their case briefs, although a significant minority does not spend class time on fact recitations. Others focus considerable time on teaching students to create proper fact recitations.

There are two types of facts reflected in court opinions: operative facts and procedural facts (also often referred to as the procedural posture or procedural history). Expert law students include both types of facts in their case briefs and know the difference between them and segregate them in their case briefs.

Operative facts are all the events that transpired before someone involved the courts. They often include information about who (what person) did what (took which actions) to whom (what person), when (the timing of the actions) and where (the location of the actions). Keep in mind that even these classifications require some thinking by the student. Sometimes, the "who" or the "to whom" can be a corporation or a governmental entity. In many such instances, the name or identity of the person who acted on behalf of the corporation or governmental entity may be irrelevant; it is the corporation or governmental entity that is the "who." In other instances, both are relevant. Sometimes, the when and where are crucial facts; sometimes, they are irrelevant and should not even be mentioned in the brief.

Nearly all law professors expect students to include only the **relevant** facts in the facts section of their briefs. For example, a party's career status may or may not be relevant.

For example, the fact that a person is a lawyer would be relevant to a case discussing the legal significance of that party telling a lie to obtain property from a client and irrelevant to a case discussing whether a party who crashed his car into the lawyer's car failed to drive his car with the requisite degree of care. Likewise, some actions, while interesting to the reader, may be legally irrelevant. For example, the fact that someone was a famous baseball player is likely irrelevant to a statement of facts about a criminal prosecution of that person for arson.

A fact is relevant if it is one of the facts upon which the court based its decision in large or small part or if the fact is otherwise a piece of information a reasonable person would need to know to be able to understand the court's decision. Most students find it helpful to write a draft of their fact section at the outset and then to revise the facts section last, after they have written their other sections. At the first draft stage, therefore, it is best to be over-inclusive. All the facts the student believes might possibly be relevant should be included and then, when the student revises the section during the final drafting stage, she can eliminate facts upon which the court did not rely.

In drafting the operative facts section of the case brief, avoid simply copy the wording and sequence used by the court in stating the facts. Expert law students write the facts in their own words. As is true of all learning experiences, people learn more when they act upon the materials than they do when they simply copy the materials. Writing facts in one's own words requires engagement and therefore enhances retention, and it helps the student recognize when the student is not understanding the material. More importantly, while most opinions include a recitation of facts early on in the opinion, that recitation is often both over- and under-inclusive. It is over-inclusive because judges have no restrictions on what they include and often include irrelevant facts. It is under-inclusive because judges often omit facts altogether that are problematic for their decisions (those facts usually can be found in a dissenting opinion) and often add important facts as part of the rationales for their decisions. Expert law students, therefore, do not simply mindlessly copy and paste the courts' initial statements of facts; they develop their own.

Figure 17 is an initial draft of the operative facts in *Parker v. Twentieth Century-Fox Corporation*. The facts that the author of this text would delete from his final version of the facts are shown with a gray background and the reasons for those deletions are shown as comments. In addition, one comment addresses a piece of information the author has added; the added piece of information has a darker gray background and the comment explaining this addition is in italic font. The author of this text has used a capital P to refer to the plaintiff and a capital D to refer to the defendant.

Procedural facts are all the facts relating to how the case moved through the legal system. Unlike operative facts, which focus on how the parties became legal antagonists, procedural facts describe what the parties, the judges and the jury did with the dispute within the legal system. Looking at the division between procedural facts and operative facts along a timeline (see Figure 18) makes the distinction more readily apparent. Procedural facts begin once the parties have completed the alleged acts that gave rise to the involvement of the judicial system. In other words, once a person who was acted upon initiates a lawsuit or once the prosecuting attorney decides to file a criminal complaint, the procedural facts have begun. The procedural facts end with the appeal to the court issuing the opinion under study.

The student also needs to know what things are NOT facts. Although the rules of law relied on by the court are matters of fact in the sense that a layperson might say so, they are not part of the "facts of the case" as a lawyer uses that term. Likewise, the issue(s)

Figure 17: Operative facts in Parker v. Twentieth Century-Fox Corporation
*with Deleted Facts Shown with a Gray Background and
the Author's Reasons for Deletions and Additions
Shown as Comments*

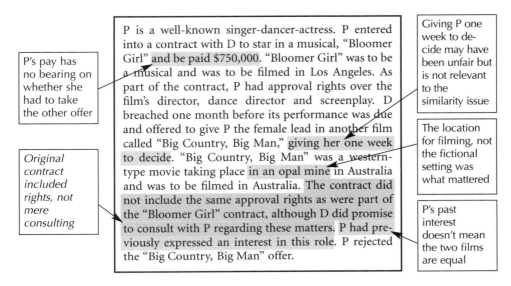

P's pay has no bearing on whether she had to take the other offer

Original contract included rights, not mere consulting

P is a well-known singer-dancer-actress. P entered into a contract with D to star in a musical, "Bloomer Girl" and be paid $750,000. "Bloomer Girl" was to be a musical and was to be filmed in Los Angeles. As part of the contract, P had approval rights over the film's director, dance director and screenplay. D breached one month before its performance was due and offered to give P the female lead in another film called "Big Country, Big Man," giving her one week to decide. "Big Country, Big Man" was a western-type movie taking place in an opal mine in Australia and was to be filmed in Australia. The contract did not include the same approval rights as were part of the "Bloomer Girl" contract, although D did promise to consult with P regarding these matters. P had previously expressed an interest in this role. P rejected the "Big Country, Big Man" offer.

Giving P one week to decide may have been unfair but is not relevant to the similarity issue

The location for filming, not the fictional setting was what mattered

P's past interest doesn't mean the two films are equal

the court is addressing, the reasons given for the court's decision and the relationship between this case and other cases the student has read are also not facts, even though each has an underlying factual basis.

Issue(s)

It is worthwhile at the outset to note that a case may have more than one issue, more than one holding and more than one rationale. While it may appear that every case ad-

*Figure 18: A Timeline-Based View of the Procedural Facts/Operative
Facts Distinction*

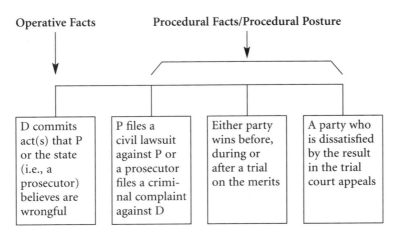

Operative Facts   Procedural Facts/Procedural Posture

| D commits act(s) that P or the state (i.e., a prosecutor) believes are wrongful | P files a civil lawsuit against P or a prosecutor files a criminal complaint against D | Either party wins before, during or after a trial on the merits | A party who is dissatisfied by the result in the trial court appeals |

dresses only one issue (based on the fact that the *Parker* opinion happens to address only one issue and that many casebook editors edit out all issues other than the one issue that caused each case to be included in the casebook), many cases address multiple issues. Consequently, expert students assess each opinion and determine how many issues the opinion addresses.

Sometimes, the task of identifying issues is a difficult one, particularly for novice law students. One hint is where the court focuses its attention. Looking at the full text of the *Parker* opinion, the court devotes most of its discussion to two topics: (1) whether Ms. Parker was legally required to take the offer of alternative employment, and (2) whether the trial court properly used a procedural mechanism called "summary judgment" to decide the first question. The discussion of summary judgment law, while important, is *not* the crux of the court's discussion and, accordingly, receives much less discussion by the court. The court focuses most of its discussion, instead, on the application of the "different or inferior" rule to the facts of Ms. Parker's dispute with Twentieth Century-Fox. For example, the court does not really relate (apply) the facts of the case to the summary judgment rule it states. Instead, the court applies the facts to the "different or inferior" rule. Another way to think about this point is to consider what new point the case teaches. The case doesn't really teach anything about summary judgment. It does, however, teach something about mitigation. Finally, the label on the outside of the casebook is of some help; the *Parker* case is included in almost every contracts casebook, and, while mitigation is a contract law concept, summary judgment is not.

Issue statements are commonly formulated in one of two ways, depending on the professor's preferences. Some professors emphasize holdings rather than issues and either do not even ask for issue statements or are satisfied with very general issue statements. Others prefer students to create fact-laden, complicated and precise issue statements. Professors also vary on the degree to which the factual descriptions within an issue statement should be the actual facts of the case or generalized statements of those facts, although a preference for the former is more common. For this discussion, we will start by learning how to create fact-laden, detailed and precise issue statements and then consider how those statements might be modified to meet the preferences of professors who are less focused on issue statements.

The following A-B-C formula[11] (see Figure 19) indicates the three elements of an issue statement and how the three are put together to form such a statement:

Figure 19: The Elements of an Issue Statement

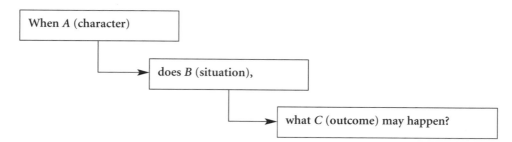

---

11. I am grateful to my colleague, Susan Keller, for allowing me to make use of this formula, which she developed as part of her regular teaching materials.

Psychology students may be familiar with a similar formula developed within the psychology field: When Actor does Behavior, what Consequence happens? From a law school perspective, either formulation is fine.

The formula translates readily into three questions a student should ask herself as she is working on her issue statement:

1. Who is A?
2. What did A do and/or have done to her? In other words, what is the situation (B)?
3. What possible legal outcome is the outcome that may be the result of the B act that A actor committed?

To make sense of this formula and the questions, it is helpful to start with a problem from outside the legal setting. Consider the following description of the "plot" of "Little Red Riding Hood:"

> Little Red decided to bring a picnic basket to her grandmother, who lived in the woods. Little Red's mother warned her to walk straight to grandmother's house and not to speak to strangers along the way. Little Red did not heed her mother's warning and spoke to a wolf along the way, who outraced her to the grandmother's house, ate the grandmother and then dressed in the grand-mother's clothes. When Little Red arrived at her grandmother's house, the wolf pretended to be the grandmother to lure Little Red towards him and then re-vealed himself and ate Little Red. Luckily, the woodcutter killed the wolf and saved Little Red and her grandmother.

An issue statement for this plot would read as shown in Figure 20, with the three elements labeled:

Figure 20: An Issue Statement for Little Red Riding Hood

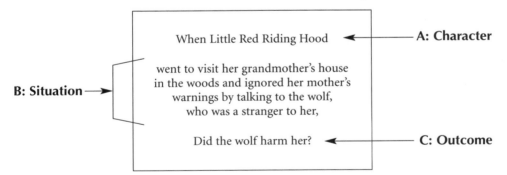

In other words, this statement answers the three questions as follows:

1. Who is A? (answer: Little Red Riding Hood.)
2. What did A do and/or have done to her? What is the situation (B)? (answer: A went to visit her grandmother's house in the woods, talked to the wolf, a stranger, even though her mother had instructed A not to speak to strangers.)
3. What is the outcome that might have happened to A because of B? (answer: the wolf may have harmed her.)

Notice that the issue statement includes the specific **key** facts and omits any fact one does not need to know to know why Little Red might die (also note that it is a matter of

Figure 21: The Elements of an Issue Statement
(Shown as Four Elements Instead of Three)

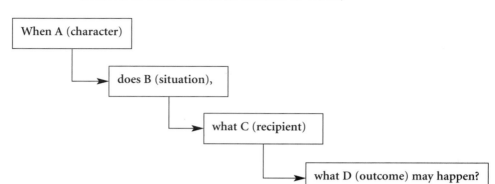

judgment to exclude the facts that grandmother's house and the wolf were located in the "woods," the wolf's dining sequence and the involvement of the woodcutter). Notice also that the other parties involved are noted (as part of the situation). Unlike stories (which often focus on the harms the characters cause themselves), legally wrongful acts always involve at least one other person who is the recipient of the wrongful act, with only a few exceptions such as victimless crimes. Many law professors therefore would modify the formula as shown in Figure 21.

Whether the student regards the "recipient" aspect as part of the "situation" or as its own separate category really does not matter, so long as the student includes the recipient in her issue statement when it is necessary.

The formula really doesn't change when the fairy tale arena is switched to the legal arena. Figure 22 on the next page shows an issue statement for *Parker v. Twentieth Century-Fox Corporation.*

There are several important points to consider with respect to the issue statement in Figure 22. First, once again, the student is answering three questions:

1. Who is A? (answer: Shirley MacLaine Parker.)
2. What did A do and/or have done to her? What is the situation (B)? (answer: Parker, a well-known singer, dancer and actress, turned down an offer from Defendant Twentieth Century-Fox to be the female lead in "Big Country, Big Man," a western-style movie which was to be filmed in Australia but over which she would have no right to approve the director or screenplay, and the offer was made by Twentieth Century as a replacement for its prior contractual obligation under which Parker would have starred in "Bloomer Girl," a musical, which was to have been filmed in Los Angeles, and which had given her approval rights with respect to the director, the dance director and the screenplay.)
3. What is the outcome that might have happened to A because of B? (answer: Parker may not be able to recover from Twentieth Century-Fox the compensation to which she was entitled under the "Bloomer Girl" contract.)

Second, because Parker is a case with many facts that are important to the court's decision and to understanding the issue, the issue statement is necessarily complex and is far from a model of excellent writing. There is no question that, from a clarity standpoint, this issue statement would be much clearer if it were broken into two or even

Figure 22: An Issue Statement for
    Parker v. Twentieth Century-Fox Corporation

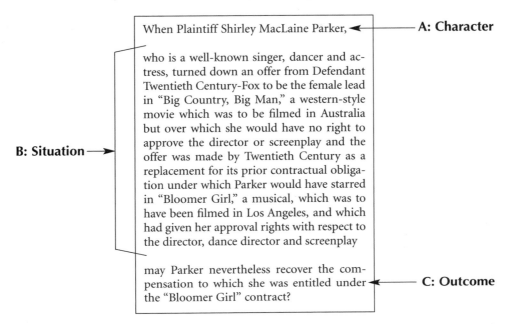

three sentences. Such issue statements are a convention in law school with a significant number of law professors, however.

Third, many professors would prefer that students integrate the legal standard into their issue statement. In the issue statement below, part C reads, "may Parker neverthe-less recover the compensation to which she was entitled under the 'Bloomer Girl' con-tract?" Using the integration of the legal standard approach, part C of a *Parker* issue statement would read, "was the alternative employment opportunity Parker rejected neither different nor inferior so that Parker must be denied her compensation under the 'Bloomer Girl' contract?"

Finally, as noted above, some professors, those more interested in holdings than issue statements, for example, prefer quite simple, general issue statements. An issue state-ment for such professors would focus on the legal issue—mitigation—and not the facts. The following issue statement is typical of what such professors prefer: "Does Parker's refusal of the 'Big Country, Big Man' offer constitute a failure to mitigate her damages?"

Holding(s)

Holdings describe the legal consequence of a generalized course of action (general-ized from the specific acts taken by the parties in the case) by a particular category of person (generalized from the status of the parties in the case at hand). Because a hold-ing describes the legal consequences of particular actions, it is, in effect, a prediction of how later courts will use the case. In other words, a holding is a statement of the prece-dential value of a case.

Some law professors say that a holding is the synthesis of the rules of law, the key facts and the court's rationale (the court's reasons for its decision). This statement is no more than a rephrasing of the notions explained in the previous paragraph. Law professors refer to the combination as a synthesis because the task of generalizing the behavior addressed by the rule and articulating the legal consequence of it requires lawyers and students to identify and articulate in general terms the commonalities or differences between the abstract statement of facts in the rule and the particular facts in the case.

Because a holding is a direct response to the question posed by the issue statement, the formula for holdings is very similar to the formula for issue statements. Figure 23 below expresses the formula for holdings:

Figure 23: The Formula for Holdings

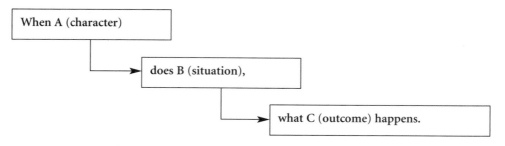

Once again, this formula can be expressed as three questions:

1. Who is A?
2. What did A do and/or have done to her? What is the situation (B)?
3. What outcome (C) happened to A because of B, if any? What did the judge(s) decide were the consequences to A because of B, if any?

Figure 24 below expresses holdings for *Little Red Riding Hood* and for the *Parker* case.

Figure 24: Holdings for Little Red Riding Hood *and the* Parker *Case*

A Holding for *Little Red Riding Hood*

When a child ignores a parent's warning not to talk to any stranger, the stranger harms the child greatly.

A Holding for *Parker v. Twentieth Century-Fox Corporation*

When an employee, employed under an employment contract for a specified period of time, rejects an offer of alternative employment from the employer after the employer breaches the parties' contract and the alternate employment opportunity is not within the employee's particular expertise, requires the employee to work in a location thousands of miles away, and affords the employee a lesser degree of control over her working conditions, the employee's rejection cannot be treated as a failure to mitigate because the alternative employment is different and inferior and therefore the employee's rejection will not result in a reduction in the employee's compensation for the employer's breach.

Note that, while detailed issue statements and holdings are very similar, there are some important differences between holdings and issue statements. The differences include the following:

(1) Holdings are statements, not questions. They express what actually happened, what the court actually decided.

(2) Holdings are usually expressed in the present tense.

(3) Holdings are expressed, not in terms of the specific facts of the case, but, rather, in **generalized terms**. Thus, for example, the holding for "Little Red Riding Hood" is so generalized that it seems to be most like a statement of the moral of the story. In fact, thinking of holdings as the moral of a story is not a complete mischaracterization. Holdings are, as noted above, statements about the precedential effect of an opinion. They are stated in generalized terms because we expect that courts will be using the holdings to resolve future disputes with somewhat different facts.

(4) In most instances, the breadth of a holding, the degree to which it can be generalized, is a matter of estimation by the student and of argument by future lawyers. Recall the prior discussion about how lawyers work with precedents. Lawyers try to stretch favorable precedents and narrow unfavorable ones. For example, can the reference to the plaintiff in Parker be generalized even further than it is in the holding above ("When an employee employed under an employment contract for a specified period of time...") to this characterization: "When a contracting party..." (so as to include all persons who make contracts and not just employees)? We, as lawyers, will not know the answer to this question with certainty until a later court answers it.

(5) Holdings usually reference the essence of the basis for the court's decision.

Of course, if there are multiple issues in the case, expert students develop multiple holdings.

Rationale(s)

A rationale explains the court's reasons for reaching its decision and therefore is sometimes called the court's **reasoning**. Courts' reasons for their decisions commonly fall into one of three categories: **rules of law, application** of the rules to the facts and of the precedent(s) to the facts — by comparing the facts of the precedent(s) to the facts of the case and analogizing to or distinguishing the precedent(s), and **public policy**. Consequently, expert law students usually include these three sub-topics in the rationale section of their case briefs.

Rules of law. Rules are relatively easy to identify. They are, as explained in Chapter 2, statements setting forth the applicable law in a particular situation. They usually are followed by a citation to a case, a statute or an authority on the law, such as a law review article, a hornbook or a treatise. What's important and somewhat harder is to identify the rule(s) on which the court is relying in the holding. For example, the full text version of the *Parker* majority opinion states the following seven rules, of which, at most, two should be included in the rule section of the student's case brief:

1. "[T]he matter to be determined by the trial court on a motion for summary judgment is whether facts have been presented that give rise to a triable factual issue."

2. "Summary judgment is proper only if the affidavits or declarations in support of the moving party would be sufficient to sustain a judgment in his favor and the opponent does not by affidavit show facts sufficient to present a triable issue of fact."

3. "The affidavits of the moving party are strictly construed and doubts as to the propriety of summary judgment should be resolved against granting the motion."
4. "The moving party cannot depend upon allegations in his own pleadings to cure deficient affidavits, nor can his adversary rely upon his own pleadings in lieu or in support of affidavits in opposition to a motion; however, a party can rely on his adversary's pleadings to establish facts not contained in his own affidavits."
5. "[T]he court may consider facts stipulated to by the parties and facts which are properly the subject of judicial notice."
6. "[T]he measure of recovery by a wrongfully discharged employee is the amount of salary agreed upon for the period of service, less the amount which the employer affirmatively proves the employee has earned or with reasonable effort might have earned from other employment."
7. "[B]efore projected earnings from other employment opportunities not sought or accepted by the discharged employee can be applied in mitigation, the employer must show that the other employment was comparable, or substantially similar, to that of which the employee has been deprived; the employee's rejection of or failure to seek other available employment of a different or inferior kind may not be resorted to in order to mitigate damages."

Rule 8 is really the only rule that directly responds to the question posed within the issue and is a basis for the court's ruling. It is helpful to include Rule 7, however, because it provides context for understanding Rule 8. It is also important for the student to **restate the rules in her own words** (to **paraphrase** them). Expert learners know that the ability accurately to translate a principle (of law, of science or of math) into one's own words shows that the student understands it. In fact, expert learners use this task as a way of monitoring their comprehension; if they cannot state the rule in their own words, they *know* they do not understand it and need to either re-read the case, obtain help from a peer or their instructor or read more about the rule in a supplemental text.

Here are paraphrases of rules 7 and 8:

Rule 7 paraphrase: For breach of an employment contract, the employee may recover as damages the contract price minus what the employee actually earned or reasonably could have earned elsewhere.

Rule 8 paraphrase: The amount of money an employee would have earned from a rejected alternative employment opportunity may be deducted from an employee's recovery of damages for his or her employer's breach of an employment contract only if the rejected position was not "different or inferior to" (was fairly alike) the position denied to the employee.

A few points are important about these paraphrases. First, the only actual language included was the standard (for which a synonym appears as a parenthetical). Because the specific words chosen by the court are so significant to its holding, it is worthwhile to include them. Second, it is probably best to include both the court's actual words and the paraphrase. Third, paraphrasing requires, in large part, simply substituting synonyms for the words used by the court. Thus, for example, the Rule 8 paraphrase substitutes "was fairly alike" for "not different or inferior," and "can be deducted" for "can be applied in mitigation." The key is to choose synonyms that do not change the meaning of the rule.

Application. Application actually involves two distinct techniques, application of rules to facts and applying and distinguishing precedent. In explaining decisions, students need to understand how the court **applied the rule to the facts of the case.** In other words, students should explain why it is that the rule the court stated warranted the result the court reached. This explanation involves identifying the key facts and explaining what aspect(s) of the facts caused the court to conclude that the factual situation required by the rule *was* present in the case or *was not* present in the case.

A consideration of how the *Parker* court applied Rule 8 above to the facts of *Parker* provides some important insights, not only into how to identify the application within an opinion but also into the skill of applying rules to facts, a crucial skill new law students must learn and which is addressed in Chapter 15. In the *Parker* case, the following two paragraphs are the application of the rule to the facts:

> The mere circumstance that "Bloomer Girl" was to be a musical review calling upon plaintiff's talents as a dancer as well as an actress, and was to be produced in the City of Los Angeles, whereas "Big Country" was a straight dramatic role in a "Western Type" story taking place in an opal mine in Australia, demonstrates the difference in kind between the two employments; the female lead as a dramatic actress in a western style motion picture can by no stretch of imagination be considered the equivalent of or substantially similar to the lead in a song-and-dance production.

> Additionally, the substitute "Big Country" offer proposed to eliminate or impair the director and screenplay approvals accorded to plaintiff under the original "Bloomer Girl" contract, and thus constituted an offer of inferior employment.

Finding the application of the rule to the facts in *Parker* is not particularly difficult. The following phrase precedes the above paragraphs in the opinion: "Applying the foregoing rules...." Most opinion authors, however, do not write in such a student-friendly way; few provide such obvious signposts. Nevertheless, it is usually easy to find the application of the rule to the facts because: (1) it is usually located within one or two lines of the statement of the rule (and well after the statement of the facts), (2) it references the specific facts of the case, and (3) it articulates the connection (or lack thereof) between the facts and the rule.

Understanding and being able to explain the court's application of the rule to the facts can be more difficult. As the *Parker* dissenting opinion points out, while the above passage *is* the majority's application of the rule to the facts, the majority did not, in fact, do a very good job of it. As the dissenting judge states,

> I believe that the approach taken by the majority (a superficial listing of differences with no attempt to assess their significance) may subvert a valuable legal doctrine. The inquiry in cases such as this should not be whether differences between the two jobs exist (there will always be differences), but whether the differences that are present are substantial enough to constitute differences in the kind of employment or, alternatively, whether they render the substitute work employment of an inferior kind.

For example, the majority opinion states that the female lead in a Western "by no stretch of the imagination" can be deemed the equivalent of the lead in a musical. What the court omits is an explanation of why the court said so, particularly given the fact that Ms. Parker appears to have once been interested in the part in the western. Such a task would not have been impossible for the court and is a likely subject for a question from your contracts professor. Thus, a good student case brief of *Parker* might point out that the role in the musical appears to be the central character ("Bloomer *Girl*") whereas the role in the western appears less central given that movie's title ("Big Country, Big *Man*"). Moreover, Parker, at the time, was known for her extraordinary skills as a dancer/singer/actress and therefore the musical made use of all of her skills whereas a western drama would only implicate her acting skills.

This thinking process, which likely would be a part of the question posing and question answering process during the reading of *Parker*, is, therefore, a worthwhile enterprise. Most importantly, the act of supplying the omitted parts of the analysis causes the student to actively engage with the material, increasing the likelihood the student will remember the case and the holding on examinations.

Finding where the court has **applied or distinguished the precedent(s)** to the facts is even easier. Courts always apply or distinguish a precedent immediately after stating the name of the precedent case and describing the key facts of that case. They then go on and either apply it or distinguish it.

It is important, of course, to know the difference between applying a precedent and distinguishing a precedent. Judges (and lawyers when they make arguments to judges) *apply* precedents that reached favorable results, i.e., the results they want to reach in their case. Applying a precedent involves identifying factual similarities between the precedent and the case for which the court is writing an opinion and then explaining why those similarities justify reaching the same result as in the precedent case. Judges (and lawyers) *distinguish* precedents that reached unfavorable results, i.e., results opposite to the results they wish to reach in their case. Distinguishing a precedent therefore involves identifying at least one factual difference between the precedent case and the case for which the court is writing the opinion and then explaining why the difference(s) justify(ies) reaching a different result than the court reached in the precedent case. Unfortunately, the *Parker* court did not use this technique at all in its opinion and therefore an example from that case is not available. Consequently, it is necessary to consider how a future court might apply and distinguish *Parker*. Consider the following hypothetical:

> An employee had a one-year contract to work as the office manager for a small clothing manufacturer. After three months, the employer informed the employee that she would no longer be able to work as the office manager but offered her a position as a salesperson (selling to retailers located within 50 miles of the manufacturer's location) at the same salary level and with the same benefits. The job would require some driving but no real travel. The employee refused to take the sales position.

This conduct by the employer would be a breach of contract, as it was in *Parker*. The issue in this hypothetical would revolve around whether the amount the employee would have earned as a salesperson should be deducted from the employee's recovery for the employer's breach. In other words, should the employee recover the rest of her nine months' worth of compensation as an office manager or recover nothing (because her pay as a salesperson would have been the same)?

A judge wishing to rule in favor of the employee would need to apply, not distinguish, *Parker* because *Parker* reached the result the judge wishes to reach. The judge therefore would point out that both cases involve terminated employees who were offered alternative employment and in both cases the alternative employment required the employee to use very different skills than the skills needed to perform the original employment and therefore denied the employee the opportunity to work within her chosen field of employment. Moreover, both alternative employment opportunities may involve work that is less attractive to the employee than the original employment and involved less convenient working conditions (Australia v. Los Angeles in *Parker* and in the office vs. driving to retailers' places of business in the above hypothetical).

A judge wishing to rule in favor of the employer in the above hypothetical would need to distinguish *Parker* because *Parker* reached a result opposite from the result the judge wishes to reach. The judge therefore would point out that Ms. Parker's unused skills were within an endeavor that required considerable expertise and hundreds of hours of study and practice whereas the employee's office manager skills did not involve a comparable degree of training or expertise and therefore the loss to the employee is much less significant. The judge would also argue that the *Parker* case involved a change of continents whereas this case involves only driving within a one hour radius of the office and therefore the employee's inconvenience would be minimal.

A few final points about the above discussion are worth noting. First, the above hypothetical is typical of law school exams, as you will learn later in this text, in the sense that the correct result is uncertain and there are good arguments for both applying and distinguishing *Parker*. Second, this indeterminacy even occurs within real court opinions. Sometimes, the majority and dissenting opinions conflict on whether the precedents are similar enough to apply them to the case before the court. Finally, the most important point for you to understand at this stage of your development is that, in some opinions, courts apply some precedents and distinguish some others.

Public policy. The third sub-topic in the rationale section of a case brief is the public policy. As explained in Chapter 2, a public policy is the social good served by a rule of law or by a precedent. In many cases, courts explicitly identify and discuss the public policy implications of the rules they state and their holdings. For example, in *Parker*, the California Supreme Court explains why courts prefer not to grant summary judgment motions—they do not want to create a "substitute for the open trial method of determining facts." The policy referenced here, our societal preference for jury trials, is fairly explicitly stated.

The *Parker* court, however, does not explain the public policy implications of the rule on which it relies—that wrongfully terminated employees need not accept substitute employment if it is different or inferior—or of its holding. The often-challenging task for the student, therefore, is to figure out what social good the court must have had in mind.

Sometimes, students can identify unstated rationales by simply thinking about why the court must have thought that its decision was a good one for society. Another, similar way to get at the policy is to consider who the prevailing party is and guess why others similarly situated (e.g., other employees in the State of California) might believe the decision was a good one. For example, employees might see the decision as a good one because it prevents employers from forcing employees to take jobs they do not like as replacements for jobs the employers had promised. More generally, it preserves employees' freedom to decide for themselves what they wish to do. Even more generally, the decision preserves freedom of action. These statements of policy are good hypotheses as to the public policy rationale for the *Parker* decision.

In other cases, the above approach is unavailing. In such cases, it is helpful to keep in mind that public policies are really arguments about what behavior should be encouraged and that such arguments almost always come in matched sets. In other words, although opinions often make it sound as if there is only one "social good" at stake in any particular case, deciding a case usually requires judges to select from competing social goods (public policies). For example, if the *Parker* court had held that employees must take any offered alternate employment opportunity or that employees never have to accept alternate employment opportunities, either rule would be premised on a social good of promoting predictability for contracting parties because everyone would always know whether the employee must take offered alternative employment. In other words, every employer and employee would know, when they made their contract and when (and if) the employer breached the contract, what would happen if the employee rejected alternative employment.

The rule actually adopted by the *Parker* court, that an employee need only accept alternative employment if it is "not different or inferior," makes the result in particular cases less predictable because of uncertainty as to what is enough of a difference for an alternative employment opportunity to be deemed "different or inferior." The rule perhaps seems fairer or more likely to produce "justice," however, because it balances society's interest in preserving the freedom to choose one's own work and society's interest in not wasting resources by having employees remain idle. Thus, the *Parker* court was faced with the need to make a trade-off between predictability and economic efficiency, on the one hand, and freedom, on the other hand. In fact, in holding for Ms. Parker, the court implicitly has chosen Ms. Parker's interest in freedom of action over Twentieth Century-Fox's interest in an efficient use of the resource that Ms. Parker represents.

Three other policy trade-offs common to legal decision-making are:

1. Encouraging competition vs. preserving individuals' rights
2. Allowing freedom of action vs. protecting society
3. Encouraging economically efficient behavior vs. preserving individuals' rights

Thus, to identify unstated public policies, it is helpful to consider alternative decisions the court could have made and the social good those alternative decisions might have served. In fact, students should identify both the policy and its traded-off match.

This list of seven policies—predictability, justice, encouraging competition, preserving individual rights, allowing freedom of action, protecting society, encouraging economically efficient behavior—is also helpful because it serves as a sort of smorgasbord from which students may select in identifying the policies implicated by a particular decision. For example, as noted above, the *Parker* decision supports a freedom of action policy because it allows employees to reject a significantly different employment opportunity while also preserving a degree of economic efficiency because employees cannot reject similar employment opportunities simply because they know they are owed money by a breaching employer.

As mentioned in the fact section discussion, once expert students complete their rationale sections, they revise their operative fact sections to reflect the actual facts on which the court relied.

Synthesis

The next crucial step in briefing cases involves reconciling the case with other cases the student has read. In some instances, the task is simple because the case the student is briefing addresses a completely different topic than all the cases that preceded it. In this situation, expert students wait until they have read several cases following the case they are briefing and then synthesize the case with those later cases.

The need for synthesis stems from the fact that the cases law students read often appear to be in conflict. For example, contracts casebooks often pair the *Parker* case with *Rockingham County v. Luten Bridge Company,* 35 F.2d 301 (1929). In the *Rockingham County* case, a bridge builder was denied damages for expenditures in working on a bridge after the county breached its contract with the bridge builder. The task of synthesis requires students to understand why the bridge builder had its compensation reduced whereas Ms. Parker did not.

There are five bases for reconciling cases. First, the courts that decided the conflicting cases may have been located in **different jurisdictions**. The term jurisdiction in this context refers to the court system in which a case is decided. In other words, for example, one case may have been decided under California law and the other under New York law. In this situation, the conflict between the two cases stems from the fact that the two jurisdictions simply have adopted conflicting rules.

Second, both cases accurately may describe the law in the same jurisdiction; the conflict may be explained as an **historical** issue. One decision may reflect the law as it was in the past and one may reflect the current version of the law. In other words, if both decisions come from the same jurisdiction, it may be because that jurisdiction changed the law at some point. In fact, even if the two decisions come from different jurisdictions, they still may reflect an older rule and a newer rule, respectively.

Third, the conflict may derive from a factual difference between the two cases and because those **factual differences** required the courts to adopt a different rule. The differences between *Parker* and *Rockingham County*, in fact, likely stem from their very different facts. *Parker* involved an employee under an employer-employee contract so that one would expect that the decision to take the original contract precluded Ms. Parker from other opportunities. *Rockingham County*, however, involved a business so that one would expect that the plaintiff would not necessarily have foregone other opportunities and would be equally happy with an award of its profit on the contract (if it did not have to do the work under the contract) as it would with the full contract price (if it still had to spend money on the labor and materials needed to build the bridge).

Fourth, the two cases may actually be stating and applying identical rules but **phrasing those rules in different language**. One court, for example, may have decided that it agreed with the other court's decision and the public policy choices that decision reflected, but the second court believed that it could phrase its rule or holding in a better way. Legal decision-making is a very difficult process, and it is hard to anticipate how later readers will understand what you write. Thus, a court facing the same problem and having the same solution in mind may simply decide that there is a better way to phrase the rule or holding.

Finally, on occasion, two decisions are **simply irreconcilable** and students simply need to say so.

Dissents and Concurrences

As explained above, many cases, like *Parker* case, include a dissenting opinion; others include a dissenting opinion and a concurring opinion or just a concurring opinion.

The student's task, when confronted with a concurrence or a dissent, is to *identify* the points of dispute between the majority opinion and the dissent or concurrence and *explain* the dissenting or concurring view. A dissenting or concurring opinion may disagree with the majority opinion's statement/description of the applicable law, its characterization of the facts, its statement of public policy or its application of law to fact or of precedent to fact.

A summary of the dissent in *Parker* should help students understand what they should be including in their summaries of dissenting and concurring opinions:

Dissent

The dissent agrees, for the most part, with the majority's statement of the facts and articulation of the applicable law; he says that the rule stated by the majority "is a serviceable one and my concern is not with its use as the standard but rather with what I consider its distortion." The error, according to the dissent, is in the majority opinion's "superficial" application of the rule to the facts of the case because the majority opinion never really explains why the differences made the alternative employment inferior. The dissent also believes that the procedural mechanism used to decide the case in the trial court, summary judgment instead of trial, was inappropriate because the facts needed to be weighed by a jury and additional facts needed to have been presented.

Conclusion Regarding Case Briefing Strategies

On the one hand, case briefing is a skill that is quite difficult to master. Most new law students do not really achieve mastery in their first semester or even their first year of law school. Briefing requires tremendous amounts of practice. Full-time law students literally read hundreds of court opinions in their first year. On the other hand, expert law students recognize that this difficulty and need for practice are simply part of the learning process, not unlike the thousands of hours of practice required to master a musical instrument or a sport. Expert law students recognize that learning to brief is not a matter of aptitude but, rather, a matter of strategic practice. Figure 25 below shows, in flow-chart form, how to create a good case brief. Exercise 9-3 in the Workbook gives an opportunity to practice case briefing with respect to the cases the student used for the pre-reading and reading strategies in Exercise 9-1.

Figure 25: A Flowchart Showing the Elements of a Good Case Brief

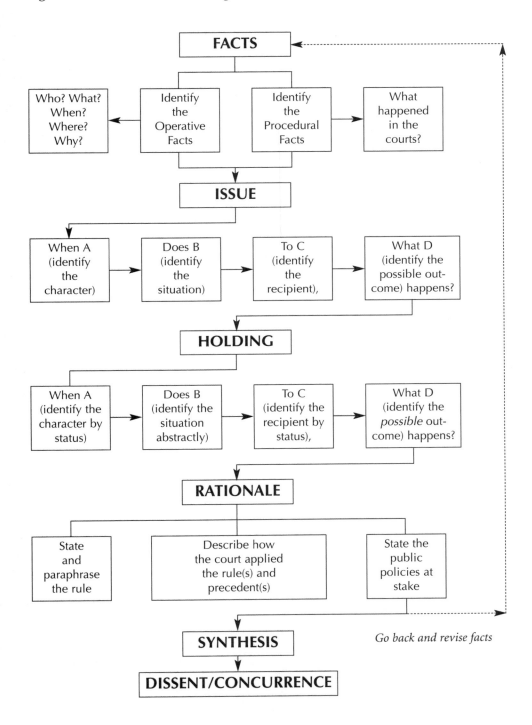

Reflection Questions

1. How are pre-reading and reading strategies with respect to court opinions similar to strategies that would also be effective for reading non-law school texts? How are they different?

2. Which of the pre-reading and reading strategies identified in this text are new to you? Of those, which would have helped you as an undergraduate student? With which of the pre-reading and reading strategies identified in this text were you already familiar?

3. Why do students who use the strategies detailed in this chapter get better grades than those who do not?

4. Select three of the pre-reading or reading strategies and explain why you believe those strategies help students understand cases better.

5. What does it mean to say expert learners "dialogue" with court opinions? Why does this strategy enhance comprehension and recall?

6. Why do many lawyers continue to brief cases even after they graduate from law school?

7. Based on your reading so far and what you know so far about lawyering, if you were a law professor, would you prefer detailed issue statements or detailed holdings or both? Why?

8. Some students mistakenly believe that policy is irrelevant, in part because many courts do not explicitly state the policy rationales for their decisions. Why are these students mistaken?

9. Why do expert learners state rules in two different ways?

10. What is the benefit of synthesizing cases?

References

Laurel Currie Coates, *Beating the Odds: Reading Strategies of Law Students Admitted Through Alternative Admissions Programs*, 83 Iowa L. Rev. 139, 158–159 (1997).

Arthur L. Costa & Lawrence E. Lowery, Techniques for Teaching Thinking (1989).

Dorothy H. Deegan, *Exploring Differences Among Novices Reading in a Specific Domain: The Case of Law*, 30 Reading Research Quarterly 154, 163 (1995).

Peter Dewitz, *Conflict Of Laws Symposium: Reading Law: Three Suggestions for Legal Education*, 27 U. Tol. L. Rev. 657 (1996).

Elizabeth Fajans & Mary R. Falk, *Against the Tyranny of Paraphrase: Talking Back to Texts*, 78 Cornell L. Rev. 163 (1993).

Anastasia S. Hagan & Claire Ellen Weinstein, *Achievement Goals, Self-Regulated Learning and the Role of the Classroom Context* in Understanding Self-Regulated Learning (P. Pintrich, ed. 1995).

Barbara K. Hofer, Shirley L. Yu & Paul Pintrich, *Teaching College Students to Be Self-Regulated Learners* in SELF-REGULATED LEARNING: FROM TEACHING TO SELF-REFLECTIVE PRACTICE 57, 76 (1998).

Mary A. Lundeberg, *Metacognitive Aspects of Reading Comprehension: Studying Understanding in Legal Case Analysis*, 22 READING RESEARCH QUARTERLY 407–415 (1987).

Frances O'Tuel & Ruth K. Bullard, DEVELOPING HIGHER ORDER THINKING IN THE CONTENT AREAS K–12 50 (1993).

Patricia L. Smith & Tillman J. Ragan, INSTRUCTIONAL DESIGN (1999).

Paul T. Wangerin, *Learning Strategies for Law Students*, 52 ALB. L. REV. 471 (1988).

Claire E. Weinstein & Richard E. Mayer, *The Teaching of Learning Strategies* in HANDBOOK OF RESEARCH ON TEACHING (M.C. Wittrock, ed. 1986).

B.Y.L. Wong, *Self-Questioning Instructional Research: A Review*, 55 REVIEW OF EDUCATIONAL RESEARCH 227 (1990).

Barry J. Zimmerman, Sebastian Bonner and Robert Kovach, DEVELOPING SELF-REGULATED LEARNERS: BEYOND ACHIEVEMENT TO SELF-EFFICACY (1996).

Chapter 10

Strategies for Learning in the Law School Classroom

Introduction

As explained in Chapter 2, most law school instruction occurs within the classroom context. For many law students, in fact, classroom instruction is their only contact with their professor, their only opportunity to practice the skills they need to be developing and obtain feedback on their progress, and their only chance to resolve confusion and ask questions. Consequently, expert law students are experts at learning what they need to learn from their classroom instruction and in recording that learning in a form they can later use.

Chapter 2 also describes what typically occurs within the law school classroom context: a law professor typically engages in a one-on-one dialogue with a selected student, asking the student to explain an assigned statute or court opinion, to dissect the court's reasoning, the public policy underlying the statute or holding and to identify and analyze the issues in a hypothetical. These distinctions among types of questions are not always clear. For example, although law professors often ask hypotheticals so that their students can practice their legal analysis skills, they also sometimes design hypotheticals to help the students identify flaws in a court's reasoning, to test students' understanding of the doctrine, or to help students discern the underlying policy implications of a court's decisions.

The questions reflect professors' underlying instructional goals, which include helping students build their doctrinal knowledge (knowledge of the rules of law), developing their skills in any or all of the following areas: case reading and briefing, synthesis, issue-spotting, factual analysis, legal reasoning and problem-solving, and beginning to adopt important professional values, such as sensitivity to facts, clients and client differences, legal ethics, thoroughness, carefulness, honesty and integrity. The variety of questions law professors ask, their likely overlap in particular instances, the likely rapid transition between goals and the fact that law professors are unlikely to note the transition and the complicated relationship between professors' questions and their instructional goals requires law students to be particularly vigilant in class. To be able to follow the discussion and produce a record in their notes that they will be able to use later, students need to be deciding, throughout the class session, what their professors are asking and to what goal they are teaching.

Figure 26 shows typical law professor questions and the corresponding instructional objectives for each.

Figure 26: Typical Law Professor Questions and Their Corresponding Instructional Objectives

Typical Law Professor Questions	Corresponding Instructional Objectives
State the facts (holding, issue, policy, reasoning) in _____ v. _____. What did the dissent say about that issue?	Case reading and briefing.
Do you agree with the majority or the dissent? Is the court right or wrong? Why? Do you agree or disagree with the court? Why?	Case reading and briefing.
How can you reconcile _____ v. _____ with this case? How does this case relate to _____ v. _____? What other case have we read where the court did _____? Why did the two courts reach a different result on this point (the same result on this point)?	Synthesis.
[A hypothetical for which the student must apply and distinguish a case or set of cases under study]. [A hypothetical to which the student must apply a rule under study].	Concept Learning (Issue-Spotting). Principle Learning (Legal Analysis). Problem-solving. Fact sensitivity.
A question about a small but significant detail in an opinion.	Thoroughness. Carefulness.

Of course, from the students' perspective, the goals of classroom instruction are slightly different. Expert law students typically have in mind four core goals in learning from lectures: (1) self-monitoring for comprehension (understanding what their professors are trying to teach), (2) help-seeking (resolving areas of confusion), (3) obtaining feedback (by comparing their answers to their professors' questions to their peers' answers), and (4) recording what they have learned in a form that allows for easy use in organizing their course materials (see Chapter 12) and studying for examinations (see Chapters 13 and 16). These goals require expert learners to prepare for class carefully, remain focused throughout the class session, ask questions and volunteer answers and take clear, succinct, well-organized notes. Novice learners, in contrast, often do not have concrete goals in mind and therefore are much less likely to be fully prepared and to remain focused. Because they are less prepared and less in control of their own learning, novice law students often try to write down everything their instructor says or simply choose to disengage during class discussions. They ask fewer questions, volunteer even less and make little effort to organize their notes.

Expert law students also do not let themselves be distracted by the instructional and personal quirks of their professors. Law professors, like all human beings, run a wide spectrum of personality types, teaching styles and political values, all of which influence the professors' interactions with their students. Over the course of their law school careers, many law students encounter an instructor whose approach is intimidating, aggravating or, at least, off-putting. Many more encounter law professors with whom they frequently disagree. For novice learners, such issues can be distracting or even can interfere with learning. Expert law students, however, by remaining focused on their short-term and long-term goals, are better able to ignore such matters, and know that, after they graduate from law school, their professional success will depend, in part, on their ability to deal with employers, judges and opposing counsel who are equally difficult to deal with on a personal level.

In the sections that follow, there is a suggested approach to taking notes in class. The techniques described below are hardly new. Rather, they reflect a synthesis of techniques that have proven successful in a wide variety of instructional contexts. The following websites provide more information about such techniques:

http://www.ucc.vt.edu/stdysk/notetake.html,

http://www.csbsju.edu/academicadvising/help/lec-note.html,

http://www.adm.uwaterloo.ca/infocs/Study/listening.html, and

http://www.d.umn.edu/student/loon/acad/strat/ss_notetaking.html.

Preparing for Class

Expert law students recognize that they will learn little in class if they simply show up unprepared and hope to be enlightened. Like any other learning experience, classroom learning is ultimately a matter of the student taking control over her own learning. Such control starts long before the scheduled start time for the class. Thus, expert law students set explicit, mastery learning goals, read and brief all of their assigned cases, review and synthesize their notes from the previous class and plan for the upcoming class by planning their notes, by deciding how they will focus their attention, by assuming they will disagree with some of what they hear, by developing questions they expect to be answered by the class discussion and by identifying any areas of confusion about the assigned materials.

Set Learning Goal

As Chapter 5 discusses, early on in every learning enterprise, a crucial prerequisite to success is setting mastery learning goals. Thus, expert law students usually set a goal of mastering the skills and acquiring the knowledge that are the subject of the particular class or lesson.

Read and Brief the Cases

Many students who were successful in college were able to succeed without having to work very hard and without doing their reading assignments before they attended class. Law school is different. Whereas, in college classes, professors devote considerable classroom time to re-explaining the knowledge already explained in the textbooks for the course, in law school classes, professors start with the assumption that all the students in the class can acquire knowledge from texts and therefore focus classroom time on student skill development. Law professors generally assume the students have acquired most of the knowledge they need to acquire from the text and focus on developing students' lawyering/analytical skills. Consequently, students who fail to prepare for class cannot follow the class discussion at all, and, therefore, expert law students know that they need to read and brief all of the cases in their assignments before class starts.

Review/Synthesize Prior Day's Class Notes

As shown in Chapter 2, humans learn new material by connecting the new material to their prior learning. By connecting the new material to their prior learning, learners are encoding the information within their existing schema. This basic principle of learning makes review and synthesis of the prior day's class notes a crucial preparatory activity. By doing so, the student is, in a sense, preparing the soil so that he or she can plant his or her new learning. Doing so creates the schemata into which the new learning will be encoded.

This activity also allows the student to engage in the necessary self-evaluation that is a part of the SRL cycle. As part of the student's review, the student is determining the extent to which she understood what occurred in the previous class session and evaluating the success of the learning strategies she used in preparing for and participating in that class session. This information assists the student in preparing for the upcoming class by allowing her to make any necessary adaptations to ensure maximized learning in the upcoming class.

Finally, this activity allows the student to identify a need for any assistance from her peers or instructor and therefore to avoid becoming completely confused as the class progresses. In this sense, law school learning is like a rapidly growing tree. Trees require regular pruning because, otherwise, they grow in ways that are either unattractive or unproductive; accordingly, knowledgeable gardeners trim unsightly branches before those branches have grown too large and become unmanageable. Confusion in one's law school learning is like an unsightly branch. Trimmed early on, confusion is no problem at all; if the student quickly resolves her confusion, it will have no effect on the rest of his or her learning. If, however, the student allows his or her confusion to persist, it becomes larger and much more difficult to resolve. Such confusion, in fact, is likely to produce additional confusion, much like an unsightly branch, not trimmed, will produce sub-branches as it grows.

Plan Notes

A particularly important activity for maximizing student learning from lectures involves planning one's notes. Expert learners do not magically produce superior notes out of thin air; their notes are the product of careful planning. Expert learners:

(1) Plan their notes in light of their goals in having notes—monitoring their learning for comprehension, obtaining help where needed, getting feedback on

their progress in the course, and having an accurate record of what transpired in class;

(2) Prepare a note-taking format that will result in a set of notes that the student readily will be able to use;

(3) Plan the structure of their notes (headings, sub-headings, use of underlining or highlighting, etc.); and

(4) Develop a set of abbreviations and a shorthand technique that allows for rapid note taking.

Planning notes to help achieve goals. Ultimately, the measure of effective notes is not the quantum of material recorded, the accuracy of their recording efforts or even the willingness of peers to ask the student to share the notes. Rather, notes are valuable only to the extent that they serve the learners' ultimate goals in creating them. Consequently, expert learners know that what works for others does not determine what they should be doing. Instead, expert learners focus on what they expect to be learning and making sure that their notes produce a record that furthers that objective.

Preparing a note-taking format. While there are a variety of note-taking formats in existence, most of them have a number of features in common. First, virtually all note-taking formats assign a separate notebook for each course and a separate page for each class session and suggest that students use full-sized (8½" x 11") notebooks. These simple strategies ensure that students readily can find all the notes for each course easily, readily identify the beginning and ending of their notes for each particular class session and have plenty of room to take their notes.

Second, expert learners never use the entire sheet of paper for their class notes; rather, they divide their paper, reserving approximately one-third of the page for writing questions they have as they are taking notes, for identifying key terms and key concepts, and for labeling the likely instructional purpose of the matters addressed in the notes. For example, as noted above, in any given class session, an instructor may be teaching students the rules of law, case reading and briefing, applying and distinguishing, legal ethics, etc. By determining and indicating the instructional goal to which the notes relate, the student makes his or her future use of those notes much easier.

This technique is a crucial one for the student to master because it not only helps law students do better in law school, but also it helps lawyers do better in law practice. Experienced trial lawyers take notes as they listen to witnesses testify (both in depositions and in court) using a very similar format. On the larger side of the page (the right two-thirds), they record what the witness said. On the smaller side (the left one-third), they note the names of additional witnesses they must depose or call, questions they should ask future witnesses, documentary and other evidence they will need to subpoena, legal research the witness' statements necessitate and the relationship between the witness' testimony and the elements of the claims and defenses at issue in the case. In other words, they take notes in much the same way expert law students take notes, using two-thirds of the page for recording what they are hearing and one-third for expressing their reflections on the implications of what they are hearing.

The best way to understand this approach is by imagining a class discussion that reflected the above and below materials on learning in the law school classroom and then considering the fictional excerpt from a student's notes about those materials as shown in Figure 27.

Figure 27: Example of Note-Taking Format

August 10, 2002

Learning in a Law School Classroom

Planning notes

Space for questions, reflections, key terms, etc.

    Keep eyes on prize

    Format

        Sep. notebk. each course

Allows for reflection

        New page each class session

        Space for questions, ideas

    Plan structure of notes

Are there common abbreviations for law school terms?

    Develop abbreviations, shorthand

Plan strategies for focusing att'n.

Planning the structure of the notes. There are two main reasons why students should plan the structure of their notes. First, doing so will help them remember what they learn. As the discussion of schema theory in Chapter 3 makes clear, humans learn new concepts better and retain that new learning better when they understand the relationships between the new concepts and the concepts they previously have studied and when they understand the relationships among the new concepts they are studying. Moreover, by planning one's notes so that they fit within a structure, rather than simply recording what the instructor says without trying to fit that information within a structure, expert law students begin to develop a schema for the new learning. In other words, the students are building a storage facility in their brains into which they can place the new learning.

Second, doing so will speed students' note taking. Experts agree that students should impose structure on their notes as they are taking notes rather than simply recording what is said in class. The effort to process the material as the student is hearing it strengthens the memory trace and thereby increases the likelihood of later recall. Consequently, developing some basic structure in advance of class will assist students in imposing that structure saving them time and mental energy.

The task is much less daunting than one might imagine. As the text explains in Chapter 9, students should pre-read their texts by reviewing their professors' syllabus, the table of contents of their texts, the table of contents of a supplemental text, the questions after the cases and by reading the supplemental text. This pre-reading not only makes it easier to understand the case but also helps the students plan the major topics and headings within their class notes. Together, these resources are very likely to result in a list of major topics, sub-topics and sub-sub-topics.

One caveat is important. Instructors are unlikely to follow the exact structure developed by the student. Consequently, it is better to develop the structure on a separate sheet of paper from which you easily can copy as you take notes.

Planning abbreviations and shorthand. Expert students recognize that note-taking speed can be helpful. Consequently, they develop abbreviations and shorthand techniques. For example, many law students, lawyers and law professors use the symbol Π or the letter P for plaintiff, the symbol Δ or the letter D for defendant and the letters ct for court. Other abbreviations used by all note-takers, both within and without the law school setting include: w/ (with), w/o (without), = (is), & (and), e.g. (example follows). Similarly, many students leave out articles (a, an, the) and otherwise write in a form that may be termed, "caveman talk." Instead of writing, "The court held that a plaintiff in a suit for negligence must prove the defendant owed a duty of care to the plaintiff," they write "Π claiming negl. must prove Δ owed duty to Π." Of course, students develop these abbreviations and shorthand over time through usage, and, most abbreviations and shorthand techniques are idiosyncratic because each student must be able to recall what he or she means by each abbreviation. Nevertheless, smart note-takers plan, as much as possible, their abbreviations for each subject area. For example, a student about to study the parol evidence rule in contracts might decide to use PER to refer to the rule, and a student about to study the tort of intentional infliction of emotional distress might decide to use IIED to refer to that tort.

Note that, in Figure 27 above, the word separate is abbreviated as "sep," the word notebook is abbreviated as "notebk," and the word attention is abbreviated as "att'n."

Plan Strategies for Focusing Attention

On the one hand, attending to law school lectures is often quite easy for most students. At any given moment, there is a risk the professor will call on the student to recite, a process that tends to keep most students focused at all times. On the other hand, most students find some aspects of the law more interesting than others. For example, a student who is planning to practice business law may not find a criminal law class particularly stimulating. Moreover, in every class, there are times when members of the class ask questions to which the student already knows the answer or a professor belabors a point the student already has mastered. For these reasons, expert law students need to plan techniques for focusing their attention when it lags. Those techniques are the same ones students use during the Performance Phase of the SRL cycle to retain focus, such as positive self-talk ("Yes, that's a key point") and self-guiding verbalizations ("Make sure you are organizing these notes").

Assume Some Disagreement

It is helpful for most students to know that they will not agree with everything their instructors and peers have to say. Legal issues have significant political implications. For example, rules of law that provide relief where one person has caused emotional but no physical harm to another person often invoke spirited debate about the best use of soci-etal resources. Expert law students assume such disagreements will occur and do not allow those disagreements to interfere with their acquisition of the knowledge and skills they need to succeed in law school.

Develop Questions to Ask and Questions You Expect to Be Answered

Just as expert readers develop lists of questions they expect to be answered by their read-ing (See Chapter 9), expert classroom learners develop lists of questions they expect to be answered by the class discussion. These questions should address areas of confusion for the student and areas the student expects the professor to address in the classroom discussion. The pre-reading question stems in Chapter 9 therefore are also helpful for this purpose.

By developing these questions, expert students not only make sure that they under-stand what they need to understand about the materials in the course, but also make sure they are actively paying attention to the classroom discussing, listening for answers to the questions they have developed.

Effective Listening

Effective listening has several components. The first component is the preparation dis-cussed above. Many of the strategies listed above, such as formulating questions, plan-ning how to focus attention during the class session, planning the structure of notes and even reading and briefing the assigned cases cause the student to effectively listen in class.

The second component of effective listening involves readying oneself mentally, in-cluding removing distractions, avoiding hasty judgments and jumping to conclusions, resisting boredom, frustration and other emotional reactions, and being physically ready (not hungry, thirsty or tired) to focus attention. These activities are somewhat akin to sweeping a floor before polishing it, as they involve readying the student's men-tal workspace to take in her new learning.

The third component is the self-monitoring that already should be a part of every learning experience in which you engage. While attending a lecture, expert learners monitor for comprehension as a means of self-evaluating their class preparation and as a way of making sure they are focusing attention on the classroom discussion. In other words, they make sure they understand what the instructor is trying to teach, evaluate whether their class preparation was effective, and make sure they do not lose their focus.

Finally, effective listening involves sense making. Effective listeners are active lis-teners who constantly strive to translate into their own words what they are hearing in class. Rather than simply recording the exact words their instructor is speaking, expert learners record their understanding of the meaning of what the instructor is saying. Of course, in law school, *sometimes the specific words do matter.* For example, law students often must know the exact phrasing of a rule statement, the name of a concept (e.g., the parol evidence rule, fee simple absolute, possession) or a defini-tion. In such instances, however, the precise term is readily available from a court opinion, secondary source or restatement, making the effort to record the exact words during the lecture a poor use of limited note-taking time. Consequently, expert students record where in their course materials they can find the requisite specific words (e.g., p. 234, 3rd ¶) and use note-taking time to translate the words into their own.

Effective Note-Taking

Focus on Key Points/Follow Cues

One of the keys to effective note taking is being able to distinguish the important points from the not-so-important points. Expert learners capture most, if not all, the key points. Studies suggest that novice learners, in contrast, record as little as 11% of the key points, leaving themselves at a huge disadvantage. Other novice learners, eager to avoid missing anything, try instead to achieve the impossible by recording every word their instructor says. These novices leave themselves in no better a position because they are completely unable to distinguish the important points from the trivial matters. In law school, writing down every word spoken is particularly difficult; unlike in college classes which usually are taught in a lecture format, students in law school classes speak as much as one-half or two-thirds of the time and some of what they say is incorrect. Consequently, law students who aspire to recording every spoken word not only fail to record every word, but also likely record some matters that are inaccurate. In other words, one of the worst things a law student can do is try to record everything spoken in class.

It is equally misguided to decide to simply listen and rely on memory and secondary sources such as hornbooks and commercial outlines to make sense of the course material. Notwithstanding anything instructors may say, studies show that students who record information themselves retain it much better than those who simply listen.

Thus, expert learners record no more and no less than the important points. This task is less daunting than it might appear at first glance. Expert law students know that instructors provide considerable guidance in this task. They know to attend to and follow the *cues* provided by their instructors. Instructors provide numerous cues about what is important in their lectures. These cues include:

(1) the things they write on the board,
(2) any outlines or other study guides they provide,
(3) the things they repeat or restate in different words,
(4) the things they summarize, and
(5) the things they review at the beginning or the end of their lecture.

Instructors use these cues to help students identify the key points in their lectures. Smart students take these cues and make sure to include such matters in their notes.

Leave Lots of Space

Studies of note-taking also reveal that students tend to fill the space they allocate to their notes, and students who leave themselves plenty of space tend to record more of the information they need than those who limit their writing space in any way. Accordingly, while expert students plan the structure of their notes, as noted above, they do not do so in a way that restricts the quantum of notes they will be taking.

Correct Confusion Regarding Rules and Holdings and Restate Them

Expert law students also use class discussions to correct their case briefs and rule statements. In many instances, instructors communicate correct statements of rules and holdings, either directly or by accepting students' rule statements or holdings. Expert law students use these statements as opportunities to correct any errors they may have made. At the same time, a crucial indicator of understanding is the ability accurately to restate a rule or holding. Consequently, expert law students use lectures both to check the accuracy of their rule statements and holdings and to develop statements in their own words of those rules and holdings.

Organize while Writing

Finally, expert students force themselves to organize the material as they take notes. In part, this effort can be made much easier by developing an outline of the key topics in advance of class, as the above discussion suggests. Even with such an outline, however, students learn more and learn it better by forcing themselves to think about and recognize the hierarchical relationships among the concepts they are studying. As Chapter 3 explains, students store learning in such hierarchical structures (called schemata); by forcing the materials into their natural structures, students assist themselves in storing the materials in their long-term memory. Figure 28 shows two sets of notes about the material in this section dealing with taking notes as if those materials were a lecture. The set of notes on the left depicts a set of notes that lacks structure, whereas the set on the right possesses such structure. Note how much clearer the relationships among the concepts appears even with these relatively simple materials. Note also that the structured notes do not include numbers or letters; students can add those later when they create their outlines; while taking notes, the minimal gain from forcing oneself to follow perfect outlining numbering simply is not worth the effort.

Finally, many expert students also incorporate color or highlighting in their note taking. For example, it may be very productive to highlight all the rules or to use different colors for rule statements, holdings, policies, examples of legal analysis and test-taking advice.

Post-Class Activities

Expert students recognize that the first few hours after class are a crucial time period with respect to their learning from class experiences. At that time, the material is much fresher and more easily remembered. Students' areas of confusion are more readily identified, and their abbreviations and shorthand more quickly recalled. Students who wait days or even weeks to review their notes often struggle to recall anything specific

Figure 28: A Comparison of Notes with Structure and
        Notes without Structure

Effective Note-Taking (*Unstructured notes*)	Effective Note-Taking (*Structured notes*)
Focus on key points	Focus on key points
Make sure all the key ideas are noted	Make sure all the key ideas are noted
Don't write everything down	Don't write everything down
Follow cues on the board	Follow cues
Follow cues from study guides	on the board
Follow cues from repetition and rephrasing	from study guides
Follow cues from summaries	from repetition and rephrasing
Follow cues from review	from summaries
Leave lost of space	from review
Correct confusion	Leave lost of space
State rules and holdings in own words	Correct confusion
Organize notes into structures	State rules and holdings in own words
	Organize notes into structures

about the class session the notes reflect, to remember what they understood and what confused them and to understand what they intended their notes actually to communicate. Consequently, expert students force themselves to review and revise their notes as soon as possible after the class session has ended. This effort actually involves three tasks, each of which is detailed below. Those three tasks are: (1) reviewing for comprehension and legibility; (2) reflecting on the student's experience of the class and note-taking strategies; and (3) transferring the notes to the student's course outline or to graphic organizer(s), such as hierarchy charts or flow charts (see Chapter 12 for a discussion of outlines and graphic organizers).

Reviewing for Comprehension and Legibility

Expert learners make sure they review their notes as soon as possible for comprehension and legibility. They first make sure they understand everything they wrote down and, where necessary, either make appointments with their instructors for assistance or send their instructors questions by e-mail. Expert students recognize that it is much easier to be able to follow a class discussion than it is to be able to understand it and use what the students have learned on examinations. They also recognize that instructors appreciate students who are eager to understand and seek help as they go. Before midterms and final examinations, instructors receive dozens of requests for assistance. Those students who seek help as they need it, therefore, are more likely to get their needs met and to inspire willingness on their instructors' parts to provide last minute help.

Likewise, expert students know that, in the rush to record what was said in class, students do not write as neatly as they could. By reviewing immediately after class, expert students ensure they can recall what they were trying to communicate.

Reflect on Your Experience of the Class

Of course, for every learning experience, expert learners include time for the reflection phase of the SRL cycle. In the context of taking lecture notes, expert learners use that time to reflect on the success or failure of their efforts to take notes and the cause(s) of the success or failure (Did they plan their notes? Were they able to focus attention throughout the lecture? Did they prepare for class sufficiently by reading and briefing the cases? Did they review the previous class session's notes before the class started? Did they take proper notes?), to attribute their successes to personal effort and their failures to their strategy selection and use and to adapt their techniques for learning from classroom instruction accordingly.

Transfer to Outline/Graphic Organizer

Finally, expert law students transfer these class notes into their ongoing course outlines and graphic organizers (see Chapter 12) as soon as possible but no later than the weekend following the class session. This quick turn around serves as a second opportunity for clarification while the material is still fresh and ensures better encoding of the new learning by ensuring its recordation in the student's ongoing course schema. Moreover, this effort connects the new learning to the student's prior learning, which also increases the speed and accuracy of later efforts to recall the learning.

Checklist of Strategies for Learning in the Law School Classroom

Figure 29 is a checklist of activities in which expert law students engage to ensure they learn everything they need to learn from their law school classroom experiences. Exercise 10-1 is an opportunity to use these strategies and evaluate practice efforts using this checklist.

Figure 29: Checklist of Activities for Learning from Classroom Experiences

Class Preparation Activities
- __ Set explicit, mastery learning goal
- __ Read and brief all assigned cases
- __ Review and synthesize notes from previous class session
- __ Plan notes
- __ Plan attention-focusing strategies
- __ Assume disagreement with some aspect of the classroom discussion
- __ Develop list of questions and of areas of confusion

Effective Listening
- __ Prepare for class as above
- __ Be ready mentally (remove distractions, avoid hasty judgments, boredom, frustration and anger and be physically ready)
- __ Self-monitor while listening (see Chapter 7)
- __ Actively listen by striving to make sense of everything the instructor says

Effective Note-taking
- __ Focus on key points and follow instructional cues
- __ Leave lots of space for notes
- __ Correct confusion and restate understanding in own words
- __ Organize while writing

Post-class Activities
- __ Review for comprehension and legibility
- __ Reflect on classroom learning experience
- __ Transfer to course outline and graphic organizer(s)

Reflection Questions

1. Why does it help students to learn better if they plan the structure of their notes and force their notes to fit an outline-like (hierarchical) format?

2. Why do lawyers use the two-thirds/one-third approach to note taking during depositions and trials?

3. How have you prepared for class in the past? Why might the strategies described in this chapter cause you to learn more and it better?

References

Donald A. Bligh, WHAT'S THE USE OF LECTURES (2000).

Barbara K. Hofer, Shirley L. Yu and Paul R. Pintrich, *Teaching College Students to Be Self-Regulated Learners* in SELF REGULATED LEARNING: FROM TEACHING TO SELF-REFLECTIVE PRACTICE 57 (D.H. Schunk, B. Zimmerman, eds. 1998).

Alison King, *Comparison of Self-Questioning, Summarizing and Notetaking-Review as Strategies for Learning from Lectures*, 29(2) AMERICAN EDUCATIONAL RESEARCH JOURNAL 303 (1992).

Claire E. Weinstein & Richard E. Mayer, *The Teaching of Learning Strategies* in HAND-
    BOOK ON RESEARCH ON TEACHING 315 (M.C. Wittrock 1986).

Paul T. Wangerin, *Learning Strategies for Law Students,* 52 ALB. L. REV. 471 (1988).

Barry J. Zimmerman, Sebastian Bonner and Robert Kovach, DEVELOPING SELF-REGU-
    LATED LEARNERS: BEYOND ACHIEVEMENT TO SELF-EFFICACY (1996).

Learning from Lectures, http://www.bradford.ac.uk/acad/civeng/skills/lectures.htm.

Reading, Listening and Notetaking, http://www.trentu.ca/academicskills/sfs/unit5_2.htm
    #st1.

Taking Notes From Lectures, http://www.d.umn.edu/student/loon/acad/strat/ss_notetak-
    ing.html.

Listening Skills, http://www.d.umn.edu/student/loon/acad/strat/ss_listening.html.

Chapter 11

Strategies for Obtaining Assistance

Introduction

As Chapters 3, 7 and 8 explain, expert learners characteristically not only recognize their need for help when it arises but also unflinchingly seek such help. There really are two steps in the help-seeking process: (1) recognizing the need for assistance, and (2) obtaining the assistance.

Expert law students recognize the need for assistance through their implementation of the self-regulated learning cycle. During the performance phase, they use self-monitoring to identify not only whether they understand what they need to understand but also whether they are developing that understanding efficiently. During the reflection phase, expert learners seek out opportunities for practice and feedback, and they evaluate their performance in comparison to their learning goals, their peers' performances in class and on coursework and their instructor's objectives. They then identify any causes of their failures to learn and revise their learning process accordingly. This frequent self-reflection and self-assessment helps expert law students obtain the help they need before their lack of comprehension causes them serious learning or educational problems.

Expert law students are also expert in the help resources available to them. Novice learners either simply accept their failure to learn or fail to seek help from appropriate resources. In contrast, expert learners recognize that help-seeking is simply another learning enterprise to which they can apply the SRL cycle. They carefully choose from the available help resources as part of the selecting strategies step of the forethought phase of the SRL cycle. The available resources include: self-help, peer help and instructor help. The materials below detail each of these resources, their strengths and weaknesses and their appropriate uses.

Self-Help

There are several reasons why self-help is not only a choice but is, in fact, the first choice for resolving law school learning problems. First, the student is, by far, the best gauge of her own learning issues and how to resolve those issues. Not only does she know when she does not understand, but, also, she is in the best position to know the particular aspect of the material that confuses her. Second, one of the most empowering experiences a law student can have is to resolve his or her own confusion. Novice learners, believing that their failure to learn reflects a defect in intellect, either seek help from others too soon and too often or simply ignore their problems. Expert learners, who know that failures to learn are a matter of strategy selection and time on task, take control over their own learning and try to resolve their confusion by changing their learning strategies and cycling through the SRL cycle a second time. Third, studies show that students are best able to recall, understand and use learning they have figured out for themselves. Accordingly, expert learners begin obtaining assistance by looking to themselves.

While self-help is the most empowering strategy for obtaining help, some novice law students overuse it at the expense of their own learning. Restudying is an inefficient tool for obtaining help with respect to matters that could be quickly clarified by checking with a peer or asking for a clarification from the instructor. Also, in instances where the confusion is great, re-studying without at least some help from an outside source may be futile.

Approach to Restudying

The principal self-help technique expert learners use is modifying their learning strategies in light of their outcome (a partial failure to learn) and then re-studying. The crucial component of this approach is the modification. Merely re-reading or re-studying material that already has confused the student is likely to produce only modest comprehension gains. The student needs to brainstorm the causes of the failure to learn and change her learning approach accordingly. Chapter 8 provides a checklist of potential causes of a failure to learn that makes this process easier.

Using Supplemental Resources Materials Effectively

The last five to ten years have witnessed an enormous proliferation of resources designed to assist law students with their self-help efforts. Legal publishers have produced a wide variety of print and electronic resources designed to help law students learn their course material better. Moreover, law professors, eager to help students develop their learning and law school skills have created law school learning web pages. Consequently, law students have ready access to a wide variety of resources to facilitate their learning.

On the other hand, the huge growth in such resources does not benefit all law students equally or at all. Law students, particularly novice legal learners, are eager, perhaps overeager, consumers of such materials. The large market, in other words, is a response to student insecurity; novice law students' insecurity about their ability to learn what they need to learn makes them a ready market for materials promising law school success. In fact, novice legal learners often spend hundreds of dollars on supplemental resources materials, some of which they never actually use.

The keys to using these resources are knowledge about what they can provide, selectivity in their acquisition and strategic use. The next sections address each of these points in turn.

Description of common secondary sources. There are so many secondary sources available to law students that a complete catalog of these resources is beyond the scope of this text. Instead, this text focuses on a list of commonly used resources. Below, six such resources are identified, described and evaluated.

Hornbooks. A hornbook is a lengthy, exhaustive recitation of the law within a given field. Often as long as 1,000 pages, these supplemental texts are characterized by completeness, thoroughness and, for the most part, accuracy. These books are excellent resources for long descriptions and explanations of current law and trends in the law and for cross-references to court opinions and important law review articles in the field. For law students, they provide much more detail than law students either can recall or are expected to recall for law school examinations. In fact, all law school courses involve a set of choices by the instructor as to what not to include; students who rely exclusively on a hornbook, therefore, actually make greater demands on themselves than their instructors have made.

Commercially Produced Outlines, Hierarchy Charts and Flashcards. Each of these tools is a commercially-created version of a learning activity commonly used by expert law students. For this reason, each can be very attractive to law students pressed for time. In fact, recent versions of commercial outlines are even available electronically. The outlines and hierarchy charts can be a helpful tool for suggesting one possible organizational structure for the course material and can be tools for clarifying certain areas of confusion. They are not as accurate as hornbooks, however, and therefore students should use them with caution. Unfortunately, some students use these tools as a substitute for creating their own outlines, hierarchy charts and flashcards, a choice that almost always is a bad one. The choice is a poor one because doing so not only cheats the student of a crucial learning experience, the creation of the student's own version of these documents, but also involves the student in adopting a product that likely does not reflect his or her instructor's particular course design choices.

Canned Briefs. Canned briefs are simply briefs of the court opinions contained in a casebook. Of all the tools designed to facilitate student learning, canned briefs are the ones most despised by law professors and for good reason. Canned briefs cheat law students of their ability to learn how to read court opinions with little gain to the student, particularly because they often are inaccurate.

Examples and Illustrations. These books are similar to hornbooks and commercial outlines except that they include more or less typical law school essay exam questions and model answers with explanations to allow students to practice their law school exam skills and self-evaluate the progression of their legal reasoning skills.

Student-Produced Resources. Nearly every law student, at some point in his or her career, is handed a student-produced outline that someone claims came from a student who received an "A" in the class. On the one hand, these resources have the benefit of, perhaps, having been created specifically for the class the student is taking. On the other hand, the recipient has no way to evaluate the truth of any of the claims about the outline, including claims about its completeness and accuracy. In fact, instructors and law schools change their course coverage from semester to semester in large and small ways so that, even if the outline had been sufficient for the session for which it was created, it may no longer reflect course content. Moreover, the recipient does not know whether the "A" student was simply lucky, actually good, or maybe both. Finally, using someone else's outline cheats the student of the learning that can come only from creating one's own organization of the course material. Consequently, expert legal learners do not rely on such outlines.

Other Resources. A complete catalog of all the resources available to law students cannot possibly address all the resources available to law students. A few free, online resources, however, are worth noting. First, two web pages created by law faculty, http://academic.udayton.edu/aep/online/ and http://www.law.umkc.edu/faculty/profiles/glesnerfines/bgf-edu.htm#STUDENTS are excellent resources for students interested in learning more about how to master law school learning. Another excellent resource for law students are the exam preparation and exam taking materials for law students located on a web page sponsored by the University of Pittsburgh School of Law called "Jurist" and located at http://jurist.law.pitt.edu/exams.htm#Guides.

How to select a supplemental resource. There are two criteria students should weigh in selecting a supplemental resource. First, the resource must be useful for that student for the particular course at issue; what works for other students or in other classes may not work for this particular student in this particular class. Consequently, expert law students try using a supplemental resource (often, copies of such resources are on reserve in the law school's law library) before buying it. Expert law students assess both whether the resource explains things in a way that make sense to the student and whether the resource accurately reflects their classroom experience. In addition, they ask their instructor for recommendations; most instructors have preferences among the various resources. Second, the benefit to the student from purchasing the resource (instead of simply using it on an as needed basis in the law library) must exceed the financial cost of that resource.

How to strategically use supplemental resources. The keys to effectively using supplemental resources lie entirely within the student's control. First, students should develop their ability to accurately and honestly monitor their comprehension and skills development (and not simply wait for the results of examinations). By actively seeking opportunities for practice and feedback and constantly self-assessing their own learning, expert learners almost always are aware not only when they are learning and when they are not but also what they are learning and what they are not learning and the causes of both their successes and failures. This optimal mix of feedback seeking, self-monitoring and assessment of learning allows students to determine both the need for a supplemental resource and the likely cause of the learning problem.

Second, the student must select a resource tailored to her particular learning issues. Having identified a learning issue and its cause(s), the student must then select a resource likely to help with the problem. For example, if the learning issue were comprehension, an expert learner would be more likely to purchase or use a hornbook. Figure 30 below contains a list of common law student learning issues matched with the resources most likely to be helpful to the student in resolving those issues.

Finally, the student must use the resource appropriately. This aspect involves a somewhat delicate balance. On the one hand, given the extraordinary time demands of law school, students should avoid, as much as possible, needless floundering on matters

Figure 30: Student Learning Issues and Resources Directed to Those Issues

Learning Issue	Resources That May Help
Comprehension of doctrine or policy	Hornbook, *Examples and Explanations*
Organization/relationships among course concepts	Commercial outline
Law school study skills	http://academic.udayton.edu/aep/online/ http://www.law.umkc.edu/faculty/profiles/ glesnerfines/bgf-edu.htm#STUDENTS

General exam writing or legal analysis	*Getting to Maybe* (short volume addressing law
	    school exam writing strategies)
	http://academic.udayton.edu/aep/online/
	http://www.law.umkc.edu/faculty/profiles/
	    glesnerfines/bgf-edu.htm#STUDENTS
	http://jurist.law.pitt.edu/exams.htm#Guides

Course specific application of doctrine/holdings	*Examples and Explanations* and some commercial outlines

that easily and speedily could be resolved by reading a supplemental resource. On the other hand, figuring out a confounding problem on one's own not only builds self-efficacy but also creates a much stronger memory trace then resolving a question through the use of a secondary source. Accordingly, a modest amount of time trying to work through a problem is a worthwhile investment.

Peer Help and Productive Study Groups

In law school, self-help efforts typically help only some of the time or only partially so. Moreover, studies of human learning suggest that students learn more, retain it better and enjoy the learning process more when they study in small groups of peers. In fact, the effectiveness of **cooperative learning groups** is "so well confirmed by so much research that it stands as one of the strongest principles of social and organizational psychology."[1] Moreover, successful practicing lawyers tend to be excellent at working in groups because so much of law practice, contrary to common images of lawyering, requires working in small groups. Lawyers form working groups to handle large litigation and transactional matters and must be able to work cooperatively, even as adversaries, in the regular course of dispute resolution. These facts help explain why law professors and law school teaching experts generally recommend that law students create and regularly use study groups. Consequently, not only do expert law students seek peer help when they need it, but, also, they do so within the context of structured study groups.

The sections below detail the characteristics of cooperative learning groups that maximize the productivity of group work and describe some common law school cooperative learning exercises successfully used by these groups.

---

1. http://www.clcrc.com/pages/CLandD.html.

Characteristics of Productive Cooperative Learning Groups

There are six characteristics of excellent cooperative learning groups. First, cooperative learning groups have **positive interdependence**. Positive interdependence means that every member of the group invests in the learning success of every other member of the group. The idea of positive interdependence is often expressed by phrases such as "It's all for one and one for all," "We sink or swim together," and "We're all in this thing together." Positive interdependence makes learning groups more productive because it eliminates social isolation and creates a safe harbor from the normal competitiveness of education (particularly legal education) so that each student can ask for help.

Positive interdependence requires effort. It requires a commitment from each member of the group. It also is inextricably linked with the other characteristics of excellent learning groups, because absent the other characteristics, such as individual accountability for doing the group's work and honest group reflection on the progress of the group, students are often unwilling to invest in each other's success. The following three activities/actions help create the requisite positive interdependence:

(1) Group learning goals at the outset of each learning experience;
(2) Group rewards for successful learning by all members of the group; and
(3) Assigned roles for group learning exercises that require each member of the group to contribute and learn.

Second, effective groups manifest their positive interdependence through **promotive interaction**. Promotive interaction involves group members supporting, encouraging, challenging, teaching and otherwise helping each other learn. In other words, members of effective cooperative learning groups promote each other's success. It requires each member to be trustworthy and trusting and an atmosphere of stimulation but low pressure.

Third, successful groups avoid what are the two most common student concerns about participating in cooperative learning experiences, "free riders" and "show-offs." Free riders let others do the group work and do little, if any, work themselves. They cause resentment and anger to build up in the group to the point where the group is unable to function. Show-offs take control of the group and participate not as a means of facilitating group learning but, rather, as a way to demonstrate their intellect. While some free riders like having show-offs in their group because the show-offs do all the work, most group members resent show-offs' insistence on always being the focal point of the discussion. The solution for both problems is **individual accountability**, the second characteristic of successful cooperative learning groups.

Individual accountability requires each member of the group not only to hold himself or herself responsible for doing group work but also to hold every other member of the group responsible for doing group work. It also means that each group member must vigilantly guard against both show-off and free-rider problems within the group. One way to avoid both problems is the development of clear group rules from the outset with respect to both issues and clearly delineated consequences, large or small, for either. Another helpful tool is the periodic assignment of one student to serve as the "group checker," the group member whose job it is to assess whether everyone is fairly contributing to the group. Ultimately, however, each group member's interest in his or her own learning should encourage him or her to address free rider and show-off behavior whenever it arises.

Forth, successful groups engage in **reflection on the group process**. In other words, during group meetings, the group reflects upon the extent to which the group is functioning effectively and efficiently and the causes of that success or failure. The focus of such discussions is more on the process than on the ultimate outcome; a successful group regularly identifies and discusses which group and individual activities and behaviors are contributing to achieving the group's goals and which are not. The group discusses how to improve the process and plans future group and individual activities and responsibilities. In other words, successful groups regularly engage in the self-monitoring step of the performance phase and the entire reflection phase of the SRL cycle. The only difference is that the monitoring and reflection are occurring on a group, rather than on an individual, level.

Fifth, group success is contingent on group members' development and use of **interpersonal and group social skills**. A range of studies has shown that groups whose members are more skilled socially actually perform better academically. The specific social skills most conducive to group success are: (1) honesty and clarity in communication, (2) acceptance and support of fellow group members, (3) trust, and (4) constructive conflict resolution.

All of these characteristics may be developed by having group members agree to and sign a group contract, in which each member promises to promote the necessary positive interdependence, promotive interactions, personal accountability, reflection on the process and communication skills. Exercise 11-1 is a form for creating a group contract.

Finally, excellent study groups are made up of at least three people and no more than six who are not homogenous but, rather, diverse. Size does matter. While groups of two can succeed, such groups generally are too small to ensure the diversity of opinions and skills typical of successful groups. Working only in a pair, students cheat themselves of the multiple sources and types of feedback available from a larger group; moreover, the smaller the group, the more likely that it is homogenous, resulting in a group where each member has the same strengths and the same weaknesses. At the other end of the scale, groups of seven or more tend to be unwieldy and less helpful to individual students. Most of us have had the experience of attending a social function in a group of seven or more. By and large, the group subdivides into two or more separate conversations because of the difficulty of accommodating such a large group. In fact, large study groups often end up focusing on the interests of one or more small sub-groups at the expense of both accountability and positive interdependence.

Diversity of group membership is, first and foremost, a matter of diversity of experiences, skills, knowledge, and interests. Where possible, diversity is also a matter of gender, race and culture. Diversity within a group has been correlated with increased achievement and productivity, creative problem solving, growth in cognitive reasoning, increased perspective-taking ability, and general sophistication in interacting and working with peers from a variety of cultural and ethnic backgrounds. It also prepares students for interacting with their colleagues and clients, who are likely to be different.

The six characteristics of effective cooperative groups are shown in graphic form in Figure 31.

Figure 31: The Six Characteristics of Effective Cooperative Learning Groups

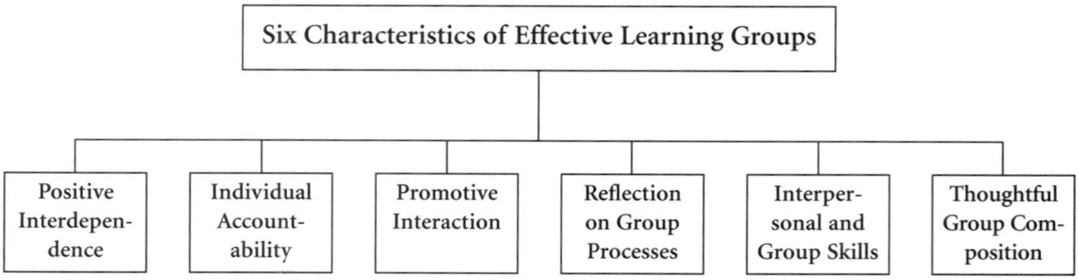

```
┌─────────────────────────────────────────────────────┐
│    Six Characteristics of Effective Learning Groups   │
└─────────────────────────────────────────────────────┘
```

Positive Interdependence	Individual Accountability	Promotive Interaction	Reflection on Group Processes	Interpersonal and Group Skills	Thoughtful Group Composition

Some Commonly Used Cooperative Learning Exercises

Over the past twenty years or so, cooperative learning experts have developed some very effective techniques for fostering the six characteristics. Below is a list of some such techniques.

Think-Pair-Share. In this exercise, each student in the group thinks through, often in writing, the analysis/resolution of the same hypothetical question. The students then pair off and exchange and try to understand and, to the extent possible, reconcile their analyses. Finally, the group as a whole discusses, tries to understand and, to the extent possible, reconciles the pairs' analyses.

Drill Review Pairs. In this exercise, students pair in sub-groups of two to analyze two short hypotheticals. For one of the two hypos, one student acts as the analyst (this person analyzes the problem) and the other as the checker (this person observes the analysis and evaluates it for thoroughness and accuracy); for the other hypo, the roles reverse. The analysts not only communicate their final analysis, but also their thinking process as they work their way through the problem. The checkers ask the analysts questions to make sure they understand the analysts' thinking processes. When all pairs have completed their answers to the hypos, the group gathers as a whole to compare and discuss thinking processes and analyses.

Roundtable. Students start with a hypothetical and a single blank pad of paper. Each student writes a portion of the analysis (one or two paragraphs) and then passes the pad onto the next student until the group has produced an answer. The group then reviews and evaluates the answer as a whole. This approach also can be done in smaller bites where each student writes one sentence.

Pass the problem. Students break into pairs and each pair is given a hypothetical clipped to the outside of a folder. Each pair writes an analysis of the problem and then puts their analysis inside the folder and passes the folder to the next pair. The next pair, without looking at the prior pair's analysis, writes their own analysis and puts it in the folder. After each pair has analyzed each problem, the group compares the pairs' analyses and tries to reach a consensus about what would be a proper analysis.

Reports. Each member creates and delivers a presentation (using a poster or handouts) on a small part of a portion of the course material. The other students must ask questions and provide the presenter with feedback on the presentation.

Cooperative learning experts also recommend doing some sort of ice-breaker (i.e., having each student interview another student and then introduce that other student to the group) when groups first form. For some students, both the exercises above and the general principles of cooperative learning groups can seem hokey; research, however, suggests that these techniques are extraordinarily effective in producing student learning.

Professorial Help

On the one hand, many professors are glad to meet with students, and many professors believe that those students who seek help from their professors outperform those who do not. On the other hand, given the facts that law professors often teach two sections of students per semester and that the typical size of first-year law school classes is at least 50 students and often twice that number, even if only half of an instructor's students sought 15 minutes of help per week, the instructor would have to hold at least twelve and one-half hours of office hours per week and as many as 25 hours of office hours per week to meet his or her students' needs. In fact, most law professors hold no more than six office hours per week. These facts suggest the very real scarcity of professorial help and the importance of students' acting professionally about their office hour meetings.

Acting professionally means that the student has tried to resolve those matters he or she can resolve without professorial intervention, that the student asks her questions with professional respect, that the student has prepared for the meeting by having specific questions (and *not* general questions asking the professor to re-explain what the class just spent three class sessions discussing) and that the student has remembered to bring the materials she needs for the meeting (a notebook for taking notes and the court opinion, paper, or examination question or answer the student wishes to discuss).

It is also worth noting that many professors are willing to (and may even prefer) to respond to questions posted by e-mail or on a course web page. This tactic allows the instructor to address the student's concerns at the instructor's leisure and gives the student the benefit of a written product from which to study. The approach also helps the professor reach students who are too shy to ask for help on their own.

Moreover, many professors have placed frequently asked questions (FAQs) and answers on their course web pages. If the student's professor has an FAQ section on his or her course web page, the student should check it out before contacting her professor for help. Students who fail to heed this advice risk annoying their professor and slowing their own learning process.

Finally, for the same reasons why it is a good practice to review class notes shortly after the class session has ended, it is also a good idea to review notes of a professorial meeting shortly after the meeting ends. Doing so allows the student to consolidate his or her understanding and makes later integration into the student's course outline easier.

Reflection Questions

1. The strategies for obtaining help addressed in this chapter are offered in a conscious order, the order the author believes students should follow in seeking help. Why is this order probably the optimal one?

2.   Why are study groups such a powerful learning tool?

3.   Why are positive interdependence, promotive interaction, individual accountability, reflection on the group process and interpersonal and group skills so important to the success of cooperative learning groups?

References

Carole Buckner, *Realizing Grutter v. Bollinger's Compelling Educational Benefits of Diversity"—Transforming Aspirational Rhetoric Into Experience*, 72 U. M. K. C. L. Rev. 1 (2004).

Gerald F. Hess & Steve Friedland, Techniques for Teaching Law (1999).

Barbara K. Hofer, Shirley L. Yu and Paul R. Pintrich, *Teaching College Students to Be Self-Regulated Learners* in Self Regulated Learning: From Teaching to Self-Reflective Practice 57 (D.H. Schunk, B. Zimmerman, eds.1998).

Vernellia R. Randall, *Increasing Retention And Improving Performance: Practical Advice On Using Cooperative Learning In Law Schools*, 16 T.M. Cooley L. Rev. 201 (1999).

Patricia L. Smith & Tillman J. Ragan, Instructional Design (1999).

Barry J. Zimmerman, *Developing Self-Fulfilling Cycles of Academic Regulation: An Analysis of Exemplary Instructional Models* in Self Regulated Learning: From Teaching to Self-Reflective Practice 1 (D.H. Schunk, B. Zimmerman, eds.1998).

Barry J. Zimmerman, Sebastian Bonner and Robert Kovach, Developing Self-Regulated Learners: Beyond Achievement to Self-Efficacy (1996).

Clifford S. Zimmerman, *"Thinking Beyond My Own Interpretation:" Reflections on Collaborative and Cooperative Learning Theory in the Law School Curriculum*, 31 Ariz. St. L.J. 957 (1999).

Chapter 12

Organizational Strategies

Introduction

As we learned in Chapter 3, students learn by causing material in their short-term memory to become stored learning in their long-term memory. More specifically, students store the new learning in schemata, which are highly organized knowledge structures. In other words, humans store new learning much like they store documents on their computers. For example, the author of this text stored this chapter of this textbook in the following way: first, all the documents his family creates on their computer are in a folder labeled "My documents." Second, because he shares his computer with his family, the chapter is in a sub-folder labeled "Mike." Then, because he also does things on his computer unrelated to his work, the chapter is in a sub-sub-folder labeled with a reference to his former law school, "Western State." Further, it is in a sub-sub-sub-folder labeled "Professional Writings" and a sub-sub-sub-sub folder labeled "Expert Learner Text." Graphically, this structure can be represented as shown in Figure 32.

Figure 32: A Graphic Depiction of a Schemata

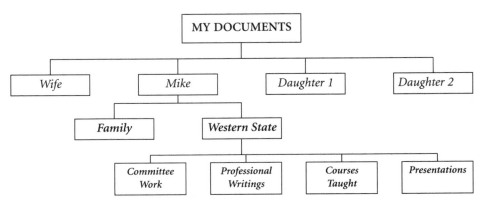

To see how schemata influence learning, imagine that the author has written a draft of a law review article. Where would he store it? He would probably choose to store it in the Professional Writings sub-sub-sub-sub folder because that is the logical place within the structure for that new information to be stored. Similarly, expert learners store new learning by encoding it in such a way that it fits within their existing schemata.

In fact, students who store their learning in multiple ways understand it better and are more likely to be able to recall and use it when they need it. For this reason, expert law students engage in multiple efforts to impose structure on their learning, devoting considerable time and effort to this project.

There is one prerequisite strategy for organizing law school materials, **deconstructing rules**. Deconstructing rules involves breaking rules down into their constituent parts or requirements. For example, the crime of burglary has been defined as "the nighttime breaking and entering of a dwelling house with the intent to commit a felony." Now imagine the following hypothetical:

> At 8:00 p.m., Samantha, planning to take Alexander's broken clock, opens an unlocked door to Alexander's vacation cabin, sticks a giant claw through the opened door and then decides not to take the clock and leaves.

To determine whether Samantha has committed a burglary, a court would first need to identify each of the requirements for the crime and then assess whether each is met in this instance. Thus, the court would divide the above definition into a set of requirements. Those requirements are:

(1) Nighttime,
(2) Breaking,
(3) Entering,
(4) Dwelling house,
(5) Of another, and
(6) Intent.

Without this organization of the definition, the court could not readily assess whether Samantha's conduct amounts to a commission of the crime. Likewise, students who fail to deconstruct rule statements into their constituent parts cannot properly analyze law school hypotheticals and bar exam questions. Deconstructing rules also helps students organize the two broad categories of organizational strategies explained in the second and third parts of this chapter: **outlines** and **graphic organizers**.

If the goal of deconstruction is to break rules into their constituent parts, the goal of outlines is to construct an organization of not only the constituent parts, but also of all the rules in relation to each other. For this reason, outlining, probably the most commonly used organizational strategy among law students, is a highly structured summary of a course or a portion of a course. Expert law students use outlines to record and organize the rules and holdings they need to know and be able to use on their law school examinations.

Graphic organizers, the second organizational strategy, are actually a set of several learning strategies, each of which involves translating words expressed in linear form (such as lists) into structures, such as the structure depicted in Figure 32 above. Expert law students, recognizing the importance of developing multiple schemata for recording their learning, frequently use graphic organizers not only to represent the material in their outlines in different forms, but also to develop alternative structures for understanding their course material.

The keys to using deconstruction, outlines and graphic organizers are careful selection and knowledgeable, thoughtful and reflective use. In other words, not only must students become expert in the use of each of these three strategies, but, also, they must use them in the context of the self-regulated learning cycle. Students must become expert in how and when to use each of these strategies, and they must continue to set learning goals, select these strategies where they are appropriate, implement the strategies while monitoring their effectiveness and then reflect and modify the strategies to make them more efficient and productive. To facilitate these efforts, the discussions below explain how to use the three strategies, as well as the most common uses and strengths and weaknesses of each.

Deconstructing Rules

Deconstructing a rule involves **translating the rule into a list of parts so that the student will be readily able to apply each part to a fact pattern.** To do so, lawyers use pattern recognition and language interpretation. Deconstructing rules involves pattern recognition in the sense that most rules fall within one of the five patterns outlined below (or a combination of two or more of those patterns). Consequently, students can deconstruct rules by analogizing the rule before them to a prototype rule. Deconstructing rules also involves language interpretation in the sense that the distinguishing features among the various types of rules, in most instances, are the conjunction used to connect the requirements (and, or, but) or the use of a "signal" word, as explained in detail below, such as "is" for definitions and "weighs" for what lawyers call "factor tests."

In addition, many rules use what might be called "language shortcuts" to communicate multiple requirements in a few words. For example, several rules include a requirement that a party have a "reasonable belief" about something. This requirement really means the party must actually believe and reasonably believe, i.e., two requirements. Another common language shortcut used in rules is to preface a list of considerations with the word "include" as in "The factors courts may consider include:…" The word "include" is a shortcut for the phrase "include but are not limited to," which means that the list which follows is incomplete and other matters not on the list may also be considered.

Using pattern recognition and language interpretation together, students should be able to deconstruct most of the rules they encounter.

Deconstructing rules is crucial to law school success, and, while the following examples and explanations may make it *seem* as if the distinctions among types of rules are easy, many law students either fail to make the crucial distinctions or do so incorrectly. As the discussion below reveals, such errors can result in students misapplying rules. In law practice, such errors constitute malpractice.

The Five Patterns

There are five common types of rules, and, while it is very common for courts and legislators to combine two or more of these patterns in a single rule, these materials will focus on simple rules in which only one, two or three patterns are combined. The task of discerning the pattern involved in a rule is a crucial one to students and lawyers because lawyers use different analytical techniques in applying each. The five patterns are explained below.

Simple rules (If A, then Z). Many rules simply identify an act or condition (*if A*) and its consequence (*then Z*). Examples of such rules from outside the legal context abound. For example, an employer might say to a salesman, "If you want a bonus, you must exceed $500,000 in sales." Similarly, a parent might say to a child, "If you stay out past curfew, you will be grounded for one week." Both rules describe the act or condition (exceeding a dollar amount in sales, staying out past curfew) and its consequence (getting a bonus, being grounded for one week).

Legal examples of simple rules include the following (explanatory material is in italic font and within parentheses for all of the rules discussed in this section of the text, and the material in bold font is simply the title of the statute):

Selling Alcohol to a Minor. It shall be a crime to sell alcohol to a minor (*act = selling alcohol to a minor; consequence = crime*).

Measure of Damages for Delay in Construction. In connection with a contract to build a building, damages for delay in completion by the contractor are measured by the rental value of the completed premises for the period of the delay (*act = delay by the contractor in completing a building construction contract; consequence = damages measured by the rental value*).

In fact, many simple rules do not explicitly identify the consequence; they simply state a requirement for action or inaction; the consequence typically is addressed elsewhere, although it may be implicit. For example, a parent might say to a child, "Clean up your room right now." The required act is cleaning up the child's room and the implicit consequence for a failure to act may be a loss of allowance or of a privilege. Similarly, an employer might say, "Your hours are 9:00 a.m. until 5:00 p.m." The required act is being on the job from 9–5, and the implicit consequence for failing to act (at least repeatedly) would be loss of the job.

Legal examples include:

When Answer Must Be Filed. An answer to a complaint must be filed within 30 days (*act = failing to file an answer within 30 days; implicit consequence = loss of the case*).

Statute of Limitations for Tort Actions. The statute of limitations for a cause of action based on a tort is one year (*act = failing to file a lawsuit; consequence explained in another statute = loss of the claim*).

Speed Limit on State Highways. The speed limit on a state highway is 65 miles per hour (*act = exceeding the speed limit; implicit consequence, if caught, = traffic ticket*).

Applying simple rules involves assessing whether the required act or failure to act is present and then explaining the consequence.

Elemental rules (If A and B and C...are present, then Z). Elemental rules are the most common rules law students learn in their first-year classes. These rules are similar to simple rules in that they also include an explicit or implicit consequence if the prerequisite condition exists or does not exist. The difference is that the prerequisite condition consists of a list of requirements, all of which must be met for the consequence to follow. Lawyers refer to each requirement as an element. Nearly all students are familiar with typical, non-legal examples of such rules, such as lists of requirements for papers, (e.g., the paper must be at least ten pages in length but no longer than 15 pages, must be in 12-point font, must have one-inch margins, etc.). The consequence typically is explicit (the instructor will not accept the paper or will deduct points).

The burglary rule expressed above is typical of legal rules, as it lists a set of elements (six in this instance). Notice that the rule can be expressed as a sentence: burglary is the nighttime breaking and entering of a dwelling house of another with the intent to commit a felony. Lawyers, however, translate the sentence into a set of elements: (1) nighttime, (2) breaking, (3) entering, (4) dwelling house, (5) of another, and (6) intent. Lawyers engage in this translation process so that they can analyze each part separately. If each part is an element, the absence of any part eliminates criminal liability for the crime. In other words, if there is no breaking or the actions occur in the daytime, the defendant cannot be convicted of this particular crime.

The key for students is the act of translation. For this reason, it is necessary to focus on the specific words used in the burglary definition. First, the use of the word "is" signaled that the words that were to follow would be the requirements for conduct to be deemed a burglary. Second, the conjunction "and" and the preposition "with" both express that the items that follow are to be added to the items that precede, thereby suggesting the rule has multiple requirements. Moreover, the words in the definition of common law burglary that are not connected directly by "and" or "with" have no connecting words at all; this usage communicates they are a part of a list.

Another point is equally crucial. Each element is, itself, a rule containing a required condition or act and a consequence (implicitly, if the requirements stated in the element are not met, the element is missing and therefore the larger, overarching prerequisite condition is not met). For example, the nighttime element has been defined as the period between sunset and sunrise when there is not enough light to discern a face. Notice that this element, itself, has two sub-elements: a time requirement (between sunset and sunrise) and a light requirement (insufficient light to discern a face), each of which must be met. Similarly, the "dwelling house" requirement actually has two sub-requirements; the homeowner must either dwell there or intend to return and the area broken into must be the house or the area surrounding it (called "the curtilage"). In this sense, as shown in Figure 33, the definition is like the sun in a solar system and each of the elements are planets (and some of those planets have moons). In other words, the definition is the hub from which sub-rules and sub-sub-rules emerge.

In most law school classes, students learn or must figure out for themselves the hub rule and study court opinions addressing each of the sub- and sub-sub-rules; expert law students must therefore put the hub together with the sub-sub-rules to ascertain how the materials fit together and can be used to analyze hypotheticals.

Other examples of elemental rules include the following:

Acceptance of Offer. To accept an offer of a contract, the offeree must manifest assent to the terms of the offer in the proper manner (*elements are: (1) manifestation of assent, (2) by the offeree, (3) to the terms of the offer, and (4) in the proper manner*).

Diversity Subject Matter Jurisdiction. Federal courts have jurisdiction where the parties are diverse and the amount in controversy exceeds $60,000 (*elements are: (1) parties are diverse, and (2) the amount in controversy exceeds $60,000*).

Battery. A battery is an intentional harmful or offensive touching of another person (*elements are: (1) intent, (2) touching, (3) the touching must be harmful or offensive), and (4) the person touched must be different than the person doing the touching*).

Adverse Possession. A trespasser to land may acquire title to that land if his or her possession of the land is (1) hostile, (2) exclusive, (3) continuous, (4)

*Figure 33: The Relationship between Hub Rules and
Sub-Rules and Sub-Sub-Rules*

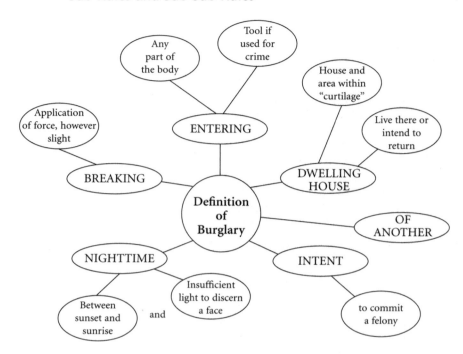

open and notorious, and (5) actual and her possession lasts for the statutory period.[1]

Factor rules (If A, B and C weighed together justify Z, then Z). Factor rules are somewhat less common then elemental rules. Factor rules consist of a list of considerations that must be weighed in deciding whether the consequence is justified. These considerations are referred to as the **factors**. Although non-lawyers seldom use the term "factors," almost everyone has had the experience of weighing considerations in making a decision. The decision of which college or law school to attend, for example, involves weighing the cost, educational programs and geographical location, among other things. Even more simply, the decision of which restaurant to go to for lunch may involve weighing the cost, quality and convenience of the various choices.

Factor rules, therefore, are similar to elemental rules in the sense that they contain a list of considerations, each of which must be analyzed to determine whether the consequence follows. The two types of rules, however, are different in one very important respect. Whereas each element of an elemental rule must be met for the consequence to come about, the absence of one or more factors does not preclude the consequence. In other words, as graphically depicted in Figure 34, whereas elements operate like the numbers in a combination lock each of which must be precisely hit or the consequence will not follow, factors operate like weights on a scale so that if the factors tip the scale in favor of the consequence, the consequence will follow and if the factors tip the scale against the consequence, the consequence will not follow.

---

1. 5–20 years depending on the state.

Figure 34: The Difference between Elements and Factors

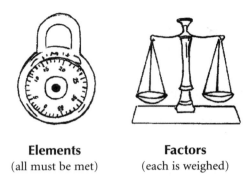

Elements
(all must be met)

Factors
(each is weighed)

An example of a factor rule is the rule commonly used by courts to determine whether a party seeking a preliminary injunction (an injunction before a full hearing on the merits of the parties' dispute) may obtain one.

> **Circumstances Relevant in Determining Whether to Grant Preliminary Injunction.** In determining whether to issue a preliminary injunction, courts weigh:
> (1) the strength of the party's claim on the merits,
> (2) the hardship to the party requesting relief if relief were denied and the hardship to the other party if relief were granted,
> (3) the extent to which the hardship to either party is compensable in money,
> (4) the practicality of enforcing the order,
> (5) public policy (what is best for society as a whole), and
> (6) the morality of the parties' respective conduct.

Notice that, as is true of elemental rules, each portion of this list is significant. In fact, sometimes, each factor may have its own definition. For example, the practicality of enforcing the order involves considering the burden on the court of supervising the order and the ability of the court to craft an enforceable decree.

Factor rules are quite often combined with a standard that the factors attempt to measure. For example, custody rules usually adopt a standard of the "best interests of the child." These rules often also articulate a list of factors that bear on the best interests of the child, including: (1) the health, safety, and welfare of the child, (2) any history of abuse by one parent or any other person seeking custody, (3) the nature and amount of contact with both parents, and (4) the habitual or continual illegal use of controlled substances or habitual or continual abuse of alcohol by either parent.

Other factor rules include:

> **Circumstances Significant in Determining Whether a Failure is Significant.**
> To determine whether a breach of contract is a material breach (*a standard*), the following circumstances (*signal of a factor test*) are significant (*another signal of a factor test*):
> (a) the extent to which the injured party will be deprived of his contract benefit (*factor 1*),
> (b) the extent to which the injured party can be compensated for that lost benefit (*factor 2*),
> (c) the extent to which the breaching party will suffer forfeiture (*factor 3*),

(d) the likelihood that the breaching party will cure the defect in his performance (*factor 4*), and

(e) the extent to which the breaching party has acted in good faith (*factor 5*).[2]

Fees for Legal Services.

A lawyer may not charge an unconscionable fee (*a standard*).

Among the factors (*signal of a factor test*) to be considered in determining the conscionability of a fee are the following:

(a) the amount of the fee in proportion to the value of the services performed.

(b) the relative sophistication of the member and the client.

(c) the novelty and difficulty of the questions involved and the skill requisite to perform the legal service properly.

(d) the likelihood, if apparent to the client, that the acceptance of the particular employment will preclude other employment by the member.

(e) the amount involved and the results obtained.

(f) the time limitations imposed by the client or by the circumstances.

(g) the nature and length of the professional relationship with the client.

(h) the experience, reputation and ability of the member or members performing the services.

(i) whether the fee is fixed or contingent.

(j) the time and labor required.

(k) the informed consent of the client to the fee.[3]

As was true with respect to elemental rules, the key to recognizing a factor rule is the words used. In particular, the word "weigh" in the preliminary injunction rule, the phrase "the following circumstances are significant" in the material breach rule, and the word "factors" in the attorney-client fee rule are typical signals that a test is a factor test. Moreover, in three of the rules above, the rule for child custody, the test for material breach, and the unconscionable fee rule for attorney-client services, the rule starts with a standard. Although, in many instances, the presence of a standard does not mean the rule will be a factor test, the use of a standard makes the need for factors to elucidate the meaning of that standard more likely.

Another way to see the significance of the language used is to consider what language would have signaled that the tests were elemental rules. For example, the material breach rule would have to say something about the plaintiff proving that the breach was material by showing that the injured party will be significantly deprived of the contract benefit, that the deprivation cannot be compensated, that the breaching party will not suffer significant forfeiture if the breach were deemed material, is unlikely to cure the defect in performance, *and* did not breach in good faith.

Alternative rules (If A or B, then Z). Alternative rules are even less common than factor rules. Students nevertheless must learn to recognize them because the analysis of alternative rules is necessarily quite different than the analysis of elemental rules. Elemental rules require the plaintiff to prove each element, and alternative rules can be met by showing that any of the alternatives is present.

Alternative rules outside the legal context are common. For example, want ads for open jobs sometimes state that applicants must either possess a particular level of educational attainment or a particular level of experience. Similarly, some parents impose

---

2. *See* Restatement of Contracts 2d § 241.
3. *See* California Rules of Professional Conduct, § 4-200.

curfew rules that require a child either to be home by the specified time or to call the parents and let the parents know the child will be late and why.

The definition of battery above includes one element that is an alternative rule. This element can be met in one of two ways—either the touching must be harmful to the victim or it must be offensive to the victim. The crucial words that signal that this test is an alternative test are "either" and "or."

Other legal examples of alternative rules include:

Punitive Damages: When Available.
A plaintiff may be awarded punitive damages if the defendant was malicious (*alternative 1*), reckless (*alternative 2*), oppressive (*alternative 3*), evil (*alternative 4*), wicked (*alternative 5*), guilty of wanton or morally culpable conduct (*alternative 6, which, itself, can be met in two alternative ways*) or (*signal of alternative test*) showed flagrant indifference to the safety of others (*alternative 7*).[4]

Remedies for Breach of Contract.
A plaintiff in an action for breach of contract may be awarded damages for the harm caused by the breach (*alternative 1*) or (*signal of alternative test*) obtain an order requiring the breaching party to specifically perform the promise (*alternative 2*).

Forcible Rape.
Forcible rape is an act of sexual intercourse accomplished against a person's will by means of force (*alternative 1*), violence (*alternative 2*), duress (*alternative 3*), menace (*alternative 4*) or (*signal of alternative test*) fear of immediate and unlawful bodily injury on the person or another (*alternative 5*).[5]

The forcible rape statute quoted above is a particularly interesting example of an alternative test because the fourth alternative itself includes three elements (fear of an immediate bodily injury, the feared bodily injury must be unlawful and the fear must be of one's own injury or of another's injury) and this third element has two alternatives (one's own injury or another's injury).

Rules with exceptions (If A, then Z, unless B). Human relations are so complex that, over time, courts and legislators find it necessary to create exceptions to many rules. Of course, rules with exceptions are also common outside the legal context. For example, college students are familiar with graduation requirements (the rule) that can be waived with approval of a dean or a department chair (the exception).

One very well known exception is the exception to the murder rules where the defendant has acted in self-defense. In this context, the rule consists of the list of the elements of the crime of murder (the (1) unlawful (2) killing (3) of another human being (4) with malice aforethought) and the exception consists of the requirements for a court to conclude that a defendant has acted in self-defense (the defendant's perception of a need for the use of force must be reasonable and amount of force must be what was reasonably necessary to avoid the threatened harm).

Other examples of legal rules that have exceptions include:

Promise to Do What One is Legally Obligated to Do. A promise to do what one is already legally obligated to do is not enforceable (*rule*), but (*signal of ex-*

---

4. *See* Dan B. Dobbs, Law of Remedies, §3.11(2), p. 468 (1993).
5. *See* Cal. Pen. Code §261 (a) (2).

ception) a similar performance is if it differs from what was required in a way that reflects more than a pretense (*exception*).[6]

Restraints on Alienation. A restraint on the alienation of property (a restriction on a landholder's ability to transfer property) is void (*rule*) unless (*signal of exception*) the present and future interests both are held by charities (*exception*).

Recovery of Property Fraudulently Taken. A person who has been induced by fraudulent misrepresentations to transfer title to property may recover that property from anyone who subsequently possesses it (*rule*) unless (*signal of exception*) that person was a bona-fide purchaser of the property (i.e., both paid for it and did not know of the victim's interest in the property) (*exception*).

Notice that the key to categorizing rules with exceptions, as is true of categorizing all types of rules, is language. In this instance, words that often signal exceptions include "unless," "except," "but," and "but if." Also notice, again, that the rule with respect to the recovery of property fraudulently taken is actually a combination rule because the exception for bona fide purchasers has two elements (payment and no notice of the victim's interest in the property).

Because the ability to distinguish among the various types of rules is so crucial, Figure 35 on the next page compares the five types of rules, their signal words and their patterns.

Combination rules. As the above discussion has noted in several places, many rules are actually combinations of the five types of rules. Thus, for example, the tort battery rule is an elemental rule, but one of its elements is an alternative rule. Similarly, the rule with respect to the recovery of property fraudulently taken is a rule with an exception, but the exception is an elemental rule with two elements.

Exercise 12-1 gives a chance for the student to practice in deconstructing a few simple rules.

Outlining Courses

The traditional method for organizing one's law school learning is to create a course outline. Outlines allow the student to both organize and include **all** the information she needs to learn for her examinations and are therefore crucial tools. They are also limited tools, in the sense that they include so much detail that the student is likely to need to use other learning tools to be able to understand and encode the relationships among all the concepts in the outline.

Goals for Law School Course Outlines

As is true of any learning task, the success of the activity of creating a course outline must be measured by the goals that prompted the student to engage in it, and, of course, setting such goals is a crucial early step in the learning process. Expert learners

---

6. *See* Restatement of Contracts 2d, §73.

Figure 35: Comparison Chart for Types of Rules

Type of Rule	Pattern	Example	Signal Words
Simple Rule	If A, then Z.	It shall be a crime to sell alcohol to a minor.	
Elemental Rule	If A and B and C..., then Z.	Burglary is the nighttime breaking and entering of a dwelling house of another with the intent to commit a felony.	and, with, all
Factor Rule	(often start with a standard) If A and B and C weighed together justify Z, then Z.	Custody shall be awarded in accordance with the best interests of the child. Factors that bear on the best interests of the child include: (1) the health, safety, and welfare of the child, (2) any history of abuse by one parent or any other person seeking custody, (3) the nature and amount of contact with both parents, and (4) the habitual or continual illegal use of controlled substances or habitual or continual abuse of alcohol by either parent.	weigh(ing), outweigh(ing), consider(ing), including (but not limited to), factors, circumstances
Alternative Rule	If either A or B, then Z.	Forcible rape is an act of sexual intercourse accomplished against a person's will by means of force, violence, duress, menace or fear of immediate and unlawful bodily injury on the person or another.	or, either
Rule with Exception(s)	If A, then Z, unless B.	A promise to do what one is already legally obligated to do is not enforceable, but a similar performance is if it differs from what was required in a way that reflects more than a pretense.	except, unless, but if

set three goals before they start working on their course outlines. Those three goals are: (1) structuring the course material, (2) recording the course material, and (3) checking for comprehension.

The first goal, structuring the course material, is quite important. Expert law students, knowing that human beings store new learning in organized structures called schemata (see Chapter 3 above), recognize that outlining courses offers them an opportunity to create structures that will increase the likelihood that they will be able to recall and use what they have learned in the courses. The hierarchy they create allows their brains to more readily store the learning. However, course outlines, because they include so much detail (given the other two goals) are, for most students, only a partial tool for achieving this goal. For most students, the level of detail in a course outline interferes with its usefulness as an organizational tool.

The second goal, recording the course material, is the most significant use of a course outline. The first task in memorizing anything is deciding what one needs to memorize. Course outlines are excellent tools for helping students make sure they know what it is that they need to know. Accordingly, expert law students use their course outlines to record everything they believe they need to know for their examinations.

The third goal, checking for comprehension, is somewhat subtler. While the obvious purposes of creating a course outline are structuring and recording the course material, the act of creating a course outline causes expert learners to assess their comprehension. In other words, each time expert law students add to their outlines, they assess whether they understand what they are adding. The normal self-monitoring that is a part of all self-regulated learning causes students to make sure they understand everything they are including in their outlines. Expert law students make sure they not only understand the words of the rules and holdings they are including in their course outlines, but also that they can develop examples and non-examples of the concepts those words describe. This effort causes expert law students to stop and obtain help when they have a comprehension issue (please see Chapter 11 for a discussion of strategies for obtaining help).

How to Create Excellent Law School Course Outlines

There are three keys to creating course outlines that help students achieve the three goals. First, and perhaps surprisingly to some students, course outlines must follow proper outline format and be highly structured. Second, course outlines must include everything the students need to know to do well on their examinations. Finally, students must check their outlines for accuracy. Each of these activities is detailed below.

How to outline. Nearly all law students create documents that they call "course outlines," mostly because it so common for law professors, "how to" books and upper division law students to recommend doing so. The fact that not all law students succeed or succeed at as high a level as they would like to succeed suggests, however, that not all course outlines are created equally. Having looked at hundreds of student outlines over the years, I have no doubt that law student outlines vary greatly in quality, quantity, depth and effectiveness.

The two most common errors made by novice law student learners in outlining their course material are failing to start early and work continuously on their outlines and failing to make the extra effort necessary to create a structured portrayal of the course material. First, many novice learners, perhaps even recognizing that a course outline is a tool for preparing for examinations, choose to delay most of the work on their course outlines until their examinations are imminent. There are numerous risks in this approach. First, at a late juncture, students have less time to think through the organization of the material. Second, rushing through the processes increases the risk of omission of key material. Third, using time at the end of the process to create an outline takes away time that could have been spent on other tasks necessary to success on examinations, including memorization and practice. Fourth, the press of time can become so great that some students simply choose to forego doing an outline altogether and try studying from their class notes, an approach that creates a risk that they will fail to see the relationships among the course concepts and be unable to focus on the materials they actually need to know. Finally and most importantly, students may either fail to identify areas of confusion in the rush to finish or may be unable to obtain access to the resources (fellow students, instructors, supplemental texts) they need to resolve any confusion they do identify.

For this reason, expert law students, rather than waiting to start their outlines at some vague future date, start working on their course outlines within the first or second week of the semester and work persistently on their outlines throughout the semester. Rather than saving their questions or not developing questions until close to exam time, they identify their need for clarification and get that clarification as the semester goes so that all their needs are met. They also strive to complete their outlines right after the semester ends at the latest so they have time to ask any final questions, work on memorization and practice using the material.

Second, novice law school learners often give up on the difficult task of creating structure and therefore create "outlines" that are not really outlines at all but are, instead, simply lists of information. This choice is a poor one for two reasons. First, the absence of structure makes their outlines much less valuable as tools for organizing and memorizing the material. Second, the struggle to identify the hierarchies is a type of deep mental processing that creates the strong memory traces that make recollection during the stress of examinations much more likely.

Expert law students therefore force themselves to follow traditional outlining principles. They try to create as many levels and sub-levels as possible. They make sure they have at least a II for every I, at least a B for A, at least a 2 for every 1, and at least a b for every a. They consider multiple ways of organizing the material and know why they have selected one method over another. They use multiple sources, their instructors' handouts and syllabi, their texts, hornbooks, and their peers to help them identify and develop their understanding of the relationships among the concepts they are learning, but they make sure they create their own understandings, recognizing that the effort to do so is, itself, crucial to their learning.

This effort is made much less arduous by the fact that every type of word-processing software has an outline feature. Students need only initiate the feature and then hit enter every time they have finished an entry and use the tab key to move to lower hierarchy levels and shift-tab to move to higher levels in the hierarchy. Moreover, the word processing software allows students to readily move things around in their outline by cutting and pasting and, in fact, automatically renumbers the outline after the student has done the cutting and pasting. For this reason, it is worthwhile for students to force themselves to devote the extra 15–20 minutes to learn how to use their word processor's outline feature (because, in the long run, this feature will save time).

What to include in outlines. Novice law students also often are confused about what they should include in their course outlines. They sometimes have trouble distinguishing things they need to know from things they really can exclude from their outlines. Part of this problem stems from the multiple objectives that law professors have in mind when they are teaching; as explained in Chapter 10, in any given class session, law professors provide instruction in case reading, synthesis, legal analysis, fact analysis and investigation, issue spotting and the doctrinal subject, i.e., torts, contracts, criminal law. In fact, not only do law professors almost never signpost their transitions among these instructional topics, but, also, they often are teaching to multiple objectives at the same time. For example, in the course of discussing the doctrine addressed in a particular case, the instructor may provide instruction in applying that particular rule or holding or in analyzing that court opinion that the instructor hopes the students will generalize to all the court opinions and doctrine they are studying.

These facts mean that smart law students often create two outlines, one outline containing the doctrinal materials they have addressed in class and one containing the skills and insights they have acquired in class. They divide their skills outlines by skills topics and sub-topics, e.g., reading court opinions, applying and distinguishing cases, applying rules to facts, etc., and they divide their doctrinal outlines by doctrinal categories, e.g., crimes against the person (homicide, battery, etc.), crimes against property (larceny, burglary, etc.), etc.

The above discussion suggests many of the things law students should be including in their outlines: (1) what their instructors communicate is important, (2) the doctrine and case holdings, and (3) instructions about performing skills. In addition, expert law students also include policy or rationale for the doctrine and holdings. This approach helps students understand the "whys" of the rules and assists students in learning to apply them. Finally, expert students include examples and non-examples of each concept with explanations as to why the examples are examples and the non-examples are non-examples so they can remember not only the words of the rules but also their use. Chapter 13 explains how to create examples and non-examples.

How to check outlines for comprehension and accuracy. Writing a course outline creates an important opportunity that expert law students recognize and use. That opportunity is the chance to make sure they understand what they have learned and to make sure their outlines are correct and complete. By doing so as they create their outlines, expert law students free up their examination preparation time for memorizing the material and practicing the skills.

Expert law students check for comprehension as they are creating their outlines as part of the normal self-monitoring process. They do so in four ways. First, they make sure they understand the words of the rules and holdings they are including. Second, they make sure they can paraphrase the rules and holdings in their own words. Third, they make sure they understand the reasons for the rules. Finally, they make sure they can generate both an example that satisfies what the rule requires and an example that does not satisfy what the rule requires (a non-example).

Additionally, expert law students check the accuracy of what they are including in their course outlines. Perfect recollection of an incorrect rule or holding is, of course, useless. Expert law students check for accuracy by comparing their work with their peers, with the statements in the court opinions recorded in their case briefs and class notes, and with their instructors by asking questions about any rule or holding about which they have doubt. Because expert law students are working on their outlines throughout the semester, they have the opportunity to ask these questions because they are not competing with their peers who have procrastinated until the end of the semester.

A website addressing law school course outlines can be found at: http://www.udayton.edu/~aep/online/exams/outlin03.htm.

The above materials are organized in outline form in Figure 36 below to show the benefits and importance of closely structuring an outline. The outline reflects an effort to create hierarchy among the topics and to organize the material such that there is at least a II

Figure 36: Summary of Key Points re Outlining Courses

I. Outlining goals
    A. Structuring the student's learning
    B. Recording what the student needs to know for her exams to facilitate studying
    C. Checking for comprehension
II. How to create excellent law school outlines
    A. How to outline
        1. Starting early and keeping up on a weekly basis
        2. Organization
            a) Following traditional outlining techniques
                (i) For every I, there is at least a II, for every A, there is at least a B, for every 1, there is at least a 2, etc.
                (ii) Thinking through all of the subcategories so that the student thinks about how all of the material fits together (doing so causes the mind to create the mental structures needed to memorize learning)
            b) Using hornbooks, commercial outlines, the textbook, syllabi, etc. as guides for the relationships among topics, but having a unique structure
    B. What to include in the outline
        1. What the instructor regards as most important (flag it)
        2. All the rules of law stated in the cases, by the professor, in the notes after the cases, and in any assigned reading from other sources, such as restatements, statutes, hornbooks, etc.
        3. An example and non-example of each concept
        4. Detailed holdings for the cases that were assigned to read (i.e., how a particular court applied the rule to a particular case)
        5. The public policy implications of the rules and holdings
    C. How to improve the accuracy of the outline
        1. Comparing the outline with the outlines of fellow students who also have completed outlines and discussing the differences
        2. Making sure that all the words, concepts, and ideas that are included are understood by the student
        3. Developing a list of questions for the professor or study group and getting those questions answered

for every I, a B for every A, and a 2 for every 1. Exercise 12-2 provides an opportunity to practice creating a course outline.

Creating Graphic Organizers

Graphic organizers are particularly helpful tools because they allow the student to structure the information in the same way that the brain structures information. As a result of creating graphic organizers, the student's mental connections are stronger and therefore the student has an easier time recalling the information on exams. Depending upon how the items are counted, (because many types of graphic organizers are similar), there are **five types of graphic organizers** useful to law students[7]—timelines, com-

---

7. A sixth type of graphic organizer, overlap charts (or as they are more commonly known, Venn Diagrams) is of only extremely limited help to law students and therefore is not addressed beyond this footnote. A Venn Diagram might be used to identify similarities and differences between

parison charts, hierarchy charts, flow charts, and mind maps—each of which is detailed below. Some good websites that provide information about and instruction to help create graphic organizers are:

http://www.graphic.org/goindex.html;

http://www.eca.com.ve/gorg/default.HTM;

http://www.writedesignonline.com/organizers/cerebralflatulence.html.

While the strengths and weaknesses of each type of graphic organizer vary, depending on the usage, a few general points about the uses, strengths and weaknesses of graphic organizers are worth making at the outset. Graphic organizers are perhaps the best tools for organizing new learning because they allow the student to create structures that reflect their schemata and to depict in one place and on one page an entire body of learning in a way that helps students identify and develop connections among the concepts they are learning. Each of the types of graphic organizers has its best uses, strengths and weaknesses. Accordingly, while students should ascertain which types of graphic organizers work best for them and use the techniques that they find most salutary, students should also tailor their selection of graphic organizer to their learning task during the forethought phase and avoid being over-dependent on a particular technique when other techniques might be more effective for the particular learning tasks in which they are engaged.

Each of the five techniques are explained and demonstrated below. These discussions also identify the most common law school uses, the strengths and the weaknesses of each technique.

Timelines

Timelines are extremely useful graphic organizers because they allow learners to organize complex material in a way that allows them to recognize the sequence of events and to identify progressions. Students can create timelines to help them make sense of factually complex cases or law school exam questions where the sequence of events is significant. For example, a successful self-defense argument depends on what transpired before the defendant took action. Similarly, in contract disputes, which often result in both parties claiming the other breached the contract first, the sequence of parties' actions and of events can be crucial. Timelines offer insights into issues of causation; by seeing the sequence of events, students can develop theories about causation. Timelines, finally, are sometimes helpful in making sense of a line of cases all dealing with the same issue in which each deals with the issue slightly differently. Such timelines allow the student to better understand how the law evolved.

To create a timeline, students simply need to draw a line and mark the earliest possible starting point at one end and the latest possible event at the other end. It is helpful

---

cases addressing the same topic, but a comparison chart would be better able to reflect even normal levels of complexities and therefore comparison charts are explained below. Figures 2 and 4 in this text exemplify a seventh type of graphic organizer, cycle charts. Cycle charts are useful to non-lawyers because they can depict processes that recur. Law study, however, really does not lend itself to cycle charts.

to then mark a few intermediate points in time (for example, in a year-long sequence, marking three, six, and nine months is helpful). The student then plots each event along the timeline, identifying both the date of the event and the nature of the event, making sure that the events are correctly sequenced along the timeline. Figures 13 and 18 in this text are examples of timelines; Figure 13 is an example of a timeline a student might create to make sense of a factually complex court opinion.

There are some important limitations to timelines. First, timelines are very limited in the quantity of information they can depict. Students can communicate only small bits of information at any given location along a timeline. For complicated matters, timelines can remove necessary complexity. Second, students cannot readily use timelines to depict events that overlap or are of long duration. Moreover, students using timelines sometimes force events into a sequence that does not reflect what really transpired. In many, if not most, human interactions, events progress in an order that does not necessarily reflect strict causation. In other words, events can cause immediate responses but also can have longer-term effects, or may not result in an immediate effect but may later produce such an effect or may produce a result that really was a cumulative result of several events. For these reasons, students should use timelines only in situations where linear sequence is important and needs to be clarified.

Comparison Charts

Comparison charts are probably the graphic organizer with which you are most familiar. Comparison charts allow you to depict the similarities and differences among concepts or ideas. The items to be compared are listed down the left hand side of the table and the bases of comparison are shown across the top. Comparison charts help identify similarities and differences between and among like things. They are particularly helpful tools for helping synthesize (identify and think through the similarities and differences between) cases. They are also helpful for preparing students to spot issues because they allow students to identify the similarities and differences among like concepts and therefore assist students in identifying which one(s) would apply in a particular context.

To create a comparison chart, the student simply needs to create a table in which she lists the items to be compared along the left side (e.g., the names of the cases that will be compared) and, across the top, lists the characteristics on which the student will be comparing the items. In the context of a case comparison chart, these characteristics will depend on the facts the courts regarded as significant in each of the cases. After the student has completed the lists of cases and characteristics, she fills in the open boxes with the relevant information.

Figures 5 and 35 in this text are both comparison charts. Figure 5 compares 41 of the learning strategies addressed in this book and shows differences in their goals, names and descriptions. Figure 35 depicts the five types of rules according to three characteristics, the pattern of each, an example of each, and signal words for each. Note that the ability to depict all five patterns together on one page provides insights into the similarities and differences that would not readily be available from either the textual material or even from an outline of the textual material.

Figure 37 below depicts a helpful use of comparison charts for law students. It shows a use of comparison charts recommended in Chapter 15 for preparing to be able to use, for analyzing a new dispute, a group of cases that all address the same legal issue but which reach slightly different conclusions. Figure 37 shows a group of cases in which the courts have applied the rule that a party may be liable for damages sustained by the other party only if those damages were "foreseeable" at the time the contract was made. This area is a complicated area of law and, while courts for the most part agree about the name of the rule, foreseeability, and its definition, they disagree about its application to particular disputes. By organizing the five cases together, however, students can gain insights into how to apply the rule and how they might apply and distinguish the five cases. For example, by looking at this chart, a student wishing to argue that a particular loss was not foreseeable would immediately be able to see that the student would have to apply the *Hadley* and *Lamkins* cases and distinguish *Victoria Laundry*, *The Heron II* and *Hector Martinez & Co.* and to identify the key facts in each case that would allow such applying and distinguishing.

Comparison charts, while helpful for certain tasks, such as applying and distinguishing cases, have only limited application to other tasks. Because the student must fit all information in a comparison chart into pre-defined categories, the student may exclude important information simply because it cannot be classified into one of the categories. In addition, comparison charts can only depict a small amount of information and only in a limited way; more complex relationships among ideas often do not fit comparison charts. Nevertheless, as Figure 37 reflects, comparison charts are useful tools for law students to include in their arsenal.

Hierarchy Charts

Hierarchy charts depict the relationships among the materials to be learned in a top-to-bottom or broadest-to-narrowest structure. The items at the top represent the broadest or highest level concepts, the items at the next level represent the next broadest or highest level concepts and so on.

These charts are helpful in a variety of circumstances, but are particularly helpful when the student needs to learn not only the concepts but also the relationships among those concepts. Hierarchy charts depict those relationships explicitly and on a single page so that students can see them easily. For this reason, expert law students always choose to ascertain the relationships among the concepts they are studying.

As explained in Chapter 15, hierarchy charts also provide some insight into issue spotting because, by knowing the relationships among concepts, students are better able to identify likely links among issues and to recognize situations where the raising of a higher-level issue necessarily (or at least usually) implicates a lower-level issue. For example, in Contract law, a recurring issue is whether a party to a contract can get a court to order a party who has breached a contract to do what he promised to do. This issue frequently implicates an issue of damages measurement because a prerequisite to getting a court to issue such an order is proving that an award of damages would not fully repair all the harms suffered because of the breach.

Finally, hierarchy charts, such as Figure 33 at the beginning of this chapter, graphically depict how students likely store their law school learning in their brains. Because hierarchy charts replicate students' schemata, they facilitate students' memorization efforts. For this reason, expert law students do not depend on outlines to depict the relationships among the concepts they are learning. An outline of a topic, which likely in-

*Figure 37: A Comparison Chart Depicting the Application
    of the Forseeability Rule*

Case	Result	Holding
Hadley v. Baxendale	Not foreseeable	Loss of profits from inability to use mill stemming from defendant's failure to deliver broken shaft to repairperson held not foreseeable because defendant only knew the shaft was broken and not that mill could not operate until it was repaired.
Lamkins v. International Harvester Co.	Not foreseeable	Loss of crop profits stemming from inability to use plaintiff's tractor at night stemming from defendant's failure to deliver lighting equipment on time not recoverable because huge difference between cost of lights and loss suffered by plaintiff suggests defendant could not foresee the loss.
Victoria Laundry, Ltd. v. Newman Industries, Ltd.	Foreseeable	Loss of profits from inability to use new boiler caused by seller's delay in delivering a functioning boiler to laundering and dying business recoverable where seller knew business would be using boiler for doing laundering and dying.
The Heron II	Foreseeable	Loss caused by dip in value of plaintiff's sugar caused by defendant's delay in delivering sugar deemed foreseeable where defendant knew plaintiff was planning on selling the sugar.
Hector Martinez & Co. v. Southern Pacific Transport Co.	Foreseeable	Reasonable cost of renting equipment to use while awaiting delayed delivery by defendant delivery company of mining equipment foreseeable where plaintiff had purchased the equipment to use it for mining.

cludes examples, non-examples and policy, seldom fits on one page and therefore is only of limited use for this purpose.

To create a hierarchy chart, the student starts with the highest-level concept. It is drawn near the top of the page and in the center of the page. Next, about one-half inch lower on the page, all of the sub-concepts for that highest-level concept are drawn. All the items on the same level need to be the same height. Lines are drawn from the highest-level concept to these second level concepts. The student then looks at each of the second level concepts individually, and determines what sub-concepts are on the level below that second level. The student draws, about one-half inch lower than the second level concepts, all of the items on this third level and then draws lines from the second level item from which each third level concept emanates to the new third level items the student has drawn. The same thing is done for each of the other third level concepts. The student continues until she has fleshed out all underlying concepts. Note: This process can be done by computer using most word processing programs.

Hierarchy charts, however, can only depict a small amount of information. While they are very useful for seeing "the big picture" of a body of law, they cannot depict all the law a student needs to know unless the student creates an enormous hierarchy chart or makes multiple charts.

Figures 11, 14 and 33 are hierarchy charts. Figure 11 shows portions of a hierarchy chart that an expert law student might create to help make sense of a torts class. This chart allows the student to see in one place all the types of intentional torts against a person, an image that will help students remember each and will serve as a checklist to use on an examination.

Flow Charts

Flow charts often look a little like hierarchy charts but differ from them in crucial ways. Whereas hierarchy charts show the relationships among concepts, flow charts show procedures, the order in which to proceed on a task. Flow charts allow students to show both simple and very complex processes, including places in the processes where decisions would lead in different directions. They are particularly effective tools for depicting the processes involved in performing legal research. They also allow students to think through how they would work their way through particular types of problems. The disadvantage of flowcharts is that they tend to restrict student thinking. Students who rely too heavily on flowcharts sometimes fail to see complexities in a rule's application or to see arguments that will take them out of the process altogether.

To create a flow chart, the student first needs to determine all the steps involved in the particular process and the order in which those steps should be carried out. Once she has determined the steps, she can use arrows to show the relationships among the steps. The student needs to be sure to indicate places where a particular result on a step will take her out of the process or allow her to skip a step of the process. There are important conventions used by some people who create flow charts with respect to the meaning of different shapes in a flow chart. For example, a diamond indicates a decision step, a parallelogram indicates a data step, and a rectangle indicates a process step.

Figures 3, 7 and 25 are all flow charts. Notice that each of these flowcharts depicts a process that is relatively simple and linear in which the student simply works his or her way from step to step. Figure 38 on the next page depicts an approach to a complicated body of contract law, the parol evidence rule. The parol evidence rule (PER) deals with a situation where the parties to a contract have created a written agreement and one party seeks to testify about an alleged term of their agreement that is not reflected in the writing. Generally, the parol evidence rule prevents the party from testifying about the term. As the chart reflects, however, the process of resolving parol evidence rule issues is quite complex. Notice that the flow chart is really an approach to problems (including exam questions) in this particular area of law and therefore, once mastered, is a helpful tool. The chart shows how law students can translate a body of law into a flowchart.

Similarly, Figure 39 depicts an approach to federal question subject matter jurisdiction. Generally, federal courts may only entertain certain types of legal disputes (certain "subjects"). One type of dispute federal courts may hear is disputes raising issues that are matters of federal law. Again, while this basic notion is easy to understand, its application by the courts is much more complex. The flowchart in Figure 39 provides students with a structured approach to these problems.

Mind Maps

Mind maps, which are sometimes referred to as "spider maps," are very helpful tools for learning. A mind map is like a hierarchy chart in that a mind map shows the relationships among the concepts that the student is learning. The differences are that the connections and relationships need not be hierarchical. The student can connect anything she wants to know about the core concept or sub-concepts regardless of hierarchy. Consequently, the process of creating a mind map is more free-flowing than the process of creating a hierarchy chart and allows the learner the freedom to create her own connections and structure, to make sense of the material for herself. Mind maps also help students avoid creating artificial hierarchies because they need not force concepts into lower and higher categories. Because mind maps are more free-flowing, however, they are less helpful for showing real hierarchies. Also, like all types of graphic organizers, mind maps only can depict a limited quantity of information.

There are several steps to creating a mind map. First, the student starts with the central concept on which she is working. Then she draws a line connecting the main idea to each category or concept that relates to that main idea (e.g., the elements, the policy and the key cases applying the central concept). Then the student draws a line connecting each of the categories or concepts to its sub-idea(s) or sub-concepts (e.g., each element connected to "the elements"). This task is completed for each category or concept. Lines are then drawn connecting each sub-idea to each of its sub-sub-ideas (e.g., each element's definition). The student continues until she has completed her depiction of the central concept.

Figure 33, near the beginning of this chapter, is a mind map that a law student might create to depict the relationships among the elements that make up the definition of the common law crime of burglary. Notice how the crime is at the center of the definition, each of the elements is arrayed around the crime, and each element's definition comes out from that element.

Exercise 12-3 provides opportunities for you to try out two types of graphic organizers.

Figure 38: An Approach to the Common Law Parol Evidence Rule in
Flowchart Form

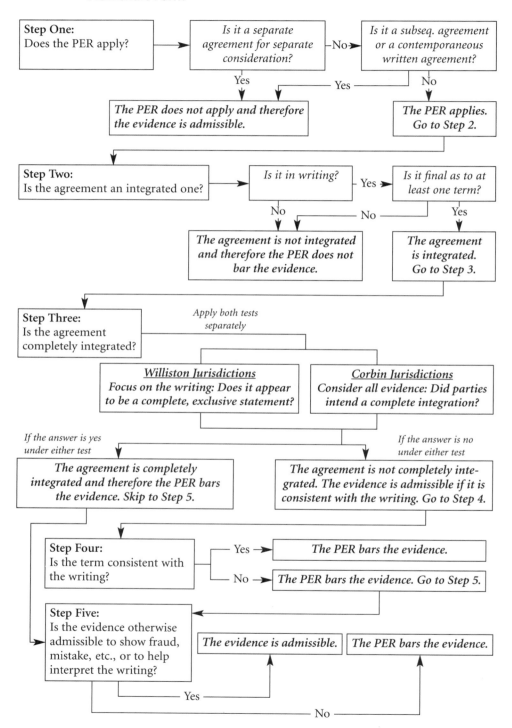

Figure 39: An Approach to Federal Question Subject Matter Jurisdiction*

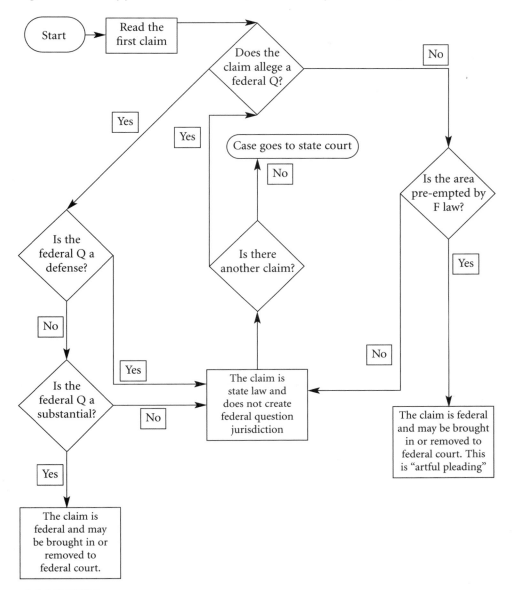

* Professor Greg Sergienko created this flowchart for his civil procedure students, and has granted permission to use this chart in this text.

Reflection Questions

1. Why is it helpful for law students to deconstruct rules? Why do they also need to be able to identify what type a particular rule is?

2. Have you ever created a course outline? For what course? Did it help you learn the course material? Did you violate any of the principles for creating an effective outline?

3. Have you ever created a graphic organizer? Which type? For what course? Did it help you learn the course material?

4. What types of students might benefit from creating graphic organizers? Why? Why might all law students benefit from creating graphic organizers?

5. (answer this question after you have completed Exercises 12-2 and 12-3) Of the strategies you tried in Exercises 12-2 and 12-3, which strategy worked best for you? Why?

References

Peter Dewitz, *Conflict of Laws Symposium: Reading Law: Three Suggestions for Legal Education*, 27 U. Tol. L. Rev. 657 (1996).

Gerald F. Hess & Steve Friedland, Techniques for Teaching Law (1999).

Barbara K. Hofer, Shirley L. Yu and Paul R. Pintrich, *Teaching College Students to Be Self-Regulated Learners* in Self Regulated Learning: From Teaching to Self-Reflective Practice 57 (D.H. Schunk, B. Zimmerman, Eds.1998).

M.H. Sam Jacobson, *A Primer on Learning Styles: Reaching Every Student*, 25 Seattle Univ. L. Rev. 139 (2001).

Rogelio Lasso, *From the Paper Chase to the Digital Chase: Technology and the Challenge of Teaching 21st Century Law Students*, 43 Santa Clara L. Rev. 1 (2002).

Cathleen A. Roach, *A River Runs Through It: Tapping into the Informational Stream to Move Students from Isolation to Autonomy*, 36 Ariz. L. Rev. 667 (1994).

Michael Hunter Schwartz, *Teaching Law by Design: How Learning Theory and Instructional Design Can Inform and Reform Law Teaching*, 38 San Diego L. Rev. 347 (2001).

Patricia L. Smith & Tillman J. Ragan, Instructional Design (1999).

Paul Wangerin, Learning Strategies for Law Students, 52 Alb. L. Rev. 471 (1988).

Claire E. Weinstein & Richard E. Mayer, *The Teaching of Learning Strategies in Handbook on Research in Teaching* 315 (M.C. Wittrock, Ed. 1986).

Chapter 13

Memorization Strategies

Introduction

It is common but by no means universal for law professors to say to their students, "I don't want you to memorize this material; I want you to *know* it." On the one hand, this statement is entirely correct; even being able to recite perfectly all the words of all the rules of law the student has learned does not equate to a passing grade in a law school class, much less an A or B. Law school examinations, as explained in Chapter 2, test the student's ability to apply the rules, not state them. In other words, on law school examinations, students must articulate and evaluate the arguments that reasonable lawyers representing all the involved parties might make.

On the other hand, the suggestion that law students should *not* memorize is perhaps the most misleading statement possible. To the contrary, nearly all law school examinations, even "open book" examinations, require students to have memorized huge quantities of information. *Expert law students memorize all the rules they have studied and the holdings for all the cases they have read.* In fact, studies of experts, not only within the legal field but also within all fields, reveal that experts not only possess more knowledge than novices, but also know it better and have organized it better.[1]

Expert law students are experts at memorizing law. They know how and when to use all the memorization techniques at their disposal, and they know which memorization techniques work best for them.

Students store new learning, as Chapter 3 explains, by making that new learning meaningful. This chapter details the five categories of techniques for making new learning meaningful so that it may be stored in long-term memory: (1) connecting new learning to the student's prior knowledge, (2) clustering and chunking, (3) associational techniques, (4) rehearsal, and (5) elaboration. For each, the chapter explains how to use the techniques in that category, when those techniques are most effective, and why those techniques facilitate recall.

Expert law students typically resort to **more** than one technique in any given circumstance. In other words, they not only connect their new learning to their existing knowledge (see below), but also they use rehearsal (see below), or mnemonics (see below) to help them memorize the new learning. They do so because they know that a

---

1. Patricia L. Smith & Tillman J. Ragan, INSTRUCTIONAL DESIGN 136 (1999).

memory trace, like a muscle, gains strength through exercise, and exercise, for a memory trace, involves processing the new learning as much and as deeply as possible.

Moreover, expert law students almost never postpone memorization until the last moment. Postponing memorization means the law student may be studying late into the night before the examination. This approach will actually decrease the student's ability to memorize because the brain works less efficiently if it has been deprived of sleep. Sleep, healthy eating and exercise have all been positively correlated with successful memorization and recall. In addition, studies have shown that **spaced study** (studying several times over a long period of time) results in students remembering more and remembering better than single event studying (also known as cramming). Consequently, expert law students space their memorization efforts throughout the semester rather than trying to memorize everything the night or even the day before the examination.

Expert law students also set mastery learning goals with respect to their memorization of course material. They do not simply decide they will study for a particular length of time or review their course materials a specified number of times. Recognizing the foolhardiness of taking chances with their learning, expert learners do not try to second guess their instructors and skip topics or legal issues on which they do not expect to be tested. Rather, they set a goal of memorizing, with 100% accuracy, everything they have learned in the course.

Finally, expert law students select memorization strategies based on their knowledge of all the strategies from which they might choose, their knowledge of the type of material to be memorized and their personal knowledge of what strategies work best for them. Accordingly, this chapter concludes with a comparative study of the fourteen memorization techniques addressed throughout the chapter.

Connecting New Learning to Prior Knowledge

One crucial way to make learning meaningful is to connect the new learning to existing knowledge. New learning can be connected to existing knowledge either directly, by identifying connections between the new learning and the prior learning, or through the use of organizational strategies.

The process of identifying connections between existing knowledge and the new learning is called **tuning**. The term tuning refers to the notion that the student is adjusting her existing schemata to accommodate the new learning. The deeper this tuning or connection (the more the student makes deeply analytical connections rather than superficial connections), the more likely the student will be able to recall that learning when the student needs it. Creating multiple connections, as noted above, between the new learning and the student's existing knowledge further increases the likelihood of recall, because it creates a greater number of mental paths to the existing knowledge.

What types of connections can law students make? First, students can make connections among their law school courses. For example, a first-year law student studying contracts might note the similarity between the contract defenses (misrepresentation, undue influence, mistake, and duress), intentional torts (battery and conversion), and crimes (larceny and burglary). In all three contexts, the party with the burden of proof must meet a series of elements based on some alleged wrongful conduct committed by the other party. The students may also be able to draw analogies between tort negligence law and contracts promissory estoppel liability. Both bodies of law impose liability for carelessness; negligence involves carelessness in conduct, and promissory estoppel involves carelessness in making promises.

Second, students can find connections between their law school learning and their undergraduate learning. Thus, students in legal writing courses who have taken rhetoric courses might note analogies between legal writing and the rhetorical techniques they have learned. Similarly, students who studied linguistics as undergraduates might note similarities between their linguistics studies and the language-focused technicalities of estates law. Students with a background in economics can draw analogies between the economic assumptions in contract and tort law and standard economics principles. Finally, history students can find connections between legal decisions and the historical context in which those decisions were made; for example, legal historians have found connections between important United States Supreme Court decisions and their historical context, such as decisions made during the Great Depression or World War II.

Third, students can make connections between what they are learning and their personal experiences, such as the legal troubles of relatives or their personal or workplace experiences. For example, a law student studying employment law may make a connection between the rule that generally allows employers to terminate employees at any time for any reason to their own experience of witnessing an employer terminate the employment of a colleague. Similarly, a student might try to reconcile his or her own experience with the legal system, such as an instance when the student received a traffic ticket for inadvertently exceeding the speed limit, to the general rule that crimes require intent (such a reconciliation *is* possible).

Sometimes, however, particularly with large amounts of new learning such as occur during the first year of law school, it is not enough simply to tune the new learning to fit within the student's existing schemata. The student, instead, needs to create entirely new schemata; this process of creating new schemata is called **restructuring**. Chapter 12 details the techniques expert law students commonly use to restructure/organize their new learning. As that chapter explains, organizational strategies help students develop the schemata so that they can store their new learning; they create the structure needed so that the student has a mental location in which to store the new learning. In this sense, by creating a mind map, hierarchy chart or flowchart, the student is building a storage facility for what they are learning, much like one might create a file drawer and set of folders to store new documents. In fact, the richness of the connections among the topics in a graphic organizer and the quality of its organization often determines whether the student succeeds in recalling the learning when the student needs it.

Moreover, the act of creating an organizational device of any type itself facilitates recall. The mental effort needed to mentally organize the material and then depict it on paper or on a computer screen constitutes a type of brain exercise that, for many students, will itself store the new learning in their long-term memories. Exercise 13-1 provides practice in connecting new learning to prior learning.

Clustering and Chunking

Expert law students recognize that it is easier to learn a large body of information in sub-groups of information than as a whole. In other words, rather than learning all the information at once, the learner remembers a series of groups. This activity of reorganizing a large amount of information into groups so it can be memorized is known as chunking. Most people have some familiarity with chunking because it is the technique that phone companies, after consulting with memory experts, adopted for phone numbers. Rather than giving a phone number as 9295550293, phone companies present phone numbers in chunks, i.e., 929-555-0293. By presenting the numbers as a series of three chunks, the phone companies make it easier for people to encode and therefore remember the number.

Clustering is a particularized form of chunking that involves organizing information into meaningful categories. In other words, the learner classifies the information into groups based on some set of criteria, such as their common features or the concepts that underlie them. For example, this chapter presents 14 memorization techniques (directly connecting to prior learning, organizational strategies, clustering and chunking, imagery, metaphor, four types of mnemonics, three rehearsal techniques and two elaboration techniques) in five clusters: (1) connecting new learning to the student's prior knowledge, (2) clustering and chunking, (3) associational techniques, (4) rehearsal, and (5) elaboration.

In law school, most of the information comes at least partially clustered, and the act of outlining or creating a graphic organizer provides the necessary associations. Thus, most texts present rules in chunks, and, even if they do not do so, students can and should readily do so, as explained in Chapter 12. Of course, the more clusters into which a student has chunked his or her learning, the more readily she or he will be able to retrieve that learning when needed.

Exercise 12-1 provided practice in clustering and chunking rules.

Associational Techniques

Associational techniques are similar to connecting new learning to prior learning. The difference is that the student creates the associations somewhat artificially and arbitrarily for the purpose of memorization, rather than as a means to facilitate understanding. There are three types of associational techniques, **images**, **analogies** and **mnemonics**.

Images

Expert law students create their own images to remember the essence of concepts they wish to remember. The student matches up the concept they wish to remember with an image that captures the key aspect of that concept. For example, a student wishing to remember the memorization concept "clustering," may imagine a star cluster. A star cluster is a group of stars from among the millions in the sky that appear to have been organized together into a particular pattern; this image helps the student remember that "clustering" is a learning technique that involves grouping information into categories based on their particular patterns or attributes.

Many legal concepts can be remembered through the use of images. For example, if a thief deposits money he has stolen into a bank account that also contains the thief's own money and then withdraws and spends some of the money in the account, the rule (in many states) is that whichever money was first deposited in the account is deemed to have been withdrawn first (the "first in, first out" rule). This rule can be remembered by imagining a bank account to be like a funnel; whatever first goes into a funnel is the first thing to come out of the funnel. Similarly, a law student can remember the parol evidence rule, a rule that prohibits the jury from hearing about contract terms not contained in the parties' written agreement, by imagining a wall dividing the terms not contained in the writing and the jury. This image is particularly apt because there are many ways to get somewhere that appears, at first glance, to be protected by a wall. A person can go over it, go around it, or even go through it (if that person is small enough to slip through a crack or strong enough to break the wall down). Similarly, there are many ways to avoid having evidence barred by the parol evidence rule. An image of keeping the evidence in a jail cell based on the similarity of the word "parol" to the word criminal law word "parole" would be an alternative powerful way of remembering the concept because it uses imagery and a mnemonic technique.

Slightly less efficacious are images based on arbitrary connections, connections that do not directly derive from the essence of the concept. For example, first-year law students learn that, to succeed on a claim for negligent misrepresentation, the fact misrepresented must be a "material fact." To memorize this rule, the student may recall that he received a sweater that appeared to be made of cashmere but which, in fact, was made of a synthetic material and may imagine the misrepresented "material" of his sweater every time he thinks about misrepresentation so that he recalls that a misrepresented fact must be a material fact. Similarly, a law student may choose to write the portion of her outline dealing with the measure of damages for breach of contract in green ink or on green paper, hoping to trigger recollections based on the association of green with money.

Images are excellent tools for remembering because they involve parts of the brain that students seldom use to remember what they need to learn. Thus, by creating a very different type of connection to the material they are memorizing, students strengthen their memory traces and ability to recall the material.

Analogies

The use of analogies as a memorization tool already has been described in the section above addressing connecting the new learning to the student's prior knowledge. The process of identifying the connections between the new learning and the prior knowledge is, primarily, a matter of analogical thinking—the student is identifying ways in which the new learning is similar to knowledge the student already possesses.

Mnemonics

A mnemonic device is a system or tool for improving recall of information. While mnemonic devices are quite powerful tools for remembering new learning, they are, for the most part, best used as a last resort methodology. In other words, experts agree that students only should use mnemonics when they cannot develop more meaningful associations. There are four types of mnemonic techniques: (1) the single-use coding method, (2) the pegword method, (3) the method of loci, and (4) the keyword technique. Generally, the selection among these methodologies depends on each student's preference. Also, learning experts agree that mnemonics can be a powerful and speedy learning tool, but they work best when each student generates personal mnemonics rather than using mnemonics developed by law school peers or predecessors.

Single-use coding. The first technique, single-use coding, probably is the only one with which you may be familiar. It actually refers to a widely disparate group of techniques. In its most common form, students first identify the first letter in a list of words or a list of sentences that they wish to remember. They then recombine the letters to create a new word or to create a sentence that uses words that begin with each of those letters. For example, many music students learned the order of notes, E-G-B-D-F, on the lines on a music staff by the sentence "Every good boy does fine."

This technique is helpful for remembering the key words in a list of elements. For example, property law students must learn the elements of a concept called adverse possession, a property law concept that allows a non-landowner to acquire title to property if the real owner ignores her property for many years while the non-landowner openly uses and improves that property. The non-landowner's use must be for the time period specified in the applicable state statute and must be (1) **h**ostile, meaning without permission, (2) **e**xclusive, meaning exclusive of the owner's use, (3) **o**pen and **n**otorious, meaning it would be visible if the true owner cared enough about the property to look, (4) **c**ontinuous, meaning without interruption and (5) **a**ctual, meaning must involve the whole area claimed. These five elements can be remembered by the following sentence: **H**is **e**nergy **on**ly **c**auses **a**nguish. Note that the first letter of each word references one of the above elements. Similarly, the elements of the common law crime of burglary are: (1) **b**reaking, (2) **e**ntering, (3) **d**welling house, (4) of **a**nother, (5) **n**ighttime, and (6) **i**ntent. These elements can be remembered by recalling that a burglar must be "**abendi.**" Although this mnemonic involves misspelling the word "abendy," it is particularly powerful memory tool because it actually combines two memory techniques, imagery, the image of a burglar bending her body to squeeze into a partially open window, and the mnemonic.

Single-use coding is also the term associated with the creation of rhymes, stories and jingles to help the learner remember something. For example, a student wishing to remember the four types of mnemonic devices might invent the following rhyme,

> *When I want to remember and cannot do so otherwise, it's mnemonics I will pick.*
> *They help me when I want to recall info that just won't stick*
>
> *The first requires using first letters to make a word or sentence I choose*
> *It doesn't matter the one I select as long as I call this method "single use."*
>
> *The second involves matching each number with one of the things I must know*
> *It's called the "pegword" method and rhyming is the best way to go.*
>
> *The third involves using my imagination to see a familiar place, room or wall*
> *It's the "loci method" when I match parts of the place to the things I must recall*
>
> *The last one involves making links that are best if they're bizarre or absurd*
> *It's a way of learning paired knowledge, and it's called the method "keyword."*

Similarly, every torts student must remember the five elements of negligence, which are: (1) the defendant must owe the plaintiff a *duty* of due care, (2) the defendant must *breach* that duty, (3) the defendant's conduct must cause **injury** to the plaintiff, (4) the defendant's conduct must be the ***proximate cause*** of the plaintiff's injury (not be too remote in the chain of causation), and (5) the defendant's conduct must be a **cause-in-fact** of the plaintiff's injury. These elements might be remembered using the following song (based on the children's song, "Mary had a little lamb").

*Mary had a little **duty,** little duty, little duty*
*Mary had a little **duty**—to use due care to Jim,*
And everywhere that Mary went, Mary went, Mary went
*And everywhere that Mary went, she **breached** that duty to him.*

*Her breach, it caused an **injury** to Jim, an injury to Jim, and injury to Jim*
*Her breach, it caused an injury to Jim that **proximately caused** his harm.*
*It also was a **cause-in-fact,** cause-in-fact, cause-in-fact,*
It also was a cause-in-fact, and so now Jim will own Mary's farm.

The pegword method. The pegword technique is a tool for memorizing items in an ordered list. It involves two phases. In Phase I, the student creates and memorizes (with a high level of automaticity) an arbitrary, rhyming association with each of the numbers within the sequence the student wishes to memorize. This phase produces a permanent set of associations that the student will use over and over again (the permanency of the associations is why a high level of automaticity is so crucial). Then, the student associates each item on the list she wishes to remember with the rhyming association (the pegword).

For example, a student who wished to memorize the nine planets in our solar system in order might remember them in the way depicted in Figure 40:

Figure 40: The Pegword Method Applied to the Order of the Planets in Our Solar System

Planet	Phase I	Phase II
1. Mercury	One is for sun	Associate sun with the **Mercury** in a thermometer rising
2. Venus	Two is for true	Associate true with true love, of which **Venus** is the Roman god
3. Earth	Three is for knee	Associate knee with kneeling down on the **Earth**
4. Mars	Four is for store	Imagine buying a **Mars** at the local grocery store
5. Jupiter	Five is for alive	Associate being alive and seeing with the giant, eye-like red spot of **Jupiter**
6. Saturn	Six is for tricks	Recall a magician doing magic tricks with rings and recall that **Saturn** has rings around it
7. Uranus	Seven is for heaven	Imagine **Uranus** sitting in the heavens between Saturn and Neptune
8. Neptune	Eight is for late	Imagine being late for a rainstorm and that **Neptune** is the Roman god of water
9. Pluto	Nine is for mine	Recall that you once owned a Disney **Pluto** stuffed animal

This method can readily be applied to aid recall of the elements of a claim or defense, although, in most instances, there is a common or even easiest order but not a required order in which you should analyze the elements. Consider the three elements of a contract claim for promissory estoppel and the possible associations depicted in Figure 41.

Figure 41: The Pegword Method Applied to the Elements of Promissory Estoppel

Element	Phase 1	Phase 2
The promisor made a promise that she reasonably could expect would induce action or forbearance by the other party	One is for sun	Associate sunlight with being able to see clearly and the requirement that the promisor should be able to anticipate (see) the action or forbearance
The promise must actually induce such action or forbearance	Two is for true	Associate true with the promisee acting true to (as a result of) the promisor's promise
Injustice cannot be avoided without enforcing the promise	Three is for knee	Imagine a knight on bended knee pledging adherence to justice

The method of loci. The third technique, the method of loci (or the place method), requires the learner to imagine a room with which she is extremely familiar, such as her living room, her bedroom or her classroom. Each has its advantages, although, if the student is readily familiar with the room in which she will be taking her examinations, that choice is probably optimal. (Of course, there may be some risk the student would be accused of cheating if her instructor sees her looking around the classroom at her fellow students or their desks.) The learner then slowly scans in her mind from one side of the room to the other, noting each thing (piece of furniture or decoration) in the room and identifying each item in her list of things to remember with something in the room. It is helpful to think of scanning the room like a movie camera might scan from one corner of the room all the way around the room and to imagine focusing on each thing in the room like a movie camera might zoom in on something important in the room. This approach allows you to organize your associations in a defined order and to create focused associations. For example, a student who wishes to learn the eight parts of speech: nouns, pronouns, verbs, adjectives, adverbs, prepositions, conjunctions and interjections, might imagine her classroom and start with the door to the classroom in her imagination.

- The first thing she imagines seeing is the classroom coat rack. She knows that coat racks are for hanging things and recalls that interjections (such as "Ouch!" or "Hey") are what writers use to hang emotions in their sentences.
- She then moves in her mind towards the student cubbyholes and recalls that cubbyholes are the place where the students place things like their backpacks and lunch boxes and recalls that nouns are persons (students), places (cubbyholes) and things (backpacks and lunch boxes).
- From the cubbyholes, her mind moves to the front of the classroom, where most of the action in the class takes place and associates that action place with verbs, which are the action words in a sentence.

- Next, her mind moves to a bulletin board on which her teacher places students' best work. She imagines the comments from the teacher on those student papers, such as "excellent" "good" "wonderful," all of which describe the papers and therefore are adjectives.
- Her mind then moves to the clock, which she recalls looking at frequently on days that are moving slowly, and she recalls that adverbs describe how actions are being performed. "Frequently" and "slowly" describe how often she is looking and how the clock is moving and therefore are adverbs.
- She then notices the candy box that her substitute teacher brought to class one day and left there, and recalls that pronouns, such as he, she and it, are substitute words used to represent previously used nouns.
- She then sees that the flag in the classroom is over the candy box and under the clock, and recalls that prepositions locate things in their place or time, just as she has located the flag over the candy box and under the clock in her imagination.
- Finally, she comes back to the front door of the classroom, which links the classroom to the rest of the school building, just as the conjunctions—and, or and but—link words and phrases.

This approach is equally effective for remembering legal rules. For example, a student who wishes to memorize the four requirements to accept an offer of a contract may use his bedroom as his focus location.

- Starting to the left of the door to his room, he first notices his dresser and recalls how he once brought a friend to his room and discovered, to his great embarrassment, that he had failed to put his clean laundry away. He may then recall his promise to himself that he would always put his laundry in the drawers as soon as he does it so that never again does a surprise visitor embarrass him. He can then associate that promise with the requirement that an acceptance express commitment.
- He then notices the poster for his favorite rock group and recalls that he was unable to get a ticket to the group's most recent concert and that only people who had a connection were able to get tickets. Similarly, the only one who can accept an offer is the person to whom the offer was made.
- Next, the student imagines seeing his bed and recalls that he had to buy the bed "on terms" because he could not afford the full price outright. He connects this recollection to the requirement that the offeree agree to all the terms specified in the offer.
- Finally, he scans towards the bedroom window. He recalls that the window often sticks closed and can only be opened if he finesses and jiggles it in just the right way. Similarly, an offer can be accepted only in a proper manner, a manner expressly required by the offer or reasonable under the circumstances.

This method works, as the above examples demonstrate, because the associations are personal to each student, have a visual component, and are easily created and easily recalled. It is, therefore, a very effective tool. In fact, the loci method was created by an Ancient Greek sect known for their ability to remember vast quantities of information.

The keyword technique. The final technique is known as the **keyword technique.** To use this method, a learner who is trying to learn a series of matched items, such as a list of elements and their definitions, associates keywords in each item of each matched set by imagining a bizarre image that combines each item in the associated pair. The student searches her brain for things that either sound like or look like each of the items in the matched set. The keys to effectiveness of this technique are the time spent on the task, the closeness of the matches between the images and the items being memorized and the vividness and uniqueness of the images.

For example, imagine that a student wishes to remember the three activities, self-monitoring, implementation and attention focusing, in which students engage during the performance phase of the self-regulated learning cycle. By identifying similar-sounding phrases, the student creates memory traces. Thus, the student associates "perfume" with "performance phase," associates "self-wandering" with "self-monitoring" and attentive locusts singing with "attention-focusing." She then puts it all together by imagining a perfumed elf wandering into a hive of attentive locusts that are singing. Law students would use this method to associate legal terms with their definitions. For example, consider Figure 42, which demonstrates the use of the keyword technique for each of the three elements of mistake, which is a defense to a claim that a party has breached a contract.

Figure 42: The Keyword Technique Applied to Each of the Elements of Mutual Mistake

Element	Definition	Associations	Image
Mistake	Both parties are unconsciously ignorant of a fact	Mistake: person saying, "Oops!" Unconscious ignorance: a person sleeping as something important happens	The parties somehow mumble "oops" in their sleep when they miss something because they are sleeping
Basic assumption	The mistake goes to the very essence of the contract	Basic assumption: base drum Essence of the contract: smell of paper	Smell of a paper drum
Material effect	The mistake has a material economic effect on the agreed exchange between the parties	Material effect: garment effects warmth greatly Economic exchange: money for goods	Exchange money for a garment that keeps you warm

The keyword technique, while helpful in certain circumstances, requires considerable effort to adapt to the complicated definitions common to legal usage and therefore may not always be a fruitful memorization tool for law students. Of course, the effort to use the technique almost always pays off because quantity of effort itself correlates with successful retention. In any event, the other mnemonics described above can be readily used in most legal contexts.

Exercise 13-2 provides practice in the use of associational techniques.

Rehearsal

By far, the most commonly used memorization technique in all learning contexts, including law school, is rehearsal. Rehearsal refers, in simplest terms, to practicing. The learner attempts, repeatedly, to speak out loud, say to himself or herself or write the information he or she is seeking to memorize. While rehearsal is the one strategy nearly all students know and use, it is almost never the best choice as a stand-alone strategy. Rather, expert students use rehearsal in tandem with other memorization strategies as described above, and only use rehearsal alone if other strategies are unavailing.

While rehearsal is not often the best strategy, it is nevertheless worthwhile knowing how to engage in productive rehearsal. Rehearsal, particularly in the law school context, can take many forms, and, in fact, there are best practices for using rehearsal. Actually, it is more accurate to state that there are worst practices for engaging in rehearsal. Rehearsal in the form of reading and re-reading one's class notes or textbook is extraordinarily inefficient and non-productive. More productive rehearsal techniques include: (1) the Gradually Shrinking Outline Technique, (2) the Course Summary Sheet Method, and (3) the Flashcard Method. Each of these techniques can be attempted by the student on his or her own or may be very successfully assisted by a family member or other loved one (friends and loved ones actually may appreciate the opportunity for interaction with the busy law student in their lives). What all productive rehearsal strategies have in common is that the student is practicing and actively testing herself as to whether she can do what she needs to be able to do during examinations—recall on command what she needs to be able to recall.

The Gradually Shrinking Outline Technique. Of the three rehearsal techniques, this method probably is the most effective because it combines self-testing with respect to the organization of the course material with self-testing of the details the student must know. To use this technique, the student must first complete her course outline (or, at least, a complete section of her course outline). The student starts this technique by going point-by-point through his or her outline to see if she can derive each of the rules from seeing the name of the concept or element. In other words, she covers up the definitions of each of the concepts with a piece of paper, book or even a hand and tests herself by speaking aloud the portion she has covered. She repeats this exercise until she can accurately recite all the rules.

The student then reduces her outline in half by only including things at a certain level of hierarchy, such as removing the elements and their definitions. She then tests her recall by speaking aloud the portion not reflected in the reduced version of her outline. Once she can do so, she reduces her outline to no more than five pages and again makes sure that she can recite the entire outline from looking at the five pages. Finally, she reduces the outline to one page and self-tests whether she can recite the entire outline from that one page.

The Course Summary Sheet Method. This approach is a variation on the gradually shrinking outline technique. At least twice during the semester (and, ideally much more often), the student forces herself to summarize the entire course (her entire course outline) on one page. She then tests herself to see if she can speak aloud the entire outline based on that summary sheet.

The Flashcard Method. Many students have used flashcards at some point in their educational careers, perhaps to memorize dates for a history test or to learn words in a foreign language. Flashcards have the advantages of being easy to create and easy to use for self-testing. On the other hand, flashcards really cannot depict the organization of a body of law and, therefore, expert law students create graphic organizers or course outlines to ensure they get the benefits of having an organized understanding of the course material.

There are two keys to successful use of flashcards. First, the student should create the flashcards for herself and not use commercially produced flashcards or flashcards created by another (or former) student. The act of creating the flashcards itself produces significant memorization (often students have memorized one-half or more of the material simply through the process of creating the cards). Recalling the material on the cards also triggers a memory of the episode of creating the card; this episodic memory is an additional memory trace. Moreover, only the creator of a set of flashcards can fully understand how the cards were intended to work and how they are organized. For example, every student leaves things out of their flashcards because they feel they already know those things, but the portion left out varies tremendously.

The second key to successfully using flashcards focuses on how the student uses the cards for self-testing. Expert learners recognize that they need to develop automaticity (see Chapter 3: How Humans Learn) to ensure rapid and easy recall during examinations. The easier it is for the student to recall her learning, the more brainpower the student can devote to the thinking demands created by the examination. This effort is crucial because law school examinations, as Chapter 2 explains, test analytical skills that require memorization of the knowledge but do not directly test the knowledge itself. In other words, memorization is a prerequisite for success but is not at all an insurer of success on law school examinations. Consequently, freeing up brainpower to focus on analytic efforts is crucial to success, and students need to develop automaticity with respect to the knowledge. This goal requires students to test themselves with flashcards until their recall is rapid and automatic with respect to every piece of knowledge they will need for the examination.

Exercise 13-3 provides practice in using rehearsal strategies.

Elaboration

Elaboration, which most expert learners automatically do, involves adding to new information to make sense of it. The learner fills in gaps, makes inferences, rephrases the information in words that make sense to the learner and imagines examples to process the new learning in her mind. Thus, for example, a student learning schema theory might infer that schema theory explains why the software designers created the folder/sub-folder organizational system on the student's computer. Similarly, a student learning the three tasks involved in the performance phase of the SRL cycle (attention-focusing, implementation and self-monitoring) might rephrase the tasks as (1) zeroing in on the learning, (2) doing the learning, and (3) making sure the student understands what she is learning. Finally, a student who learns that expert students seek opportunities for practice and feedback might recall examples from the student's past learning experiences in which the student either sought feedback or avoided it.

Elaboration is, in fact, an excellent learning tool, perhaps even the best memorization tool for law school learning, because it can produce both memorization and understanding of the material. From an understanding perspective, elaboration is the way learners make sense of new information; they attach their own independent meaning to the learning to reconcile the new learning with what they already know and understand. In fact, to be able to generate both an example of a concept and a non-example of that concept (a situation similar to the example, except as to the aspect critical to the concept), learners need to understand the concept well. Likewise, to be able to accurately paraphrase a principle, the learner must possess an accurate understanding of it. From a memorization perspective, elaboration facilitates recall in large part because the learner, by engaging in elaboration, is connecting the new learning to the learner's prior knowledge. Moreover, the deeper processing produced through elaboration, which involves more of the brain and greater mental effort than merely memorizing the information itself, also facilitates recall.

In the law school context, there are two particularly effective approaches to elaboration. The first technique involves **paraphrasing**. The student translates the words of the rule into his or her own words. The two crucial aspects of this technique are: (1) accuracy (which requires the student not only to study the words in the rule but also to study the cases that have applied the rule) and (2) using one's own words (rather than someone else's). Accuracy is crucial because a paraphrase is useless if it is wrong. Thus, expert law students may develop tentative paraphrases which they then test (and usually revise) as they read the cases that have applied the rule. Using one's own words (rather than adopting someone else's paraphrase) is crucial because the struggle to create the paraphrase is a large part of what creates the memory trace.

For example, nearly all contracts students studying contract formation read the Second Restatement of Contracts, which states that an offer of a contract is a "manifestation of willingness to enter into a bargain so made as to justify another person in understanding that his assent to that bargain is invited and will conclude it."[2] A student who has mastered this definition after studying it and reading the cases might paraphrase the rule as a "communication of commitment." Notice that this paraphrase boils down a very complicated rule into three simple words. Students in a criminal law class learn that a breaking, which is one of the elements of the common law crime of burglary, is "the application of force, however slight." A student who has mastered this definition after studying it and reading the cases might paraphrase the rule as "any volitional touching producing movement."

Exercise 13-4 provides practice in paraphrasing.

The second technique involves generating **examples and non-examples** of each of the concepts the student must learn. An example of a legal concept is a hypothetical situation that includes each attribute required by the rule defining that concept, and a non-example is a hypothetical situation that includes every non-critical attribute of the example but not all the critical attributes.

Thus, a law student studying the above definition of "offer" and having read the cases addressing the issue of offer might generate the following example and non-example:

Example: A says to B, "I promise to sell you my compact disc player for $40."

Non-example: A says to B, "I might sell you my compact disc player for $40."

Notice first that the example appears to include the crucial components of an offer; it is communicated (from A to B) and it expresses a completed decision to sell to B ("I promise"). Notice also that the non-example includes all of the non-critical attributes (both situations involve a proposed sale of a compact disc between the same parties at the same price). The non-example also contains a critical attribute, as it is communicated (from A to B). The non-example, however, communicates an undecided, rather than decided, state of mind and therefore lacks the second critical attribute, commitment.

---

2. RESTATEMENT 2D CONTRACTS §24 (1978).

Similarly, a law student studying the "breaking" element of burglary and having read the cases addressing the issue of breaking might generate the following example and non-example:

> *Example:* B kicks down the closed door to A's home, walks into A's house because he's planning to steal A's $5,000 stereo system, and he does so.

> *Non-example:* B walks in through a wide open door to A's house because he's planning to steal A's $5,000 stereo system, and he does so.

Notice the example includes the critical attributes of the breaking element; B uses (applies) force (in the form of a kick). Notice the non-example possesses all the non-critical attributes of the example, same parties (A and B), B has the same plan of action (stealing A's stereo), same additional actions (walking in and taking A's stereo). The difference, of course, is that the non-example omits any application of force; it is unnecessary because the door is already "wide open." The non-example requires a few additional comments. First, the non-example may nevertheless describe a burglary under modern statements of the definition of burglary, which generally omit the breaking element. Second, even at common law, even if the absence of a breaking would make B's actions a non-burglary, that conclusion would not have prevented B from being convicted of another crime, larceny. The important point is that the non-example accurately depicts a situation where there has been no breaking and therefore no burglary (assuming a breaking was a required element of burglary).

The final point worth noting is that the effort to generate examples and non-examples is a powerful tool for learning by law students because the student must know and understand the rule to generate each. Moreover, the example and non-example serve as additional paths to the words of the definition, thereby increasing the likelihood of recall. For this reason, this approach is a technique commonly used by successful law students to memorize their materials.

Exercise 13-5 provides practice in creating examples and non-examples.

Selecting Memorization Strategies

Ultimately, the selection of memorization strategies is task- and individual-specific. Each student needs to be an expert in his or learning preferences and make selections most likely to help the student achieve her mastery memorization goal. To facilitate that effort, Figure 43 takes a comparative look at the memorization strategies addressed in this chapter.

Figure 43: A Comparative Look at the Common Memorization Strategies

Strategy	Benefits/Strengths	Limitations/Weaknesses
Connecting in general to prior learning/analogizing	Reflects how information is stored in the brain	May be overdone and therefore may create misunderstanding No analogies may be availing for very new learning
Connecting to outlines and G.O.s	Reflects how information is stored in the brain	Can be difficult for learners with limited visual learning skills
Chunking and clustering	Reduces information to pieces that can be memorized	Does not address how the information will be stored
Imagery	Uses parts of the brain not commonly used for legal studies	Many legal concepts are difficult to reduce to images
Single use coding: first letter mnemonics, rhymes, and songs	Ease of use and familiarity; Songs and rhymes use parts of the brain not commonly used for legal studies	Connections are arbitrary and therefore less meaningful
Pegword Method	Ease of use	Connections are arbitrary and therefore less meaningful
Method of Loci	Powerful and easily adapted to law school learning	Connections are arbitrary and therefore less meaningful
Keyword technique	Powerful and often fun to use	Connections are arbitrary and therefore less meaningful. Requires particularly great mental effort to adapt to law school learning
Gradually shrinking outline	Easy to use and allows for easy checking of accuracy	Slow and can be less stimulating
Course summary sheets	Excellent tool for focusing on the most important points	May be too reductionistic
Flashcards	Excellent tool for drill and allows for ready check of mastery	Provides no information about organization of the material
Paraphrasing	Serves dual memorization and comprehension goals	May not equate directly to mastery memorization
Creating examples and non-examples	Serves dual memorization and comprehension goals and creates different type of memory trace	May be slow May not always equate to mastery memorization

Reflection Questions

1. Why is connecting new learning to one's prior knowledge a helpful learning tool?

2. What is the relationship between the organizational strategies you learned in Chapter 12 and memorization?

3. How does clustering facilitate memorization?

4. For what types of students is imagery a particularly powerful learning tool?

5. Why are mnemonics and rehearsal less favored memorization techniques?

6. Why are paraphrasing and generating examples and non-examples regarded as particularly effective memorization tools?

7. (answer this question only after you have completed Exercises 13-1 to 13-5.) Now that you have tried each of the memorization strategies described in this chapter, you can begin evaluating which of the techniques work best for you. Rank the techniques in order of your preference for using that technique. Explain your rankings.

References

Barbara K. Hofer, Shirley L. Yu and Paul R. Pintrich, *Teaching College Students to Be Self-Regulated Learners* in Self Regulated Learning: From Teaching to Self-Reflective Practice 57 (D.H. Schunk, B. Zimmerman, eds.1998).

Michael Hunter Schwartz, *Teaching Law by Design: How Learning Theory and Instructional Design Can Inform and Reform Law Teaching*, 38 San Diego L. Rev. 347 (2001).

Patricia L. Smith & Tillman J. Ragan, Instructional Design (1999).

Claire E. Weinstein & Richard E. Mayer, *The Teaching of Learning Strategies* in Handbook on Research in Teaching 315 (M.C. Wittrock, ed. 1986).

How to Study for and Take College Tests, http://www.partnershipforlearning.org/article.asp?ArticleID=757.

Remembering What You Read, http://www.csbsju.edu/academicadvising/help/remread.html.

Chapter 14

Strategies for Excelling in Legal Research and Writing Classes

Introduction

In many respects, legal research and writing (also known as "Professional Skills") courses are the most difficult courses a student will take during the first year of law school. In part, this difficulty stems from the fact that all of the other classes (known as "doctrinal" or "substantive law" classes) will be more similar to each other than they are similar to the legal research and writing courses. Doctrinal courses tend to focus on teaching students issue spotting and legal analysis skills, policy analysis skills, case reading and synthesis skills and a lot of knowledge about the particular doctrinal area under study (e.g., criminal law, contracts, torts). While legal research and writing courses focus on the foregoing list of skills, they also teach students legal research skills, citation skills and the drafting skills involved in creating particular types of legal documents, such as objective memoranda, written court arguments called "briefs," client letters and contracts. These courses also assume students have already developed excellent writing, paragraphing and grammatical skills.

Legal research and writing courses are also difficult because each of the course-specific tasks, e.g., legal research, objective memorandum writing, brief writing, writing client letters, is unique and exacting. Legal research is not exactly like any other form of research. It requires extensive brainstorming, a wide-variety of search strategies and substantial crosschecking to make sure the list of sources found is current and complete. The particular and specialized legal documents the student must learn to write have unique formats and require particularized language and writing style. Likewise, legal citation form requires a particularly high level of detail and accuracy, and legal research and writing instructors expect student papers to be error-free in this regard. Finally, legal research and writing professors expect law school papers to have flawless grammar, paragraphing, diction, word choices and sentence structures.

Because practicing lawyers regularly do all these things—perform legal research, use proper citation form and create the documents students learn to create in their legal writing courses—the importance of developing these skills and of legal writing courses cannot be exaggerated. In other words, the legal writing course is probably the most important first-year course students take in terms of preparing for the practice law.

Developing these skills will require you to develop a whole set of new learning strategies. For this reason, this chapter is divided into three sections: (1) strategies for learning legal research, (2) strategies for learning legal citation form, and (3) strategies for learning to write excellent law school papers. The purpose of this chapter is not to teach you legal research, citation or legal writing; that instruction is a part of your legal research and writing classes and is far beyond the possible scope of this book; rather, this chapter focuses on helping you become a thoughtful, reflective learner of each of the skills you need to learn and use in your legal research and writing course.

Strategies for Learning Legal Research

While, as noted above, legal research has many unique features, the keys to successfully learning this skill are the same as the keys to learning any other type of skill. First, from the outset, expert law students adopt a **mastery-focused** approach to their research projects, rather than aspiring merely to completing their assignments, passing their classes or getting good grades. Excellent research skills are among the most crucial skills for new lawyers because they are the ones employers expect recent law graduates to already possess. Moreover, by overlearning the recurring aspects of legal research, students free up brainpower to focus on the analytical demands of their research. In other words, students who have memorized the steps involved in finding cases and statutes can focus more on brainstorming topics, sub-topics and key words that will lead them to finding the cases and statutes for which they are looking.

Second, like most forms of research, a key to successful legal research is being **systematic**. In other words, expert law students work through the steps involved in pursuing their particular research goals in an organized, methodical and thorough way. They translate research approaches into checklists or flowcharts (see Chapter 7 for a discussion of "systematic guides" and Chapter 12 for a discussion of flowcharts) and then use those checklists to make sure they perform each step. For example, a somewhat simplified version of the steps involved in finding a statute might be:

1. STEP 1: If you know the citation for an applicable statute, go directly to the volume in which the statute has been published and get the statute.
2. STEP 2: If you do not know the citation of an applicable statute, brainstorm a list of words and short phrases describing the situation for which you are looking for a statute. Consider as possibilities abstract descriptions of your factual situation or basic principles or areas of law that you suspect apply.
3. STEP 3: Find the statutory index for the jurisdiction and look for the words and phrases you have brainstormed. If you find the words with a statute or statutes listed next to them, list all the statutes and go to the volume in which each appears and get that statute.
4. STEP 4: If you cannot find any of the words and phrases you brainstormed, brainstorm additional words and short phrases and then repeat step 3 above.
5. STEP 5: If, after performing step 4 above, you still cannot find a statute, look for the words and phrases in a treatise or other secondary source (which may either list applicable statutes or, at least, suggest additional words and phrases you might look for in the statutory index).
6. STEP 6: If you still have not found statute, your search is flawed or there is no statute on point or you will only be able to find a statute by first reading cases. Go to case research procedure.

As a checklist, this approach might look like Figure 44 below.

Figure 44: A Checklist for a Simple Statutory Research Project

☐ Do I already have a statute on point?
    ☐ **Yes.**   Get the statute.
    ☐ **No.**   Go to next task.

☐ Brainstorm applicable words and short phrases
    Word or phrase 1:   Word or phrase 2:
    Word or phrase 3:   Word or phrase 4:

☐ Find the statutory index and look for the words and phrases.
    Did I find any statutes using the above words and phrases?
    ☐ **Yes.**
        List all the statutes I found.
        Get each statute.
    ☐ **No.**   Go to next task.

☐ Brainstorm alternative words and phrases.
    Word or phrase 1:   Word or phrase 2:
    Word or phrase 3:   Word or phrase 4:

☐ Find the statutory index and look for the alternative words and phrases.
    Did I find any statutes using the alternative words and phrases?
    ☐ **Yes.**
        List all the statutes I found.
        Get each statute.
    ☐ **No.**   Go to next task.

☐ Search a treatise for all the words and phrases I have brainstormed.
    Does the treatise contain any of the words and phrases I brainstormed?
    ☐ **Yes.**
        Read the applicable sections and search those sections for statutory references.
        List all statutes referenced, if any.
        Get each statute.
    ☐ **No.**
        Go to case research procedure.

Exercise 14-1 gives an opportunity to try to translate a simple case-finding procedure into a checklist or flowchart.

Expert law students also check their work as they go (self-monitor—see Chapter 7). In fact, expert law students check their research several times while the research is in progress (as they work their way through each of the steps, for example) and after they finish, to make sure both that they have found all the resources they needed to have found and that the resources they have found still reflect current law.

Third, expert law students are **persistent**. Legal research, like all forms of research for all researchers, is a trial and error process. Some research paths inevitably fail, even for expert legal researchers; consequently, *almost all beginning legal researchers go down some research paths that prove useless.* Because expert law students expect to encounter some useless paths and possess the self-efficacy to believe they can and will find authorities they can use, they persist even when they repeatedly encounter difficulties. Moreover, because expert learners expect to encounter difficulties, they discover their errors at a time when they can still rectify them. Novice learners, in contrast, see difficulties as failures and as a reflection of their inadequacies and, as a result, either give up in frustration too readily or assume they are finished too soon.

Fourth, expert law students **organize** their research during all phases of the research process. They use the organization strategies discussed in Chapter 12, including outlining, mind mapping, flow-charting and hierarchy charting both to plan their research processes and to help them identify the structure of the legal materials they are researching. For example, a student researching a torts question might create the hierarchy chart depicted in Figure 11, and a student researching common law burglary might create the mind map depicted in Figure 33. By identifying the structure of those materials, i.e., how the various research topics fit together, they ensure that they identify all the issues and sub-issues raised by the materials, improve their understanding not only of the materials but also of how those materials fit together, and help themselves organize what they find in a way that makes the writing process better and speedier. In other words, just as expert law students in doctrinal courses must organize the law they are learning, expert law students in legal writing courses also organize the law they are learning.

Fifth, expert law students do not hesitate to engage in **help seeking**. They recognize their need for help and seek the help they need from whatever resources are permissible within the scope of the class. Thus, when they encounter difficulties, expert law students seek help from their texts, their peers, their professors and from their law school's librarians, a resource that tends to be particularly underused by law students.

Finally, expert law students are **reflective** researchers. While they are researching, they are constantly reflecting on and learning from their success and errors, planning how they will alter their future research approaches based on their results. They keep careful research records, by using charts such as the chart in Figure 45 below, to record their selected research methods, their initial perceptions and ultimate perceptions of their results and their time on task. They dedicate a small notebook to such record keeping so that the notebook can serve as a tool not only for their law school legal research efforts but also for their efforts as new lawyers. After they have obtained feedback from their professors about the success of their efforts, they study their logs and reflect on how they can improve their research skills and on the accuracy of their perceptions of the success or failure of their selected strategies. Accuracy in students' perceptions of the effectiveness of their research efforts is a crucial skill for legal researchers because it allows them to know when they need to keep researching and when they can confidently stop researching, knowing they have found everything they needed to have found. Expert students, in other words, use their logs as a resource for planning future new research projects. Where possible, they analogize new research projects to past successful research projects and adopt methodologies that proved successful in the past. If the closest analogy is a less successful project, they reflect on, brainstorm and systematically plan alterations to those less successful approaches. This thoughtful approach allows the students to refine their research skills and increase their success levels and speed.

Exercise 14-2 allows you to use the research log in Figure 45 for your first research assignment in law school.

Figure 45: A Model Research Log

Research Topic[1]	Strategy Used[2]	Time[3]	Initial Result[4]	Final Result[5]

---

1. Write the specific subject you are researching. Make sure you write the subject each time because, as you become more expert in the subject, you will be refining your understanding of the topic.

2. List separately each specific strategy, including the specific resource (AmJur, Witkin, etc.) that you are using. List each strategy on its own line so you will later be able to evaluate its effectiveness. Note that, for each research project, you will need to use multiple strategies. For example, you often may start by reading a treatise to gain background insight into the subject and to identify the most significant cases in the general subject area before you look for statutes or cases on point in a code or case index.

3. Record the amount of time you spent on this approach.

4. State your initial impressions of whether your approach was successful. Did you find what you were trying to find?

5. Indicate whether you have found everything you were supposed to have found, what you did not find (if anything), and why your approach either succeeded or did not succeed.

Strategies for Learning Legal Citation Form

Students' difficulties in learning legal citation form stem less from problems in comprehension than from issues of goal setting, diligence, attention to detail, and self-checking. In other words, students who choose to learn citation form inevitably do so.

Thus, setting a mastery goal is a crucial prerequisite for success. Students who set a mastery citation goal, in fact, engage in a very similar set of behaviors. They memorize all the major citation rules, force themselves to look up any rule about which they are uncertain and practice not only by doing any assigned exercises from their instructors, but also the lessons available developed by the Center for Computer-Assisted Legal Education (CALI) at http://lessons.cali.org/cat-lwr.html. CALI lessons have been developed and are available at the above-referenced link for both of the two major citation formats used in legal education, the Harvard Bluebook, and the ALWD Citation Manual.

Students who master citation also recognize that success requires not only mastery of the rules relating to *citation form*, but also mastery of the rules relating to the citation usage. For a very simple example, if a student quotes directly from an opinion, the student must not only provide a general citation to the opinion, but also the specific page(s) on which the words appear. Similarly, even if the student paraphrases the words used by a source into her own words, she nevertheless must cite the authority, even if the student is describing, in her own words, the current or former state of the law.

In addition to setting a mastery goal, expert law students recognize that diligence and attention to detail are the keys to using accurate citation form. In other words, nearly all citation questions can be answered by reference to the proper section of the citation manual assigned to the course. By being diligent, students therefore always can ascertain the format most appropriate to the resource to which they are citing. Having found the proper format, accuracy then primarily becomes a matter of attending to details with respect to the following matters:

(1) capitalization,
(2) parentheses,
(3) commas,
(4) periods,
(5) abbreviations,
(6) spacing,
(7) font style (e.g., the use of italic font style), and
(8) required information (what information about the source should be included).

Finally, expert law students always double-check their citations before they hand in their papers. Citation form is a matter that students readily can address correctly through effort. In many respects, the points or credit allocated by professors to citation form provides an easy way for students to get points on their papers.

Strategies for Learning to Write Excellent Law School Papers

Writing excellent law school papers helps students achieve multiple goals, including goals that extend well beyond the particular class for which the papers were written. First and most obviously, the effort involved in producing excellent law school papers helps students master skills crucial to their success as lawyers and achieve excellent grades in their legal research and writing courses. For many employers, grades in these courses are an important measuring stick of students' potential as lawyers. Second, many students use their papers as writing samples in their applications for clerking experiences while in law school and for jobs after they graduate. Third, many employers view participation on a law school's law review as a benchmark of student excellence, and most law schools' law reviews require students to participate in a writing competition as a condition of participating on the law review. Students who write well do well in these competitions. Law students, therefore, have many reasons to master legal writing skills.

Mastery of legal writing skills is a function of two things: (1) mastery of the issue spotting, legal analysis and legal reasoning skills that will be a focus of your legal research and writing courses (which are beyond the scope of this chapter and text), and (2) mastery of the two phases of legal writing—a preliminary phase, in which students plan their writing process, and a trans-writing phase, in which students engage in a series of behaviors designed to insure they produce an excellent final product. Fortunately, mastering the two phases is a matter of effort, not aptitude.

There are three steps in the preliminary phase. They can be remembered by imagining the start of a race. The starter says, "On your marks, get **SET**, and go!" The preliminary steps reflect how law students "get set;" they are:

(1) Set mastery goals,
(2) Exert control over where work will be done, and
(3) Take control over the time.

The activities in the second phase describe behaviors that occur while the student is writing and therefore may be termed "trans-writing activities," activities in which students should be engaged throughout the writing process. These activities can be remembered with the following mnemonic—FORCE:

(4) **Following** instructions from the professor,
(5) **Organizing** and planning before, during and after writing,
(6) **Reflecting** on the process, progress and results throughout,
(7) **Caring** to systematically revise and edit the work, and
(8) **Emulating**, *properly*, expert legal writers.

Each of the eight activities in the preliminary and trans-writing phases is described below.

Preliminary Writing Activities

Success on law school papers depends, in significant part, on how students start their writing process. A student who starts her writing process improperly is like a branch of a tree that starts growing in an awkward direction; it is virtually impossible for either the branch or the student to end up in the proper position.

Setting mastery goals. As is true of all learning tasks, expert students begin by setting mastery goals (see Chapter 5). In the writing context, a mastery goal plays a crucial role throughout the process. Law students who set mastery goals are more likely to plan their writing process, adjust that process as they work and reflect on the process after they have completed it, all of which are keys to success on law school papers. In fact, for legal writing assignments, students need to set not just one, but multiple goals. The goals should include goals that address the various aspects of writing a law school paper, including issue spotting, legal analysis, legal reasoning, case analysis and synthesis, writing, paragraphing, organization, word choice, usage and grammar, and citation form.

Exerting control over the writing environment. Expert learners also recognize that writing papers requires them to pay particularly close attention to issues of environmental control. Selecting an appropriate location, allowing time for rest, sufficient sleep and nutrition all bear on the success of law school papers. Moreover, many students find that they efficiently and effectively can write in the same location where they study. Finally, while students on their own must do most legal writing assignments, students sometimes may have permission to collaborate in whole or in part. Expert law students always take advantage of such collaboration opportunities, recognizing they can produce a superior product in a small group to any product they could have produced on their own.

Managing time. Time management is a particularly crucial strategy. Nearly all of the strategies discussed in this chapter assume the student has carefully managed her time so that she has sufficient time to engage in each. All new law students struggle to find the time to complete all their work. In the context of legal writing papers, one of the most crucial issues is planning. Students writing legal writing papers must learn to work backward from their assignment due dates and plan their time so that they have the time they need for brainstorming, research, writing, reflection and re-writing.

For example, imagine that a student has received a legal writing assignment that is due in two weeks. To produce an excellent paper, the student will need to devote time to at least the following tasks:

1. Reading the assignment and any background materials.

Figure 46: A Calendar for a Hypothetical Two-Week Legal Writing Assignment

Monday	Tuesday	Wednesday	Thursday	Friday	Saturday	Sunday
Receive and read assignment; identify issues	Develop research plan; begin research	Complete research; check results	Reflect on research; read and analyze authorities	Read and analyze authorities; apply to assignment	Plan and organize paper (develop detailed outline); begin writing first draft	Write first draft; follow-up research
Finish follow-up research; edit first draft	Reflect on first draft; begin writing second draft	Finish second draft	Edit and reflect on second draft	Write third draft	Edit third draft; check authorities and cites; do final research	Write final draft; copying

2. Brainstorming and identifying the legal issue(s) raised by the assignment.
3. Developing a research plan.
4. Performing the research and checking those results for completeness and accuracy.
5. Reflecting on the research results.
6. Reading and analyzing the authorities the student has found (cases, statutes, law review articles, etc.).
7. Analyzing the implications of those authorities for the assigned legal issue(s) (in other words, applying the legal authorities to the facts of the hypothetical dispute assigned to the student).
8. Planning the paper.
9. Writing multiple drafts of the paper spaced out over several days.
10. Performing any additional research that (often) becomes necessary.
11. Editing the paper, not only for errors in legal writing, but also for errors in grammar, diction, usage, punctuation, sentence structure, paragraphing, and organization.
12. Reflecting on the drafts.
13. Checking the accuracy and continuing validity of the citations upon which the student has relied.

These thirteen activities must be spaced throughout the two weeks assigned for the paper so that the student is able to complete all the tasks, complete the work assigned in all other courses, fulfill any responsibilities the student has to the significant others in her life and get sufficient sleep, food and exercise. Moreover, just as spacing produces better learning in the context of studying, it also produces better learning in writing papers. Spaced time allows students more time for reflection and more opportunity to check their research results for completeness, their writing for grammatical accuracy and their citation for form.

For this reason, expert law students become expert at managing their allotted time for legal writing papers. The moment they receive an assignment, they pull out their calendars and budget their time. They work backwards from the due date, estimating the time required for each of the tasks and spacing the tasks throughout the two weeks to allow for the necessary reflection and thinking time. The calendar in Figure 46 suggests one set of possibilities.

In looking at Figure 46, it is important to keep in mind three things. First, the point of Figure 46 is not to suggest that every law school paper should be produced according to this particular schedule. There are many scheduling issues that might alter the above schedule. For example, although Figure 46 reflects an attempt to assign larger portions of the work to weekend days, some students may choose to do even larger chunks of the work on weekend days and smaller chunks on the other days. This choice would be particularly wise if the students have midterms or other assignments in their other classes. Second, law school projects vary greatly in their degree of research and analysis difficulty, and expert law students know that they need to apply any schedule flexibly. In other words, some projects may require more research time or more thinking time than the hypothetical project in Figure 46. Finally, law school papers inevitably require students to make adjustments as they work on the project; the ability to adapt, both in terms of research and analysis and in terms of scheduling and planning, therefore, is crucial. For these reasons, the real lesson of Figure 46 is that expert law students do not procrastinate with respect to their legal research and writing assignments and always allocate time for adapting, editing, analysis, organization, reflection and rewriting, all of which are crucial to success on law school papers and many of which are omitted by novice law students.

Exercise 14-3 provides practice in using a calendar to plan a legal writing paper.

Trans-Writing Activities

Because legal writing is such an adaptive process, students need to engage in most of the strategies that are key to success on law school papers throughout the process. These trans-writing activities require students to work back and forth from their research, their notes, their assignment materials and their outlines and graphic organizers.

Following instructions. It may surprise new law students to find out that as many as **one-third** of their peers will lose points on their assignments simply because they did not follow their professor's instructions. Most legal writing assignments include easily-complied with specifications regarding number of pages, margins, fonts, collaboration restrictions, due dates and times and other similar matters. Because courts will refuse to accept court filings that violate similar court prescriptions, most legal writing professors either refuse to accept papers that violate these requirements, or they deduct points from the students' scores for such violations.

Most assignments also constrain the breadth of the students' tasks. These directions specify matters such as jurisdiction (the body of applicable law) and the issues the students must analyze. The directions may even provide research guidance or steer students away from problematic research paths. Most importantly, the directions include the facts of the legal matter the students must research. Many law students err either by omitting from their papers key facts stated in their assignments or by including facts not stated in their assignments.

For these reasons, expert law students devote considerable time not only to reading, taking notes on and analyzing their assignments when they receive them, but also to re-reading the materials and to checking and rechecking their work product against the requirements to make sure they have fully complied with the assignment instructions.

Organizing and planning. Novice legal learners also tend to underestimate the importance of an in depth effort at organizing and reorganizing their papers. Even those who claim they "outline" their papers tend to treat outlines as a place to list topics, rather than as a detailed structure that identifies not only topics but also the flow and connections between topics. As a result, many novice legal writers, including many who claim to write from outlines, write by what might be termed a "stream-of-consciousness method." Having produced only a skimpy plan for their essays, these students link sentences only in the sense that each sentence generates the next one and connect ideas solely by the order in which the student had the ideas. Their papers therefore reflect little choice and less self-control. In legal writing, this approach is particularly problematic because clarity and organization are both crucial and closely related.

Expert law students develop highly-structured, detailed outlines to plan their papers, planning the order in which they will address the issues, how they will present the issues, and where and how they will integrate the cases, statutes and other authorities upon which they base their arguments and explanations. These outlines are created on their computers so that the students can expand them, add topics, insert sub-topics and otherwise edit their outlines. In fact, expert law students revise and expand these outlines throughout the period of time they have allocated to work and reflect on their projects, even after they have completed the first few drafts of their papers. Sometimes, students' outlines cause them to make revisions in their papers, and sometimes the drafts cause them to make revisions in their outlines. In other words, expert law students' outlines serve as a check on their papers, allowing the students to make sure they have included everything they needed to have included and have organized their efforts in a way that is easy for the reader to follow.

In many legal writing courses, professors provide considerable and explicit guidance as to the overall organization of student papers and as to the structure and format students should use in writing various aspects of their papers. Expert law students, of course, integrate these structural requirements into their outlines.

Reflecting. In all writing contexts, both within the legal field and outside it, reflection characterizes good writing. Excellent legal writing, like all good writing, always reflects a large set of **choices**, choices about the organization of the paper, about how to meet the needs of the readers and about the readers' reading comprehension skills, about the structure of sentences and paragraphs, about the relative persuasiveness and ordering of arguments, about the inclusion and omission of particular matters, and about the use and reliance on authorities. For example, this book reflects dozens of small outlines, revisions and reorganizations, thousands of rewritten sentences and dozens of reorganized paragraphs. It reflects choices about sentence length and about the need to include analogies, examples and graphic illustrations. It also reflects many assumptions about the readers' interests and abilities.

In fact, in some law schools, students are encouraged to include comments on their papers or attach memoranda to their papers in which the students explain their perceptions of the sets of choices open to them and their reasons for making the particular choices they have made. Even at law schools where students cannot do so, expert law students write and think about their papers as if they are required to make such submissions.

Reflection also requires students to be **teachable**. Being teachable means the student is open to learning, receptive to feedback and unafraid of criticism. Many writing professors will say that being teachable is the most important quality of successful legal writing students. This skill is particularly crucial because legal writing students almost always receive frequent and detailed feedback about their work. In many instances, the sheer quantity of feedback can be daunting or frustrating, particularly for students who are used to receiving mostly positive feedback on their writing.

Most importantly, legal writing is a conscious, systematic process over which the most successful learners exert considerable and continuous **control**. Most novice legal writers regard writing as an almost mystical process in which the student awaits inspiration until shortly before the paper is due and, once inspiration hits, writes continuously until the student has finished the entire paper. They are wrong. Expert legal writers engage in a constant dialogue with their papers, their research and their thoughts, asking themselves questions during every phase of the writing process. Figure 47 below suggests some questions the student can ask herself before she writes, while she is writing, and while she is revising her paper.

Systematically revising and editing the paper. Nearly every text, article and website addressing legal writing (and, for that matter, all writing) emphasizes the importance of editing. In fact, most writing experts agree that editing is the key to successful writing. Even the best writers cannot produce a flawless first draft. Rather, expert writers *plan* for revision, not only by assigning blocks of time to the task but also by leaving space in their drafts for making revisions by skipping lines. In fact, as they are writing (see the above section on reflection), expert writers identify places in their drafts that are particularly troublesome and leave extra space in their drafts to remind themselves later that they felt those sections required particular attention and to allow for such revisions.

Many writing experts make a distinction between revising and editing, using the term revising to refer to changes to the work that address the organization and content of the paper and the term editing to refer to changes addressing matters of style and writing propriety, including diction and usage, word choice, sentence variety, paragraphing, grammar and punctuation. Because legal writing instructors grade law students both on the organization and content and on the style and writing propriety of their papers, law students must engage in both revision and editing, and this chapter uses the terms interchangeably.

While every writer edits her work differently, there are best practices with respect to how to approach the editing process. Experts agree that the following seven techniques facilitate the editing process:

- *Work from a hard copy, not on a computer screen.* Reading printed text is easier and increases both the accuracy and amount of editing.
- *Take a break before moving from the drafting to the editing process.* Do not go immediately from writing the paper to editing it. Space the writing and editing by at least two hours (and, preferably, one day). This technique, of course, requires students to plan their process to allow for such a break.
- *Read the paper aloud.* Reading aloud helps students identify errors and awkward sentences because it engages both the visual processing and the auditory processing parts of their brains.
- *Re-read the paper multiple times, focusing on a different writing issue each time.* Singleness of purpose as the student reads makes it easier to identify problems. Thus, read once for sentence issues, once for paragraphing issues, once for transitions between sentences, once for citation, once for proper legal analysis, etc.
- *Revise sentence-by-sentence and word-by-word.* It is much harder to identify errors in one's own work than to find errors in someone else's work. Consequently, self-editing requires more work. Students must force themselves to read their papers one sentence at a time and reflect on each sentence before moving on to the next one.

Figure 47: Reflection Questions for Legal Writing Papers

While reviewing the assignment and planning my research
1. Do I understand what I am being asked to do? Who is my imagined reader?
2. When have I written something similar to this paper?
3. What do I predict is the proper analysis of the issue(s)?
4. What alternative research approaches are possible? Why do I believe my research plan is the best approach?
5. On what skills am I being evaluated by this assignment? What are my professor's expectations for this project?

While doing the research and analyzing the facts in light of the research results
6. Is my research approach working? If not, how should I change it?
7. Do I understand the authorities I am reading? If not, where can I get help?
8. Why have the courts (or why has the legislature) decided _____ issue in this way?
9. What could I be researching that I am not researching? Why have I chosen not to do this additional research?
10. What is the broadest possible interpretation of the authorities I am reading? The narrowest?

While planning my paper
11. What are the possible ways I could organize my paper?
12. Why have I chosen to organize my paper this way as opposed to any other way?
13. (for each point I plan to make or decide not to make) Why am I including _____ point? Why am I not making _____ point?

While writing my paper
14. (for each sentence) Why am I including this sentence? How else could I phrase this? Would that alternative phrasing be better?
15. Is my discussion logical? Would my imagined reader understand each point?
16. Would I feel comfortable making this point in speaking with a judge?
17. (for each point or sentence I chose not to include) Why am I not including _____?
18. What paragraphs in my paper feel wrong or off to me? What sentences or words sound wrong or off? (highlight them, circle them or underline them and move on)
19. Where will I need to expand on the next draft? What will I need to revise?

While editing and rewriting my paper
20. What are the flaws, if any, in each of my arguments? My paragraphs? My sentences? My word choices?
21. Is my paper persuasive? Well-written?
22. What could have I done differently? Why do I believe the choices I made were the best ones?
23. How do I predict I will do on this assignment? Why do I predict I will receive that grade?

While reviewing my instructor's feedback on my paper
24. How did I do on this assignment? Did I do as well as I had predicted? Why or why not?
25. What were the most significant weaknesses/biggest errors in my paper? How can I avoid making those errors in the future?
26. What will I do differently on the next project? What will I do the same?

- *Read the paper as an intended reader.* For editing purposes, students need to read out-of-character; they need to imagine themselves as the reader and not the author. This task is made particularly difficult because law school papers have an imagined reader and an actual reader. The identity of the imagined reader will come from the assignment; the assigning materials will designate whether the student should write her paper as if it will be read by a judge, by a client or by another attorney, such as the student's employer or the attorney representing an opposing party. The actual reader, of course, will be the student's legal writing instructor. To apply this technique properly the student must imagine herself in both roles.
- *Work from a checklist.* Many writing instructors disclose the criteria by which the student's paper will be evaluated. Those criteria are an excellent starting point for the creation of an *editing checklist.* Students then can expand their checklists by adding details. For example, if one grading criterion is writing propriety (as it likely will be), students can create a checklist of writing issues to look for, such as the checklist reflected in Figure 48 below.

Exercise 14-4 gives an opportunity to try using the checklist in Figure 48 in connection with the student's first legal writing paper.

Emulating the experts the right way. Finally, expert learners emulate expert legal writers. They do so, however, carefully, selectively and systematically. First, they identify (always in consultation with their instructors) examples of excellent work on the particular type of project they have been assigned. This admonition is particularly crucial because, for example, most court opinions, even those generally agreed to be excellent legal works, are poor models for legal writing assignments. Judges writing court opinions are engaged in a very different task for very different readers. They make choices about including and excluding information and discussions that students preparing legal writing papers should avoid at all costs. Even papers students find on law student internet sites or in legal writing texts may not reflect particular instructors' images of what makes for an appropriate paper or at least may adopt conventions not appropriate to the particular task assigned to the student.

Second, expert learners carefully analyze what makes the examples excellent, asking themselves questions as they read the paper, such as:

- Why is this paper an example of excellent work? In what ways, if any, is it flawed?
- What stylistic, organizational and analytical choices must the author of this paper have made? Why did she make those choices?
- Which aspects of this example work apply to all similar projects? Which aspects are unique to this particular project?
- What do the papers have in common? How are they different? Why are they different?

Lastly, expert law students emulate judiciously. They avoid simply copying words, formatting, phrases and sentences, and focus instead on emulating the thinking, organization and reflection demonstrated in these papers. Each legal writing paper requires a slightly different approach, slightly different organization and largely different analysis. Consequently, you must make conscious choices both to emulate aspects of the experts' work and to deviate from what the experts did.

An aside for students who enter law school with weaker writing skills. As Chapter 2 and the above materials explain, success in legal writing courses requires the student to have mastered basic writing skills. Legal writing papers must have excellent paragraphing, sentence structure, diction, usage, punctuation, etc., and law students who enter law

Figure 48: A Sample Checklist for Self-Editing Legal Writing Papers

Assignment Checklist
- ✓ Have I responded to all the issues and answered all the questions?
- ✓ Have I complied with all the formatting requirements?
- ✓ Have I either used or consciously chosen not to use all the information?

Organization Checklist
- ✓ Have I followed the organization I planned to follow? If not, why not?
- ✓ Have I addressed all the subjects I intended to address?
- ✓ Have I articulated all the points I intended to have articulated?

Analytical Checklist
- ✓ Have I included every step of my reasoning?
- ✓ Have I used the analytical style my instructor wanted me to have used?
- ✓ Have I discussed in depth all the important authorities?

Writing Propriety Checklist
- ✓ Do I have any typos?
- ✓ Have I grammar-checked, spell-checked and "think-checked" (checked for errors that spell-checkers and grammar-checkers do not catch)?
- ✓ Are all of my sentences complete sentences and not run-ons?
- ✓ Is my spelling correct?
- ✓ Have I avoided the use of jargon?
- ✓ Is my punctuation correct?
- ✓ Did I use words properly?
- ✓ Are my sentences parallel?
- ✓ Are my pronoun references proper?
- ✓ Do my verbs and subjects agree?

Writing Style Checklist
- ✓ Does my sentence structure vary?
- ✓ Is my writing interesting?
- ✓ Does it flow logically? Is it easy to read? Are there good transitions between ideas, sentences and paragraphs?
- ✓ Do I avoid falling into writing patterns, such as overusing semi-colons, certain phrases, certain words?
- ✓ Do I avoid using meaningless words like "certainly" and "obviously"?
- ✓ Is my writing overly cute? Sufficiently formal?

Citation Checklist
- ✓ Is my citation form proper? Have I properly used abbreviations, commas, parentheses, fonts (i.e., italic font, underlined font)?
- ✓ Do I provide authority for every assertion of law in my paper? Of fact?
- ✓ Do I place quotation marks around every statement that is not my own?

school with weaker writing skills need to quickly ascertain this weakness and get help. Some law schools provide such help in the form of on-campus writing centers. Even in such schools, however, students need to make their own efforts to remediate their deficient writing skills. Fortunately, there are numerous books and websites that are helpful in this regard as discussed in Chapter 2.

Conclusion

In many respects, the keys to success in all aspects of legal research and writing courses are the same as in all courses: planning, reflection, time on task, practice and effort. At the same time, legal research and writing courses make unique demands on new law students. These courses require law students, very early in their legal careers, to imagine themselves as professionals, working for real clients who have real legal problems and to hold themselves up to a high standard of professionalism. The courses require students to stop thinking of themselves as students and start thinking of themselves as legal experts, who will be held accountable for every error in their work. These shifts in students' self-images are what make legal writing courses so demanding and so exciting.

Reflection Questions

1. Why do expert law students keep a research log?

2. Why is time management a crucial factor for success on legal writing assignments?

3. What should students learn from the instructions for their legal writing assignments? How do expert law students use those instructions?

4. Why do expert law students organize their papers before, during and after writing them?

5. Why is reflection crucial to success on legal writing papers?

6. Why is good basic writing a part of students' grades in legal writing courses? (Hint: Consider who will be reading your legal writing once you start practicing law.)

References

Steve Graham, Karen R. Harris and Gary A. Troia, *Writing and Self-Regulation: Cases from the Self-Regulated Strategy Development Model* in SELF REGULATED LEARNING: FROM TEACHING TO SELF-REFLECTIVE PRACTICE 20 (D.H. Schunk, B. Zimmerman, eds.1998).

Elizabeth Fajans & Mary R. Falk, *Against the Tyranny of Paraphrase: Talking Back to Texts*, 78 CORNELL L. REV. 163 (1993).

Richard Michael Fischl & Jeremy Paul, GETTING TO MAYBE (1999).

Barbara K. Hofer, Shirley L. Yu and Paul R. Pintrich, *Teaching College Students to Be Self-Regulated Learners* in SELF REGULATED LEARNING: FROM TEACHING TO SELF-REFLECTIVE PRACTICE 57 (D.H. Schunk, B. Zimmerman, eds.1998).

Maureen Straub Kordesh, *Navigating the Dark Morass: A First-Year Student's Guide to the Library*, 19 CAMPBELL L. REV. 115 (1996).

Suzanne E. Rowe, *Section III: Gaining Lawyering Skills: Legal Research, Legal Writing, and Legal Analysis: Putting Law School into Practice,* 29 STETSON L. REV. 1193 (2000).

Michael Hunter Schwartz, *Teaching Law by Design: How Learning Theory and Instructional Design Can Inform and Reform Law Teaching,* 38 SAN DIEGO L. REV. 347 (2001).

Patricia L. Smith & Tillman J. Ragan, INSTRUCTIONAL DESIGN (1999).

Claire E. Weinstein & Richard E. Mayer, *The Teaching of Learning Strategies* in HANDBOOK ON RESEARCH IN TEACHING 315 (M.C. Wittrock, ed. 1986).

Barry J. Zimmerman, Sebastian Bonner & Robert Kovach, DEVELOPING SELF-REGULATED LEARNERS: BEYOND ACHIEVEMENT TO SELF-EFFICACY (1996).

Chapter 15

Strategies for Learning Legal Analysis

Introduction

Law professors almost universally refer to their task as teaching their students to "think like a lawyer" or teaching their students "legal analysis." While many law professors do not do a very good job defining for themselves or their students what either of these terms either means or involves, nearly all believe they have designed their classroom teaching to produce such learning and even more believe their exams assess whether students have developed this set of skills. Consequently, expert law students know they must become expert in developing legal analysis skills.

Teaching all the analytical nuances and intricacies that together constitute legal analysis is far beyond the scope of a chapter or even an entire book; for the most part, the entire first year of law school is devoted to teaching students these skills. For this reason, this chapter covers only the rudimentary basics, leaving the bulk of the instruction to your first-year instructors. The chapter is organized into three sections, each of which addresses one of the three basic skills involved in legal analysis: issue spotting, applying rules to facts and applying and distinguishing cases. A fourth skill, public policy analysis, is equally important but beyond the scope of this text. Each section explains the skill, provides examples of the proper application of that skill and identifies the similarities between the skill and skills all of us already possessed before we went to law school. Each section also provides a blueprint for learning the skills, focusing on what expert students do to develop their issue spotting, applying rules to facts and applying and distinguishing skills.

Spotting Issues

Introduction

Law professors are like traffic cops.[1] Traffic cops wish to ensure that all drivers slow down and drive within the speed limit. They recognize, however, that there are

---

1. I am indebted to my colleague, Professor Susan Keller, for this analogy.

so many drivers on the road that it is impossible to catch every person who speeds. For this reason, traffic cops are forced to hope that drivers who see the officers pulling over other speeders will perceive a threat that they, too, may be pulled over and therefore will slow down. Law professors are similar to traffic cops because they know that, on a three-hour exam (the typical length of law school final exams), it is impossible to test students on every legal concept the class has studied over the course of the semester or year. For example, most contracts students develop course outlines as long as 50 or 60 pages and include hundreds of legal rules and/or holdings. Most law school exams require students to apply much less than one-half of these rules. Law professors, therefore, are forced to hope that the threat that students might be tested on any of the rules causes the students to slow down and study all of the rules.

Because law school exams test only a subset of the rules the students learn and because that subset changes every semester (because every law professor writes new exams every time and most law professors try to vary what they test), law students must be able to "spot" (identify) the particular set of rules raised by their exam questions. This task requires students to know all the legal concepts they have studied, to understand the relationships among all those concepts and to recognize which particular concepts are being tested on the particular exam question they are reading. In shorthand, this task is referred to as "issue-spotting."

The task is not unlike what practicing lawyers must do every time they get a new case; when a new case comes to a lawyer, the lawyer must identify the particular legal problems and issues raised by that client's problem. In many ways, the task for law students is much easier than the task faced by lawyers. Law school exams always come with labels (e.g., "Torts Final Exam" or "Civil Procedure Final Exam"); these labels tell the students that all the legal issues on the exam will only be in that particular subject area. A client, of course, comes to her lawyer with no labels, and most client problems do not confine themselves to one subject area. For example, a client who has been in a simple car accident and wishes to sue the driver of the other car is likely to require the attorney to consider issues relating to tort law. The client's problem, however, almost certainly also will require the lawyer to analyze issues relating to civil procedure law (e.g., where to sue, when to sue, how to sue), evidence law (how will the lawyer present all the evidence she needs to present) and remedies law (how will the client's injuries be compensated).

Issue spotting is a lot like figuring out where any kind of problem lies. People who regularly cook, for example, issue spot when they decide what spice a particular dish is missing. People who have played a sport, such as basketball or golf, know that there are times when their shooting or their swing stops working right, and they have to figure out what they are doing wrong. People who sing or who play musical instruments sometimes must identify where their efforts have gone wrong; they must ask themselves: why doesn't the song or musical piece sound right?

Most significantly, college students take many tests that require them to apply some but not all the concepts they have learned. For example, most high-level math tests, such as tests in calculus courses, do not require students to apply every math principle the students have learned. Similarly, most literature tests do not ask questions about every aspect of each of the novels, plays or poems the students have read.

Example

To understand this process in the law school exam context, take a look at the one-paragraph statement of facts in Figure 49 below. The short story in Figure 49 raises three of the approximately fifteen crimes the students probably considered in their criminal law course and one of the many defenses. The story raises particular questions about aspects of those crimes and that defense, i.e., is the breaking element of burglary met if the door is already partially open and the defendant just pushes it open the rest of the way? Is the intent element met even if the intent is formed after the entering? Can a person abandon a crime after completing it and avoid criminal liability? Is it nighttime at 8:00 p.m. in April if the defendant needed to use a flashlight? Each of these questions, while expressed in the abstract, might just as readily be related to a case the students had read. For example, if the students had a read a case where the court held that turning a knob constitutes a "breaking," the facts in Figure 49 would raise the issue of whether pushing open a partially open door is sufficiently similar to turning a knob. In Figure 49, the facts that raise issues are highlighted and the issues are identified.

Figure 49: A Criminal Law Hypothetical with Possible Issues Identified

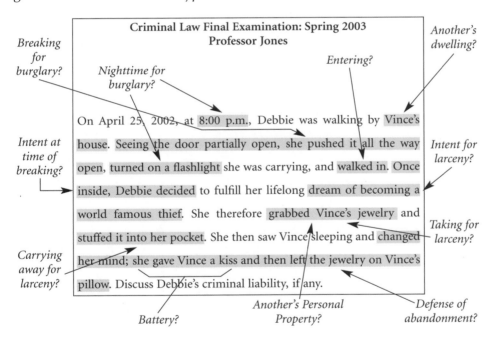

The Keys to Developing the Ability to Spot Issues

Spotting issues involves a number of distinct, but related, skills. First, spotting issues requires students to **possess excellent knowledge of the legal rules and case holdings** they have studied over the course of the semester. This knowledge is indispensable because it serves as an issue-spotting checklist. For example, the hypothetical in Figure 49 required the learner to know of the existence of the three crimes it addresses: burglary, larceny and battery and the defense of abandonment. Moreover, a student addressing the hypothetical in Figure 49 would also need to know the elements of each of the three crimes and the definitions of each of those elements. For example, a student who knew that the definition of breaking is "the application of force, however slight" would be more likely to recognize the need for a discussion of whether pushing an open door all the way open is a breaking. In the alternative, a student who recalled a case in which the defendant turned the doorknob of an unlocked door and recalled that the court analyzed whether turning a doorknob was enough force would also be likely to spot this issue. For these reasons, expert law students strive to overlearn the rules and holdings so that they can recall this information automatically.

For the same reason, many law students develop a **checklist of potential issues** as part of their examination preparation. They use their checklists, which they often remember using mnemonic or organizational strategies, as a way to make sure that they mentally consider all possible issues before consciously deciding not to address particular ones.

Second, spotting issues requires students to **understand the connections among the topics** that have learned. For example, as you learned in Chapter 12, the elements that make up a rule and the definitions of those elements are always linked. Moreover, common law burglary requires intent to commit a common law felony; expert students studying criminal law would recognize the likelihood that an exam question would link one of those other common law felonies with common law burglary. For these reasons, graphic organizers, such as mindmaps, are particularly helpful tools for building issue-spotting tools. In particular, mindmaps that depict connections between concepts, such as the connection between burglary and the other common law felonies (as shown in Figure 50), are particularly powerful learning issue spotting tools.

Figure 50: The Elements of Common Law Burglary

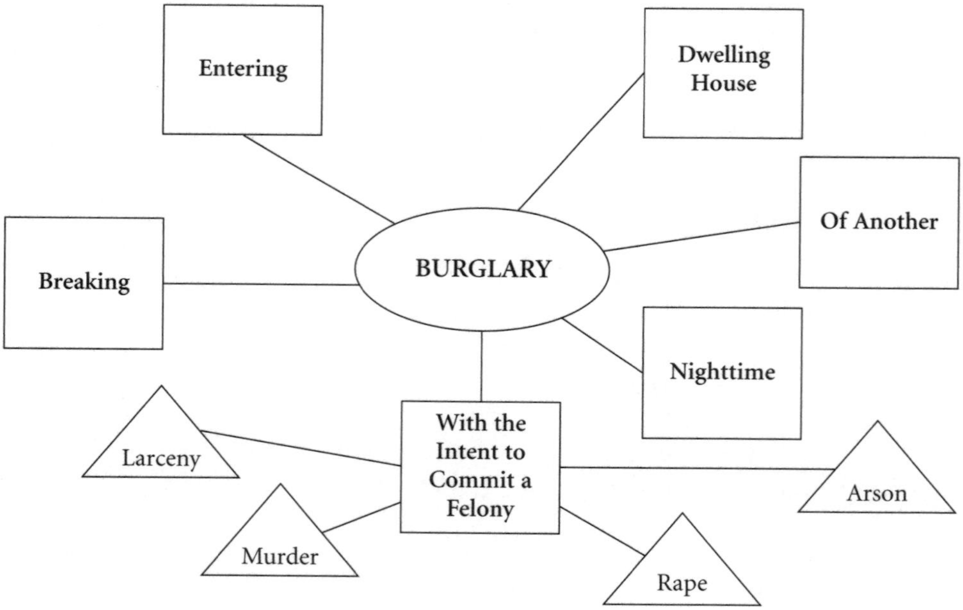

Figure 50 depicts a very elementary and obvious set of connections. Expert law students also look for more complex relations among the concepts in their courses. For example, course material in Civil Procedure and Contracts classes can be depicted along a timeline. For Civil Procedure, a partial timeline begins with the law that governs decision as to the courts that may properly hear a lawsuit (subject matter and personal jurisdiction and venue), continues with the decisions relating to whom the plaintiff may bring together in one lawsuit (joinder and class action law) and ends with the binding effect on future cases of the decisions made in a prior case (issue and claim preclusion). In Contracts, a partial timeline would start with how parties can create a contract (contract formation), continue with defenses parties can assert against enforcement of the contract (contract defenses), add in how courts determine interpret the meaning of the contracts that are enforceable (contract interpretation) and how courts determine which party breached (contract performance) and end with what a party can get from the courts if the other party does not perform or improperly performs her contract promises (remedies for breach of contract).

Still other connections among topics are possible. For example, a major recurring theme in most contracts classes is the interpretation of language; it is an issue in connection with contract interpretation, many types of regularly disputed contract terms and even contract formation. In torts, the topics fall broadly into two categories: claims and defenses. Because such connections both increase the memory trace and assist with issue-spotting, expert law students organize and re-organize their course material in multiple ways.

Third, spotting issues requires students to **attend closely to the details in the fact pattern**. Like most law school examinations, Figure 49 is dense; almost every phrase includes facts that students must recognize as issue signals. Law professors sometimes refer to this skill as "fact sensitivity" because the skill involves paying close attention to each fact, each piece of information contained in the hypothetical. One way to understand this point is to imagine your law professor writing your exam question. Law professors, being careful people, consciously chose and discard each word in their examination questions; thus, imagine your professor sweating over each word, consciously choosing what to include, what to delete and how to phrase each sentence.

In other words, the care with which your professors construct their examination questions tells you something about the care with which you should read those questions, and spotting issues therefore involves using many of the reading techniques you learned in Chapter 9, including

- reading the questions at the end first,
- developing, as you read, hypotheses about the issues you expect to be addressed by the facts and then testing those hypotheses,
- reading line-by-line and word-by-word,
- developing graphic depictions of the facts to help you make sense of them (where necessary), and
- dialoguing with the facts as you read them.

For these reasons, expert law students always force themselves to use reading comprehension strategies when they read examination questions and read their examination hypotheticals slowly, carefully and multiple times.

Fourth, spotting issues involves **recognizing patterns**. The intellectual task of matching up the facts of a hypothetical with the abstract statement of facts in a rule or with the facts of a case requires students to identify what these things have in common. For example, as noted above, the students may only have read a burglary case where the defendant turned the knob of a closed but unlocked door. To spot the issue, the students would need to recognize the similarity between turning the knob of a closed door and pushing open a partially closed door. In other words, the students would have to recognize that both involve using a part of the defendant's body to create the physical access through which the defendant entered the dwelling. Similarly, the students may not have read a battery case where the only touching was a kiss, but they may have read a case where the touching only involved a light punch. By focusing on what these two stories have in common, a touching that does not physically hurt the victim, the student can spot the issue. By knowing the key facts of the cases they have read cold, expert law students set themselves up to analogize between their exam questions and those cases.

Fifth, because spotting issues is a form of brainstorming, expert law students, as part of their normal examination preparation, **anticipate all of the ways issues might appear on an examination question.** For example, contract law express conditions issues require students to identify language from a contract that has, as at least one possible connotation, that one party will not have to perform her contractual promises absent the occurrence of some event. Thus, students would anticipate the following on an examination question testing this issue: (1) language from a contract, (2) the language references some event—getting a loan, winning the lottery—and (3) the language communicates one party will not have to perform unless the event occurs.

Sixth, expert law students try to **create as many of their own examination questions as possible,** recognizing that the mental effort a student would use to create an examination question is identical to the mental efforts in which their professors engage. As a result, students are able to anticipate the most logical combinations of issues and identify those patterns on their examinations.

Finally, because legal issue spotting is mostly a new skill and because it involves pattern recognition, expert law students **practice the skill in multiple ways.** Because issue spotting is a form of concept learning, they use elaboration memorization techniques, such as *paraphrasing* and *developing their own examples and non-examples* (see Chapter 13), to make sure they not only understand the concepts and the essential features of those concepts but also rapidly can recognize the patterns those concepts take in hypotheticals. They also *practice issue-spotting old exam questions* in study groups (and on their own) to get the benefit of the collective brainstorming possible in small groups. Old exams are available from a wide variety of sources, including:

(1) students' instructors or from other students,
(2) law schools' bookstores and/or libraries, and
(3) online resources, such as **http://jurist.law.pitt.edu/Guides** (which has links to old essay examinations from fifteen different law schools).

Exercise 15-1 requires the student to find and spot the issues on at least three hypotheticals for each of the courses she is taking.

Applying Rules to Facts

Introduction

Like the issue spotting skill, the skill of applying rules to facts involves skills the student has been using all her life. The skills the student needs to be able to use include careful reading, knowledge of the rules of law she has learned, the ability to identify similarities and differences, the ability to draw inferences from facts, and the skill of explaining her thinking. Applying rules to facts is like all types of application skills, and, like all types of application skills, it involves analogical reasoning.

One concrete example should help you see how you already have done things very similar to applying rules to facts: Imagine you had an 11:00 p.m. curfew. Your parents, however, recognized that, on rare occasions, you cannot reasonably be home by 11:00 p.m. so they told you that you can violate curfew if you "have a good reason" and "let them know." Note that the above sentence describes a rule. Note also that this rule describes two requirements: (1) a good reason and (2) notice. These two requirements are abstract statements of facts; in other words, the former requirement, a "good reason" does not identify every situation that would constitute a good reason but, rather, simply requires that the particular situation meet the abstract description "good reason." Likewise, the notice requirement does not state a particular time for notice but, rather, simply describes the requirement as "notice."

Now, imagine a hypothetical. Imagine you are still 17 years old, and, one night, you missed the 11:00 curfew because a friend's significant other ended a one-month relationship with your friend and you stayed with your friend until 11:30 p.m. to comfort her. Also assume you thought your friend would be OK with you leaving on time (you would have needed to leave her house at 10:55), but, at 10:50, she started crying again, and so you didn't call your parents until 11:10 p.m. because you did not want to call until she had stopped crying. First, note the similarity between this hypothetical and what you know about law school essay examinations. Law school exams, as explained in Chapter 2, tend to raise issues that could go either way. Is a sad friend a "good reason"? Does it matter that the relationship was only one month old? Was calling after 11:00 adequate "notice" because you waited until the friend had stopped crying?

What would your parents argue as to why you violated the curfew rule? Keep in mind that they would need to argue that you did not have a "good reason" for staying out beyond 11:00 and did not give the required "notice."

Your parents would probably first note that you came home at 11:30 (identifying the specific fact, 11:30, and noting its difference from the required time, 11:00) and they therefore would assert that, unless your conduct meets the two requirements for excuse—"good reason" and "notice"—you have violated curfew. They then would point out that your friend was only crying (a fact) and argue that people cry or feel sad all the time; they will argue this problem was not a big deal. They would also note that you were comforting a friend because of the loss of a relationship that had lasted only one month (identifying facts that bear on the good reason issue). They would argue that a one-month relationship cannot be very serious (drawing an inference from the facts) and that the friend adequately can be comforted over the phone or the next morning (drawing more inferences). Note that these arguments suggest some refinements of the rule; your parents are arguing that "good reason" means that your excuse must involve a significant problem (not, for example, merely a break-up of a one month relationship) and that other means of achieving the goal that caused you to violate the curfew must not have been available.

Your parents would also note that you did not call until after 11:00 (identifying a fact that may distinguish this case from the required state of "notice"). They will assert that you could have made a quick call any time before 11:00 and your friend would have understood (identifying another distinguishing fact and drawing an inference [a quick call was possible]). They also suggest a refinement of the "notice" standard to require a call before 11:00.[2]

What would you argue as to why you did not violate the curfew rule? Keep in mind that you would need to argue that you had stayed out beyond 11:00 for a "good reason" and gave proper "notice."

With respect to the "good reason" issue, you would argue that your friend was sad (a fact) and therefore needed comforting, which is something kind people should do (inferences from the fact). You would also reply to your parents' "only a one month relationship" argument by saying that a break-up can make a person feel very sad even if the relationship was a short one (another inference).

With respect to the notice issue, you would argue that you called within 10 only minutes of the curfew (a fact), so your parents would know you were late and why (an inference). You might also argue that you had a good reason for not calling sooner— your friend was crying from before 11:00 until past 11:00 (a fact), and you would make her feel worse if you left while she was still crying (an inference). In addition, you would note that you only discovered you would be violating curfew at 10:50 (when your friend started crying again and did not stop) (a fact) and called only 10 minutes after 11:00 (a fact), that you called within ½ hour of discovering you would be late (a fact) and therefore you gave notice within a reasonable time after discovering the need to give such notice (an inference). These arguments would be arguments to refine the notice rule so as to define "notice" to mean reasonably proximate to curfew under the circumstances and given the time when you discovered that you will be missing curfew.[3]

Applying legal rules to facts involves similar skills. Consequently, it is worthwhile to take a close look at what is going on in each of the above arguments. Both you and your parents are starting with the same rule and the same set of facts. Both you and your parents are also engaged in a process in which you:

- focus on the abstract rule (e.g., "good reason")
- identify facts that you believe either suggest your situation does live up to what the standard requires (the fact that your friend was crying) or does not live up to the standard (the fact that she was crying over a one-month relationship)
- explain what it is about the facts that you have identified that justifies the conclusion that your situation does meet the standard (helping others in need is a kind thing) or does not (people cannot be too sad if they lost a relationship that only was one month long).

While both you and your parents start with the same facts, note that you choose to emphasize different facts (length of the relationship vs. crying) and draw different inferences (crying happens all the time vs. crying means the person could use some comforting).

---

2. They also would probably make what law professors would label "policy arguments." They would argue that, if they excused you for helping this friend, they would have to excuse you anytime you found even a sad friend (a common lawyer "floodgate" argument—if they make an exception in this case, it would open a flood gate of exceptions). They also would argue that the reason they require a call as soon as possible is so they will not have to suffer worry, and excusing you now would encourage you to wait until after curfew to call.

3. You, too, would make policy arguments. You would argue that your parents want you to be a nice person and a good friend (using the common lawyering technique of asserting a counter-policy). You also would argue that 10 minutes is not a long time to wait (replying to your parents' parental worrying policy argument, another common lawyering technique).

The Basics of Applying Rules to Facts

A legal rule is simply a statement of an abstract set of facts that a court, legislature or administrative agency has determined must be present to produce a specified legal consequence. In other words, if a court finds that the facts of a particular situation (the facts of a dispute or alleged crime) match up sufficiently close to the required abstract set of facts, the court will attach the specified legal consequence. For example, recall the common law rule of burglary noted elsewhere in this book. The rule provides that a burglary is:

    (i)   a nighttime
    (ii)   breaking
    (iii) and entering
    (iv) into the dwelling house
    (v)   of another
    (vi) with the intent to commit a felony.

Note that the only difference between the above rule and the curfew rule is the number of requirements.

Focus now more specifically on the second requirement, a breaking, which courts have defined as "the application of force, however slight." That rule is an abstract description of the required action (using force to get into a dwelling) and therefore covers a wide range of conduct that courts might denominate a breaking, including: blowing up a door with a bomb, knocking down a door, pushing a door open, or even just turning a doorknob (because of the word "slight"). Notice the similarity between the analysis above with respect to the hypothetical curfew rules and the standard for breaking. Both the curfew rules and the definition of breaking describe the requirement abstractly (e.g., "good reason" "some force, however slight"). Likewise, to apply either to a particular instance, you must "match up" the facts of particular circumstances (e.g., staying out beyond 11:00 to comfort a sad friend; turning a doorknob) to the abstractions ("good reason"; "some force, however slight").

It is extraordinarily common for law students and law professors to refer to the process of applying rules to facts as "IRACing" or "using IRAC." IRAC is a mnemonic that refers to a commonly-used organizational format for answers to law school and bar exam essay questions. Figure 51 below explains the IRAC mnemonic and provides suggestions for doing each part well.

The IRAC formula is described above as "commonly used" because dozens of law school professors tell their students that they hate IRAC (however, notwithstanding professorial statements of disdain for IRAC, exams that include paragraphs written in the IRAC form, *where it is appropriate to do so*, often receive good marks). The dislike many law professors feel for IRAC stems not really from proper uses of IRAC, but, rather, from how students abuse and overuse IRAC. In other words, what law professors who complain about IRAC are really saying is that they dislike poor, thoughtless uses of the IRAC formula.

Here is a list of the six most **common errors in students' use of IRAC.**

    1.   Making the entire essay one gigantic IRAC in which the first paragraph states every issue, the second states every rule, etc. Remember—**IRAC is a tool for constructing paragraphs of an exam answer, not a list of the four paragraphs of a good exam answer.**

Figure 51: Basic IRAC

Issue	Start the *paragraph* by identifying the particular legal question the student is about to discuss. In nearly all instances, the issue stated will **not** be the larger legal claim, i.e., not "burglary" or "negligence" or "subject matter jurisdiction" or "contract formation." Rather, the issue is the particular aspect of the larger legal rule the student plans to analyze, such as the "dwelling house" element of burglary, the "duty" element of negligence, the "complete diversity" element of diversity subject matter jurisdiction or the "consideration" element of contract formation. Professors vary in the degree of specificity they want from students' issue statements. Some want case brief level detail (see Chapter 9 above) whereas others encourage students to simply identify the name of the element or claim they are about to analyze and underline it, e.g., *"duty"; "complete diversity."*
Rule	Next, *accurately* state or paraphrase the particular rule the student plans to apply. Many professors accept accurate paraphrases; some, however, want exact statements of rules.
Analysis	Immediately following the rule should be the analysis of the **facts of the particular situation** described in the fact pattern. Because the analysis portion of IRAC is the part weighted most heavily in students' grades, the discussion below details the steps involved in doing analysis in the context of applying rules to facts.
Conclusion	The final sentence or sentences of each paragraph should state and defend the student's prediction as to how a court would decide the particular issue. The conclusion should follow from the analysis, and, if the analysis identifies arguments for both parties, the conclusion should explain why the student believes one set of arguments are more persuasive.

2. Ignoring all other principles of writing, organization and exam taking. Some students, for example, include only IRAC paragraphs in their essays and never actually respond to the question posed by the exam. Other students fail to include introductions and conclusions in their papers and omit introductions to each of the sections of their exam answers. **IRAC, at best, summarizes a large part of what makes for effective exams, but good writing also helps make for good exams.**

3. Using IRAC for questions of law. Some exam questions require students to analyze which of two or more rules a court should apply to the parties' dispute rather than how a court would apply a particular rule to the parties' dispute. **IRAC is a tool for applying rules and holdings, not for deciding questions of law.**

4. Using IRAC for questions of policy. Some exam questions require students to analyze whether a particular rule is good public policy (see Chapter 9 for an explanation of the role of policy in deciding cases and creating legal rules). **IRAC is a tool for applying rules and holdings, not for analyzing questions of policy.**

5. Labeling the pieces of the IRAC. Some students literally write: "Issue: The issue in this case is…" **IRAC works best as a guide inside your head, not as a set of labels** for each of the paragraphs or sentences in your essay.

6. Giving equal weight, length and time to each of the pieces of IRAC. Some students assume each piece of IRAC should be one sentence long. In fact, **the analysis portion of IRAC counts for 2/3 to 4/5 of students' grades; it therefore should be that much more extensive than the other portions (see below for an explanation as to what to include).**

Figure 52: The Four Steps of Applying Rules to Facts

(1)	Identify and list (on a separate sheet or in your head) all facts that tend to prove or disprove the state of facts required by the rule;

	**Hints:
❏	Read the facts carefully and repeatedly. Facts are in the fact pattern for you either to use or to recognize as irrelevant.
❏	As you read, look for evidence on which either or both parties might rely. Try to avoid thinking of yourself as an advocate for either party. Look for facts that help both parties.
❏	Mark each fact with a highlighter pen, like this, as you use the fact so that, by the end of the examination, you visually can make sure you either have used or have dismissed as irrelevant every fact in the fact pattern.
❏	Consciously decide to use or disregard each fact.

(2)	State one fact or set of facts that tends to prove or disprove the existence of the state of facts required by the rule;
(3)	Explain *why* the fact or set of facts tends to prove or disprove the existence of the required abstract set of facts. This step often involves first drawing factual inferences and then connecting the factual inferences to the rule's requirements by using a synonym that references the key facts for the key requirement of the rule.
(4)	Repeat Steps 1–3 for each additional relevant fact or set of facts.

	**Hints:
❏	Keep in mind that you are explaining why you felt the fact was a significant one. Ignore the fact that your reader is a law professor; rather, imagine your reader is someone, not completely unlike the stereotype of a three year-old, who keeps asking you "why" in response to whatever you say. In other words, explain every step of your reasoning.
❏	Make sure you identify arguments each of the parties involved (there may be more than two) would make.
❏	Watch out for facts both parties may use but from which they would draw opposite inferences.

As the curfew discussion should suggest, the IRAC formula actually omits the most important part. It does not tell how an application of a rule to a set of facts is done. In other words, the label "analysis" fails to explain what is involved in applying a rule. Applying rules to facts requires the student to engage in a further, four-step process, which is detailed in Figure 52. Use Figure 52 as a "cheat-sheet" whenever you are practicing applying rules to facts.

The combination of IRAC and the four steps outlined above ensures that the student does all of the things she needs to do to succeed on her examinations: spotting issues, stating the rules, identifying all of the relevant facts, drawing factual inferences, arguing both sides, explaining every step of her reasoning, reaching a conclusion and justifying the conclusion.

At this time, three more warnings about common student errors are necessary. First, **never begin discussing the facts until after the rule has been identified.** Arguing the justice or injustice, rightness or wrongness, fairness or unfairness of the facts or the parties' behavior, without reference to a rule (or at least to a policy that you have connected with a rule), is a waste of time. Second, **arguments need to be made as though they will be read or heard by a judge or jury.** If you could not make the

Figure 53: An Image Depicting the Key to Effective Legal Reasoning

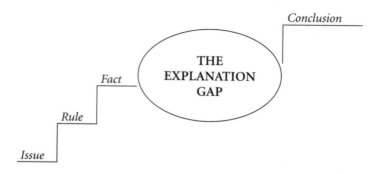

argument with a straight face to a judge or jury, it should not be made in an exam answer. Third, **explain the reasoning rather than assuming the reader will know what is in your mind.** The key to good grades on exams, in fact, is each of the student's explanations as to why a fact is legally significant, why it tends either to prove the existence of the required state of facts or to prove the non-existence of that required state. For this reason, many law students find it helpful to use imagery (such as the image depicted in Figure 53) to make sure they include such explanations every time they mention a legally significant fact. Figure 53 shows the explanation as the largest part of the process (because it is the most important part) and also shows what happens if the explanation is missing from a student's analysis (she falls into a gap).

Figure 54 below is a model IRAC paragraph. It addresses one narrow issue, the "nighttime issue" with respect to a hypothetical raising a burglary issue. For purposes of instruction, Figure 54 explicitly identifies each of the IRAC elements and each of the four steps of legal analysis in parentheses using bold font. Real exam paragraphs would, of course, omit this information.

The hypothetical addressed in Figure 54 points out that the police were unable to determine the time of day when the events described in the facts occurred, but they found strong evidence that the alleged burglar carried a lit torch both before she entered the alleged victim's house and while she was inside the house.

As shown in the IRAC paragraph in Figure 54, there are conventions of legal writing that make it easier for the reader to know what the writer is doing. For example, the paragraph transitions from the rule statement to the analysis through the use of the phrase "in this case." Students typically signal that they are about to begin their analysis by the use of phrases such as "in this case" or "under these facts" or "here." Similarly, Figure 54 involves a situation that requires the writer to consider both sides of the argument and therefore adopts a second commonly used convention—introducing the arguments with the phrases "On the one hand" and "On the other hand." Finally, the paragraph is preceded by a heading, a recommended practice, because it makes it easier for the reader to know the topic the student is about to address. While each of these usages is no doubt unoriginal, the choice to follow these conventions makes sense given the real purpose of IRAC paragraphs—making it easy for a law professor to follow the discussion.

Second, while the paragraph purports to objectively analyze the facts, it nevertheless is a form of persuasive writing. Law professors often refer to exam writing as requiring

Figure 54: A Model IRAC Analysis of a Criminal Law Issue

Nighttime Element

The first element of burglary requires that the alleged conduct have occurred during the "nighttime." (**Issue**—identification of legal question) Common law courts defined "nighttime" as "the period between sunset and sunrise when there is not enough light to discern a face." (**Rule**—statement of the applicable rule) In this case, on the one hand (**Signal of start of analysis section and of plan to argue both sides**), the facts do not state the time of day so it is difficult to know whether the acts occurred after sundown or when there was not enough light to see a face (**Analysis STEPS 2–3: identification of the absence of a key fact—time of day—and explanation of its significance to the question of whether the element is met**). On the other hand (**Signal of start of counter-argument**), the facts state defendant carried a lit torch both before she entered the alleged victim's house and while she was inside the house. (**Analysis STEPS 2–3: We have identified and listed a relevant fact.**). Lit torches only have utility if a place is dark enough such that the person carrying it feels she cannot see without it, and, if it was dark enough to need a torch to see, it likely was too dark to see much of anything, including a face. (**Analysis STEP 3 (in part)**—Drawn inferences from the fact and connected those inferences to the "too dark to discern a face" standard by substituting a synonym, "see much of anything," for the definition). Moreover (**signal of start of a second argument**), the facts state she carried the lit torch before she entered the house, suggesting that, even outside, she perceived a need for light to be able to see, which suggests it was dark outside and was after sunset. (**Analysis STEPS 2–3: Identification of a second relevant fact and connecting directly to the abstract condition required by the rule**). Accordingly, because it almost certainly was after sunset and too dark to discern a face, it seems likely a court would conclude it was nighttime. (**Conclusion**—author's predicted result identified using the language of the key requirements of the rule and the facts).

students to objectively analyze the issue; this assertion is correct in the sense that the student must analyze the facts unemotionally and try to accurately predict how a court would decide the issue. The writing is also persuasive, however, because the author's goal is to convince the reader that the author has correctly analyzed the facts and has accurately predicted how a court would decide the issue.

Figure 55 is a second example of an application of a rule to a set of facts. This discussion involves an element of "misrepresentation," a defense a party to a contract might use to avoid having to perform a contract. Misrepresentation deals with the situation where one party has misstated a fact to the other party while the parties were negotiating their agreement, and the other party made the contract in reliance on that misrepresentation. The misrepresentation defense has five elements:

(1) the defendant made a false statement of fact, opinion or future intention,
(2) the falsely stated fact was a material one,
(3) the misstatement was made with the requisite state of mind,
(4) the party claiming misrepresentation justifiably relied on the misrepresentation, and
(5) the party claiming misrepresentation suffered an injury as a result of the misrepresentation.

Figure 55 focuses exclusively on the second element, the requirement that the misrepresented fact must have been "a material fact." Although not all courts agree, a majority of courts have held that a fact is material if, under the circumstances, a **reasonable person** would regard the fact as **important** to her decision to make the contract. In other words, courts ask: Would a reasonable person, in deciding whether to have entered into this contract, have cared if the true facts were different from the facts as represented by the other party? The words "reasonable person" and "important" are in bold font above. These words are the touch points upon which good lawyers would make arguments. To clarify the connection between the facts of a hypothetical and its analysis in an IRAC format, Figure 55 shows both the facts of the hypothetical and the analysis.

Like Figure 54, Figure 55 adopts the "In this case" convention. Figure 55, however, involves an issue for which a reasonable counter-argument is not possible and therefore Figure 55 does not use the "On the one hand" convention. Also, although Figure 55 still uses the IRAC format, it consists of two paragraphs. As noted above, clarity matters; in this instance, there are two paragraphs because the division makes the reasoning easier to follow. Finally, because Figure 55 deals with an issue that only could be resolved in one way, some law professors would not want their students to address it all. Most, however, would deduct points from students who omitted the issue or any argument it addresses. Law professors have two good reasons for requiring such discussions: (1) the discussion still allows the student to demonstrate analytical reasoning and understanding of the rule, and (2) material fact is an element that must be proved or the misrepresentation claim would fail and therefore real lawyers would always analyze it.

As shown in the IRAC in Figure 55, the analysis explains every step of the analyst's reasoning. Notice also that the fact that Betty refused to perform is not identified as a relevant fact. The fact is not relevant because it does not bear on the question of what a reasonable person would do; Betty may be an unreasonable person or may have acted unreasonably this one time.

The facts also contained information with which the student could have analyzed other issues, such as the question of whether Betty justifiably relied on Larry's representation (element #4 above), and, in fact, the analysis of whether a reasonable person would consider the fact important does not address the question of whether Betty acted reasonably in choosing to rely on Larry's representation (instead of investigating the title herself, for example). That argument addresses a different element, the requirement that the victim justifiably rely, and that element (element #4 above), again, is not within the scope of the issue. **Many students err in combining issues instead of analyzing each separately.**

The Keys to Learning How to Apply Rules to Facts

The prior materials make it clear that, in applying rules to facts, expert law students **use some form of IRAC and the Four Steps of Applying Rules to Facts.** IRAC provides a structure that is familiar to law professors and therefore makes it easier for them to credit students with having done what they needed to have done. The four steps make sure that each student's "A," the analysis, possesses the requisite depth.

For these reasons, most law students find it helpful to **memorize the components of IRAC and of the Four Steps** as soon as possible and certainly no later than the end of the students' second week of class. By doing so, students can use IRAC and the Four Steps as a systematic guide as they talk themselves through the analysis of hypotheticals. In other words, IRAC and the Four Steps serve as a checklist to help students make sure they are including everything they need to include in their analysis. In fact, it is also helpful for students to know the six common students errors in using IRAC as a reminder of what students should not be doing.

Figure 55: A Model IRAC Analysis of a Contract Law Issue

HYPOTHETICAL

Larry Landowner was negotiating with Betty Buyer for Betty to buy, for $50,000, Purpleacre, a tract of farm land on which a corn crop is growing. Betty, who owns a chain of ice skating rinks, was planning to use the land to open an ice skating rink. During negotiations, Larry falsely told Betty that the land was zoned for such a use. Betty thereafter agreed to buy the land from Larry. Three weeks before the sale was to close, Betty discovered the land was zoned exclusively for farming, and she would have to pay at least $25,000 for the surveys, plans, zoning applications etc. necessary to get the zoning changed. Betty refused to perform the contract. Discuss.

Material Fact Element

The question is whether the fact misrepresented by Larry was a material fact (**Issue**). A material fact, according to the majority rule, is a fact a reasonable person would consider important in deciding to enter into the contract (**Rule**). In this case (**signal**), Betty owned a chain of ice skating rinks and therefore was purchasing Purpleacre for $50,000 solely for the purpose of developing an ice skating rink, and Larry falsely represented the tract was zoned for such a use (**Analysis STEPS 1–2, ID relevant facts and state first relevant set of facts**). Because the zoning of a tract controls its use, a person who was purchasing a tract of land on which to open a business would consider how the tract is zoned in deciding to purchase it (**Analysis STEP 3, Part 1: Draw inference from the fact**). Accordingly, a prudent businessperson planning to build an ice skating rink on Purpleacre would consider the fact that the property was zoned exclusively for farming and not for Betty's intended use to be a major factor in deciding whether to buy the property (**Step 3, Part 2: Connect inference to requirement of rule by using a synonym that references the key requirement of the rule**).

Moreover, the facts state the contract price was $50,000 and a zoning change would cost $25,000 (**Analysis STEPS 1–2, ID relevant facts and state second set of relevant facts**). Because the zoning change costs one-half the probable value of the entire property, a person considering buying the property and using it for a commercial site would have to increase her or his investment substantially to use the site as planned, making the site much less desirable (**Analysis STEP 3, Part 1: Draw relevant and reasonable inference from fact**). Such an increase in cost would cause a prudent businessperson to be very concerned about purchasing the property. (**Analysis STEP 3, Part 2: Connect inference to requirement of rule by using a synonym that references the key requirement of the rule**). Accordingly, because a reasonable person would regard the zoning issue and the increased cost of development as important in deciding whether to buy the property, the misrepresented fact was a material fact (**Conclusion**).

Of course, mastery of IRAC and the Four Steps is a waste of time unless the students also have learned to **spot the issues** and have **correctly memorized the rules**. Spotting the issues is a prerequisite skill because an analysis of something that is not an issue is a waste of time; it's like playing the wrong musical note perfectly on an instrument—it *sounds* good but misses the point. Errors in memorization are equally problematic; the Four Steps require students to match up the facts of the hypothetical to the abstract statement of facts in the rule; an erroneous rule statement, therefore, will result in erroneous analysis.

Nothing, however, is more important to learning this skill than **practice**. Applying rules to facts is a new skill and therefore students must frequently practice it if they wish to master it. Nearly all first-year law students have a hard time applying a rule to a set of facts if they have not practiced applying that particular rule. Consequently, expert law students, particularly in their first year of law school, make sure they *practice applying each rule they study.*

Exercise 15-2 provides several opportunities to practice applying rules to facts.

Applying and Distinguishing Cases

Introduction

It is helpful, in trying to develop this skill, to begin by defining the key terms implicated by this skill. The term "cases" refers to legally binding precedents. The term "applying" involves explaining why the specific facts of a hypothetical are sufficiently similar to the facts of the precedent such that a court should decide the hypothetical case in the same way the court decided the precedent. In the real world of law practice, lawyers try to apply precedents that reached a result similar to the result their clients want. The term "distinguishing" involves explaining why the specific facts of a hypothetical are sufficiently different from the facts of the precedent such that a court should NOT reach the same decision in the hypothetical case that the court reached in the precedent case. Thus, lawyers try to distinguish precedents that reach a result that is different from the result their clients want.

In many ways, applying and distinguishing is actually an easier skill to learn than the skill of applying rules to facts. Both involve matching facts and explaining the significance of similarities and differences. Applying rules to facts requires students (1) to match up the abstract statement of facts contained in a rule (e.g., "the period between sunset and sunrise when there is not enough light to discern a face") with the facts of a hypothetical (e.g., time was 8:00 p.m., month was April, defendant carried a flashlight), and (2) explaining why a court might conclude the facts satisfy the requirement stated in the rule and why a court may conclude the facts do not satisfy the requirement stated in the rule. Applying and distinguishing cases involves (1) matching up the key, real world facts of a case the student has read, the precedent, (e.g., a case where the court held that opening a closed, but unlocked door was a breaking) with the facts of the hypothetical (pushing open a door that already was partially open) and (2) explaining why a court might conclude the facts are sufficiently similar for a court to reach the same result in both cases and why a court might conclude the facts are too different to reach the same conclusion in both cases (both cases should reach the same result because both involve using the defendant's body to allow the defendant to pass into the house vs. the precedent case involved creating the opening whereas, in the hypo, the opening already existed, suggesting the homeowner in the hypo, unlike the homeowner in the precedent, was inviting or at least was unconcerned about preventing entry).

Applying and distinguishing is easier than applying rules to facts because the matches are easier; it is easier to match a concrete set of facts to another concrete set of facts than it is to match a concrete set of facts to an abstract statement of facts. As this discussion reflects, applying and distinguishing is, like applying rules to facts, an application skill and requires analogical reasoning.

An example from outside the legal context makes it clear that most people already possess at least a rudimentary level of this skill. Imagine a parent lets a 10 year-old child stay up past her bedtime one Saturday night because the family is seeing a play for which the parents had purchased tickets. Two nights later, the child wants to stay up late to watch the end of a television show the family is watching. The child likely would say something like, "On Saturday, you let me stay up late so I could see the end of a show we were all watching. You should do the same thing now. Otherwise I will not know how the show ends, and I'll have a hard time getting to sleep because I'll be wondering about it." Notice that the child, who wants the parents to reach the same result as in the "precedent case," identifies similarities between the precedent case and the new case (both involve shows, both involve shows the whole family was watching). Notice also that the child offers what the child believed to be the reasons why the parents made the decision they made in the precedent case (finding out how the show ends so the child can get to sleep easily).

The parents, however, likely will say, "Saturday was not a school night and therefore you could sleep in on Sunday and still get the rest you need to be healthy. If we let you stay up late, you still will have to get up early tomorrow for school or you will be late for school and you will be tired all day. Also, on Saturday, we were seeing a play, something we don't do often, and so it was a special occasion. Finally, we paid money for you to see the play which would be wasted in part if you didn't see the end of the play; we are watching the television show for free so, if you miss the end of the television show, there's no waste of money." The parents identify what they believe to be the key differences between the precedent and the new case (not a school night vs. a school night, something the family doesn't do often vs. an every day event, paid money vs. didn't pay money). They also explain why these differences justify a different result (on school nights the child cannot sleep in so child will not be well-rested, plays are rare, special events and not seeing the end of the play would waste money, which is not true about not seeing the end of a television show).

The Basics of Applying and Distinguishing Cases

The discussion of IRAC above also is relevant to applying and distinguishing cases. The "Issue" part of IRAC, in fact, is exactly the same for both applying rules to facts and for applying and distinguishing cases.

The "Rule" part is a bit trickier. In many instances, students must apply and distinguish cases that have applied a particular rule; in such instances, stating the rule in this context is very much the same as stating the rule for applying rules to facts. Because the student will not be applying the rule, but, rather, applying and distinguishing a precedent, the student needs to then state a holding for that precedent (see Chapter 9 for a discussion of how to write holdings). In other circumstances, there is no "rule" at all; instead, students only state the holding of the precedent case.

The "Conclusion" part of applying and distinguishing also requires some explanation. Like the conclusion section of an application of rules to facts discussion, the student must explain why she reached the particular conclusion that she reached. In other words, having identified the parties' respective arguments in the analysis section, the conclusion explains why one argument is more persuasive than the other. The only difference between the two types of conclusions is one of focus. In the context of applying a rule to a set of facts, conclusions focus on the fit between the rule and the facts and explain why a court would be most likely to conclude that the facts of the hypothetical either meet or fail to meet the requirements stated in the rule. In the context of applying and distinguishing a case, however, conclusions focus on the fit between the facts of the precedent and the facts of the hypothetical and explain why a court would be most likely to conclude that the facts of the hypothetical justify either reaching the same result the court reached in the precedent case (i.e., justify applying the precedent) or justifying reaching a different result than the court reached in the precedent case (i.e., justify distinguishing the precedent).

The greatest difference between an application of rules to facts IRAC and an applying and distinguishing IRAC is in the analysis section. Figure 56 on the next page describes the Four Steps of Applying and Distinguishing Cases. As you review Figure 56, it is helpful to compare each of the steps to the child's and the parent's arguments regarding the bedtime issue above and to identify each of the steps described in Figure 56 in those arguments.

Students make many of the same errors in applying and distinguishing cases that they make in applying rules to facts. For example, some students combine issues rather than analyzing each issue distinctly. Likewise, some students devote so much attention to properly stating their holdings or to reaching what they believe to be the "correct" conclusion that they fail to devote adequate time and mental energy to filling the explanation gap, which, of course, is the key to performing well.

A few examples may help clarify these points and make the Four Steps more concrete. Figure 57 below is an excerpt from a law school essay examination question and answer.[4] The question required, among other things, students to apply and distinguish a particular case the students had read and studied, *Asahi Metal Industry Co. v. Superior Court of California*, 480 U.S. 102; 107 S. Ct. 1026; 94 L. Ed. 2d 92 (1987). A bit of background information about the legal issue addressed in the *Asahi* case and the hypothetical will make it easier to follow the discussion in Figure 57. The issue raised in *Asahi*, addressed in the hypothetical and requiring analysis involves a question of the propriety of requiring the defendant to participate in a lawsuit filed in a state in which the defendant does not reside. The United State Supreme Court has held that requiring a defendant to appear in a court in a state with which the defendant has had insufficient contact violates the due process clause of the Fourteenth Amendment of the Constitution. This rule is known as the "minimum contacts" rule. As the discussion below explains, the Supreme Court has held that minimum contacts must have a basis in "some act by which the defendant purposefully avails itself of the privilege of conducting activities within the forum State, thus invoking the benefits and protections of its laws."[5]

The *Asahi* case involved a lawsuit by an individual who crashed his motorcycle and claimed the crash was caused by a defective tire. The individual sued the tire manufacturer in California, and the tire manufacturer tried to bring Asahi into the lawsuit because Asahi had supplied the tire manufacturer with a component of the tire and the manufacturer claimed Asahi's part was the cause of the accident. Asahi successfully argued that it could not be sued in California because it had insufficient contact with the state of California.

Figure 57 adopts the same convention used in the above discussion of applying rules to facts with respect to placing comments and explanations in parentheses and bold font. It also adopts the law school writing conventions explained above, such as "here" and "on the one hand." Figure 57 uses every fact contained in the hypothetical that relates in any way to the business arrangements addressed in the hypothetical. The effort to identify the absence of facts, particularly because the absence of facts was relevant in *Asahi*, is also included. Finally, there is an explanation of why the differences are legally significant.

---

4. I am grateful to my colleague, Glenn Koppel, for this hypothetical and its analysis, both of which are used with his express permission.
5. 480 U.S. at 109.

Figure 56: The Four Steps of Applying and Distinguishing Cases

(1)	Recall each fact that influenced the court's decision in the precedent case (i.e., each key fact) and why that fact influenced the decision;

> ****Hints:**
> ❑ If you memorized all your holdings, this task will require minimal mental effort.

(2)	Looking at the list of facts you develop in STEP (1) above,
	a. identify each fact in the hypothetical that is similar to or identical to a fact you identified in STEP (1), and
	b. identify each fact that is different;

> ****Hints:**
> ❑ Create a chart with four columns, two of which you will label and fill out at this time: (1) "Key Facts of Precedent Case" and (2) "Key Facts Of Hypothetical." Be sure to match facts from the hypothetical with facts of the precedent and to note, where appropriate, any absence of facts (either in the hypothetical or in the precedent).
> ❑ Read the facts carefully and repeatedly. Facts are in the fact pattern for you either to use or to recognize as irrelevant.
> ❑ As you read, look for evidence on which either or both parties might rely. Try to avoid thinking of yourself as an advocate for either party.
> ❑ Mark each fact with a highlighter pen, like this, as you use the fact so that, by the end of the examination, you visually can make sure you either have used or have dismissed as irrelevant every fact in the fact pattern.

(3)	For each fact you identified in STEP 2, decide (1) whether you believe that fact is sufficiently similar to a fact in the precedent case to justify reaching the same conclusion, and (2) why or why not;

> ****Hints:**
> ❑ Possessing broad and narrow holdings for each case (see Chapter 9) makes this step much easier.
> ❑ The keys to both of the above decisions are the reasons the precedent court regarded each fact as important in the first place. If those reasons would also apply to the hypothetical, the fact is sufficiently similar. If not, it isn't sufficiently similar.
> ❑ Label and fill out the other two columns in your chart as follows: (1) "Is the Fact in the Hypothetical Sufficiently Different?" and (2) "Why or why not?"

(4)	Using all the facts and explanations you identified in STEPS 1–3, explain why a court might decide the facts are sufficiently similar and why a court might decide the facts are not sufficiently similar.

Figure 58 is another law school exam-type hypothetical and answer.[6] Figure 48 deals with an issue of property law. The question requires students to apply and distinguish a very interesting case, *Moore v. Regents,* 271 Cal. Rptr. 146, 793 P.2d 479 (1990). A bit of background is helpful in understanding Figure 58. In *Moore,* the plaintiff consented to have his doctor perform necessary surgery to remove the pa-

---

6. I am grateful to my colleague, Greg Sergienko, for this hypothetical and its analysis, both of which are used with Professor Sergienko's express permission.

Figure 57: Applying and Distinguishing Civil Procedure Hypo and Model Answer

---

HYPOTHETICAL

While living in California, Paul had smoked cigarettes manufactured by Lorelei Cigarettes, Inc. from 1955 to 1998, when he quit smoking. In 1999, Paul was diagnosed with a form of lung cancer caused by exposure to asbestos. Paul died in April 2000 of lung cancer. In 1954, Lorelei had entered into an arrangement with Best Asbestos Manufacturing Company ("Best") to develop a "Micronite Filter" for cigarettes manufactured by Lorelei. The Micronite Filter contained asbestos. Lorelei and Best jointly owned the resulting patent for the filter, and Best sold over 10 billion of the filters to Lorelei during the 1950s and 1960s knowing they would be incorporated into Lorelei cigarettes to be made in Lorelei's Pennsylvania manufacturing plant and sold throughout the United States. Best is incorporated in Arizona and has its offices and manufacturing plant in Arizona. Wanda, Paul's widow, has sued Best in a court in California, alleging that the asbestos fibers in the filters caused Paul's death. Best moved to dismiss the suit on the grounds that the court lacked personal jurisdiction. Discuss.

Purposeful Availment (**Issue**). The Supreme Court has held that merely placing a product in the stream of commerce, even if the manufacturer knows the product will end up in the forum state, is not enough to be a purposeful availment. The defendant must engage in conduct that indicates a purpose of serving the market in question (**Rule**). In Asahi (**signal holding is coming**), the court held that, where a party manufactured, outside the state, a component of a tire (tire stems) and its only contact was that it could anticipate some of the tires would be sold in the state, it violated due process to require that party to defend a suit filed in the state (**Holding**). Here, on the one hand, just as Asahi just sold tire stems to a tire manufacturer outside the forum, Best just supplied a component part (the filters) to a manufacturer outside the forum state (Lorelei in Pennsylvania). Also like Asahi, Best sold nothing directly to customers in California, conducted no marketing in California, had no distributors, sales agents or customer network in California, and didn't design its product to comply with any California law (**List of similarities**). Just like Asahi, there was, in other words, no act by Best from which a court could conclude Best chose to exploit this market (**Explaining significance of similarities**). On the other hand (**transition**), unlike Asahi (**signal distinction is coming**), which had no close business ties to the tire manufacturer, Best had a close business relationship with Lorelei. Unlike Asahi, which merely supplied tire stems, Best was in a partnership with Lorelei for distribution of the filter in Lorelei's cigarettes (**List of differences**). Best's financial gain from the development and manufacture of the filter depended upon the success of Lorelei's national marketing. For this reason, this case is distinguishable from Asahi, where the manufacturers had an arms length relationship from which only an inference of indirect intent could be inferred. Here, Best and Lorelei's joint venture warrants attributing Lorelei's marketing to Best (**Explaining significance of differences**). For this reason, a court would likely conclude that Best has chosen to aim its business at California and therefore the facts meet the purposeful availment test (**Conclusion**).

---

tient's spleen. During the operation but without the patient's knowledge or consent, the doctor took spleen cells from the excised spleen and then established a medically important cell line from the cells and sold cells from that line to others. The patient sued the doctor, asserting that the doctor wrongfully had taken (converted) the patient's cells. To prevail on that claim, the patient argued that he possessed a property interest in his spleen cells. The California Supreme Court rejected the patient's claim, holding that a patient does not possess an ownership interest in "the disposition of human biological materials."

*Figure 58: Applying and Distinguishing Property Law Hypo and
            Model Answer*

HYPOTHETICAL
On Halloween, Anthony and Deborah got drunk and, as a prank, went to a church graveyard and dug up a recently buried coffin and took it and the body inside from the graveyard. The body was that of Paula's recently deceased husband's body. Discuss whether Paula possesses a property interest in her recently deceased husband's body.

Does Paula possess a property interest in her deceased husband's remains? (**issue phrased as a question**) In *Moore* (**almost no professor expects students to cite cases in full on an exam**), the Court held that a doctor who, after removing his patient's spleen with the patient's consent, had used the patient's spleen cells, without the patient's knowledge or consent, to conduct what proved to be profitable research was not liable for converting the spleen cells because the patient did not possess an ownership interest in "the disposition of human biological materials" (**holding**). On the one hand (**signal**), Paula would seem to have an even weaker claim to a property interest than did the plaintiff in *Moore* because Paula's husband's body is valueless whereas the spleen cells had value for research (**factual similarity — this technique, arguing that the case under analysis is even stronger than the precedent case, is a common one**). The absence of value suggests an absence of a property interest (**explanation of significance of factual similarity**). Moreover (**signal that a second argument is coming**), the language used by the *Moore* court, "the disposition of human biological materials" encompasses the body of a deceased person (which is involved here) (**fact**) because a deceased body is simply decomposing body parts (**more of an applying rules to facts explanation**). On the other hand (**signal**), people, like Paula, who bury their loved ones, wish the loved ones' bodies to remain where they are buried, whereas people who have bodily tissue removed, like the plaintiff in *Moore*, almost never assume anything or show any interest in how their removed tissue will be disposed of (**factual difference**). Thus, while Moore might be said to have abandoned his spleen tissue, Paula could not be said to have abandoned her husband's body (**explanation**). Moreover, grave robbing has no social utility whereas medical research does (**factual difference**). Consequently, there is no benefit to protecting the conduct at issue as there was in the *Moore* case (**explanation in terms of the court's reasons for its decision**). Accordingly, Paula should be deemed to have possessed a property interest in her husband's remains (**Conclusion**).

In looking at Figure 58, it is important to note the continued use of conventions. It is even more helpful, however, to notice both what arguments the author makes and what ones the author does not make. As to arguments not made, the omission of one particular argument is instructive. The hypothetical in Figure 58 involves a taking of an entire body, as opposed to a few cells. Undoubtedly, the quantum of body parts taken is a difference between the two cases. The author of the answer to the hypothetical, however, does not mention this difference. Why not? The court's reasoning did not lead the author to believe that the difference was a legally significant one. By recalling that distinguishing a case requires *both* identifying factual differences and explaining why those differences are legally significant, the author was able to make the proper choice not to discuss this factual difference. Raising a factual difference that is not legally significant would be no different than arguing, in connection with the bedtime hypo above, that the child was wearing different clothing on the two occasions in question.

Exercise 15-3 provides several opportunities to practice applying and distinguishing cases.

The Keys to Learning to Apply and Distinguish Cases

In many respects, the keys to learning this skill are the same as the keys to learning how to apply rules to facts. In fact, expert law students recognize that the most significant difference between the two skills is the difference between matching the facts of the hypothetical to the abstract statement of facts in a rule and matching the facts of the hypothetical to the concrete facts of the precedent. Consequently, in performing this skill, expert law students **use some form of IRAC and use the Four Steps of Applying and Distinguishing Cases.** Similarly, most law students find it helpful to **memorize the components of IRAC and of the Four Steps** (to use as systematic guides) as soon as possible and certainly no later than the end of the students' second week of class.

Because one of the keys to developing this skill is the systematic comparison of the key facts in the precedent with the key facts in the hypothetical case, expert law students use the **comparison chart** approach described above and integrated into Exercise 15-3 in the Workbook to insure they consider all relevant facts.

Issue spotting and memorization are also crucial to the development of this skill. Students who fail to spot issues miss opportunities to demonstrate this skill, and students who have failed to memorize holdings for each of the cases they have read possess nothing that they can either apply or distinguish. Many expert law students, in fact, find it helpful to develop **broad and narrow holdings** (see Chapter 9) for each of the cases they will need to be able to apply and distinguish. Broad holdings help the student know which facts to use in an argument applying a precedent whereas narrow holdings help the student know which facts to use in an argument distinguishing a precedent.

Most importantly, expert students also frequently **practice** the skill. In most law school classes, law professors' in-class questions are opportunities for every student to practice the skill and obtain feedback by comparing their answers with their peers' answers. In other words, students who play along in their heads, who try to answer their professors' in-class hypotheticals have countless opportunities for practice and feedback. Of course, nothing replaces the more in depth practice possible from writing out answers to practice examinations.

Exercise 15-3 offers you multiple opportunities for practicing this skill.

Reflection Questions

1. In what ways is issue spotting similar to something you learned before you went to law school?

2. Think of and describe an example from your own life when you have applied a non-legal rule to a set of facts.

3. Think of an example from your own life when you have applied or distinguished a non-legal precedent to a set of facts.

4. Why are practice and feedback so crucial to your development of the skills addressed in this chapter?

References

Richard Michael Fischl & Jeremy Paul, GETTING TO MAYBE (1999).

Suzanne E. Rowe, *Section III: Gaining Lawyering Skills: Legal Research, Legal Writing, and Legal Analysis: Putting Law School into Practice*, 29 STETSON L. REV. 1193 (2000).

Michael Hunter Schwartz, *Teaching Law by Design: How Learning Theory and Instructional Design Can Inform and Reform Law Teaching*, 38 SAN DIEGO L. REV. 347 (2001).

Paul T. Wangerin, *Learning Strategies for Law Students*, 52 ALB. L. REV. 471 (1988).

Chapter 16

Strategies for Preparing for and Taking Law School Examinations

Introduction

While the real bottom line in all learning contexts is whether the students have learned the skills and knowledge they were supposed to have learned, the measure of whether a class of students has achieved that bottom line are the examinations. In many law school classes, the final examination is the sole determinant of each student's grade in the course. In nearly all other law school classes, the midterm and final examination together determine each student's grade. In other words, excelling on law school examinations is essential to law school success.

This chapter therefore identifies and explores the strategies expert law students use to prepare for and take law school exams. This discussion has been divided into two main topic areas: strategies for preparing for law school exams and strategies for taking law school exams. The discussion of strategies for preparing for law school exams addresses four main topics: dumping the negatives, studying for law school exams, self-assessing the student's learning in the weeks and days leading up to the examination and learning from midterms and taking and learning from practice examinations. The discussion of strategies for taking law school examinations addresses three topics: dealing with exam stress, taking law school multiple choice tests and writing answers to the various types of law school essay tests.

Strategies for Preparing for Law School Exams

Introduction

Law school examinations are marathons, not sprints. Unlike students in some (or, perhaps, even many) college-level courses, law students cannot excel on law school exams simply by reserving hours or even days of "cramming" time at the end of the semester. Nor does real law school studying have much in common with its media depictions, such as those in movies like *The Paper Chase* or *Legally Blonde*. There is no way to make law school easy or to reduce, significantly, the amount of work required; it is **not** true that smart law students either do not need to work very hard or that they avoid having to work hard in law school by dividing up the work among members of a study group.

As this text explains elsewhere, expert law students do work less hard than their novice peers, and they do participate in study groups. However, even very gifted law students must work incredibly hard in law school, and they and their fellow study group members do not divide up the work. Rather, expert law students start studying for their examinations right from the beginning of the semester and continue throughout, using each other as tools for acquiring the knowledge and for practicing the skills on which they will be tested.

In short, the process of exam preparation in law school itself requires thought and self-reflection, planning, self-assessment and lots of practice and feedback.

Dumping the Negatives

Expert law students avoid, at all costs, negative feelings about themselves, negative people and negative activities. Rather than focusing on their fear of failing, they focus on showing how well they have learned. Rather than imagining the consequences of failure, they envision the pleasure of success. Rather than spending time with people who do not believe they can succeed, they choose to be with people who believe they will succeed. Rather than wearing out their bodies with unhealthy food or drink, such as sugar and alcohol, and with sleep deprivation, they focus on eating brain-strengthening food and drink, such as fish, milk, fruits and vegetables, and try exercising regularly—even if they only can manage a single five minute walk per day.

The reason to avoid negative feelings about oneself stems from the well-established fact that self-efficacy, believing that the student can and will succeed, is better correlated with success in educational settings than scores on standardized tests, such as the LSAT. Students with low self-efficacy, because they doubt whether they can ever learn, study less hard than they need to study or do not persist with their studying when they encounter the inevitable difficulties all law students encounter. They also are less likely to seek the help they need because they perceive, incorrectly, that their peers are superior students and do not need or seek such help. Similarly, they are less likely to self-assess their learning or to write and obtain feedback on practice examinations because they excessively fear critical feedback. Finally, students with low self-efficacy are less likely to adopt the recommendations detailed below in this chapter because they believe their results are outside their own control and, therefore, any efforts towards preparing themselves are a waste of time. The saddest part of all of these consequences is that students with low self-efficacy, because they do not engage in the behaviors most likely to prepare themselves for their examinations, usually get the grades they expect, poor ones; in fact, even when such students get good grades, they almost always attribute their success to luck or error and, as a result, miss out on the pleasure that comes from crediting themselves for their success.

It is equally negative, however, for law students to possess unrealistically high perceptions of self-efficacy. Nearly all law students enter law school having enjoyed considerable success at the high school and undergraduate levels. Hundreds, if not thousands, of law students, however, draw a poor and unreasonable inference from these past results. They assume their high school and college successes mean that their methods of studying were effective and efficient. In many instances, those methods were simply good enough, effective enough and efficient enough for them to get good grades but by no means effective or efficient in an absolute sense. They therefore assume their current learning strategies do not need refinement. Unfortunately, too many law students do not discover this error until it's too late, until after they receive grades that do not reflect their capacity for success in law school. Some simply get B's when they could have had A's; others, however, risk academic dismissal.

The key, from an exam preparation perspective, is for the student to possess the belief that *she can learn*. In other words, students study appropriately and productively for examinations when they feel confident that they can learn *if they do the work*.

For different but related reasons, eating healthy food, consuming only low levels of alcohol, getting plenty of sleep and rest and even exercise all help students ready themselves for law school examinations. Law school examinations are long and therefore require stamina; most are at least three hours and some exceed four. Law school exams also require students to operate at peak mental efficiency. Eating healthy food, drinking only small amounts of alcohol, exercising and sleeping well all stimulate the brain and all allow students to perform at their best. In fact, studies in other educational disciplines show that students who are the most mentally fit in these ways do better on examinations. Unhealthy eating, excessive alcohol or drug use, poor sleep and lack of exercise, in contrast, have been associated with higher levels of depression, muddled thinking and slower mental processing speed.

Specific Studying Strategies

Planning studying. Studying for examinations is no different than any other learning task. It begins with planning. The difference is that the time frame within which the students must do the planning is much broader. Just as experts law students plan their legal writing papers by starting from the due date and working backwards, they also plan their examination preparation by working backwards from the date of their examination. This planning is crucial for a number of reasons. First, students who plan their studying can take advantage of the benefits of **spaced learning**. As you learned in Chapter 2, a student who studies one hour per night for three nights will learn more and better than a student who studies three hours for one night. Second, students who plan their studying make sure they include time for healthy eating, plenty of sleep and exercise. Third, students who plan and space out, through the semester, their exam preparation, seek help as they discover they need it. At the end of the semester, while their peers compete for the shrinking amounts of professorial time available, they, having already had all or nearly all of their questions answered over the course of the semester, can devote themselves to more productive exam preparation activities. It might even be true that students who have sought help throughout the semester actually receive more help at the end of the semester as well because their professors, being human, respect and appreciate their semester-long diligence. Finally, students who plan their studies cope better with unplanned events, personal crises, extra assignments and other such matters.

The Studying the Student Has Done so Far. If the student has followed the recommendations of this text, she has already engaged in many of the activities in which expert students engage to prepare for their law school examinations. For example, by carefully reading and briefing the cases, the student has ensured that she understands the rules and has given herself the base level tool for being able to apply and distinguish the cases. Applying and distinguishing is impossible unless she understands both the results the courts reached in all the cases and the courts' reasons for reaching those results. Moreover, even in courses in which the student is not expected to apply and distinguish cases (but are expected to apply rules to facts), the cases play an important role in learning and skill development. The cases provide examples of how legal experts have applied the rules, and therefore serve as models. As shown in Chapter 9, however, sometimes law professors assign cases that are examples of ineffective application of the rules; in such instances, students develop their ability to apply the rules by figuring out, through the class discussion and on their own, what an effective application might have looked like. Thus, both the excellent cases and the poor ones teach students lessons about how to apply the rules.

Deconstructing the rules the student has learned also has helped prepare the student to apply rules. For each class, the student has been deconstructing the rules into their constituent parts. This task prepares her to be able to isolate each aspect (i.e., element, factor) of every rule so that she is able to apply each separately. This approach prepares expert students to do well on their examinations. As Chapter 15 explains, many law students perform poorly on their examinations because they fail to analyze each element or factor separately.

The student has also created outlines and graphic organizers, activities that prepare the student to be able to quickly recall the rules and holdings when she needs them (by creating schemata for storing the learning) and to be able to spot issues (because she knows and understands the relationships among the concepts she has learned). In fact, studies of experts in all fields reveal that experts possess highly organized knowledge of their fields. The high degree of organization allows the expert to more readily identify, analyze and solve problems within their field, just as law students must be able to identify, analyze and solve the legal problems described in law school examinations.

Likewise, by memorizing the rules and/or case holdings (depending on the expectations of the professor), the student has insured that she possesses the knowledge that is a necessary, but not sufficient, component of success on law school examinations. Experts in every field are characterized not only by their skill and the organization of their knowledge but also by the depth and breadth of their knowledge; studies show that experts do know more. Expert law students, therefore, possess more knowledge and deeper understanding of that knowledge.

Instructor Study. In most respects, nearly all law professors expect their students to do the same things on their examinations and define excellence in very similar ways. Consequently, it is possible to write a book like this one and describe the expectations and testing methodologies of law professors. At the same time, expert students in all learning contexts know that instructors do vary in their expectations because subject matters vary, political views vary, interests and goals vary and instructors' perceptions of students vary. In other words, expert law students both recognize the commonalities among their professors and make sure they know what each of their professors expect on the examinations.

In the law school context, this task is made more difficult because, while law school professors mostly teach in the same way, a practice that might lead students to expect that they would all test the same way, in fact, law school instructors do not all test in the same way. As detailed below, while there clearly is a most prevalent approach to designing law school examinations, law school exams can and do take one of several different forms, all of which can and do overlap. In fact, even professors who administer similar examinations in terms of style may expect different things from their students. Figure 59 depicts the potential for variation. In the broadest terms, law school exams always involve hypothetical factual stories that the students must "analyze." Analyze, as explained in Chapter 15, involves identifying issues, applying rules to facts, applying and distinguishing cases and performing policy analysis. The variation, therefore, comes in part from the mix of these expectations, in how much weight each instructor assigns to each task, both in terms of constructing the exam (e.g., how many issues, how much depth of analysis) and in terms of grading the exam (i.e., how much demonstration of each of the skills bears on the students' grades on the examination). Moreover, some but not all law professors expect their students to be able to integrate discussions of policy in their legal analysis or to be able to use their knowledge and skills in the context of lawyering tasks other than applying rules to facts or applying and distinguishing cases, such as creating client letters, constructing documents that might be submitted in court or drafting other legal documents. Accordingly, Figure 59 depicts the various ways of testing law students as a series of boxes that can be the central focus or attached to one of the other testing approaches. Particular exams, in other words, can test in all of the areas identified, in some of the areas or in only one area.

This variation makes teacher study an important skill. Sometimes, the task is an easy one; some instructors are explicit. They tell their students whether the students are expected to apply and distinguish cases or not, whether they should be integrating public policy in their analyses or not and whether with the exams will test lawyering skills other than applying and distinguishing or application of rules to facts. Most law professors, however, are much less forthcoming. Many, however, give multiple hints about their examinations, both in terms of the testing topics depicted in Figure 59 that they are likely to test and in terms of the relative weight assigned to each topic. These hints take the form of course and topic-by-topic objectives, classroom and office hour discussions and past and practice examinations. The widespread absence of explicitly stated expectations makes such teacher study a crucial skill.

For these reasons, expert students use their class notes not only to record what they are learning about the subject areas and skills addressed in class but also to record their instructors' examination hints and the students' reflections and questions about their instructors' examination expectations. Thus, expert students who are watching a peer be questioned by their instructor focus on discerning what reasoning techniques appear to produce instructor approval. While they are listening in class or reading an answer to a past exam question, they ask themselves questions such as:

(1) What types of student classroom responses elicit positive comments from the instructor? What types of responses elicit criticism?
(2) Which court opinions does the professor believe to be well reasoned? Which does the instructor believe to be poorly reasoned?
(3) (if the instructor communicates dissatisfaction with a student response) How should the student have answered the question?
(4) What would a written answer to this question look like? What would it include? Exclude?

In other words, expert students frequently use the 1/3 of their classroom note-taking designated for "reflection" and "questions" (see Chapter 10) to record what they are learning about their professor's exam-related expectations.

Expert law students also get their hands on every exam question ever authored by each of their professors. Notwithstanding the fact that nearly all law professors devise

Figure 59: Variations in the Types of Law School Examinations and Expectations for Student Performance

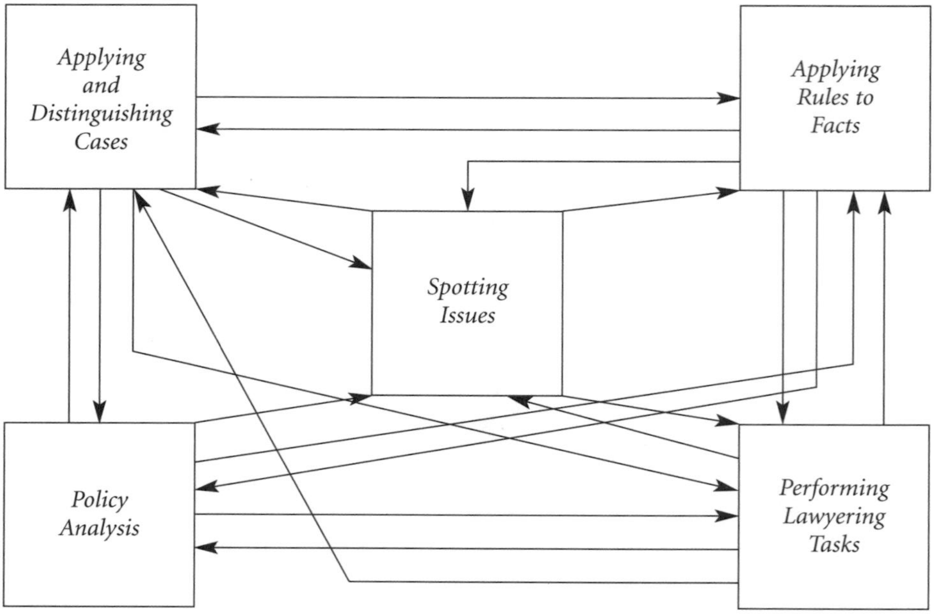

new questions every semester, past exams provide crucial insights. At a minimum, such review allows students to review the instructions their instructors commonly include with their exams. Moreover, in many instances, reviewing past exams provides students with insights into their instructors' formatting preferences and helps students get used to their instructors' exam writing style. The review also allows students to identify the skills and knowledge their instructors have emphasized in the past. (This knowledge is somewhat of a double-edged sword because some professors keep testing the same subjects over and over, others try to make each exam entirely unique and still others strive for a perfectly random combination of reuse and novelty in their testing.)

Overlearning. As Chapter 3 explains, expert law students strive to overlearn what they need to know and be able to do for their examinations. Law school examinations require students to apply their knowledge, not simply recite it. Moreover, law school examinations are complex and dense and therefore test not only the students' lawyering skills but also their speed. A typical law school essay exam question is at least three-quarters of one page single spaced and as long as two or three pages. In the assigned one hour, students must be able to read the hypothetical facts, identify what question(s) they are being asked, discern which details are important and which are not, identify which topics, from among all the topics they have studied, are being tested by the exam, plan and organize an analysis of the exam, recall and accurately state all the relevant rules and holdings they have studied over the course of the semester and write a coherent essay in which they demonstrate the ability to apply what they have learned to this unfamiliar set of facts.

In other words, during law school examinations, students simply do not have time or mental resources to spend struggling to recall the knowledge or to remember how to perform the skills. They need to free up as many mental resources as possible for thinking, brainstorming, analogizing, reasoning and writing. Consequently, expert law students try to so master their knowledge of the rules and holdings and to become so competent at performing legal analysis that the knowledge and skills come to them **automatically**, without great mental effort. Just as anyone who has mastered reading does not need to "sound out" words and therefore possess the mental resources necessary to think about the substance of what they are reading, so do law students strive for a level of knowledge and skill development that frees up their brain to focus on the substance of their exam task. Expert law students strive for the law school equivalent to what expert athletes call "The Zone," a mental state in which athletes are so immersed in their sport that they play without thinking consciously about what they "should" be doing.

As explained below, overlearning is one of the best if not the best tools for dealing with examination stress. Students who have overlearned their course material are less likely to forget what they have learned, even under the stress of the examination. They also are more confident (because they are confident that they know the material well) and, therefore, they are less likely to fear failure or to feel stress. They also are more likely to have an initial success on the examination, such as by spotting an issue or by recalling a case analogous to the hypothetical on the examination. This initial success builds their self-efficacy, causing the students to be more likely to persist, even in the face of difficulty on the examination, because they believe their persistence will pay off. And, of course, such persistence does pay off when they get their grades, which further builds their self-efficacy and willingness to persist and further reduces their examination stress (unless they have chosen not to properly prepare for their examination).

In contrast, students who fail to overlearn are more likely to feel anxious going into the examination because they recognize their vulnerability. They also are less likely to feel self-confidant, to have an initial success or to persist in the face of difficulty on the examination. For these reasons, expert law students strive to overlearn their course material as part of their regular examination preparation.

This overlearning or automaticity requires students to devote more effort to memorization than they would normally need to devote. In other educational settings, expert students continue memorizing until they can demonstrate to themselves the ability to recall everything they need to know for their exams (such as by being able to accurately paraphrase all their flashcards). Expert law students, however, need to go further. They need to continue memorizing until they have achieved a higher level of recall, until they not only are able to recall everything by looking at their flashcards but also are, in fact, able to rapidly recite everything without even looking at the flashcards at all (or, perhaps, by only looking at a very skeletal, one page outline). Students' efforts towards this goal are made much easier if they have already used the organizational and memorization strategies addressed in Chapters 12 and 13. These efforts will also be greatly supported by the reorganization activities described below.

Reorganizing. In addition to organizing their learning, by creating outlines and graphic organizers as they are learning each topic, expert law students also reorganize their learning as part of their examination preparation. The initial organizational efforts facilitate the development of the students' schemata for storing the new learning, prepares students to be able to spot issues on their examinations and helps them better understand the learning. The reorganizing increases these benefits.

By creating new schemata structured in new ways, students are creating alternative paths within their brains to the information. Much like knowing alternative routes to work or school helps one get to school or work on time when one encounters traffic, possessing alternative mental paths to information increases the likelihood that a student will be able to recall it during the examination. In fact, just as an alternative path to work or school allows a person to get to work or school faster when there is some blockage impeding the normal route, so do alternative mental paths allow to more quickly access the knowledge needed. To see how powerful a memorization tool reorganization is, try this experiment: think of your favorite movie. How did you recall the name of the movie? Most people recall the name of their favorite movie by simply accessing their mental file for a list of movies, recalling those movies that have stood out in their minds and then selecting from among the movies. If you wished to remember for a long time the particular movie you selected this time, you would simply remember it in additional ways (other than in your mental list of favorite movies). For example, you could and likely already have associated the name of the movie in your brain with this chapter and/or this book. Depending on the movie, you also could store it in your brain with other movies starring the same actor or actress or directed by the same director. You could store it in your brain by associating it with other movies made the same year or having the same theme, having similar plots or being in the same genre (westerns, comedies, etc.). You could even store it in your brain by associating it with other performance favorites, including your favorite song, play, novel and television show episode. The larger the number of associations you make, the more likely you will be to be able to recall it if asked later in this book to do so.

Reorganizing also increases the likelihood that students will spot issues on their examinations. By reorganizing their learning, students can identify connections among the subject areas they have studied that were not apparent when they first studied the material. These connections will suggest to the student different ways their instructors can combine the topics on their examinations. In other words, students can anticipate possible combinations of topics that their instructors might choose.

Finally, reorganization helps students better understand the material. Reorganization allows students to identify connections among course materials that were not apparent during their initial study of the material and therefore it helps students better understand each topic. For example, one common policy rationale for contract doctrine is economic efficiency. It plays a role in a wide variety of contract rules and court decisions. By identifying all of the areas of contract law for which economic efficiency explains the law, students can see how each rule is a part of an overall approach to solving contract disputes and thereby better understand each individual rule.

The two graphic organizers in Figure 60 illustrate some of these possibilities. The two graphic organizers depict two very different ways of organizing materials relating to the contract law topic known as express conditions. The first shows a traditional organization of the course material that a contracts student would be likely to create during an initial study of the subject. It shows how express conditions law fits within the overall topic of contract law looked at as a series of subjects along a timeline from cradle (contract formation) to grave (remedies to a victim of a breach of contract). Express conditions law is depicted as being part of contract performance and breach, as a subcategory equivalent to "constructive conditions" and "excuse and discharge of conditions." The second shows an entirely different view of express conditions in which express conditions law is shown as one of many contract law topics in which the courts interpret the parties' contractual language. By reorganizing the material in this way, a contracts student would better see the similarities and differences among this wide variety of topics not commonly considered together.

Figure 60: Two Graphic Organizers Integrating Express Conditions Law

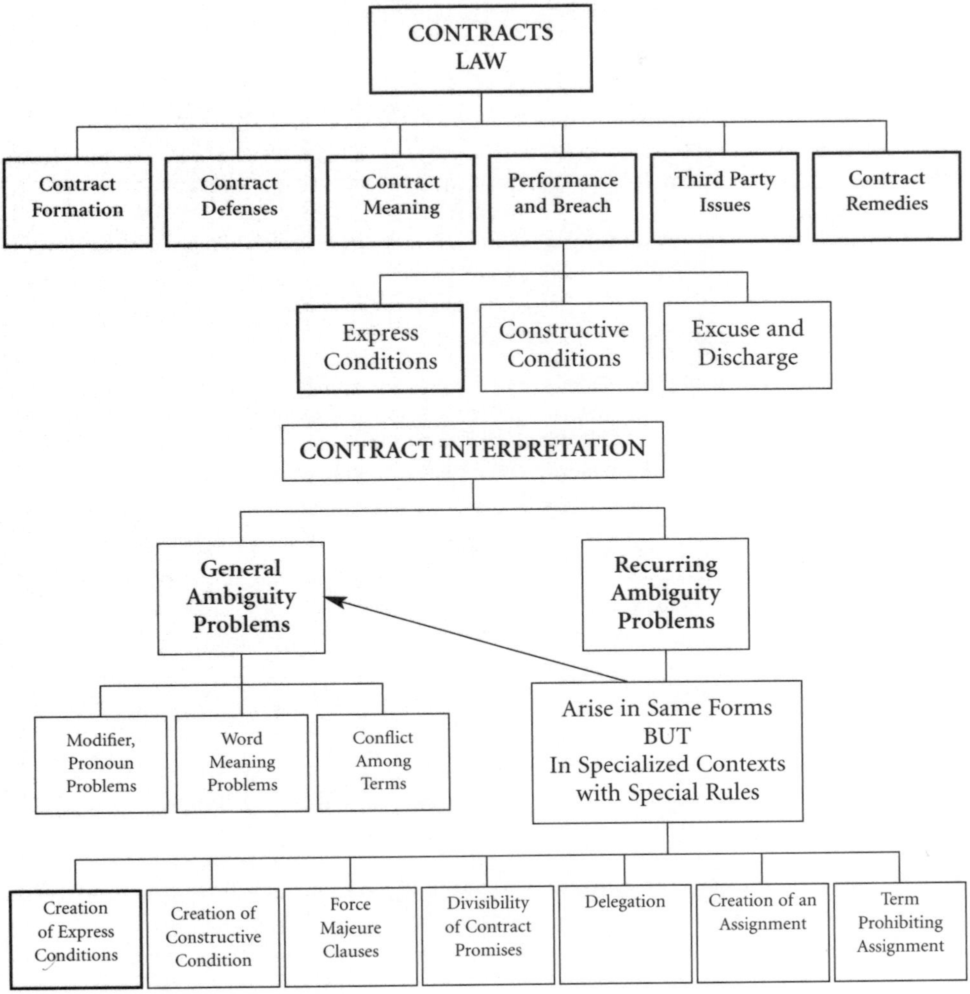

In many courses, a wide variety of combinations are possible. At the simplest level, by looking at the outlines of a variety of hornbooks, texts and other commercial products, students can see the variety in how law professors have organized the topics in the course. Copying someone else's reorganization, however, creates a much weaker mental trace and therefore is not a recommended practice. More complex combinations are also possible. For example, as explained in Chapter 9, public policy rationales often come in matched sets, in which the selection of a rule involves choosing one social good over another. For example, courts' dislike of contract defenses reflects a choice that the social good of making contracts predictable is more important than the social good of allowing people out of unfair contracts. One possible reorganization of the contract rules is to organize together those rules that reflect a decision that predictability is more important than fairness and to organize elsewhere those rules that reflect a decision that fairness is more important than predictability. Holdings may also be organized according to the party in whose favor the court ruled. This task would make the task of applying and distinguishing easier.

Regardless of the particular form students' efforts at reorganization take, there is no question that such efforts pay off on examinations. Accordingly, expert law students reorganize their learning as part of their examination preparation.

Learning Self-Assessment

Pre-exam self-assessment is a crucial component for success on law school exams. Self-assessment, of course, is a part of the SRL Cycle and therefore is a component of students' learning efforts throughout the semester. As exams approach, however, self-assessment assumes even greater importance. Expert law students determine whether they understand everything they need to know for their examinations and make sure they obtain the assistance they need if they do not.

As exams approach, expert law students use three techniques to self-assess their learning: (1) comparing their skills and knowledge against the professor's instructional objectives (if any are provided), (2) using elaboration techniques and checking them for accuracy, and (3) creating and analyzing their own mock exam questions.

Self-assessment using the professor's learning objectives. If their professor has provided detailed learning objectives, expert law students measure their learning against those objectives, asking themselves whether they know and are able to do everything their professor expects them to know and be able to do. In this way, the objectives serve as an exam preparation checklist; if the student has not yet mastered any of the skills described in the objectives, she knows she is not yet ready for the examination and needs to continue studying. Exercise 16-1 provides an opportunity to practice self-assessing learning from objectives.

Self-assessment by creating rule and holding paraphrases. Expert law students also use an elaboration technique (see Chapter 13), translating rules and holdings into their own words, to make sure they understand the rules and cases. If the student cannot accurately state a rule or holding in her own words, the student does not understand it. Creating accurate paraphrases therefore is, perhaps, one of the best ways of making sure the student not only knows the words of the rules but, also, understands what those words mean. Expert law students use their study groups or peers in the class to check the accuracy of their paraphrases.

Self-assessment by creating and analyzing mock essay exam questions. Most importantly, in addition to brainstorming examples and non-examples of each individual concept as part of their memorization efforts (which, as explained in Chapter 14, is another elaboration technique), expert law students also create their own, complete practice exam questions. This technique is different from brainstorming examples and non-examples to memorize concepts. Creating examples and non-examples requires considering each concept in isolation from all the other concepts the student has learned. It involves identifying the essential attributes of the concept and then creating an example that possess all the essential attributes and a non-example that is identical (or, at least, similar) to the example in all trivial respects but is missing one or more essential attributes. The goal is to create fact patterns that indisputably either possess the required attributes or indisputably do not possess the required attributes. In other words, the student is making the concept make sense to herself (see Chapter 2 for more information about constructivist learning theory and the importance of making one's learning personally meaningful).

Creating exam questions is quite different in several respects. It involves engaging in a role shift. The student must imagine herself as her own professor and try to construct exam questions that her professor might create. For this task, the student is not trying to demonstrate understanding of the concept by seeing if she can think of an example of it. Rather, she is trying to anticipate how her professor may test her. The student is trying to think like her professor, a particularly beneficial approach given that the student will soon face an exam drafted by that professor.

The task also involves thinking more broadly about the course material because exam questions combine concepts, almost always in ways the student has never seen them combined before. In other words, example and non-example fact patterns are shorter and simpler and give rise only to one issue whereas exam questions are longer, more complicated, and have multiple issues. To draft exam questions, students must not merely understand each concept individually but also must understand the relationships among all the concepts in the course. This thinking will prepare the student for an exam question that forces the student to do the same thing.

Most significantly, whereas examples and non-examples have clear, correct and indisputable answers, law school examinations (and therefore the questions students create as part of their examination preparation) often do not have clear and indisputable answers. In fact, as explained in Chapter 3, the correct answer on law school exams is, at best, a prediction of how a court would rule and, often, even a moderate degree of certainty as to how a court would actually resolve all the issues on the exam is impossible. Law school exams test students' ability to develop and evaluate the arguments reasonable lawyers might make in response to hypothetical fact patterns; consequently, the exams provide sufficient information for good students to develop persuasive arguments on behalf of all parties involved in the fact pattern. This aspect of law school exams, which law professors call "testing on the line," "creating debatable issues," or making students "argue both sides" requires a higher level of understanding and therefore is a particularly effective examination preparation tool. To create a good exam question, students must understand the concepts, must see where the line is located between a set of facts for which there is a clear answer and one about which reasonable lawyers would argue, and must be able to add or eliminate facts as needed to achieve a proper position along the line. This difficult mental task is, in fact, more mentally tasking than answering the actual exam question. Consequently, it both makes the exam-taking process easier and helps the student develop her sensitivity to small factual differences, a crucial skill on law school exams.

For these reasons, creating exam questions is both extraordinarily difficult and extraordinarily important. Many students find it helpful to approach the task in one of the several ways their professors do it; those ways are described below. Regardless of which approach the student takes, the student's learning experience is likely to be a rich one. A few caveats about writing exam questions apply to the design of all questions and are worth noting at the outset. First, a crucial component of the learning process is planning a model answer while the student is drafting the question. Most law professors have discovered, at one time in their teaching careers, that, if they do not plan an answer as they write, they discover, either after a lot of work or, worse yet, while grading the students' answers, that a question that sounded great actually was a poor question. This approach is particularly important to law students because the purpose of the process is to create a representative exam and to learn from the process of creating one. Second, the learning goal for this task is always the following: creating an exam question that accurately reflects how the student might be tested on the examination. Consequently, students need to pay careful attention to how they are likely to be tested (see the above discussions of teacher study and types of exam questions) and therefore to create a question reflective of how they expect to be tested. Third, most law professors revise their questions several times and therefore students should do the same. Finally, most professors have a peer review the question. Expert students do something similar but different in an important way—they have a peer answer the question.

Three approaches law professors use to create essay exam questions. One way professors create essay exam questions is to start by selecting the areas in which they would like to test the students. After selecting a topic, the professor brainstorms a story that gives rise to issues in the areas in which the professor wishes to test the students. Many professors initially just try to get a story from any source (newspaper articles, current events, subjects relevant to law students) from which they can work. The professor then starts editing the story to make sure the story includes issues about which reasonable lawyers could argue on behalf of the fictional parties in the story. The professor adds and deletes facts to give the students information they need to build arguments, to clarify the story or to otherwise make the test as fair as possible.

A second approach involves starting from the cases the students have read over the course of the semester. In fact, if the instructor has emphasized applying and distinguishing skills during the course, this approach is likely one their instructor will adopt. After selecting a case, a set of cases, multiple cases or multiple sets of cases as a starting point, the instructor will begin combining the issues while altering the facts to make the exam question sufficiently unique. Much like the professor poses difficult hypotheticals in class that requires the student to apply or distinguish a case the class has just discussed, the professor will alter the facts of the case(s) in ways that make the "correct" answer difficult and open up possibilities for arguments on behalf of all the parties described in the hypothetical. Almost always, by the time the professor is done, the exam question looks only a little like the case(s) from which the instructor started.

A third approach involves performing legal research. The professor decides what areas in the field she might be interested in testing and then performs searches in those areas to find recently-decided cases, older, interesting cases, or even news stories that the instructor can use as a starting point for creating the exam. What the professor finds becomes the starting point for the creation of an exam question. Once again, the professor alters the facts of what she finds to add issues the professor is interested in testing and to make the exam question more challenging, more interesting, or otherwise more appropriate.

A student who adopts any or all of these approaches is likely to be engaging in a learning process that will help prepare the student for her exam. In fact, if a student can create appropriate essay exam questions, there is no doubt that she has mastered the material. Nevertheless, all other things being equal, the approach in which the student starts by finding a case is probably the most helpful because it has an added benefit; the approach causes the student to read additional cases relating to the topics on which the student will be tested. These additional examples will increase the student's understanding of the subject area. Exercise 16-2 gives an opportunity for the student to practice creating her own exam-type hypothetical questions.

Learning from Taking Tests

Choosing to take practice tests. Dozens of professors have authored law review articles detailing a crucial failure within legal education: students are given almost no opportunities to practice the skills on which they will be tested and therefore receive little, if any, critical feedback on their development of legal analysis skills. Novice law students simply accept this status quo without question. Their fear of or discomfort with negative feedback and their lack of knowledge of the learning process cause them to practice their legal analysis skills only when forced to do so and to avoid, at all costs, feedback.

Expert law students know better. Critical feedback is crucial to the development of any skill. To understand this point, try to imagine an athlete who never obtained coaching, a mathematician who never received teaching or a musician who never gets a music lesson. Feedback helps students know what they are doing well and what they are doing poorly. It guides students' studying and future practice efforts. Expert students therefore ask for practice and welcome feedback from anyone who might be willing to give it, including their professors, study groups, and even whoever takes the seat next to them in class.

Expert law students also do not fear or even feel uncomfortable when they receive harsh feedback because they expect it as a part of the learning process. For this reason, some expert law students even encourage their practice exam readers to be critical. Interestingly, law professors characterize such students not as being "pesky" or "demanding" but as being "teachable."

Of course, because expert law students practice more often and receive more feedback, they are able to correct errors, improve their skills and minimize exam anxiety. These factors, of course, have the ultimate result of causing the expert learners to perform better on exams than their novice peers. They also enjoy the learning process more and feel better about themselves (because they do not experience any ego deflation when they receive critical feedback).

Selecting appropriate practice tests. Although taking almost any practice test helps, expert law students devote some care to the selection of appropriate questions. The two best sources of exam questions are the student's professor and any collection of past exams given by that professor. In fact, as noted above in the discussion of teacher study, expert law students review every past exam question authored by their professors that they can find. Other sources include other professors' past exams and exams posted on websites such as the Jurist website (see Chapter 12). Exercise 16-3 gives an opportunity to practice finding/selecting appropriate practice exams and writing answers to those exams.

Self-assessing results. As shown in Chapter 8, the feedback the student receives on exams and practice tests plays a crucial role in her learning process. Equally important is the student's own effort to assess her results. The student's grade and her professors' comments will give her some insights into what she did well and what she did poorly on the exam question. Neither the grade nor the comments, however, will identify for the student the cause(s) of her success or failure or help her plan her future studying efforts to continue engaging in practices that worked and change practices that did not work. As the best authority on their own learning process, expert law students are ideally suited for this evaluative and reflective process. Moreover, each law professor sees only the one exam the student wrote for that professor. Consequently, the professor is unable to make connections and see patterns within the student's exam results or to evaluate whether a particular result at a particular time reflects progress.

Accordingly, expert law students typically plan for how they will learn from their examinations. The approach reflected in Figure 61 is typical of students who maximize what they learn from reviewing their exams. Such students carefully evaluate their results, review all their professors' comments to assess what they can learn from this feedback, and attribute their successes to strategy selection and effort and their failures to

Figure 61: How Expert Law Students Plan Their Learning from Feedback

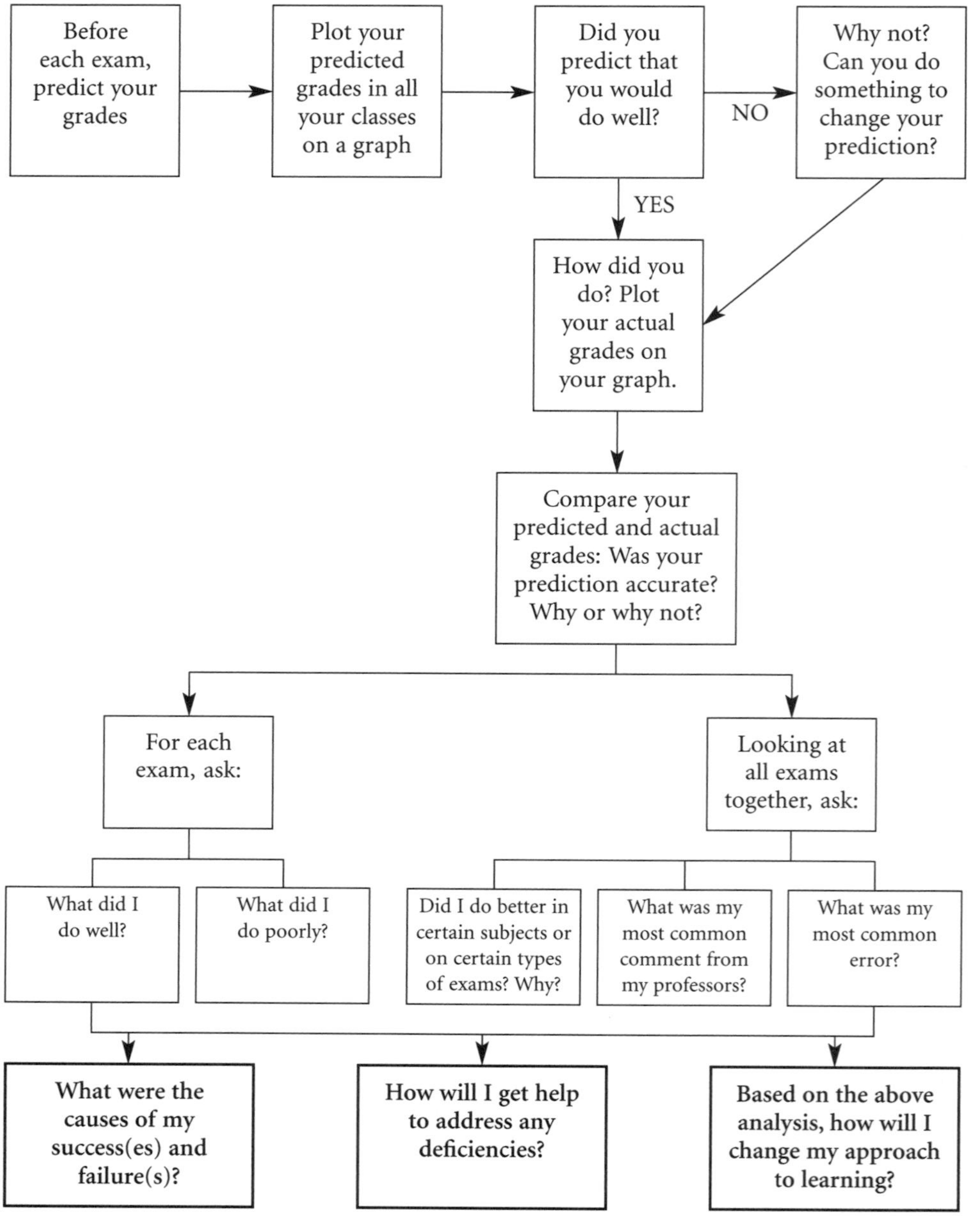

curable errors such as mistakes in strategy selection or lack of sufficient effort. Most of all, expert law students use the feedback they get as a tool for identifying their strengths and weaknesses, planning how they will address any weaknesses in the future and adapting their studying approach to improve their future outcomes. Exercise 16-4 gives an opportunity to apply this approach to the student's first set of law school examinations (or practice examinations, if the student's law school provides such opportunities).

Strategies for Taking for Law School Exams

Introduction

Ultimately, successful exam day strategies come from excellent preparation. Students who plan their studying well in advance, who seek opportunities for practice and feedback, who overlearn their course material and reorganize it, who carefully self-assess their learning by using their instructors' objectives, by paraphrasing the rules and holdings and by drafting their own exam questions, and avoid the negatives, such as self-doubt, sleep deprivation and unhealthy food and drink, inevitably select excellent strategies on the day of their exams. Being well prepared academically, well rested, and healthy physically, they experience less stress, manage their exam time better and are able to adapt to whatever their exam requires of them. Most of all, students who take all of the above suggestions and who combine them with high self-efficacy do well.

At the same time, there are effective tools for dealing with exam stress, for managing your time during an examination and for dealing with the two most common forms of law school exams: essay questions and multiple choice tests.

Dealing with Exam Stress

General approaches. Almost all students experience some exam stress. In fact, a moderate amount of stress, well managed, may actually improve performance by helping students stay focused and on task. Thus, the discussion below focuses only on techniques for dealing with excessive, debilitating exam stress, for handling the type of stress that may cause students to perform more poorly than they otherwise would have performed. There are six techniques generally deemed by experts to be effective tools for dealing with exam stress right before an exam:

1. *Invoking self-efficacy:* Invoking self-efficacy by recalling past successes helps reduce stress because it helps the student remember that she can and should succeed on the exam.

2. *Overlearning:* As explained above, overlearning is a powerful tool for dealing with exam stress. Overlearning increases confidence and usually produces early success on exams thereby increasing students' self-confidence.

3. *Reframing:* Students experiencing extreme exam stress often obsess about the exam and the possibility of failure. Reframing involves redirecting this stress; instead of worrying about the exam, the student strives to substitute an alternative mental state, one that will replace this debilitating doubt and fear. For example, some students have had success imagining themselves to be excited about the exam and by thinking of the exam as an opportunity to show off what they have learned. Other students find it helpful to make themselves angry about the exam and to adopt an "attack the exam" mental focus. These seemingly irreconcilable mental states have one thing in common that explains why they work. In both situations, the student is substituting productive sets of strong emotions for unproductive exam stress emotions.

4. *Planning and Using Attention-Focusing Strategies:* As Chapter 7 explains, when expert law students are engaging in any learning activity, they use strategies to focus their attention, including systematic guides and positive self-talk. Each of

these techniques is an effective tool for dealing with exam stress. Systematic guides, such as exam checklists, IRAC and the four-step approaches to applying rules to facts and to applying and distinguishing cases, give students tools for staying on task instead of focusing on their exam stress. Positive self-talk allows students to catch themselves succeeding as they work on their exam answers and thereby calm their anxiety.

5. *Perspective:* While law school exams are important, they are not a matter of life and death. The most meaningful things in life, such as family, friends, health, etc., are never resolved during three-hour exams. Smart students focus on what they can control, their effort and preparation, and then they celebrate the fact that they have done their best. Moreover, high law school grades do not predict success in legal practice or in life and low law school grades do not predict failure. In short, while preparing earnestly for examinations is an incredibly valuable, rewarding task, worrying about exam results serves no purpose.

6. *Relaxation techniques:* Women and men who have been through Lamaze or other similar child-birthing processes already possess or are aware of the benefits of using relaxation techniques as a tool for reducing anxiety. The deep breathing commonly recommended involves taking **deep, slow breaths**, focusing on taking air in through the nose and breathing out through the mouth. **Progressive relaxation** is another technique for reducing stress. The student works upward from her toes, focusing on, tensing and then relaxing, one-by-one, every muscle from the muscles connected to the student's toes to the muscles on her forehead. This technique both relaxes tense muscles and distracts the student from the anxiety.

A few students do not need to use any of these techniques or need to use only one of them. Many students, however, use several of these techniques at once, and still others use them all. The key to avoiding or minimizing stress is planning how you will deal with it well *before* the exam. Exercise 16-5 gives you an opportunity to plan your strategies for dealing with exam stress before your first set of law school examinations.

Getting unstuck. Even students who are usually calm during exams or who have used one or more of the above techniques to calm themselves before an exam still get stuck during an exam. There are three keys to getting unstuck. First, expert students use one of the above techniques to try to get themselves unstuck. The relaxation techniques, in particular, are effective tools for getting unstuck. Second, expert students remember that each exam question is an opportunity. They force themselves to look only at what is in front of them; they neither look backwards at questions they already answered nor look forward at what is coming up ahead. Finally, they devote no more than four minutes to their effort to get unstuck. If they cannot get unstuck in those four minutes, they move on to the next question, figuring they will do better on the current question after they have been away from it for a while.

Time Management

Law school exams almost always put time pressure on students and therefore require students to manage their exam time. Primarily, this task requires law students to apportion their time based on the relative weights of the questions they are answering. As a general rule, students should devote more time to questions that count for a larger share of their grades and less on questions that count for a smaller share of their grades.

For example, if a question is worth 50% of the student's grade on the final, the student should be spending 50% of her exam time on the question. This approach makes sense because law professors assign weights based on degrees of difficulty and time required for the task.

More difficult and more subtle time management is also required. On any given law school essay exam question, there are issues of varying degree of difficulty. Generally, law students can expect that greater grading weight will be assigned to those issues requiring greater thought and more discussion and lesser grading weight will be assigned to more simple issues. In particular, issues about which lawyers representing both parties would have a great deal to say tend to be assigned greater grading weight. Consequently, in addition to managing time among the various questions according to each question's relative weight, students must apportion their time within each question, spending more time on issues most likely to bear on their final grade. Any person who has ever participated in or watched an Easter egg hunt has an excellent metaphor for this approach. Every child who has ever participated in an Easter egg hunt knows that the largest quantity of candy and the best prizes can be found in the largest plastic eggs. For this reason, children go for the "big eggs" first. Law students should do the same on exams; they should make sure they get to all the "big eggs" (the major, most difficult issues) on the exam at all costs. While the smaller issues, the little eggs, do matter, students' grades usually are made or lost on the big eggs.

Finally, managing time requires students to pay attention to the passage of time while they are taking the examination. For the most part, students simply need to force themselves to look at the clock periodically to confirm that they are on track.

Taking Law School Multiple Choice Tests

This section provides some guidance in taking multiple-choice tests. It contains three sub-sections. The first subsection, The Structure of Law School Multiple Choice Questions, makes explicit how law professors structure multiple-choice questions. The section also discusses the various aspects of an answer to a multiple-choice question that can cause an answer to be wrong. The second sub-section, The Skills Tested by Law School Multiple-Choice Questions, focuses on the particular skills commonly tested by multiple-choice questions. The final section, Multiple-Choice Test-Taking Strategies, details the basic, across-the-board test-taking strategies that are specific to multiple-choice tests.

The Structure of Law School Multiple-Choice Questions. Law professors have adopted, either consciously or unconsciously, a set of conventions that guide the look and feel of law school and bar exam multiple-choice questions. Quickly identifying the type of question helps you know what to look for in the question that might be incorrect. Questions come in one of three forms.

The first and most common form of law school and bar exam multiple-choice question (Type 1) looks like the question in Figure 62 below.

Notice the common features of Type 1 questions: they include a Story, a Query and a set of answers, most of which include both a Stem and an Explanation. A slight variation on Type 1 questions involves basing several questions on one story. Law professors signal to you that they are giving you a multi-question story by adding the following

Figure 62: Type 1 Law School Multiple Choice Questions

> Jack and Jill went up the hill to fetch a pail of water. They were very thirsty, and they knew that the best water in the town could be found at the top of the hill. Jack fell down and broke his crown and Jill came tumbling after. Jill sustained a severe injury to her left leg; as a result, Jill now has a permanent limp and has been forced to give up her career as a professional basketball player, at which she earned $150,000 per year plus the additional $500,000 per year she had been earning from endorsing products. Jill has sued Jack for hill negligence. (*this part of the question is "The Story"*)
>
> In Jill's suit against Jack, Jill will (*this part of the question is "The Query"*)
>
>   a. Win (*this part of the answer is "The Stem"*), because Jack should not have fallen down the hill (*this part of the answer is "The Explanation"*).
>   b. Lose, because Jill voluntarily went along.
>   c. Win, because Jack fell first.
>   d. Lose, because Jack was careful.
>   e. None of the above.

words right above the story (often in bold): **Questions ___ through ___ are based on the following facts.**

An answer to a Type 1 question can be wrong because either the stem or the explanation is incorrect. For example, in the above question, two of the answers have the correct stem and two have an incorrect stem. Some law school multiple choice questions have three or four answers that share a stem paired with one or two other stems.

Type 1 questions sometimes do not use the stem/explanation structure, but, instead, take the form of a "best or worst argument" or a "least or most likely result" query or some other, similar query. Such questions require you to compare the arguments or results and select the best, worst, least likely, or most likely answer.

Type 2 questions are similar but have some important differences; they also include a story, but their structure and answers are much different. They look like the question in Figure 63.

Type 2 questions are similar to Type 1 questions in terms of the analysis required to answer them correctly, but they are both harder and easier. They are easier because they usually only have two or three substantive statements, e.g., I, II and III, and they are harder because the student needs to analyze correctly all three statements to select the right answer.

Type 3 questions are much simpler in form but require a higher degree of analysis. These questions look like the question in Figure 64.

Type 3 questions do not require the student to recall a detailed story. However, Type 3 questions usually require the student to analyze four or more hypothetical questions as opposed to one as in Type 1 or Type 2 questions.

The Skills Tested by Law School Multiple-Choice Questions. Multiple-choice questions can test a wide range of skills. Understanding the range of skills tested by multiple-choice questions may help the student distinguish correct from incorrect answers.

First, they test skills the student may have developed before she ever came to law school, such as her reading comprehension skills. Answers to Type 1 or Type 2 ques-

Figure 63: Type 2 Law School Multiple Choice Questions

> Jack and Jill went up the hill to fetch a pail of water. They were very thirsty, and they knew that the best water in the town could be found at the top of the hill. Jack fell down and broke his crown and Jill came tumbling after. Jill sustained a severe injury to her left leg; as a result, Jill now has a permanent limp and has been forced to give up her career as a professional basketball player, at which she earned $150,000 per year plus the additional $500,000 per year she had been earning from endorsing products. Jill has sued Jack.
>
> Consider the following statements about Jill's claim against Jack and determine which are true.
>
> > I. Jill can recover her salary as a basketball player.
> > II. Jill can recover her pain and suffering.
> > III. Jill can recover the $500,000 she made from endorsements.
> >
> > a. Only I is true.
> > b. Only II is true.
> > c. Only III is true.
> > d. Only I and II are true.
> > e. I, II and II all are true.

Figure 64: Type 3 Law School Multiple Choice Questions

> In which of the following cases would Jill be most likely to succeed if she brought a claim against Jack for hill negligence:
>
> > a. Jack and Jill went up the hill to fetch a pail of water. Jack fell down and, as he was falling, grabbed Jill's crown so they both went tumbling after.
> > b. Jack and Jill went up the hill to fetch a pail of water. Jack fell down and broke his crown, and Jill, who thought the whole thing looked fun, chose to come tumbling after.
> > c. Jack and Jill went up the hill to fetch a pail of water. Jack fell down and broke his crown, and Jill immediately started running down the hill to try to help Jack, tripped and came tumbling after.
> > d. Jack and Jill went up the hill to fetch a pail of water. Jack fell down and broke his crown, and Jill came tumbling after.
> > e. Jack would not be liable for hill negligence in any of the above situations.

tions can be incorrect, for example, because they misstate the facts in the story. Likewise, multiple-choice questions can test memorization skills; Type 1 or Type 2 answers can be incorrect because they misstate the law the student has learned or the holding of a case she studied. Such questions can be tricky; the misstatements included as wrong answers are likely to be based on common student errors or confusion and even may be what students might perceive to be minor points.

Second, multiple-choice questions can test issue-spotting skills. A set of answers each can correctly state (and even correctly apply) the law, but only the correct answer identifies the issue raised by the facts.

Third, multiple-choice questions can test the student's analysis skills. The Type 3 example above shows how easy it is to create a Type 3 analysis question. However, it is equally easy to create Type 1 and Type 2 analysis questions. For example, an Explanation to a Type 1 question can be incorrect because it involves an incorrect application of a rule or an improper basis for distinguishing or applying an authority.

Multiple-Choice Test-Taking Strategies. There are several well-known strategies for taking multiple-choice tests. Although a student may have learned many of these strategies in high school, college, or in connection with a prep course for a standardized test such as the SAT or the LSAT, the following strategies are worth remembering because they also apply to law school exams.

Know the materials well. To make sure the student gets the answer correct on a question that requires knowing the law, students must know the law cold. To do so, methods should be used that actively test the student's knowledge of the rules, such as creating and going through flashcards, trying to recite course outlines from memory, developing mnemonic devices, etc. (see Chapter 13).

Read the facts and the question carefully. Reading carefully not only helps the student correctly answer reading comprehension questions, it also helps her spot issues and identify both the relevant and the irrelevant facts.

Read every answer to each question, even if the first answer seems correct. Most law school tests and the bar exam require the student to select the "best" answer. The term "best" suggests that more than one answer may be correct and the student's task is to select the best correct answer. Moreover, a later answer may cause the student to reconsider her original inclination.

Come up with tentative answers to those questions that are completely baffling and then move on. The time pressure on multiple-choice tests is significant. Students have, on average, two minutes to answer each question. Students therefore do not have time to linger over any one question; once students have answered all the questions, however, students can take the time for greater reflection and contemplation. Students should generally not skip confusing questions; rather, they should decided upon a tentative answer, make a note to herself to come back to the question, and then go back to the question(s) at the end if time permits.

The student needs to plan, before the test, how she will signal to herself that she needs to come back to a question. Students should avoid using test-taking time planning how they will signal to themselves that they need to come back to certain questions, such as by marking a dot next to the answer, marking the question, or writing down the number of the question on a scratch paper.

With difficult questions, the student should start by eliminating the answers she is fairly certain are incorrect. For some very hard questions the answer may not jump out. To make progress with such questions, the student will need to start by eliminating the answers she knows to be incorrect. Then, the student needs to do her best to select from the remaining answers.

Taking Law School Essay Tests

Aside from the discussions and explanations of IRAC, issue spotting, applying rules to facts and applying and distinguishing cases discussed in Chapter 15, there are only a few general principles applicable to taking all types of essay exams. Each of those principles is listed and explained below.

Principle 1: Answer the call of the question. The call of the question is the statement at the end of the hypothetical that tells the student what she should do with the story told in the hypothetical. The student is graded, in part, by how well she responds to that call.

Perhaps most importantly, the student gets NO CREDIT for addressing things not reflected in the call of the question. In fact, some law school essay exam questions raise more issues than can be addressed within the time allotted; for such questions, the call of the question tells the student what she needs to do to be able to finish the exam in the time allotted. For this reason, most expert law students read the call of the question first.

Principle 2: Make the essay readable. If an instructor cannot read what the student has written, the professor cannot give the student credit for it. The student needs to write neatly as she can. In fact, if the student can type her exam without losing any speed, she should do so. The student's essay should be organized before she writes it. Headings should be used to make the organization visually obvious. The tendency of some novice law students to underline words should be avoided. Because analysis, not knowledge, is the key to success on law school exams, the use of particular words is seldom important. Students reveal a misapprehension of their assigned task when they choose to use a lot of underlining.

Principle 3: Don't lead the exam; follow it. It is tempting to take an essay examination as an opportunity to show the professor the student has learned everything covered in the course, even though no law school exam tests everything the students have studied in the course. It is also tempting to try to relieve stress by developing a plan of action (sometimes called an "exam approach") and then sticking to that approach regardless of what the student finds on the exam. Both strategies don't work. Accept that law school exams do not test knowledge but only require it, and, while it is often helpful to have a checklist of issues and sub-issues in mind, student cannot be slaves to those lists. The ultimate source of the topics students must discuss is the exam itself. If students discuss matters beyond what the exam question requires, they are not only likely to see that error reflected in their grade but also are unlikely to finish the exam in the allotted time.

Principle 4: Analyze, don't just recite, the facts. Student are not writing court opinions. Moreover, professors already know the facts because they wrote the exam question. Students therefore should **not** do what courts do and include a recital of the facts in their answers. In the answers, a fact should never be stated until the student has **first** stated a rule or holding with which to analyze that fact. In addition, students should never state a fact without **following** that fact statement with an analysis of whether that fact satisfies the requirements reflected in the rule.

Principle 5: Populate the answer with IRACs for each element, at least each element about which reasonable lawyers would argue. In other words, students' answers should not be single, giant IRACs in which, for example, the students state all the rules relating to battery at one time, or all the holdings of all the relevant cases at one time. Rather, examination answers should consist of a series of IRAC paragraphs in which the student analyzes each element separately and in which the "R", the rule, is the definition of the element or a sub-rule (such as one of the transferred intent rules) relating to that element or the one specific holding the student is about to apply or distinguish.

Principle 6: Be sure to make a conscious decision about the legal significance of each fact in the hypo. As you use each fact in the hypo in your answer, highlight it using a highlighting pen. By the end of the examination, all the facts should be highlighted except those you have **consciously** decided are not relevant, given the call of the question or the issues.

Principle 7: Avoid the crazy-makers. In the minutes before the exam, the student should try to avoid discussing what she has learned with her fellow students and, in the minutes after the exam, the student should try to avoid torturing herself with a postmortem of what she and others did. The student needs to do her best, stay calm and remember, when it is all over, that no one asks the lawyer who has just won a big case what grade she got in her contracts class.

Principle 8: Work carefully and systematically. Excellent law school exam answers reflect careful thought and great sensitivity to factual nuances. Consequently, expert law students read the entire question at least twice and work systematically to make sure they use every fact in the exam question.

Reflection Questions

1. Why do the behaviors designated "the negatives" in this chapter interfere with student learning and success?

2. Have you ever planned how you will prepare for an examination? Describe what you did.

3. Why do expert law students self-assess their learning?

4. Why do expert law students take practice exams? Why do novice learners avoid them?

5. Compare the strategies you have used in the past to deal with exam stress and the strategies described in this chapter. Which of the strategies in this chapter might work for you? Which might not?

References

Richard Michael Fischl & Jeremy Paul, Getting to Maybe (1999).

Barbara K. Hofer, Shirley L. Yu and Paul R. Pintrich, *Teaching College Students to Be Self-Regulated Learners* in Self Regulated Learning: From Teaching to Self-Reflective Practice 57 (D.H. Schunk, B. Zimmerman, eds.1998).

Philip C. Kissam, *Law School Examinations,* 42 Vand. L. Rev. 433 (1989).

Kurt M. Saunders and Linda Levine, *Learning to Think Like a Lawyer,* 29 U.S.F.L. Rev. 121 (1994).

LaVergne Trawick & Lyn Corno, *Expanding the Volitional Resources of Urban Community College Students* in Understanding Self-Regulated Learning 57 (P. Pintrich, ed.1995).

Claire E. Weinstein & Richard E. Mayer, *The Teaching of Learning Strategies* in Handbook of Research on Teaching (M.C. Wittrock, ed. 1986).

Chapter 17

A Chapter for the Family and Friends of Law Students

Introduction

(I co-authored this chapter with my wife, Dr. Stacey Hunter Schwartz. Dr. Schwartz has particular expertise relevant to the matters discussed in this chapter. She has a Ph.D. in counseling psychology from the University of Southern California School of Education, and is a college dean. She and I met while I was in law school, and we are still together today.

We have written this chapter solely for the significant people in law students' lives—their husbands, wives, partners, sons, daughters, parents, grandparents and others. Law students: ask all the significant people in your lives to read this chapter—it will make your adjustment to law school and their adjustment to living with a law student much easier.)[1]

Law school can be hard not only on law students, but also on their relationships with others! We are writing this chapter for you, the significant others of law students, because we would like the primary readers of this book, law students, to do well. Law students do better in law school when they do not have to worry about their personal relationships. We also believe having a loved one in law school need not result in relationship strife but can, in fact, bring you closer. To achieve both these goals, you need to know more about what law students experience in law school, how their experiences can alter your relationship and what you can do to use law school to strengthen what you have.

Almost everyone has heard or seen something that purports to explain what law school is like for new law students. The first year of law school, in fact, has been depicted in movies, television shows and novels and other books. Many people also hear things about law school from family, friends and acquaintances, even from people who have never been to law school and have no idea what law school is really like. Many of these reports bear little resemblance to the modern law school experience, having been over-blown for dramatic purposes.

This chapter therefore begins by describing the law school process in a way that makes sense to non-law students, to people who really do not know what law students go through in law school and even for those who have some familiarity with law school

---

1. Dr. Schwartz has granted express permission for the inclusion of her ideas in this book.

but have not seen law school in its current form. The chapter explains law school by focusing on the five characteristic difficulties that first-year law students encounter: (1) the difficult and enormous workload, (2) the law professors' expectations, (3) the law school's testing and grading practices, (4) the changes in how students think and analyze problems, and (5) the stress produced by all these issues.

The chapter then addresses how these difficulties and other matters relating to law school can alter your relationship with the law student in your life and suggests what you can do to preserve and even strengthen your relationship.

The Five Characteristic Difficulties Encountered by New Law Students

There is a reason why the first year of law school has been the focus of so much literary interest: the first year of law school is just plain hard. Most law students experience their first year as the most difficult and stressful educational experience of their lives. In fact, it is that difficulty and stress that prompted this book in the first place.

The first year is so hard and has become such a subject of myth, lore and fear, that, in addition to the many and expensive required texts new law students must buy, they can spend even more money on optional books written solely for first-year law students. Legal publishers, cognizant that an anxious, reading-oriented group such as new law students constitutes a ready market, offer first-year law students hundreds of books on which the students could spend thousands of dollars.

This section explains the things that make law school so hard, so famous and so much a trap for the fearful.

Law School Workload

First-year law students take two types of courses. "Doctrinal" courses focus on the law applicable to specific subject areas regarded as crucial to students' knowledge base as future lawyers, such as contract law, criminal law and constitutional law. The word doctrine, in fact, is a synonym for the "rules of law." "Skills" courses focus on teaching law students lawyering skills, such as legal research and legal writing. These labels, however, are somewhat misleading because skills instructors teach their students doctrine (because the students must use doctrine in their legal writing papers) and doctrinal instructors teach students lawyering skills (because success in doctrinal courses depends on students' ability to do legal reasoning, to be able to **apply** the legal rules the students are studying and not simply to **know** the words of the rules).

While the focus and emphases of the two types of courses are different, both make huge time demands on law students. In fact, law students' workloads are considerably greater than the workloads of undergraduates or those attending many other, but not all, types of graduate schools. During the regular part of the semester, law students are expected to devote 3–4 hours outside of class for every hour they are in class. Thus, a full-time law student taking a typical 15-unit class load, should be studying at least 45 hours per week and as many as 60 hours per week. Before examinations, those numbers get even higher.

Most law students do not find it difficult to fill the 45–60 hours. The law school reading load is quite heavy. For **each** of their doctrinal classes (full-time students typically take four such courses per semester whereas part-time students take two such courses per semester), students must read at least 60 pages and, sometimes, in excess of 100 pages per week. Moreover, the print in law school texts is tiny, and law school texts include almost no pictures, charts or graphs.

The reading is also very dense, particularly for new law students, who, because of their unfamiliarity with legal materials, must frequently use law dictionaries while they are reading, just like students learning a new language must use foreign language dictionaries. The concepts addressed in the reading are very difficult and require multiple readings to be understood. In other words, legal materials cannot be read in the same way one might read a novel or newspaper; law students cannot skip or otherwise ignore the many unfamiliar words they encounter. Rather, law students must quickly become experts in this new language and become adept at using it.

Classroom experiences in doctrinal classes do not always help students increase their understanding. Many law students report that their classroom experiences often leave them more confused rather than less confused because their professors assume students have understood this difficult reading and focus on testing students' ability to use what they have learned to analyze new legal problems. These new problems are difficult for new law students because they require them to use materials with which they may not yet be comfortable, because they often do not have a clear, right answer and because they require the students to use a skill, legal reasoning, that the students are still learning. Moreover, many law professors never let their students know whether they have correctly analyzed the problems, instead asking the students additional and even more difficult questions.

In addition, most law professors, unlike college instructors, seldom lecture. Instead, they devote most of every class session to asking students questions about their reading material. Students must infer what they need to learn from those discussions and their peers' responses. This teaching technique is stressful on students, not in small part because most law students experience anxiety about being asked questions in class. In fact, for some law students, the fear of being called upon next is so great that they have a hard time focusing on what their peers or the professor is saying.

The reading and classroom teaching for the legal research and writing courses tends to be more straightforward. The work, however, often proves at least as difficult and time consuming as the work in the students' other classes. For their legal research and writing courses (both full-time and part-time law students typically take one such course per semester), students must write multiple lengthy papers (as many as five ten-page papers in a 14-week semester), most of which require extensive research and highly technical citation and word processing formats. Legal research, while similar to other types of research, has its own, unique techniques and materials. Many law students have difficulty knowing when they have finished doing their research; they have trouble being sure they have found every resource they needed to have found. Even after they have finished their research, students must go back and check to make sure, for each source they have used in their papers, whether that source is still good, a process that itself can be painstaking. Finally, excellent content is not enough; students must make sure their papers have flawless grammar, punctuation, paragraphing and word usage. Professors assume students have written and re-written their papers multiple times.

Law School Professors' Expectations

As the previous section suggests, law professors expect a great deal of their students. First, by choosing to use questions to teach the material and skills, law professors are assuming their students possess considerable and well-developed learning skills. In any given class, most professors ask questions of 6–10 students; in other words, law professors assume the other 50–90 students in the class can learn "vicariously" by watching how their peers answer the questions. Second, they also assume their students can learn what they need to learn from the reading, on their own, outside of class. Finally, many law school instructors devote little time to questions that teach the students the skills on which the students will be tested on their exams. Rather, they devote class discussions to questions of what lawyers call "policy." Policy refers to the reasons underlying the law, the reasons why courts and legislators enact one rule of law instead of another.

Law professors also expect students to prepare diligently for every class session. In college, many students do not prepare for class at all and do most of the course reading only shortly before their examinations. Law students who fail to prepare for class not only are unable to learn what they need to learn in class, but also may actually be dismissed from their classes.

Finally, law professors expect their students to be able to memorize enormous quantities of information. Typically, students must memorize 40- to 80-pages of dense outlines for each of their courses that they are expected to develop on their own during the course of the semester. Thus, students taking five classes must memorize 4 or 5 such outlines.

Law School Testing and Grading Practices

How are law students tested? Law school final examinations are unique. Not only must law students, as noted above, memorize an enormous amount of material in the short time before their examinations, but also they must prepare themselves to deal with examinations that often are only vaguely connected to the focus of their classroom discussions, are determinative or largely determinative of their entire grade for an entire year's worth of material (or at least a semester), and are challenging, often having no "right" answer and often lasting 3–4 hours.

While law school classroom discussions often focus on "policy," most law school essay exam questions are unlike the classroom discussions and unlike, at least in some important aspects, anything they would have to do as practicing lawyers. The exams are unlike the classroom discussions because they focus on the application of the rules the student has studied in the course to hypothetical factual situations significantly unlike other factual situations they have studied over the course of the semester or year. Thus, classroom discussions often fail to prepare students for their final examinations, and, even in courses where there is congruity between the classroom discussion and the final examination, the actual final examination questions are nevertheless significantly different from the hypotheticals the students have discussed in class. Law professors justify this testing approach by asserting that they are assessing the extent to which their students are able to think under pressure and apply what they have learned.

Exam questions are unlike what lawyers do because the questions are often more factually intricate (although, certainly, some law practice problems are even more complicated, but it is worth noting that such questions are handled in practice by people with more than one year of law school under their belts). Moreover, particularly with respect to complicated questions, practitioners have more than one hour (the time assigned for most law school essays) in which to analyze the legal issues.

Law school exams are also extraordinarily difficult because of their significance to students' course grades. Many (if not most) law professors only test their students once over an entire semester or even an entire year. Students who have a "bad day" are simply out of luck.

Finally, law school examinations are intellectually challenging. On most law school examinations, there is no "right" answer to the question; rather, students must determine the kinds of arguments all of the lawyers involved in handling the dispute would be likely to make and assess the persuasiveness of all answers. This assessment is particularly difficult because law professors design their exams so that the likely result in the hypothetical dispute is unknown or at least uncertain, even to the professor! Thus, an excellent law school examination answer is not one that "correctly" decides who would win, but, instead, makes plausible arguments for each of the parties described in the hypothetical. In fact, one of the most highly regarded books written about law school exams is called *Getting to Maybe*.[2] This title reflects the common law professor belief that the ultimate answer to a law school examination that raises a question of whether the plaintiff would win the lawsuit or the defendant would be convicted of the alleged crime is "maybe."

How are law school examinations graded? Law school grading is not really unusual; it is merely stingy. While most graduate students' grades are higher than their college grades, law students' grades typically are one-half to one full grade point lower. Consequently, law students, nearly all of whom excelled in college, do "worse" in law school. Moreover, law schools get some of the very best college students so that the competition for grades is much stiffer. Thus, law school grades surprise both law students and the significant others in their lives. Former "A students" learn to feel proud of "C" grades.

Law school results (grades), can be particularly confusing to students. Law students often incorrectly predict their results on examinations. These predictive inaccuracies occur because law students assume that, if they felt the exam was easy, they must have done well and, if the exam seemed hard, they must have done poorly. In many instances, however, struggling with an exam reflects the fact that the student correctly perceived its difficulty and a lack of struggle may reflect a failure to recognize the complexity of the examination. Moreover, law students often assume that, if they have memorized the material perfectly, they are certain to do well on the examination. However, as explained above, while law school examinations require memorization, excellent grades on examinations depend on the extent to which the student's exam answer reflects excellent, thoughtful analysis.

How Law School Changes People

In general, all graduate school experiences change people. In fact, because of the changes wrought by graduate school, more than one-half of all marriages do not sur-

---

2. Michael Fischl and Jeremy Paul, GETTING TO MAYBE (1999).

vive having one spouse obtain a graduate degree. Law school produces a particular set of changes that can be challenging to a law student's significant others.

First, law school causes students to become more analytical. Lawyers must be able to find flaws in their opponents' legal arguments. Law students learn this skill by criticizing court opinions. In fact, many classroom discussions in first-year law school classes focus on the task of finding flaws in courts' legal reasoning. This skill is like a newly-developed muscle for new law students; they often cannot help but flex their new critical skills in their interactions with their peers and significant others. You peers, however, may not appreciate these critiques.

Second, having been subjected to critical questioning and having witnessed it in all their classes, law students are more likely to question things they hear and read. They are less likely to accept matters at face value and more likely to insist that things make sense to them. In their classes, their professors have insisted they discern the rationale underlying every court decision. This process causes law students to search for rationales with equal vigilance in all aspects of their lives.

Third, in the competitive environment typical of law school, where higher grades lead to more exciting employment opportunities, many law students become highly competitive. The competition is invigorating for some law students but depressing for others.

Finally, as the next section explains, for all the reasons detailed above and more, most law students experience considerable stress.

Law School Stress

For all of the reasons discussed above, most law students experience considerable stress, particularly in their first year of law school. In particular, the difficulty and amount of work required, the pressure to succeed, the competitiveness of the law school environment and the teaching methodology commonly used by law professors combine to produce a high level of stress. Considering also the high cost of graduate education and the students' and his or her loved ones' expectations, it is easy to see why law school puts great stress on interpersonal relationships. The key for loved ones is to recognize this fact, to try to be supportive and to be forgiving.

Challenges to Your Relationship and What You Can Do to Make Things Better

Problems and Solutions Applicable to All Loved Ones

You probably thought that it was a good idea for the student to go to law school. You also probably want to be supportive and certainly do not want to interfere with the law student's studies. But, what does being supportive really mean? This section explores the challenges you will be facing and suggests some solutions.

Problems Caused by Not Understanding. For all non-law students, one major problem is not understanding. Many law students perform poorly in law school because they and their loved ones do not understand how law school changes things. They had no idea what the law students would experience, and, as a result, they put pressure on the law students to continue devoting the same amount of time and effort to familial obligations that the student devoted prior to law school. They also put excessive pressure on the law students by expecting them to achieve the same grades in law school that the students had obtained in the past.

Your choice to read this chapter suggests you care about helping the law student in your life succeed. What you do with this information, however, remains completely within your control; you can act on this knowledge or ignore it. We hope, obviously, that knowing what to expect helps you not only accept what will be happening but also to find ways to be supportive.

Problems Caused by Law Students' Lack of Time and Energy. Another problem is the dramatic decrease in time the student will be spending with you. Law students have little time and even less energy to devote to their relationships. Understanding this fact, however, does not replace what you have lost. You will find that the law student in your life will need to miss family gatherings, such as holiday parties or Sunday dinners. The law student may fail to call on birthdays or other special occasions or to return phone calls for several weeks. Even when they do call, they will have little time to talk.

Recognizing these limitations, of course, does not equate to enjoying them. It does help to know, however, that law school is a three- or four-year experience, not a lifetime sentence. Law students' lack of time does not reflect a lack of priorities, but, rather, a shifting of priorities to meet new demands, and law students' lack of attentiveness does not reflect a lack of interest or caring, but only a lack of time and energy common among all law students. There's nothing personal involved.

Thus, people who successfully support law students volunteer to take over chores for the students. They offer to act as liaisons to groups of friends or family so that the law student can maintain relationships with others without devoting time to communicating with so many people individually. They ask the law student to name convenient times to discuss conflicts, to socialize or to perform necessary tasks. They do not make the student's lack of availability become an issue in their relationship because they realize that they are not personally being rejected; they know the student would rather be with them. They don't try to induce "guilt trips" in students who may already feel guilty about their neglect of relationships.

Supportive family members and friends do not second-guess the amount of time the law student spends studying by saying things like, "You must have studied enough by now. Don't you think you're being obsessive? Exams are still several weeks away." They recognize that proper preparation takes a great deal of time and all semester- or year-long.

Problems Caused by Law Students' High Level of Stress. Competitive pressure, fatigue, deadlines, and performance anxiety all have the potential to put people in a bad mood. Try combining all four for weeks on end! With such a combination of stressors, it is easy for law students to forget why they signed up for law school in the first place.

Supportive family members try to let grumpy or even hostile comments from students fall off their backs, recognizing that the amount of pressure on the law students is to blame. (Of course, emotional or physical abuse should never be tolerated.) Instead of engaging in defensive posturing, supportive family members reframe outbursts or depressive behavior by responding with remarks like, "I know that you're under a tremendous amount of stress right now. Please let me know tonight when might be a better time to talk to you."

Problems and Solutions Applicable to Spouses and Significant Others

Ever tried to have a partnership with someone who does not pull his or her weight? If you measure your partner's participation in your relationship as you have done in the past, you have a formula for resentment. Instead, you will have to view law school studies as a part of work for the partnership. When you have taken out the umpteenth bag of trash or have had to be the parent who has to help your daughter with yet another school project, you may feel like your partner has deserted you. You will have to remind yourself that you wanted the person to go to law school in the first place and will have to remember the ultimate goal.

You may also resent all the time the law student spends with study group partners and even resent the bonds these students share. They are sharing a unique emotional experience, and you are bound to feel like an outsider, maybe even jealous. Be sure to communicate these feelings to your spouse at an appropriate time in a calm, not accusatory manner. You want this experience to help your relationship grow, too, and expressing such feelings honestly can bring you closer together.

As law school continues, so does your life. You will encounter your own challenges and joys. You may feel yourself slipping away emotionally from the ever-absent law student. You will need to establish a support system for yourself. Take care to include the law student in your important decisions, even if scheduling an appointment is necessary.

Conclusion

It is impossible, of course, to describe every challenge you and the law student in your life will face over the next few years. Relationships are often difficult, and law school makes things harder. At the same time, it also can make things better. The law student in your life is following a dream of bettering his or her life. Law school requires only three or four years; looking backward, we believe that you will regard your investment of time, effort and patience as an excellent one. Loved ones who support law students receive a level of appreciation you cannot now imagine, end up improving their relationship and help the law student attain a better, richer life.

Reflection Questions

(For the significant others of law students)

1. Why did the law student in your life decide to go to law school?

2. Why do you want the law student in your life to go to law school?

3. What are your normal expectations of the law student in your life in terms of daily chores, emotional support, time with you in person, phone calls to you, income, etc.? Which of these expectations are you willing to give up to support the law student in your life?

4. What are you willing to do to support the law student in your life?

References

Lawrence S. Krieger, *What We're Not Telling Law Students—And Lawyers—That They Really Need to Know: Some Thoughts Toward Revitalizing the Profession from Its Roots*, 13 J. L. & HEALTH 1 (1999).

Bridget A. Mahoney, *Distress Among the Legal Profession: What Law Schools Can Do About It*, 15 NOTRE DAME J.L. ETHICS & PUB. POL. 307 (2001).

Making Docile Lawyers: An Essay on the Pacification of Law Students, 111 HARV. L. REV. 2027 (1998).

Cathleen A. Roach, *A River Runs Through It: Tapping into the Information Stream to Move Students from Isolation to Autonomy*, 36 ARIZ. L. REV. 667 (1994).

Appendix A

Time Management/ Self-Monitoring Log

You should make additional copies of this log for your use throughout this course and the school year. The format of this log was developed based on logs recommended by experts in teaching expert learning skills; studies undertaken by these experts show that students who complete such logs (students who engage in such self-monitoring) greatly outperform those who do not do so. *See* Chapters 5 and 7 above.

Concept/Skill to be Studied[1]	Learning Goal(s)[2]	Strategy(ies) for Learning[3]	Place for Studying[4]	Time Planned for Studying and for Break[5]	Actual Study Time and Study Break[6]	Actual Time Getting Help and Source of that Help[7]	Ability to Focus During Study[8]	Steps Used to Study the Material[9]	Effectiveness of Study Techniques[10]

1. This column requires you to identify what you need to learn — in most cases, that information will come from your professor's syllabus or from your efforts to pre-read the cases.

2. This column requires you to set an explicit goal or goals for learning the material. Setting the right type of goal has been shown to improve student performance; you therefore will learn how to set learning goals for yourself. Initially, just force yourself to state some sort of goal. After you have completed Chapter 5, force yourself to set a proper, mastery-learning goal.

3. This column requires you to plan your strategy for achieving your learning goal(s). In this text, you will be learning a variety of learning strategies for each type of learning task and how to select from among those choices. *See* Chapters 9–16. Describe how you plan to study the material.

4. Identify where you plan to study in this column. *See* Chapter 5 for more information about environmental strategies.

5. State the specific hours you have designated for study and when you plan to take study breaks in this column. For a discussion of study planning and study breaks, *see* Chapter 5.

6. In this column, report when you actually studied and took your study breaks. This information will allow you to compare what you did with what you wanted to do.

7. As is true of any type of learning, students cannot learn everything on their own; they sometimes need help. In this column, report the time you spent getting help and from whom you got the help. *See* Chapter 11.

8. In this column, you will rate your ability to focus on your studies while you were studying as low, medium or high. Expert students monitor their attention. *See* Chapter 7.

9. This column allows you to record the steps you took in implementing the learning strategy you selected. This activity will help you focus your attention on your learning tasks. *See* Chapter 7.

10. A crucial component of expert learning is reflection; this column requires you to reflect upon the effectiveness of your learning strategies so you can retain or alter them as needed. *See* Chapter 8.

Concept/Skill to be Studied	Learning Goal(s)	Strategy(ies) for Learning	Place for Studying	Time Planned for Studying and for Break	Actual Study Time and Study Break	Actual Time Getting Help and Source of that Help	Ability to Focus During Study	Steps Used to Study the Material	Effectiveness of Study Techniques

Concept/Skill to be Studied	Learning Goal(s)	Strategy(ies) for Learning	Place for Studying	Time Planned for Studying and for Break	Actual Study Time and Study Break	Actual Time Getting Help and Source of that Help	Ability to Focus During Study	Steps Used to Study the Material	Effectiveness of Study Techniques

Concept/Skill to be Studied	Learning Goal(s)	Strategy(ies) for Learning	Place for Studying	Time Planned for Studying and for Break	Actual Study Time and Study Break	Actual Time Getting Help and Source of that Help	Ability to Focus During Study	Steps Used to Study the Material	Effectiveness of Study Techniques

Concept/Skill to be Studied	Learning Goal(s)	Strategy(ies) for Learning	Place for Studying	Time Planned for Studying and for Break	Actual Study Time and Study Break	Actual Time Getting Help and Source of that Help	Ability to Focus During Study	Steps Used to Study the Material	Effectiveness of Study Techniques

Concept/Skill to be Studied	Learning Goal(s)	Strategy(ies) for Learning	Place for Studying	Time Planned for Studying and for Break	Actual Study Time and Study Break	Actual Time Getting Help and Source of that Help	Ability to Focus During Study	Steps Used to Study the Material	Effectiveness of Study Techniques

Concept/Skill to be Studied	Learning Goal(s)	Strategy(ies) for Learning	Place for Studying	Time Planned for Studying and for Break	Actual Study Time and Study Break	Actual Time Getting Help and Source of that Help	Ability to Focus During Study	Steps Used to Study the Material	Effectiveness of Study Techniques

Concept/Skill to be Studied	Learning Goal(s)	Strategy(ies) for Learning	Place for Studying	Time Planned for Studying and for Break	Actual Study Time and Study Break	Actual Time Getting Help and Source of that Help	Ability to Focus During Study	Steps Used to Study the Material	Effectiveness of Study Techniques

Concept/Skill to be Studied	Learning Goal(s)	Strategy(ies) for Learning	Place for Studying	Time Planned for Studying and for Break	Actual Study Time and Study Break	Actual Time Getting Help and Source of that Help	Ability to Focus During Study	Steps Used to Study the Material	Effectiveness of Study Techniques

Appendix B

Exemplar Case:
Parker v. Twentieth Century-Fox Corporation

Appendix B contains two versions of the exact same case, *Parker v. Twentieth Century-Fox Corporation*, Cal.3d 176; 474 P.2d 689; 89 Cal. Rptr. 737 (1970). The first version depicts how this case might appear in a law school casebook, and the second shows how the case appears in its full form as it was written by the judge who authored it (with only the footnotes and citations to other cases omitted).

It is worth noting the many differences between the two versions and how the case would appear slightly differently online or in a legal reporter. The two versions below, for example, do not include a summary or headnotes. All casebooks omit summaries and headings, both for copyright reasons and to encourage students not to use the summaries and headnotes as alternatives to reading the full text of the opinions. It is also noteworthy that the textbook version omits citations. Casebook editors often omit many or most of these citations because they are unnecessary to student readers who are unlikely to read them. The casebook version also omits many of the references to summary judgment. This choice is based on the fact that many of the students reading the case will be unfamiliar with summary judgment and therefore may be distracted by their efforts to understand what is an important, but non-contract law, concept. Most significantly, the casebook version omits the dissenting opinion. Usually, casebooks editors include dissenting opinions in their casebooks, but not always.

Version 1: *Parker* in Casebook Form

Parker v. Twentieth Century-Fox Film Corporation
Supreme Court of California
3 Cal. 3d 176; 474 P.2d 689; 89 Cal. Rptr. 737
September 30, 1970

Burke, J.—Defendant Twentieth Century-Fox Film Corporation appeals from a summary judgment granting to plaintiff the recovery of agreed compensation under a written contract for her services as an actress in a motion picture. As will appear, we have concluded that the trial court correctly ruled in plaintiff's favor and that the judgment should be affirmed.

Plaintiff is well known as an actress, and in the contract between plaintiff and defendant is sometimes referred to as the "Artist." Under the contract dated August 6, 1965, plaintiff was to play the female lead in defendant's contemplated production of a motion picture entitled "Bloomer Girl." The contract provided that defendant would pay plaintiff a minimum "guaranteed compensation" of $ 53,571.42 per week for 14 weeks commencing May 23, 1966, for a total of $ 750,000. Prior to May 1966 defendant decided not to produce the picture and by a letter dated April 4, 1966, it notified plaintiff of that decision and that it would not "comply with our obligations to you under" the written contract.

By the same letter and with the professed purpose "to avoid any damage to you," defendant instead offered to employ plaintiff as the leading actress in another film tentatively entitled "Big Country, Big Man" (hereinafter, "Big Country"). The compensation offered was identical, as were 31 of the 34 numbered provisions or articles of the original contract.[1]

Unlike "Bloomer Girl," however, which was to have been a musical production, "Big Country" was a dramatic "western type" movie. "Bloomer Girl" was to have been filmed in California; "Big Country" was to be produced in Australia. Also, certain terms in the proffered contract varied from those of the original.[2] Plaintiff was given one week within which to accept; she did not and the offer lapsed. Plaintiff then commenced this action seeking recovery of the agreed guaranteed compensation.

The complaint sets forth two causes of action. The first is for money due under the contract; the second, based upon the same allegations as the first, is for damages resulting from defendant's breach of contract. Defendant in its answer admits the existence and validity of the contract, that plaintiff complied with all the conditions, covenants

---

1. (Footnotes are renumbered to follow the numbering in this text) Among the identical provisions was the following found in the last paragraph of Article 2 of the original contract: "We [defendant] shall not be obligated to utilize your [plaintiff's] services in or in connection with the Photoplay hereunder, our sole obligation, subject to the terms and conditions of this Agreement, being to pay you the guaranteed compensation herein provided for."

2. Article 29 of the original contract specified that plaintiff approved the director already chosen for "Bloomer Girl" and that in case he failed to act as director plaintiff was to have approval rights of any substitute director. Article 31 provided that plaintiff was to have the right of approval of the "Bloomer Girl" dance director, and Article 32 gave her the right of approval of the screenplay.

Defendant's letter of April 4 to plaintiff, which contained both defendant's notice of breach of the "Bloomer Girl" contract and offer of the lead in "Big Country," eliminated or impaired each of those rights....

and promises and stood ready to complete the performance, and that defendant breached and "anticipatorily repudiated" the contract. It denies, however, that any money is due to plaintiff either under the contract or as a result of its breach, and pleads as an affirmative defense to both causes of action plaintiff's allegedly deliberate failure to mitigate damages, asserting that she unreasonably refused to accept its offer of the leading role in "Big Country."

Plaintiff moved for summary judgment under Code of Civil Procedure section 437c, the motion was granted, and summary judgment for $ 750,000 plus interest was entered in plaintiff's favor. This appeal by defendant followed.

As stated, defendant's sole defense to this action, which resulted from its deliberate breach of contract, is that in rejecting defendant's substitute offer of employment plaintiff unreasonably refused to mitigate damages.

The general rule is that the measure of recovery by a wrongfully discharged employee is the amount of salary agreed upon for the period of service, less the amount which the employer affirmatively proves the employee has earned or, with reasonable effort, might have earned from other employment. (citations omitted) However, before projected earnings from other employment opportunities not sought or accepted by the discharged employee can be applied in mitigation, the employer must show that the other employment was comparable, or substantially similar, to that of which the employee has been deprived; the employee's rejection of or failure to seek other available employment of a different or inferior kind may not be resorted to in order to mitigate damages. (citations omitted)

Applying the foregoing rules to the record in the present case..., it is clear that the trial court correctly ruled that plaintiff's failure to accept defendant's tendered substitute employment could not be applied in mitigation of damages because the offer of the "Big Country" lead was of employment both different and inferior, and that no factual dispute was presented on that issue. The mere circumstance that "Bloomer Girl" was to be a musical review calling upon plaintiff's talents as a dancer as well as an actress, and was to be produced in the City of Los Angeles, whereas "Big Country" was a straight dramatic role in a "Western Type" story taking place in an opal mine in Australia, demonstrates the difference in kind between the two employments; the female lead as a dramatic actress in a western style motion picture can by no stretch of imagination be considered the equivalent of or substantially similar to the lead in a song-and-dance production.

Additionally, the substitute "Big Country" offer proposed to eliminate or impair the director and screenplay approvals accorded to plaintiff under the original "Bloomer Girl" contract, and thus constituted an offer of inferior employment. No expertise or judicial notice is required in order to hold that the deprivation or infringement of an employee's rights held under an original employment contract converts the available "other employment" relied upon by the employer to mitigate damages, into inferior employment which the employee need not seek or accept.... The judgment is affirmed.

Version 2: *Parker* in Full-Text Form

Shirley Maclaine Parker v.
Twentieth Century-Fox Film Corporation
3 Cal. 3d 176; 474 P.2d 689; 89 Cal. Rptr. 737; 44 A.L.R.3d 615 (1970)

Opinion: Defendant Twentieth Century-Fox Film Corporation appeals from a summary judgment granting to plaintiff the recovery of agreed compensation under a written contract for her services as an actress in a motion picture. As will appear, we have concluded that the trial court correctly ruled in plaintiff's favor and that the judgment should be affirmed.

Plaintiff is well known as an actress, and in the contract between plaintiff and defendant is sometimes referred to as the "Artist." Under the contract dated August 6, 1965, plaintiff was to play the female lead in defendant's contemplated production of a motion picture entitled "Bloomer Girl." The contract provided that defendant would pay plaintiff a minimum "guaranteed compensation" of $53,571.42 per week for 14 weeks commencing May 23, 1966, for a total of $750,000. Prior to May 1966 defendant decided not to produce the picture and by a letter dated April 4, 1966, it notified plaintiff of that decision and that it would not "comply with our obligations to you under" the written contract.

By the same letter and with the professed purpose "to avoid any damage to you," defendant instead offered to employ plaintiff as the leading actress in another film tentatively entitled "Big Country, Big Man" (hereinafter, "Big Country"). The compensation offered was identical, as were 31 of the 34 numbered provisions or articles of the original contract.

Unlike "Bloomer Girl," however, which was to have been a musical production, "Big Country" was a dramatic "western type" movie. "Bloomer Girl" was to have been filmed in California; "Big Country" was to be produced in Australia. Also, certain terms in the proffered contract varied from those of the original.[2]

Plaintiff was given one week within which to accept; she did not and the offer lapsed. Plaintiff then commenced this action seeking recovery of the agreed guaranteed compensation.

The complaint sets forth two causes of action. The first is for money due under the contract; the second, based upon the same allegations as the first, is for damages resulting from defendant's breach of contract. Defendant in its answer admits the existence and validity of the contract, that plaintiff complied with all the conditions, covenants and promises and stood ready to complete the performance, and that defendant breached and "anticipatorily repudiated" the contract. It denies, however, that any money is due to plaintiff either under the contract or as a result of its breach, and pleads as an affirmative defense to both causes of action plaintiff's allegedly deliberate failure to mitigate damages, asserting that she unreasonably refused to accept its offer of the leading role in "Big Country."

Plaintiff moved for summary judgment under Code of Civil Procedure section 437c, the motion was granted, and summary judgment for $ 750,000 plus interest was entered in plaintiff's favor. This appeal by defendant followed.

The familiar rules are that the matter to be determined by the trial court on a motion for summary judgment is whether facts have been alleged, which give rise to a triable factual issue. The court may not pass upon the issue itself. Summary judgment is proper only if the affidavits or declarations in support of the moving party would be sufficient to sustain a judgment in his favor and his opponent does not by affidavit show facts sufficient to present a triable issue of fact. The affidavits of the moving party are strictly construed, and doubts as to the propriety of summary judgment should be resolved against granting the motion. Such summary procedure is drastic and should be used with caution so that it does not become a substitute for the open trial method of determining facts. The moving party cannot depend upon allegations in his own pleadings to cure deficient affidavits, nor can his adversary rely upon his own pleadings in lieu or in support of affidavits in opposition to a motion; however, a party can rely on his adversary's pleadings to establish facts not contained in his own affidavits. (citations omitted)

As stated, defendant's sole defense to this action, which resulted from its deliberate breach of contract, is that, in rejecting defendant's substitute offer of employment, plaintiff unreasonably refused to mitigate damages. Also, the court may consider facts stipulated to by the parties and facts, which are properly the subject of judicial notice. (citations omitted)

The general rule is that the measure of recovery by a wrongfully discharged employee is the amount of salary agreed upon for the period of service, less the amount which the employer affirmatively proves the employee has earned or with reasonable effort might have earned from other employment. (citations omitted) However, before projected earnings from other employment opportunities not sought or accepted by the discharged employee can be applied in mitigation, the employer must show that the other employment was comparable, or substantially similar, to that of which the employee has been deprived; the employee's rejection of or failure to seek other available employment of a different or inferior kind may not be resorted to in order to mitigate damages. (*citations omitted*)

In the present case defendant has raised no issue of *reasonableness of efforts* by plaintiffs to obtain other employment; the sole issue is whether plaintiff's refusal of defendant's substitute offer of "Big Country" may be used in mitigation. Nor, if the "Big Country" offer was of employment different or inferior when compared with the original "Bloomer Girl" employment, is there an issue as to whether or not plaintiff acted reasonably in refusing the substitute offer.

Despite defendant's arguments to the contrary, no case cited or which our research has discovered, holds or suggests that reasonableness is an element of a wrongfully discharged employee's option to reject, or fail to seek, different or inferior employment lest the possible earnings therefrom be charged against him in mitigation of damages.

Applying the foregoing rules to the record in the present case, with all intendments in favor of the party opposing the summary judgment motion—here, defendant—it is clear that the trial court correctly ruled that plaintiff's failure to accept defendant's tendered substitute employment could not be applied in mitigation of damages because the offer of the "Big Country" lead was of employment both different and inferior, and that no factual dispute was presented on that issue. The mere circumstance that "Bloomer Girl" was to be a musical review calling upon plaintiff's talents as a dancer as well as an actress, and was to be produced in the City of Los Angeles, whereas "Big Country" was a straight dramatic role in a "Western Type" story taking place in an opal mine in Australia, demonstrates the difference in kind between the two employments; the female lead as a dramatic actress in a western style motion picture can by no stretch of imagination be considered the equivalent of or substantially similar to the lead in a song-and-dance production.

Additionally, the substitute "Big Country" offer proposed to eliminate or impair the director and screenplay approvals accorded to plaintiff under the original "Bloomer Girl" contract (see fn. 2, *ante*), and thus constituted an offer of inferior employment. No expertise or judicial notice is required in order to hold that the deprivation or infringement of an employee's rights held under an original employment contract converts the available "other employment" relied upon by the employer to mitigate damages, into inferior employment which the employee need not seek or accept. (citations omitted)

Statements found in affidavits submitted by defendant in opposition to plaintiff's summary judgment motion, to the effect that the "Big Country" offer was not of employment different from or inferior to that under the "Bloomer Girl" contract, merely repeat the allegations of defendant's answer to the complaint in this action, constitute only conclusionary assertions with respect to undisputed facts, and do not give rise to a triable factual issue so as to defeat the motion for summary judgment. (citations omitted)

In view of the determination that defendant failed to present any facts showing the existence of a factual issue with respect to its sole defense—plaintiff's rejection of its substitute employment offer in mitigation of damages—we need not consider plaintiff's further contention that for various reasons, including the provisions of the original contract set forth in footnote 1, *ante*, plaintiff was excused from attempting to mitigate damages.

The judgment is affirmed.

Dissent: Sullivan, Acting C. J. The basic question in this case is whether or not plaintiff acted reasonably in rejecting defendant's offer of alternate employment. The answer depends upon whether that offer (starring in "Big Country, Big Man") was an offer of work that was substantially similar to her former employment (starring in "Bloomer Girl") or of work that was of a different or inferior kind. To my mind this is a factual issue, which the trial court should not have determined on a motion for summary judgment. The majority has not only repeated this error but has compounded it by applying the rules governing mitigation of damages in the employer-employee context in a misleading fashion. Accordingly, I respectfully dissent.

The familiar rule requiring a plaintiff in a tort or contract action to mitigate damages embodies notions of fairness and socially responsible behavior, which are fundamental to our jurisprudence. Most broadly stated, it precludes the recovery of damages which, through the exercise of due diligence, could have been avoided. Thus, in essence, it is a rule requiring reasonable conduct in commercial affairs. This general principle governs the obligations of an employee after his employer has wrongfully repudiated or terminated the employment contract. Rather than permitting the employee simply to remain idle during the balance of the contract period, the law requires him to make a reasonable effort to secure other employment. He is not obliged, however, to seek or accept any and all types of work which may be available. Only work which is in the same field and which is of the same quality need be accepted.

Over the years, the courts have employed various phrases to define the type of employment which the employee, upon his wrongful discharge, is under an obligation to accept. Thus in California alone it has been held that he must accept employment which is "substantially similar" (citations omitted);"comparable employment" (citations omitted); employment "in the same general line of the first employment" (citations omitted); "equivalent to his prior position" (citations omitted); "employment in a similar capacity" (citations omitted); employment which is "not...of a different or inferior kind...." (citations omitted).

For reasons which are unexplained, the majority cite several of these cases yet select from among the various judicial formulations which they contain one particular phrase, "Not of a different or inferior kind," with which to analyze this case. I have discovered no historical or theoretical reason to adopt this phrase, which is simply a negative restatement of the affirmative standards set out in the above cases, as the exclusive standard. Indeed, its emergence is an example of the dubious phenomenon of the law responding not to rational judicial choice or changing social conditions, but to unrecognized changes in the language of opinions or legal treatises. However, the phrase is a serviceable one and my concern is not with its use as the standard but rather with what I consider its distortion.

The relevant language excuses acceptance only of employment which is of a *different kind.* (citations omitted). It has never been the law that the mere existence of *differences between two jobs in the same field* is sufficient, as a matter of law, to excuse an employee wrongfully discharged from one from accepting the other in order to mitigate damages. Such an approach would effectively eliminate any obligation of an employee to attempt to minimize damage arising from a wrongful discharge. The only alternative job offer an employee would be required to accept would be an offer of his former job by his former employer.

Although the majority appear to hold that there was a difference "in kind" between the employment offered plaintiff in "Bloomer Girl" and that offered in "Big Country" (*ante,* at p. 183), an examination of the opinion makes crystal clear that the majority merely point out differences between the two *films* (an obvious circumstance) and then apodictically assert that these constitute a difference in the *kind* of *employment.* The entire rationale of the majority boils down to this: that the *"mere circumstances"* that "Bloomer Girl" was to be a musical review while "Big Country" was a straight drama "demonstrates the difference in kind" since a female lead in a western is not "the equivalent of or substantially similar to" a lead in a musical. This is merely attempting to prove the proposition by repeating it. It shows that the vehicles for the display of the star's talents are different but it does not prove that her employment as a star in such vehicles is of necessity different *in kind* and either inferior or superior.

I believe that the approach taken by the majority (a superficial listing of differences with no attempt to assess their significance) may subvert a valuable legal doctrine. The inquiry in cases such as this should not be whether differences between the two jobs exist (there will always be differences) but whether the differences which are present are substantial enough to constitute differences in the *kind* of employment or, alternatively, whether they render the substitute work employment of an *inferior kind.*

It seems to me that *this* inquiry involves, in the instant case at least, factual determinations which are improper on a motion for summary judgment. Resolving whether or not one job is substantially similar to another or whether, on the other hand, it is of a different or inferior kind, will often (as here) require a critical appraisal of the similarities and differences between them in light of the importance of these differences to the employee. This necessitates a weighing of the evidence, and it is precisely this undertaking which is forbidden on summary judgment. (citations omitted)

This is not to say that summary judgment would never be available in an action by an employee in which the employer raises the defense of failure to mitigate damages. No case has come to my attention, however, in which summary judgment has been granted on the issue of whether an employee was obliged to accept available alternate employment. Nevertheless, there may well be cases in which the substitute employment is so manifestly of a dissimilar or inferior sort, the declarations of the plaintiff so complete and those of the defendant so conclusionary and inadequate that no factual issues exist for which a trial is required. This, however, is not such a case.

It is not intuitively obvious, to me at least, that the leading female role in a dramatic motion picture is a radically different endeavor from the leading female role in a musical comedy film. Nor is it plain to me that the rather qualified rights of director and screen-play approval contained in the first contract are highly significant matters either in the entertainment industry in general or to this plaintiff in particular. Certainly, none of the declarations introduced by plaintiff in support of her motion shed any light on these issues. Nor do they attempt to explain why she declined the offer of starring in "Big Country, Big Man." Nevertheless, the trial court granted the motion, declaring that these approval rights were "critical" and that their elimination altered "the essential nature of the employment."

The plaintiff's declarations were of no assistance to the trial court in its effort to justify reaching this conclusion on summary judgment. Instead, it was forced to rely on judicial notice of the definitions of "motion picture," "screenplay" and "director" (citations omitted) and then on judicial notice of practices in the film industry which were purportedly of "common knowledge." (citations omitted) This use of judicial notice was error. Evidence Code section 451, subdivision (e) was never intended to authorize resort to the dictionary to solve essentially factual questions which do not turn upon conventional linguistic usage. More important, however, the trial court's notice of "facts commonly known" violated Evidence Code section 455, subdivision (a). Before this section was enacted there were no procedural safeguards affording litigants an opportunity to be heard as to the propriety of taking judicial notice of a matter or as to the tenor of the matter to be noticed. Section 455 makes such an opportunity (which may be an element of due process, see Evid. Code, § 455, Law Revision Com. Comment (a)) mandatory and its provisions should be scrupulously adhered to. "[Judicial] notice can be a valuable tool in the adversary system for the lawyer as well as the court" (citations omitted) and its use is appropriate on motions for summary judgment. Its use in this case, however, to determine on summary judgment issues fundamental to the litigation without complying with statutory requirements of notice and hearing is a highly improper effort to "cut the Gordion knot of involved litigation." (citations omitted)

The majority does not confront the trial court's misuse of judicial notice. They avoid this issue through the expedient of declaring that neither judicial notice nor expert opinion (such as that contained in the declarations in opposition to the motion) is necessary to reach the trial court's conclusion. *Something*, however, clearly *is* needed to support this conclusion. Nevertheless, the majority makes no effort to justify the judgment through an examination of the plaintiff's declarations. Ignoring the obvious insufficiency of these declarations, the majority announces that "the deprivation or infringement of an employee's rights held under an original employment contract" changes the alternate employment offered or available into employment of an inferior kind.

I cannot accept the proposition that an offer which eliminates *any* contract right, regardless of its significance, is, as a matter of law, an offer of employment of an inferior kind. Such an absolute rule seems no more sensible than the majority's earlier suggestion that the mere existence of differences between two jobs is sufficient to render them employment of different kinds. Application of such per se rules will severely undermine the principle of mitigation of damages in the employer-employee context.

I remain convinced that the relevant question in such cases is whether or not a particular contract provision is so significant that its omission creates employment of an inferior kind. This question is, of course, intimately bound up in what I consider the ultimate issue: whether or not the employee acted reasonably. This will generally involve a factual inquiry to ascertain the importance of the particular contract term and a process of weighing the absence of that term against the countervailing advantages of the alternate employment. In the typical case, this will mean that summary judgment must be withheld.

In the instant case, there was nothing properly before the trial court by which the importance of the approval rights could be ascertained, much less evaluated. Thus, in order to grant the motion for summary judgment, the trial court misused judicial notice. In upholding the summary judgment, the majority here rely upon per se rules which distort the process of determining whether or not an employee is obliged to accept particular employment in mitigation of damages.

I believe that the judgment should be reversed so that the issue of whether or not the offer of the lead role in "Big Country, Big Man" was of employment comparable to that of the lead role in "Bloomer Girl" may be determined at trial.

Index